Whitman

AND THE IRISH

Whitman
AND THE IRISH

JOANN P. KRIEG

Ψ

UNIVERSITY OF IOWA PRESS

IOWA CITY

University of Iowa Press, Iowa City 52242
Copyright © 2000 by the University of Iowa Press
All rights reserved
Printed in the United States of America
Design by Richard Hendel
http://www.uiowa.edu/~uipress

The publication of this book was generously supported
by the University of Iowa Foundation.

Printed on acid-free paper

Library of Congress
Cataloging-in-Publication Data
Krieg, Joann P.
Whitman and the Irish / by Joann P. Krieg.
p.   cm.
Includes bibliographical references and index.
ISBN 0-87745-729-8 (cloth),
ISBN 0-87745-730-1 (pbk)
1. Whitman, Walt, 1819–1892—Friends and
associates. 2. Whitman, Walt, 1819–1892—
Knowledge—United States. 3. Whitman, Walt,
1819–1892—Knowledge—Ireland. 4. Poets,
American—19th century—Biography. 5. Irish
Americans—Biography. 6. Ireland—Biography.
I. Title.

PS3233.K75   2000
811'.3—dc21
[B]
00-044345

00 01 02 03 04 C 5 4 3 2 1
00 01 02 03 04 P 5 4 3 2 1

For John, in loving memory

CONTENTS

Introduction *ix*

1. Historical Background *1*

2. Time Line *12*

3. New York City *16*

4. Boston, 1860 *75*

5. Washington, D.C. *103*

6. Boston, 1881 *129*

7. Camden & Eminent Visitors *163*

8. Dublin *190*

9. Coda *232*

Notes *239*

Index *267*

INTRODUCTION

On May 27, 1846, just four days short of his twenty-seventh birthday, the editor of the *Brooklyn Eagle*, Walter Whitman as he was known then, informed his readers that "'Valentine M'Clutchy, the Irish Agent' . . . a well-printed book . . . from the pen of one of the most popular Irish writers, the author of 'Fardorougha, the Miser,'" was available at a local bookstore. The editor had "no doubt" that it would "be found good reading."[1] The unnamed author, whom Whitman seems to assume his readers will know, was William Carleton (1794–1869), one of Ireland's finest nineteenth-century novelists. Whitman's recommendation was made on the basis of his own and his readers' familiarity with Carleton's *Fardorougha*, which had an American edition in 1840 and was widely read. In fact, Carleton's novels were so popular in America that a collected works had five American editions between 1856 and 1885.[2]

On another occasion many years later, in 1888, Whitman was deep in memories of his dearest companion Peter Doyle after having read over again an old letter from "Pete." Speaking of Doyle to Horace Traubel, the young man who was to become the chronicler of his final days, Whitman (sounding like Matthew Arnold at his accommodationist best) attributed Pete's finest qualities to his being Irish: "The real Irish character, the higher samples of it, the real Keltic [*sic*] influences: how noble, tenacious, loyal, they are!"[3] Then, suddenly, adding:

> You should read — you probably have not read — a book called The Collegians, printed some fifty years ago. I can't think of the author's name — my memory plays me such shabby tricks these days — (though I should know it — it is a familiar name). . . . It is a beautiful study of Irish life, Irish character — a little uncanny, but very important for some of the things it discloses. I am not a voracious novel reader — never was — but some of the few novels I have read stick to me like gum arabic — won't let go. The Collegians was one of them.[4]

Like Carleton, Gerald Griffin was also a writer popular with the general public in America as well as with Irish readers. The works of both men were serialized in New York newspapers and magazines, Carleton's running in *Brother Jonathan* early in the 1840s when Whitman published two of his early poems there. While he makes no mention of it, Whitman may also have read John M. Moore's *The Adventures of Tom Stapleton*, which began serialization in *Brother Jonathan* in January 1842, the same month Whitman's poem "Ambition" appeared there.

Whitman's references to these Irish novelists somewhat undermine his claim not to have read many novels. They better support a counterclaim he made at another time and which Traubel also reports, that Whitman had read "cartloads" of novels when he was young and that they were "a most important formative element" in his education.[5] While we are aware of his love for the novels of Eliot, Dickens, and Sand, it is clear from these references to two Irish novelists, who are admired yet for their skill at characterization, that whether he read many or a few, Whitman had an innate critical sense of what made a novel good — its faithful depiction of human nature. Certainly his high praise of *The Collegians*, Griffin's 1829 novel of Irish country life (which years later would have its parallel in Theodore Dreiser's *An American Tragedy*), has been seconded by literary critics of the caliber of William Butler Yeats, who included it in his list of the best Irish books, and Padraic Colum, who called it "the best of the Irish romantic novels."[6] As for Carleton, Yeats so admired his writing that he edited the anthology *Stories from Carleton* (1889). In an article where he extolled Carleton as "the peasant Chaucer of a new tradition," Yeats, quite coincidentally, created an undeniably Whitmanian catalog of Carleton's novelistic offerings: "[Carleton] was able to give us a vast multitude of grotesque, pathetic, humorous persons, misers, pig-drivers, drunkards, schoolmaster, labourers, priests, madmen, and to fill them all with an abounding vitality."[7] Small wonder Whitman found Carleton "good reading."

If not from the New York publications, Whitman may have become aware of Griffin's *The Collegians* through his friend Edward H. House, an habitue of Pfaff's, the Broadway restaurant (actually more of a pub) where Whitman spent many nights in the late 1850s and early 1860s. House is believed to have collaborated with Dion Boucicault in the creation of *The Colleen Bawn*, the very popular stage version of Griffin's novel, which Whitman, a frequenter of the theater and familiar with Boucicault's work, probably saw.[8] Whitman also loved Scott's novels and may have noticed the similarity of *The Collegians* to *The Heart of Midlothian*, his particular favorite among Scott's works, and may even have found something reminiscent of the farmers on his native Long Island in Griffin's depictions of eighteenth-century Ireland's country people. We do not know if Whitman was aware that the author was born in Limerick, birthplace of his friend Peter Doyle, but he makes it clear that he saw in Pete the same characteristics that are presented in Griffin's tale and that he found these characteristics highly impressive whether encountered in fiction or in life.[9]

Griffin made much of "national" characteristics, a topic of great interest to nineteenth-century Americans, which is discussed in chapter 1 in some detail. Despite this interest, we do not find the Irish well represented in American literature prior to the twentieth century, their depiction, like that of blacks, having been left largely to the popular stage. In his poetry Whitman presents both blacks and the Irish, though the latter appear mainly in his lengthy catalogs and are thus not easily discovered. If he cast about for literary precedents, Hugh Henry Brackenridge's Teague O'Regan in *Modern Chivalry* (1792–1805) must surely have come to mind, for he is one of the most delightful characters to be encountered in early American fiction. Teague's opportunistic but beguiling attempts to rise in the loosely ordered frontier society of eighteenth-century Pennsylvania are the occasion for great humor but also allow Brackenridge to lecture him, and the reader, on the need for a rational approach to democracy and the elevation to public office of those who are best prepared for the responsibility. While Teague's political ambitions are treated with indulgent amusement, they signal what will later become a genuine fear in American society, the highly politicized Irish immigrant male eager to avail himself of democratic prerogatives.

The late eighteenth century offers another portrait of an Irish immigrant, less well known than O'Regan but more interesting for the psychological complexity with which he is drawn. Clithero Edny (whose surname is an anagram of "deny") in Charles Brockden Brown's *Edgar Huntly, or, Memoirs of a Sleep-Walker* (1799) is both a victim of his lowly birth among the peasantry of Ireland's County Armagh and the victimizer of the family of an English landlord whose wife seeks to improve Edny's condition. Though Edny harbors murderous intent, Brown's protagonist, the humanitarian Edgar Huntly, seeks only to reach the Irishman on a humane level, a rationalist approach which he learns too late is foolhardy.[10]

Not so easily discerned is the culpability of another character in the book known only as Dr. Sarsefield, who becomes a father figure to both Huntly and Edny. While he is never identified as Irish, his name suggests it, for it echoes that of Patrick Sarsfield (?–1693), who achieved heroic status when he and his Irish cavalry defended Limerick against the forces of William of Orange following the defeat at the Battle of the Boyne. In a romance infused with the shadowy influences of denied or unacknowledged evil and dominated by the fear of various kinds of "others" (immigrants, American Indians, those who manifest such disorders as sleep walking), Sarsefield, a physician, is the supposed example of the truly rational man, yet he bears a good deal of responsibility for the tragedy that concludes the tale.[11] He and Edny are thus twinned villains and are perhaps of the same national origin.

Whitman created no Irish characters in his early works of fiction but did include the Irish as part of the democratic portrait of America he draws in *Leaves of Grass*. He could hardly have done otherwise. In 1855 when the first edition of *Leaves of Grass* was published, 72 percent of New York's workers were foreign born, and of these the Irish formed about 45 percent; of the city's total population, 30 percent were Irish.[12] The Irish moved into the workforce wherever they were welcomed, as day laborers, bricklayers, servants, carters, ferrymen, and longshoremen. In the years before the Civil War New York was a workers' city, with a working-class culture that inspired Whitman and to which he responded joyfully. Within this environment the Irish, as the city's largest ethnic group, maintained a cultural identity of their own. Crowded into the lower Manhattan districts of the First, Fourth, and Sixth political wards, they re-created there the familiar, the world of church and public house, and added the new-found joys of inexpensive entertainment and engagement in politics. All of this "Irishness" swirled about Whitman as he trod the streets of his "Mannahatta," and it became part of him and his poetry. In his private life his contacts with the Irish and Irish Americans were among the most important, and the most satisfying, of his life experiences. In general, Whitman's remarks about the Irish are so generous that they offset the effect of the one incident most often referred to as evidence of his antipathy for them, an 1842 attack in the *New York Aurora* on Bishop John Hughes. The contradiction, if real, needs explanation and is addressed in chapter 1.

The overall need for a work such as this became clear to me in 1996 when I was asked by my friend and colleague Maureen Murphy, who is a specialist in Irish studies, to make some welcoming comments to members of the International Association for the Study of Anglo-Irish Literature at their annual conference. The association was meeting that year at Hofstra University on Long Island, New York, where Murphy and I are on the faculty. Since Long Island is Whitman's birthplace, it seemed appropriate to comment on Whitman and the Irish. To my surprise, I found no definitive published scholarship on which to draw except for studies that included reference to such events as Edward Dowden's 1871 appreciation and Oscar Wilde's visit in 1882. Terence Diggory's critical study, *Yeats and American Poetry*, included Whitman but was narrowed by its subject matter. Drawing together some remarks for the occasion, I began then to outline a study of Whitman's connections not only to the literary people at Trinity College and to the Irish literary revival but also to the Irish and Irish Americans with whom he came in actual contact. Not surprisingly, these latter connections became the major portion of the study and now constitute the first five chapters of this book. Despite attempts to trace all of the individuals with obviously Irish surnames with whom Whitman was in contact, some remain elusive. One of these is the Frank Sweezey (or possibly Sweeney) in New York to whom Whitman claimed to have told the full story of the unknown "Ellen Eyre," who wrote Whitman a highly suggestive letter in 1862. If the same occupational stereotypes held then as now, Sweezey may have been a bartender, for Whitman appears to have confided in him because he "talks very little."[13] Other Irish connections, such as with the Irish-born David Goodman Croly, editor of the *New York Daily Graphic*, where Whitman published a number of poems in the 1870s, proved insignificant.

While the book is by no means a biography of Whitman, of necessity it has required a presentation of background on his life and work so that the reader is properly situated in each chapter. I have been keenly aware in writing it that a book of this kind draws two distinct audiences, as represented by the title. My task has been to interest both groups while filling in, to the best of my ability, gaps that may exist within the respective compasses of each. I must admit, however, to a greater knowledge of American studies than Irish studies; further, much of what is presented here is by way of narrative, establishing the kinds of links between Whitman and the Irish upon which subsequent critical and theoretical studies can be built.

The format governing the chapters is geographical rather than biographical, which allows an examination of Whitman's connections with the Irish and Irish Americans in those United States cities where they were located in large numbers. While Washington, D.C., does not fit the schema in that it did not have a large number of Irish, it is important because of two Irish friends there who were especially close to Whitman, William Douglas O'Connor and Peter Doyle. New York and Boston are natural sites for him to have made Irish contacts, but one regrets the lack of a chapter on Philadelphia, another city with a large Irish population and located just across the Delaware River from Camden, New Jersey, where Whitman spent his final years. Whitman's personal contacts in Philadelphia were few, however, and with the exception of the visiting Irish American sculptor William O'Donovan and perhaps of some working men, did not include, so far as I have been able to determine, any Irish.

I hope that the reader will not be disconcerted by the interweaving of fact and supposition in chapter 1. While we know of certain connections Whitman had to New York's Irish, his early years in Brooklyn and New York still have large gaps in factual information, though it is always hoped that scholarship will fill these blanks. Many links are suggested here on the basis of Whitman's enormous interest in everything that took place in New York City and the involvement of the Irish in so much of what went on there. The first of the two Boston chapters brings Whitman into the abolitionist activities of that city and their impact on the Irish. It examines attitudes toward the Irish revealed by leading New Englanders and draws some parallels between Whitman's abolitionist sentiments and those of Boston's Irish immigrants. The second Boston chapter revisits William O'Connor's role in defending Whitman against the suppression of the 1881 *Leaves of Grass*. This is a familiar matter to Whitman scholars, but the chapter also lays out for the first time Whitman's friendship with another Irishman, one of Boston's outstanding figures in his time, John Boyle O'Reilly.

Chapter 5 moves in the direction of the leap across "the pond" that occurs in the final chapter by bringing together accounts of visits to Whitman by three Irishmen, Oscar Wilde, Bram Stoker, and William Summers. In the case of Wilde, it also examines the Irish writer's role in the Swinburne "defection," as it has been called, the change of heart toward Whitman by the English poet Algernon Charles Swinburne. The final chapter takes us to Dublin, where a coterie of Whitman admirers formed around Edward Dowden at Trinity College, and establishes the roles of Standish James O'Grady, Thomas W. H. Rolleston, William Butler Yeats, and others in furthering an appreciation of Whitman among Europeans. It also examines Yeats's changing reactions to Whitman, in whose work he seems to have seen a harbinger of the fate of culture in a modern society. Fearful, perhaps, of an approaching democratic state, Yeats chose to turn to his country's past rather than risk further loss of Irish culture to a poetic voice that may not have resonated with the Irish people. In what might be termed the final chapter of Whitman's life, the years 1889 to 1892, there were other, though not highly significant, Irish connections that deserve to be mentioned here. Late in 1889 Whitman decided on the site at Harleigh Cemetery, outside Camden, where he wished to be buried. Some of the cemetery personnel had tried to convince him that the site should be prominent and highly visible, with no trees about to obscure the view. Only one man on the staff understood his feeling, that nature should be kept "in her own character — not to have her spoiled, deflected."[14] That man was Ralph Moore, the cemetery superintendent whom Whitman spoke of as "an Irishman of the better kind: I like him." He urged Horace Traubel to introduce himself to "Mr. Moore," adding, "you will like him — he has a genuine way — and as engineer, gardener, has a good deal to tell."[15] Moore was able to understand Whitman's desire to go deep in the woods and agreed with the poet that it was necessary to keep the trees.

The sympathy between the two men seems to have been so well established that Whitman was able to sum Moore up for Traubel: "Moore is not bitten with the art-side of life: not sacrificed to that band of all literary, artistic ambition: elegance, system, convention, rule, canons. In that respect he is our man."[16] Whitman so trusted Moore that in signing a contract for the tomb he appended a note leaving the details of the design and layout to him. This proved to be a mistake, for Moore allowed the cost of construction to outrun the agreed-upon sum. Yet when the tomb was completed and the bill was more than Whitman could pay, Whitman refused to believe that Moore was involved in any deceit. The matter was finally settled to Whitman's satisfaction, and Ralph Moore's name cleared. Though younger than Whitman and, according to Traubel, "a giant, rosy with health," Moore died unexpectedly in December 1891, three months before Whitman's death.[17]

The tomb plans brought another Irishman into Whitman's life. At the suggestion of Whitman's friend Thomas Donaldson, a Philadelphia sculptor came to discuss the design of the burial vault. He was John J. Boyle (1851–1917), an Irish American born in New York City, who grew up in Philadelphia. Originally a stonecutter, he studied sculpting at the Pennsylvania Academy of the Fine Arts and in Paris.

In 1880 he had completed a bronze group, *Indian Family, or The Alamo*, for Chicago's Lincoln Park and later a bronze, *Stone Age in America*, for Philadelphia. Whitman was hesitant about having a recognized sculptor's opinion on the matter of the vault, since he feared "the temptation [of sculptors] to make their work genteel," but Boyle pleased Whitman with his suggestion "simply to have a rough boulder with a bronze leaf somewhere carelessly disposed."[18] Though it is not certain that Boyle did design the tomb, Whitman was well disposed toward him and his ideas, and Traubel records the advice he (Traubel) gave the sculptor: "Make the vault *elemental*— keep it strictly to elements: it more fits Whitman's character and tastes than anything else."[19] The tomb as it stands fulfills these instructions. It's comforting to know that Whitman had a few good Irishmen to help him in this important decision of where and how he would spend eternity.

Finally, some explanation must be offered of terms used throughout this book. "Irish" and, at times, "the Irish," are most often used in the same all-encompassing sense that Whitman and those of his time used it, to refer to those born in Ireland, either north or south, Protestant or Catholic, and to Irish Americans, whether naturalized or born in the United States of Irish parents. Where necessary, the term is modified textually for greater specificity and at times is set off by quotation marks to indicate Whitman's rather stereotypical references to the Irish people. In the historical discussions the term "Anglo-Irish" is used with reference to the Protestant community that came to the foreground in Ireland in the eighteenth century when they became the principal landowners. Though few in number, they are said to have "ascended" economically, educationally, and politically above the Catholic Irish, a position they continued to hold until late in the nineteenth century. In the literary sense, "Anglo-Irish" also refers to the literature of Ireland written in the English language.

There are many people who helped me in researching and preparing this book. I wish first of all to thank Maureen Murphy for reading the manuscript, offering advice and encouragement, and for being my friend. Julie Jones was an enthusiastic listener and saw to it that I was introduced to professors of literature at Trinity College who shared her enthusiasm for this project. Thomas Heffernan and the members of the Columbia University Seminar in Irish Studies were most helpful, as were the members of the International Association for the Study of Anglo-Irish Literature and the Irish American Heritage and Culture Week Committee of the Board of Education of the City of New York. Various libraries and their curators and librarians provided vital information, among them Trinity College Library and the National Library, Dublin; the New York Public Library; the Library of the Religious Society of Friends in Ireland; Boston College Library; the New-York Historical Society Library; the Donald and Joan Axinn Library at Hofstra University; and the American Irish Historical Society. Thanks are due, too, to John Ridge, Craig Rustici, Thomas D'Agostino, Richard Ryan, and Albert von Frank. In Dublin I was warmly and graciously entertained by Annette, Bridget, and Una O'Connor, the "Three Graces," as James Joyce would have dubbed them. The suggestions of readers and editors at the University of Iowa Press were invaluable, as was the work of Robert Burchfield. The loving support of my husband, John, during the writing of this book, in what proved to be the final summer of his life, will always be remembered.

Whitman

AND THE IRISH

1

HISTORICAL BACKGROUND

Ask most Americans at what point their nation's history first touched Ireland's and the answer will likely be, "At the time of the Irish famine when all the immigrants came here." Few realize the Irish were in America before the American Revolution and that many were involved in the revolution. In fact, countless episodes of Irish history, and the history of the Irish in America, remain obscure to the average American. While nineteenth-century Ireland is somewhat scantily known for its Fenianism and for Charles Stewart Parnell, twentieth-century Irish history has been so romanticized in film and song as to cast it, as well, into a shadowy light. With this in mind, and conscious that the narrative of Walt Whitman's connections to and influence on the Irish must be placed against a backdrop of historical events, a brief overview is offered of events pertinent to that narrative.

The earliest point at which America can be said to have played a role in Irish history was when the Irish saw in England's distraction, at the time of the war between France and England from 1793 to 1802, an opportunity to press their own claims. Because of the similarities between their colonial status and that of the North Americans, Irish sympathy lay heavily with the colonies at the time of their rebellion. When American independence signaled to England the instability of its position relative to its colonies, there was a movement on the part of the Westminster Parliament to allow the Irish Parliament legislative autonomy. Ireland's parliamentary government was a product of the Middle Ages and represented the acknowledgment of a common need among the disparate peoples of that time. Under England's rule, however, the Dublin Parliament had lost the freedom to legislate for its own people.

Concessions made by England revived the spirit of a people who, in ancient times, had belonged to independent kingdoms until raiding Danes and Norsemen disturbed their civilization. The great Irish hero Brian Boru routed the Danes in the eleventh century, but by 1171 Henry II, with the blessing of a papal bull, began the conquest of Ireland for his Norman lords. For another hundred years the English and the Normans fought to retain hold of Ireland, with the English barely managing to hang on and, by 1400, reduced to inhabiting a circumscribed area around Dublin known as "the Pale."

Under succeeding kings, England managed to gain greater advantage and exert increasing control over the Irish, but things took a radical turn in the sixteenth century when Henry VIII separated his country from Roman Catholicism and established himself as head of the Church of England. The Irish, however, remained loyal to Rome. When Henry VIII made the Protestant Church of Ireland their official church they suffered for their resistance by having their lands taken from them and by being denied the right to hold public office. Never ceasing to agitate and never deserting their faith, the Irish rebelled repeatedly and each time were punished by the loss of more freedoms. The worst such punishment came when Oliver Cromwell landed at Dublin in 1649 and conducted a campaign of conquest that included the massacre and dispossession of thousands of Irish.

In the decade between Cromwell's arrival in Ireland in 1649 and the restoration of the English monarchy in 1660, Joseph Whitman moved, in 1657, from Connecticut to Huntington, Long Island, New York. Joseph was nephew to John Whitman, who had arrived from England in 1635 on the *True Love* and settled in Massachusetts. Before long Joseph Whitman would own a very sizeable portion of the West Hills area surrounding Huntington, where Walt Whitman was born.

Later in the century Ireland thought it saw an opportunity to gain ground by welcoming England's Catholic king, James II, when he was forced to abdicate; however, both the Irish forces and James's were beaten at the Battle of the Boyne in 1690. This defeat, bitterly remembered by the Catholic Irish, was triumphantly celebrated by the Protestant Irish on each anniversary of the date. In the nineteenth century these celebrations, brought by immigrants from both sides of the religious conflict to the streets of American cities, became the cause of violent riots. The defeat at the Boyne would echo through the streets of New York City every July for a good part of the nineteenth century, with at least one such reminder terminating in a riot severe enough for Walt Whitman to comment on. On these occasions Ulster Orangemen (named for William of Orange, James II's Protestant son-in-law who helped drive the king from his throne) paraded through the most densely populated Catholic Irish areas of the city, a practice continued in Northern Ireland to this day. The penal laws that followed the defeat of the Jacobites aimed at eradicating Catholicism in Ireland. Meanwhile, Scottish Presbyterians, who were planted in northern Ireland after what is known as the "Flight of the Earls" (the exodus of the most powerful northern families after their defeat in a futile effort against a southern enemy), took control of the land so that the 59 percent of Irish soil that had been owned by Catholics in 1641 fell to 14 percent by 1703.[1]

In 1780, just a year after the birth of Walter Whitman Sr. and two years before Cornwallis's surrender to the revolutionary forces in America, Henry Grattan, a member of Parliament from Dublin, moved for an independent Irish legislature. Although the motion failed, it was successful in 1782, and for a time relations between the two parliaments improved. The revolution in France, however, reawakened a thirst for independence, which led an Irish barrister, Theobald Wolfe Tone, to argue for sweeping reforms of a kind the English Parliament was not ready to grant. Tone saw an advantage in uniting the interests of two groups, Irish Catholics and Protestant radicals who refused the claims on their allegiance of the established Anglican church. He also sought the help of France and in 1798 undertook a rebellion, which failed when the small number of French who arrived in August of that year were defeated along with the Irish revolutionaries in September. The rebellion was brutally put down, and Tone committed suicide rather than allow the English to hang him. In New York Rufus King, then serving as United States minister to England, learned that the British planned to banish the captured Irish rebels to America and protested against the United States becoming a new penal colony for England. In 1803 Robert Emmet attempted to revive the revolutionary fervor of 1798 but was hanged and beheaded for his fruitless efforts. While no direct evidence of this exists, it seems likely that Walter Whitman Sr. would have been as supportive and admiring of this revolutionary attempt as he was of all others directed against European tyrannies. It was in this democratic and dissenting atmosphere that Walter Jr. spent his formative years and which led to his veneration of such freethinkers as Thomas Paine and Frances Wright. Later he would add to these the Irish who fought to secure for themselves their own native land.

The immediate result of the 1798 rebellion was an enforced Act of Union in 1800 that created a United Kingdom in which Ireland's Catholic population was a minority among the combined Protestant populations in England, Scotland, and Wales. This United Kingdom of Great Britain lasted until Ireland gained independence in 1922. Ireland's north became the industrialized region, and Belfast soon took precedence over Dublin. Under the Union, Protestants were privileged over Catholics in all social and political institutions; most eggregious was the stipulation that Catholics were not allowed to serve in Parliament, a provision that was remedied in 1829 with the passage of the Catholic Emancipation Bill for which Daniel O'Connell, a Catholic lawyer and head of the Catholic Association, had fought for more than a decade.

Once emancipation was won O'Connell soon took his fight in a new direction, leading a movement to repeal the Act of Union by constitutional means. Though the movement was slow to gather momentum, by 1840 he had enough support to launch a Repeal Association. The association attracted a group of young literary men, Catholic and Protestant, who acquired the name "Young Ireland." This group was not interested in constitutional reform, and saw repeal as only a half-way measure toward full separation of Ireland from England. In the event of such a separation, however, they wished to see neither religious faction gain an ascendency in Ireland, so they sought to focus attention instead on a common national culture of history and literature.

One of their leaders was a Protestant attorney, Thomas Davis, who, with Charles Gavan Duffy, founded the *Nation*, a periodical devoted to fostering their ideals. Through the pages of the widely read *Nation* Davis became the spokesperson for a cultural nationalism, the aim of which was to free the Irish people of their cultural dependency on Britain and provide them with a set of values that were distinctively Irish. After Davis's death in 1845 Duffy assumed leadership of the group and split with O'Connell over the issue of O'Connell's determined belief in constitutional nationalism as the only viable position.

In these same years Walt Whitman was making his first impress on the city of New York, soon to become the refuge of thousands of Irish. In May 1841 he went to work in the printing office of the *New York New World*, a weekly newspaper, and in July he gave a speech at a Democratic Party rally in City Hall Park. These newspaper and political activities were leading Whitman in new directions so that he came to know such Irish champions of democracy as Mike Walsh, of the New York Spartan Band and one of the "Bowery b'hoys," and John L. O'Sullivan. O'Sullivan, best remembered for originating the words "Manifest Destiny," owned and edited the highly influential *United States Magazine and Democratic Review*, where Whitman published fiction pieces. After becoming editor of the *New York Aurora* in 1842, however, Whitman came out against the Irish in New York, a position he took because of strong democratic reasons of his own.

Soon after, in Ireland, both the Repeal movement and Young Ireland were overshadowed by a natural disaster of such proportions that it swept away all other concerns. In 1845 the potato crop was destroyed by a fungal disease that caused black spots to appear on the leaves of potato plants and the potatoes to wither and rot. These were the first signs of the famine that would blight large portions of Ireland in that year and again in 1846, 1848, and 1849. By the end of the decade the population of Ireland had declined by 1.6 million people who died of famine-related disease and starvation or who left the country. During these famine years mass emigration brought thousands of Irish to America, most of them from the country's southern counties where Catholics predominated. In New York Whitman became increasingly aware of the plight of these immigrants, finding himself particularly sympathetic to the public exposure of Irish women seeking employment.

The famine destroyed O'Connell's Repeal Association, and with his death in 1847 the movement came to an end. Young Ireland attempted an uprising in 1848, and a number of its leaders, notably John Mitchel, were arrested while others fled the country, some finding refuge in America. Mitchel was sent to prison in Van Diemen's Land (Tasmania) but escaped and made his way to New York in 1853. There, among the large population of Irish immigrants and with the help of other revolutionaries who had fled Ireland, he began raising funds for an organization that would undertake to free Ireland. Many years later, in 1881, Walt Whitman formed a close friendship with a veteran of that same prison in Van Diemen's Land, John Boyle O'Reilly, who, like Mitchel, had been sent there for revolutionary activities and had likewise escaped to America.

When Mitchel had sufficient funding he returned to Ireland, in 1858, to found the Irish Revolutionary Brotherhood; a year later an American branch of the brotherhood, the Fenian Brotherhood, was established in New York. The dreamed-of revolution never took place and, except for the production of such remarkable leaders as John O'Leary and Jeremiah O'Donovan Rossa, the brotherhood languished in Ireland. It rapidly gained momentum in America, however, where small militia groups formed and a rhetoric of Irish liberty developed. After the American Civil War began these militia quickly swelled the ranks of enlisted men (in armies of both North and South) in the belief that America's gratitude for such service would lead to full support of a military action against Britain. While serving as a hospital visitor in Washington, D.C., throughout the war years, Whitman met and tended to many an Irish and Irish American soldier. When he published *Drum-Taps*, a collection of poems related to the Civil War, he included his poetic tribute to Ireland, "Old Ireland." During these same years Whitman developed intense friendships with two men of Irish ancestry, Peter Doyle and William Douglas O'Connor.

At the war's end many former soldiers returned to Ireland ready to fight for its freedom. They were dependent on their American counterparts for arms, however, and with insufficient support from the American Fenians the idea collapsed. Before that, in 1866, the Irish Fenians undertook an attempted assault on Great Britain by invading Canada. The invasion was thwarted, but another attempt was made in 1870; equally unsuccessful, it heralded the decline and eventual end of the Fenian Brotherhood.

In Ireland, the decade of the 1880s was dominated by the land wars. The Protestant ascendancy of the late eighteenth century had been largely the result of their landownership. A century later these landlords controlled the Irish Parliament, while most of Ireland's large population in the south was forced by lack of industry to subsist mainly by land tillage. Industrial growth in the north gradually led to that region's becoming the provider of goods for both north and south, and the earlier reliance on land there was diminished. In the famine years, thousands in the south who were unable to pay rent were evicted; many never really had an opportunity to catch up even after that disaster had passed. In the postfamine years a change in family practices of land transfer, which posited ownership with one son rather than parcelling the land among many, proved to be a move toward stabilization and toward focusing greater power within the ranks of tenant farmers. Such stabilization was needed, for an unofficial policy developed of agrarian disturbance, which sometimes became violent, directed against landowners, many of whom were English. This unofficial policy was replaced in 1879 by the founding of the Irish National Land League, which sought specific objectives and had as its ultimate goal Irish ownership of Irish land. Though not Irish himself, James Redpath, friend and active supporter of

Whitman, became a partisan of and fundraiser for the Land League, bringing to it the full force of his skills as writer and speaker.

It was two former Fenians, Michael Davitt and John Devoy, both of whom had been imprisoned for their activities in the brotherhood, who saw in the question of land distribution an issue that could influence the outcome of the larger political objective, Home Rule for Ireland, which in the minds of most Irish meant complete independence. The president of the Land League, Charles Stewart Parnell, took up what had been mainly an issue in the western counties and made it the Irish land issue by advocating fixed rents and an eventual right of landownership by the peasant population. In short, the object of the Land League was the abolition of landlordism and the return of the land to those who worked it. Parnell went to America in 1880 to raise funds for the Land League. While there he addressed Congress on the Irish issue and organized an American Land League that was strongly supported by the Irish population in America. A more revolutionary movement in both Ireland and America was the Clan na Gael, founded in 1867 and later led by Rossa, who instituted a terrorist campaign of dynamite sabotage against Londoners in the 1880s.

By this time Walt Whitman had gained a following among students and professors at Trinity College, Dublin. Included was Thomas W. H. Rolleston, who wrote letters to Whitman in which he told of the purposes and activities of the Land League, winning for this cause Whitman's heartfelt support. Land League activities included boycotting, or shunning those who took up tenancy on a farm from which a poor farmer, unable to pay rent, had been evicted. In this way the league exerted a moral force, but mass rallies at which Parnell pushed the objective of Irish land for the Irish people brought the league and its president into direct conflict with England's prime minister, William Gladstone. Gladstone became prime minister in 1868 and, with the help of the Liberal Party, which took up the cause of Irish Catholics as part of its opposition to the Whig Party and its support of the Protestant ascendancy, in 1869 succeeded in disestablishing the Church of Ireland, the first of many steps Gladstone would take to ameliorate conditions in Ireland. Ultimately, Gladstone's Land Act of 1881 went a long way toward correcting the rent problem, but before that was accomplished, continued disturbances led to severe action by the government.

In 1881, just a year before Whitman welcomed Oscar Wilde in

Camden, New Jersey, Parnell was arrested for publicly denouncing these repressive measures. His imprisonment called forth the Land League's "No Rent Manifesto," exhorting no payment of rents until the government acceded to the league's land policies. Gladstone was forced into releasing Parnell early and had to agree to work with him in formulating legislation that would further address the land problem. A brief setback to this spirit of cooperation came just after Parnell's release from prison in 1882, when two government officials were murdered in Phoenix Park by extremists acting in the cause of independence. But Parnell was now ready to take another, nonviolent, step toward independence, the Home Rule movement.

In 1884 the Irish National Land League was superseded by the National League, with Parnell at its head, and Home Rule, or self-government, became the avowed objective. Two years later Gladstone introduced a Home Rule bill that included provision for an Irish Parliament that would attend to all Irish matters, leaving other matters to the English Parliament. It was defeated by Gladstone's own Liberal Party, whose members feared an independent Ireland. Again, in 1893, Gladstone offered the third Home Rule bill, which was also defeated. Home Rule was defeated by more than the Liberals, however; it fell along with Parnell, who suffered disgrace and the loss of his position when, in 1890, he was named in a divorce action by the husband of Katharine O'Shea, Parnell's mistress for many years.[2] In America Whitman was among the many who supported Parnell, but he came to believe that for the good of the cause of Home Rule Parnell must step aside. The point became moot when Parnell died in 1891 of natural causes, contributed to, no doubt, by the disgrace he suffered.

There was no political leader to take Parnell's place, and Irish politics splintered into dissenting groups. Strangely, it was a literary force that gave direction in the early years of the twentieth century by attempting to replace political nationalism with cultural nationalism. The Irish literary revival had its beginnings as early as Standish O'Grady's *History of Ireland* published in 1878. Although nationalist, like the earlier Young Ireland movement, its aim was to revive the submerged culture of the Irish and thus foster a new sense of nationalism. O'Grady was among many of the writers and thinkers in Ireland who in these years were admirers of Whitman. Their leaders, mostly Protestants, held to a firm belief that Ireland needed its educated Protestant class in order to command respect from other nations.

The clear leader of this literary movement was William Butler Yeats, early on a Whitman follower who later turned away because of what he perceived as Whitman's failure to gain an audience among his countrymen and women. Yeats's nationalism had been awakened by contact with the great Fenian revolutionary John O'Leary. While Yeats revered O'Leary's devotion to Ireland, he believed that the Young Ireland and Fenian movements had been far too romantic in their vision of Ireland and too uncritical of its reality. Yeats founded the Irish Literary Society in London in 1891 where he and others attempted to wrestle with questions of what constituted Irish culture and Irish literature and what each of those entities would be in the future. Their objective was an Irish literature that would take its place among those of other nations and command their respect. Though a nonspeaker of Irish, as were most of those who followed him in the revival, Yeats supported the Gaelic League, which sought to revive that language and to produce a literature in Ireland's own tongue.

In 1905 Arthur Griffith founded Sinn Fein (Ourselves alone). A nationalist movement, it had as its vision an independent Ireland unified politically as well as culturally. This vision was opposed by the Ulster unionists, who prized their connection to the United Kingdom. While the question of Irish independence continued to dominate the national discourse, a labor movement was forming strength under the leadership of James Larkin and James Connolly. Connolly, a socialist, had attempted to establish an Irish Labour Party, a move that challenged the Labour Party of Great Britain. He and Larkin were successful, however, in organizing the Irish Transport and General Workers' Union. In 1913 and 1914 Larkin and Connolly led strikes during which they attempted to inspire the workers with Whitman's words. The strikes caused widespread disruption in Ireland but brought little change for the workers.

The year 1916 is indelibly stamped in Irish history by the events in Dublin during the Easter Rising, a rebellion against the British government. The nationalist Sinn Fein believed that the Irish volunteers fighting in the World War should not have been so engaged anywhere until the battle for their own national independence had been won. The Sinn Fein were joined in rebellion by an Irish Citizens Army, formed to protect strikers during the 1913 lockout. The strikers, members of the Irish Transport and General Workers' Union, were aided by other republican organizations and may have received aid and support from Fenian Irish Americans. The rebellion centered on the capture of the General Post Office, from the steps of which one of the rebel leaders, Patrick Pearse, read a proclamation declaring an Irish republic. The rebellion lasted only six days before being put down by the British.

The British moved swiftly against the rebels, and court martial trials of key figures in the rising were followed by executions that roused the passions of the Irish populace. James Connolly was one of those executed; another who was sentenced to die, Eamon De Valera, was spared because of his American citizenship, a consequence of his New York birth. As a result of the Easter Rising, Sinn Fein became the political force of revolutionary nationalists, eventually replacing the Irish Party and the Irish Republican Brotherhood. In 1917 de Valera was elected president of Sinn Fein.

In 1918, with the British army taxed heavily by the war, the United Kingdom decided to extend conscription to Ireland, which had been exempted until some form of Home Rule could be enacted. The Irish refused to accept Prime Minister Lloyd George's conditional offer of partial Home Rule, and conscription was not instituted. However, in 1919 an underground military force made up of the Irish Republican Army and, under Michael Collins, the Irish Republican Brotherhood began a guerrilla war against the British government. The objective was to prove to the British that they were not capable of governing Ireland, and in this the guerrillas enjoyed the wide support of the populace. The British retaliated by sending additional forces, the Auxiliaries and the Black and Tans, the latter so named for the colors of their uniforms, who were responsible for atrocities against the general populace as well as against the rebels.

Late in 1920 the Government of Ireland Act ended the hope of a united independent Ireland by acceding to the Ulster resistance to Home Rule, partitioning the country into north and south, and establishing parliaments in Dublin and in Belfast. These two bodies were empowered to exert control in local matters, but the United Kingdom Parliament could still interfere and held supreme authority. The following year, in the face of continued agitation in the southern counties, the United Kingdom offered a treaty stipulating dominion status similar to that of Canada, Australia, New Zealand, and South Africa. It amounted to near independence for the southern counties, though with sworn allegiance to the king and continued separation for Northern Ireland.

A team of negotiators, including Michael Collins, agreed to the offer, but de Valera and the Republicans rejected it because a Free State was not a republic. They further rejected the oath of allegiance to the king required by the terms of the treaty. The Irish Parliament accepted the treaty, as did a majority of the Irish people. Conflict over the two positions led to a civil war of largely guerrilla actions. Despite the Republican rejection, the Anglo-Irish treaty held, and in 1922 Ireland became the Irish Free State. The loss of the dream of an Irish republic was a terrible blow to the revolutionaries, for whom the division of the country was of lesser importance.

In 1937 the Irish Free State's (Eire's) constitution became effective, and in 1949 Eire was formally declared a republic, the Republic of Ireland. The division of north and south remained in place, with Northern Ireland still a part of the United Kingdom until such time as its Parliament should demand a change. In November 1985 the British and Irish governments signed the Anglo-Irish Agreement by which the British allowed the Irish government some sway over the affairs of Northern Ireland in exchange for Irish cooperation in rooting out terrorists. The terrorism, mostly directed against the British army in Northern Ireland, continued, and long years of violence ensued. Whitman's prayer of "God-speed," uttered in support of the Land League, appeared to have been thwarted by the enduring enmity of the two sides.

TIME LINE

1819

Whitman born (May 31) on Long Island, N.Y.; family moves to Brooklyn, N.Y., four years later

1823–1830

Whitman and family live in various places in Brooklyn, including the vicinity of the Brooklyn Navy Yard located very near the heaviest concentration of Irish in Brooklyn

1840s

In Ireland, the Young Ireland revolutionary movement flourishes; one of its writers is "Speranza," Lady Jane Francesca Wilde, mother of Oscar Wilde

1841

Address from the People of Ireland to their Countrymen and Countrywomen in America is issued by Irish and American abolitionists calling on Irish to support abolitionism; Whitman begins working for the *New York New World* and becomes active in the Democratic Party, political home to most of the city's Irish; he publishes for the first time in John O'Sullivan's *United States Magazine and Democratic Review*

1842

Whitman becomes editor of the *Aurora*, a New York daily, and writes editorials attacking New York's Irish and Bishop John Hughes

1844–45

The great Irish famine migration begins, bringing Irish in record numbers to the United States

1847

Whitman, now editor of the *Brooklyn Daily Eagle*, adopts the Free Soil position supported by Irish workers; Whitman recommends books by William Carleton to *Eagle* readers and editorializes on problems of Irish laborers and their attempts to unionize

1848

Whitman writes sketch of Irish drayman for the *New Orleans Daily Crescent*; back in New York later this year Whitman has his head "read" by a phrenologist and becomes an advocate of this pseudoscience, which contributed to notions of national characteristics

c. 1850

Whitman writes an unpublished account of the plight of Irish women seeking new positions as servants through an emigrant agency

1854

Whitman may have written "Poem of Apparitions in Boston," later known as "A Boston Ballad," in this year at the time of the trial in Boston of fugitive slave Anthony Burns; an attempt by abolitionists to rescue Burns leads to the death of Irishman James Batchelder

1855

Whitman publishes *Leaves of Grass*; this and succeeding editions of *Leaves* contain references to the Irish and to New York employment, activities, and events that included many Irish

1858

The Fenian Brotherhood, an Irish American revolutionary society, is founded in the United States

1859–1860

At Pfaff's, a New York restaurant, Whitman is friendly with Fitz-James O'Brien, writer of short stories

1860

In Boston for the publication of a new edition of *Leaves*, Whitman meets William Douglas O'Connor

1861

Whitman publishes "Old Ireland" in the *New York Leader*; firing on Fort Sumter begins the Civil War; New York's all-Irish Sixty-ninth Regiment enters the war

1862

Whitman goes to Washington, D.C., and takes a government position while volunteering as a hospital visitor to Civil War wounded; renews friendship with William Douglas O'Connor

1863

Conscription Act brings four days of rioting in New York City in which Irish play a major role

1865
Whitman meets Irish-born Peter Doyle in Washington, D.C.,
beginning a long and intimate relationship

1866
William Douglas O'Connor publishes *The Good Gray Poet* defending
Whitman, who has been dismissed from a government position

1869
The Fenians invade Canada for a second time (the first was in
1866); John Boyle O'Reilly, just escaped from an English prison,
accompanies invasion as a reporter for the *Boston Pilot*

1871
In July Whitman writes letters to Peter Doyle and William Douglas
O'Connor describing the riot that occurred in New York City
on Boyne Day; Edward Dowden publishes "The Poetry of
Democracy: Walt Whitman"; Yeats, at first an admirer of
Whitman, later challenges Dowden's views and rejects
Whitman as a model for a national poet

1879
National Land League formed in Ireland

1880
American Land League founded; Charles Stewart Parnell
arrives in New York

1881
In Boston to deliver his Lincoln lecture, Whitman meets
John Boyle O'Reilly, now editor of the *Boston Pilot*;
Whitman grants permission for Russian translation
of *Leaves* to John Fitzgerald Lee, a student at
Trinity College, Dublin, and to Thomas W. H.
Rolleston for a German translation

1882
Oscar Wilde visits Whitman in Camden, New Jersey; murder of
government officials in Dublin's Phoenix Park; *Leaves of Grass* is
suppressed in Boston and in the library of Trinity College, Dublin

1884
Whitman meets Abraham (Bram) Stoker; Stoker has admired
Whitman's poetry since 1872 and had written to him in 1876

1889
William Douglas O'Connor dies in Washington, D.C.

1890
John Boyle O'Reilly dies in Boston
1892
Whitman dies (March 26) in Camden, New Jersey, and is buried
in Harleigh Cemetery, Camden, in a spot recommended to
him by an Irish cemetery worker, Ralph Moore

3

NEW YORK CITY

"Immigrants arriving,
fifteen or twenty thousand in a week . . ."
"Mannahatta"

Although the events of 1871 are not especially memorable in American history, the year offers a good starting place for a consideration of relationships between Walt Whitman and the Irish. Essential to this consideration are two letters written by Whitman in the summer of that year, each of which suggests he had found in New York's Irish community verification of his long-held faith in the gradual absorption by his country's immigrants of the principles and practices of democracy. It could not have come at a better time for the poet of democracy, who in the same year published *Democratic Vistas*, a somber prose meditation revealing a generally bleak outlook on the nation's future. That we should see in Whitman's private letters a glimmer of hope occasioned by the sight of New York City's Irish policemen, even while he publicly castigated American society as "canker'd, crude, superstitious, and rotten," is not something to be ignored.[1] The glimmer is especially significant because Whitman had not always been so sanguine about the city's Irish immigrants, especially the Irish Catholics. Indeed, his earliest published utterances on them were filled with the kind of venom most often associated with nativism. Unfortunately, the alteration was not so public as had been his earlier attack, appearing as it did in private correspondence rather than, as before, in a public newspaper. In truth, it must be allowed that his warming toward the Irish may have been somewhat influenced (since Whitman was susceptible to such influences) by a show of appreciation for his work coming at about this time from a group of writers and scholars in Dublin. Certainly he was influenced by his deep love for particular Irish friends, some of whom were born in Ireland and others born in America. But there is no reason to doubt that Whitman was also genuinely impressed in 1871 by the changes that time had wrought in the condition and the character of New York's largest ethnic group. There is, in fact, reason enough to believe he welcomed the thought that his early belief in the democratic impulses of the Irish immigrants was vindicated by those changes.

Whitman's exposure to the Irish in the cities of Brooklyn and New York spanned the years before and after the great migration spurred by the famines in Ireland that began in 1845. In New York the pre-famine Irish population has been estimated as high as twenty-five thousand, or one-fourth of the city's total.[2] Mostly Protestant, either Anglican or Presbyterian, the earliest immigrants joined the middle class in Brooklyn and New York. Some of those who came after the 1798 uprising, men like Thomas Addis Emmett and William James Mac Nevin, were by their culture and refinement considerably more aristocratic than their revolutionary activities would indicate. De Witt Clinton, United States senator, mayor of New York City, and governor of New York, was of Irish descent. When he initiated New York's great engineering project, construction of the Erie Canal (completed in 1825), he coincidentally opened up employment opportunities for hundreds of Irishmen.

In subsequent decades Catholic Irish immigrants were increasingly among the poor who gathered in neighborhoods on the fringes of middle-class enclaves. Whitman's recollection, in 1889, of a family by the name of Murphy whom he had known "in New York 30 or 40 years ago — famous men in their line — stationers," is an indication of the prosperity attained by the earlier arrivals.[3] An 1866 *New York Times* description, however, of the Irish living in the area just south of the Brooklyn Navy Yard, where the largest allotment of poor Irish were found and not far from where Whitman's family was living, offers a different picture, one that Whitman could not have ignored:

> Here homeless and vagabond children, ragged and dirty, wander about; here the utterly poor congregate; and here accumulate all the causes of pestilence or disease; decaying garbage, dead animals, filthy and unclean privies, with crowds of unwashed human beings packed together, and houses badly arranged for ventilation. Here the drainage or sewerage is usually imperfect and the whole soil is thus ripe for diarrhea or cholera.[4]

In New York City conditions were no better. Edgar Allan Poe described an Irish squatter camp in the southern portion of the site where Central Park was later built. By Poe's account, a typical Irish shanty there was about "nine feet by six, with a pigsty applied externally, by way both of portico and support." Built entirely of mud, the shanty, as Poe recalls it, would seem to have been "erected in somewhat too obvious an imitation of the Tower of Pisa."[5] In other parts of the city the Irish were crowded into buildings and neighborhoods never designed to hold such large numbers of people. One result of this, as the *Times* noted, was contamination of the city water supply drawn from shallow wells. When cholera struck the worst neighborhoods of the city in 1832 and 1835 as the result of the contaminated water, the Irish who lived there were believed to be the cause of the contagion.[6] Cholera, a concomitant of poverty and, more specifically, of a lack of sanitation and pure water, spread rapidly among the Irish. As a result, their poverty became so linked with the disease in the minds of the city's more fortunate that cholera came to be looked upon by many as a necessary scourge of nature eliminating the poorest, and least "desirable," members of society.

Whitman seems not to have been completely immune to this line of reasoning. Though he was in the safer regions of Brooklyn and Long Island while the epidemic raged in 1832, he later worked it into one of his fiction pieces, presenting the disease in such a way as to somewhat uphold the belief that epidemics can function as a means of moral cleansing. In the summer of 1845 he published "Revenge and Requital; A Tale of a Murderer Escaped," in John L. O'Sullivan's *Democratic Review*. It is the story of Philip Marsh, a man who commits murder and escapes the law before punishment can be meted out. Marsh finds redemption for his guilty soul by nursing cholera victims in the "dirtiest and wretchedest section of the city, between Chatham and Centre streets." The location was on the fringe of Five Points, in the Sixth Ward — known as the "Bloody Ould Sixth" — where the poorest of the city's Irish were congregated, the same area to which Jacob Riis would turn for material for his 1890 exposé of conditions among the city's poor. Though it is unlikely it was his first visit, given his journalistic career, Whitman mentioned going to the Five Points area in September 1868, claiming the visit was "instructive but disgusting."[7] While Marsh's redemption, gained through selfless contact with contagion, is not the interpretation of cholera's purgative effects adopted by the morally righteous of the city, it partakes of the generalized belief that such widespread disasters can offer opportunities for moral redemption and cleansing; indeed, Whitman describes the murderer as an "unterrified angel of mercy and charity" and as a "messenger of health."[8]

In 1849 when cholera struck New York again, Whitman became

concerned for the inhabitants of Brooklyn and two years later wrote an article in that city's daily *Advertiser* (June 28, 1851) on the need for pure water to be supplied by the city, as New York had done for its citizens by building the Croton reservoir. Later, in "Song of Myself," Whitman identified not with the healer, as in his story of Philip Marsh, but with the victims of the disease:

> Not a cholera patient lies at the last gasp,
>> but I also lie at the last gasp,
> My face is ash-color'd, my sinews gnarl . . .
>> away from me people retreat.
> Askers embody themselves in me, and I am embodied in them,
> I project my hat and sit shamefaced and beg.[9]

Since the subject of cholera is encompassed in the poem by a wider identification with other unfortunates, such as the imprisoned and street beggars, it is possible to see in these lines an oblique reference to the city's Irish, who in their poverty are embraced by the poem's persona as selflessly as are the cholera victims by Philip Marsh. Whitman's identification with the Irish poor may have stemmed from an early association with them in Brooklyn, where he and his family barely managed to remain above the level of poverty that obtained in the immigrant neighborhoods. Brooklyn's "Irish Town" was located near the navy yard, not far from where the Whitmans lived in the 1820s and where Walt's brother Jesse worked for a time. The family was still in Brooklyn in 1855 when the Irish made up Brooklyn's largest foreign-born element, numbering 56,753 out of a population of 205,250.[10]

In the 1850s when he was fashioning the all-encompassing poetic voice he believed America needed, Whitman experimented by assuming a fluid, flexible persona. Among the many tentative lines written in this manner in his notebook is one in which he directly associates that persona with the newly arrived Irish: "The poor despised Irish girls and boys immigrants just over."[11] New York was by then at a saturation point, having absorbed thousands of famine exiles in the preceding four years, and the newly arrived Irish were indeed poor and despised. The 1855 edition of *Leaves of Grass*, however, contained a direct reference to these immigrants that subtly reminded them that for all their troubles in America, they were still better off here than at home. The reference appears in the poem later titled "The Sleepers," a marvelous evocation of sleep and its dreams, where the narrator is capable of entering the night visions of the sleepers whose dreams he describes. Among such visions are those in which "ships make tacks in the dreams . . . the sailor sails . . . the exile returns home, / The fugitive returns unharmed," and "the immigrant" (suggesting the many songs of exile fashioned by the Irish in America) "is back beyond months and years; / The poor Irishman lives in the simple house of his childhood, with the well-known neighbors and faces, / They warmly welcome him . . . he is barefoot again. . . . he forgets he is welloff . . ."[12]

As the immigrants were forced into ever tighter precincts the Irish neighborhoods of the midcentury became the worst slums of the city. In 1871, however, by which time the United States had absorbed, subsequent to the 1845 famine, some 2.5 million Irish emigrants, conditions had improved considerably for most of New York's Irish. They formed 21 percent of the city's population, and as a consequence of their numbers and their political aspirations, they had moved into the mainstream of its life. In fact, the Irish had become a potent force in what was still a workers' city. They had moved ahead in the workforce to become tailors, shoemakers, metalworkers, and masons, while still filling those roles they had earlier claimed as carters, coachmen, housemaids, longshoremen, and ferrymen. The city's largest union, the Laborers' Union Benevolent Society, was made up mostly of Irish members, and by the end of the 1860s nearly all the officers of New York's unions were Irish, either native or descendent.[13] By 1872 the "Tammany Tiger" was headed by its first Irish Catholic leader, John Kelly, paving the way for the election in 1880 of New York's first Irish mayor, shipping magnate William Grace.

The years just prior to 1871 also had wrought some changes in Whitman's life, not all of them welcome. Most had been within his family structure. Thomas Jefferson Whitman, or Jeff, the brother to whom he had felt closest since their six-month sojourn in New Orleans in 1849, had moved to St. Louis with his wife and two daughters. There Mattie, Jeff's wife, had developed a persistent throat ailment from which she would die in 1873. Louisa Whitman, the poet's mother, widowed since 1855, was also beginning to show signs of poor health and of wearing down under the pressures of caring for her son, Edward, who had mental and physical disabilities, and worrying about the deteriorating mental health of another son, Jesse, her eldest.[14] The child of yet another son, Andrew, who died in 1863, had been run over and killed by a cart while playing in the street, the result of his mother's drunken neglect.

As counter to these there were the upswings in Whitman's authorial life. *Leaves of Grass* had seen its fourth edition in 1867, and he continued to work on poems to be added to the next edition. Through the good offices of the publisher of the magazine *Galaxy* he had published two essays in 1867, "Democracy" and "Personalism," which had been fused into the soon to be published *Democratic Vistas* (1871). In the same year he would produce *Passage to India*, the title poem of which is arguably the last of his great poems. Since the publication of some of his poems in England in 1868, he had become a focus of attention for a number of prominent figures there, among them a female admirer, Anne Gilchrist, who sent an impassioned marriage proposal he did not accept. In the summer of 1871 Edward Dowden, professor of English literature at Trinity College, Dublin, issued a significant essay, "The Poetry of Democracy: Walt Whitman," which reflected a growing admiration for the American bard among Irish literati. In 1871 he would also be hailed by the English poet Algernon Charles Swinburne and receive warm letters from that country's poet laureate, Alfred Lord Tennyson.

Although he had lived in Washington, D.C., since 1863, Whitman was still a son of "Mannahatta" and returned often to visit friends there and his mother in Brooklyn, as he did in 1871. New York, then as now, had a tendency to believe itself the center of the world, but Whitman would have been quite conscious of the fact that the District of Columbia had been provided for the first time with a form of territorial government. Other events that would not have escaped his attention in 1871 included the establishment of the first Civil Service Commission, though Congress, not able — until the assassination ten years later of President Garfield — to see the need to replace the spoils system, failed to continue its support; the organization of the country's first professional baseball association, displacing amateurs; and the fire in Chicago that destroyed an area of more than three square miles, consuming human lives and property including the original draft of Lincoln's Emancipation Proclamation. Of more immediate interest to the vacationing Whitman would have been some New York events of that summer: work on the bridge between the cities of Brooklyn and New York entered the second of its fourteen years; more than a hundred people were killed when a boiler exploded aboard the *Westfield*, a Staten Island ferry; and at least fifty people were killed in a riot involving Irish Catholics and Irish Protestants. All of these events would have impressed Walt Whitman, but we have his comments on only one, the Irish riot.

On June 20, 1871, Whitman returned to Brooklyn on his annual vacation from his position as clerk, third class, annual salary of sixteen hundred dollars, in the Attorney General's office in Washington, D.C. Just three months earlier he had been declared dead by the *New York World*, which ran a lengthy obituary in the mistaken belief that he had been killed by a railroad train in Croton, New York. Though to one correspondent he claimed the false report kept him from "hardly stir[ring] out in New York," it was really his mother's illness that kept him close to home.[15] While in Brooklyn Whitman wrote regularly to his beloved friend in Washington, Peter Doyle, being careful to set Pete's mind at ease about his health by assuring the younger man that he was doing very little work and spending most of his time at home caring for his mother. When not with her, Walt told Pete, he was riding the ferry and visiting Coney Island. On Sunday, July 16, he even wrote a letter to Pete while on the sands of Coney Island, expressing the time-honored sentiment, "Pete, I wish you were with me."[16] Two days earlier he had written Doyle and another friend, the Irish American William Douglas O'Connor, news of quite a different sort, the murderous riot that took place July 12 in New York City at the annual parade of the city's Orangemen commemorating the Battle of the Boyne in 1690. Both of the friends to whom he wrote were "Irish" (as Whitman used the term), and Whitman seems to have felt the particular need to share with them his feelings on the subject. To Pete he wrote:

> There was quite a brush in N.Y. on Wednesday — the Irish lower orders (Catholic) had determined that the Orange parade (protestant) should be put down — mob fired & threw stones — military fired on mob — bet. 30 and 40 killed, over a hundred wounded — but you have seen all about it in papers — it was all up in a distant part of the city, 3 miles from Wall street — five-sixths of the city went on with its business just the same as any other day — I saw a big squad of prisoners carried along under guard — they reminded me of the squads of rebel prisoners brought in Washington, six years ago —.[17]

Whitman wrote much the same thing to O'Connor, only emphasizing to him the peculiar manner in which so much of the life of a big city can go on unconcernedly while mobs riot and the police and militia kill.[18]

The riot in New York on that July day in 1871 was actually a repeat of what occurred at the previous year's Boyne Day. Orangemen, originally members of an Ulster Protestant Society in Ireland dating to

1795, were, in the United States, members of an ethnic organization whose principal activity was its annual celebration of the Battle of the Boyne. The 1870 observance had been given an extra boost by the fact that in May President Grant had declared the government would no longer tolerate the Irish Catholic Fenian Brotherhood functioning as a kind of separate government within the United States.[19] Actually, it was an empty gesture, for the Fenians had ceased some years before to wield the force of numbers they had once commanded, but the Orangemen took it as a token of further Catholic defeat. On July 12 they had a procession up Eighth Avenue to a park located at Ninetieth Street, where a picnic and dance were to be held. One report credits twenty-five hundred men, women, and children with parading to tunes of "Boyne Water," "Derry," and others "obnoxious to the Catholics."[2] As it passed a road construction site where a large number of Irish were employed, the procession attracted unfavorable attention and was soon followed by the workers and other Irish Catholics. The Metropolitan Police were notified, but by the time they reached the park a shower of stones was falling on the Orangemen. A general melee followed, with clubs, sticks, and anything that could serve as a weapon being brought to bear. The militia were called, but by the time they arrived the injured were scattered about the streets. Groups from both sides of the combat tried to crowd into horsecars to escape, and as the fighting continued it brought wreckage to the cars and animals as well as to innocent passengers. Eight people died as a result, fifteen were wounded, and only six arrested; a subsequent investigation cast doubt on the willingness of the city's police to put down the rioters.[21] New York's Irish waited to see what the following year would bring.

At the time, the New York Irish were as closely linked to the powerful Tweed Ring as any politically motivated ethnic group could hope to be. William M. Tweed was Grand Sachem of Tammany Hall, deputy street commissioner of New York City, and New York state senator. Peter Barr Sweeny, one of the original Ring organizers, was a Tammany sachem and city chamberlain, and Richard B. Connolly was the city comptroller. The Irish had been in America long enough to be able to see some of their number move up into the ranks of the well-to-do, and some even became Republicans. For example, in 1871 Edward Gleason, superintendent of the Union League Club, a highly respectable Republican political group, was able to build a house on 128th Street near Fifth Avenue. Though the location was considered "in the country," the house was designed by the prestigious architects Calvert Vaux and Frederick Withers. Vaux and Frederick Law Olmsted designed Central Park, and he and Withers had just completed the plan of the spacious estate Olana in Hudson, New York, for landscape artist Frederick Church.[22]

Despite the evidence of economic gain, most of the city's Irish still toiled as laborers at low wages, competing always with the latest immigrants and with free blacks. Labor activism among Irish immigrants throughout the midcentury had focused mainly on improved wages, and this limited objective hampered any strides toward overall improvement of working conditions. In addition, Irish workers originally impeded their own progress by forming rival groups and secret societies whose memberships were determined by place of origin in Ireland.[23] Only gradually did the idea of benevolent societies replace these secret organizations. Benevolent societies, forerunners of organized labor unions, had political and religious as well as occupational roots. In March 1846 Whitman wrote in the *Eagle* of a meeting of laborers held at Carroll Hall (a conservative Catholic political society often opposed to Tammany Hall) for the purpose of forming a benevolent society that would care for sick members and bury its dead, "as well as to regulate the prices of work." One speaker who, Whitman says, addressed the gathering "in very animated language" was Michael F. O'Connor. A partial victory was claimed by reading aloud letters from contractors who had agreed to the demanded wage, among them Messrs. Collins, Brady, S. and P. O'Donnell, Quinn, and Burns. While Whitman makes no mention of this, note the Irish names of the contractors, who may have been Americans born to immigrant parents and who are indicative of entrepreneurial advancement possible in a labor-dominated economy that was beginning to break down, creating the need for unions.

Craft workers, among whom the prefamine Irish immigrants numbered highly, were essential to the working class that developed in New York from the 1790s to the mid-nineteenth century. Whitman was part of this working class; because of his particular craft, printing, he was aware of the encroaching mechanization that would revolutionize the very character of work and create a new social and economic order based on what Sean Wilentz has labeled "capitalist conceptions of wage labor as a market commodity," where the worker's labor was no longer his or her own.[24] In the mid-1830s the city's unions had maintained that those workers who attained the status of journeymen had the right to determine the worth of their labor, which was said to be their own "property."[25] By the time Whitman was writing about unions in the *Eagle*, in 1846, unions represented not just the city's craftworkers but also laborers such as the stevedores and dock builders, where the influx of Irish was just beginning to be felt.

In his *Eagle* article Whitman warmly supported the organization of a benevolent society but denounced the attempt to regulate wages, which he saw as similar to tariffs, fair trade laws, and other such restrictions on business, to all of which he was opposed. He examined the case of the workers, however, and found it worthy of attention, pointing out that they labored from sunrise to dark for sixty-four and a half cents and were docked exorbitantly for being only minutes late. "And," he exclaimed, "many of these men have families of children to feed, and clothe, and *educate*—and potatoes are a dollar a bushel, and flour and beef unusually high! . . . Let our philanthropists not go to oppressed England and starving Ireland for samples of scanty comfort."[26] A month later Whitman was not so sympathetic. He editorialized that the new Laborers' Association had not only set its own prices and hours but the men now refused to work unless all were employed, which, he says, the city's requirements did not at the time justify. He regretted that the laborers were "going to the very excess of injustice which they complained of in their own former employers."[27]

The following day the editor reported that several of those in the association had called upon him and made him realize he had not done its members justice, for they were in fact ready to receive any work when available. One supposes that the contingent of workers with whom he met included more than a few Irish, for Whitman went on to a lengthy discussion of the condition of Irish laborers. Whigs and nativists, he claimed, say the Irish are a "low ignorant set" who do not belong in the country. He argued that though they were ignorant in "book-lore" and "perhaps uncouth in manners," they had come here "pining and panting for a new and better home" and were opposed to "all kinds of tyranny." Largely because of this last-named quality, Whitman professed to have felt great pride when in a political meeting he had seen "a mortar-stained laborer coolly taking his prominent part in the proceedings." He thought he was witnessing "the budding in a fellow creature's long darkened breast, of the seeds of freedom, and of a knowledge of his own rights." There is, Whitman claimed, a glory to such a dawning "even in the despised hod-carrier."[28]

The same spring of 1846 brought a strike at Brooklyn's Atlantic

Dock by Irish dock construction workers seeking higher pay. There was violence, especially when the construction firm brought in German workers to replace the striking Irish. In the *Eagle* Whitman claimed the disturbances were not caused by Brooklyn workers but by "blustering rowdies" from New York "who seize every occasion to fan the flames of riot."[29] Late in his life Whitman claimed to have been familiar with the dockworkers, "the Be-Jesus boys," he called them, "in New York — stevedores on the wharves: I am soft for them, too — the real genuine fellows: but there's a rough gang, set, in New York . . . a dangerous gang."[30] Dangerous they no doubt were, and the violence of their strikes was far from Whitman's vision of comradely workers. In the Atlantic Dock strike German workers were attacked and badly beaten, for which a number of Irish were indicted. The indictments broke the strike, and though many of the Irish returned to their jobs, the workforce was carefully set at half Irish, half German, which meant that many Irish workers lost jobs. Most devastating, however, there was no increase in salary for the laborers on land, who were mostly Irish, while the dredgemen, all Germans, received an increase of five cents an hour, bringing their hourly rate to eighty-five cents, five cents more than the Irish were paid.[31]

In editorializing on the worst aspects of the dock strike Whitman pointed out that, "with all their faults, the Irish are a warm-hearted people." He then told of a striking Irishman who found some forty or so non-English-speaking Germans (scabs called in to replace the strikers) who had finished work but were fearful of crossing the picket line to get to the ferry and return home to New York. The Irishman took the Germans to the boat and saw them safely across the river, where, with no common language in which to do so, they made every effort to convey to him their gratitude.[32]

Consideration of this type did not extend to black workers, however; the Longshoremen's United Benevolent Society, formed in 1852, operated exclusively for the Irish dockworkers but proclaimed its willingness to accept any white workers it deemed worthy of working the docks. The key word here is "white," for in 1850 the Irish dockworkers had gone on strike to force the firing of a black worker. Subsequent strikes, in 1852, 1855, 1862, and 1863, though undertaken for higher wages, also involved violence aimed at black workers brought in to replace the strikers.[33]

On principle, in the 1840s and 1850s Whitman did not support the idea of organized labor, which he saw as an attempt to interfere with business and manufacturing. There was always the hope, however, that the narrowness of focus that shaped the views of most immigrants would expand under the influence of democracy. About 1856 Whitman noted to himself what he believed to be the "Gist" of his work: "To give others, readers, people, the materials to decide for themselves, and *know*, or grow toward *knowing*, with cleanliness and strength."[34] Below this he lists a number of New York newspapers and their street addresses, perhaps with a view of finding in at least some of them outlets for his proposed educational program. The only ethnic paper on the list is the *Irish-American*, at 116 Nassau Street, and while there is no direct evidence that Whitman actually published in it, the paper was the one Irish newspaper in New York that would have welcomed such a liberal approach.[35]

The *Irish-American* began publication in New York in the summer of 1849; its owner and editor was Patrick Lynch, former editor of the Boston Irish Catholic newspaper, the *Pilot*. In Boston Lynch had used his paper to support revolutionary movements in Europe and repeal of the enforced union of England and Ireland. These positions made him unpopular with the Roman Catholic hierarchy of Boston, who feared seeing their people in the States thrust into dangerous situations if they adopted Lynch's views. Lynch learned from his experience, and in moving to New York to begin publication of the *Irish-American*, he made an effort to reconcile Irish American republicanism and Roman Catholic interests. In the first issue of the paper he indicated he would support democratic-republican principles but would not forsake Catholicism, and in later editorials he scrupulously defended the honor of the Church.[36] Nevertheless, Lynch's republican tendencies were strong, and though his newspaper bore on its masthead the motto "neutral in religion and politics," it was not long before it clearly demonstrated its editor's leanings. These sympathies may have led Whitman to see the paper as a possible outlet for his own democratic proselytizing, a way of placing in the hands of its readers "the materials to decide for themselves" and thus hasten the democratization of the Irish in America.

The process of democratization, Whitman knew, had begun long before among the Irish Protestants who had arrived in the States earlier. It could continue among the more recent Catholic arrivals, he believed, if the influence of their priests could be overcome. The Irish had started coming to North America before that continent boasted a free and independent nation. The first to arrive were mostly Protestants — Ulster-Scots who were Presbyterian (Andrew Jackson's parents were among these) and others who were Church of

Ireland or Anglican. Many proved themselves valiant in both the Revolutionary War and the War of 1812. A slow but steady immigration rate continued, with an upsurge early in the 1840s that seemed to signal the spiraling rate of increase that would follow the famines in Ireland. Among those who came in the years of a declining economy in the southern counties of Ireland, immediately preceding the famine, were Catholics who then found themselves at odds with the already established Protestant Irish when such issues arose as the controversial move to fund parochial schools with public tax monies. The famine, of course, brought the great waves of Catholic immigration. In the years between 1847 and 1851, 848,000 Irish entered New York City's port. So many of them remained in the city that in 1860 New York was the most Irish city in the United States, with the Irish population totaling some 200,000 out of a total population of 800,000.[37]

Census figures for 1870 show a New York City Irish-born population of 201,999.[38] At that time roughly 75 percent of New York's Irish voted Democratic (the remainder, Protestants for the most part, made up the Irish wing of the city's Republican Party), though there was some discontent that the Democrats did not see fit to run an Irish candidate for mayor.[39] Nonetheless, the Irish vote in New York (11 percent of the state's total population and 21 percent of the city's) was strong enough to secure the elections in 1870 of Democrats A. Oakey Hall as mayor and John T. Hoffman as governor.[40]

The Irish had played a vital role in shifting the political power base away from Albany and toward New York City. The earliest Irish immigrants found their way into whichever of the parties suited their political philosophy, but as the immigrant population increased and especially as it became clear that the immigrants intended to remain in the city, they were viewed by the Democratic Party as a means of gaining power through sheer force of numbers. This brought the Irish into the rivalry between upstate and downstate politicians in which Albany Whigs, later Republicans, sought to keep the city submissive to the state government. Already highly politicized when they arrived in America because of their own country's forced subservience to England, the New York Irish allied with the Democrats, who were fighting to gain control of city politics. When the doors to the Tammany Society and the Democratic Party were opened to them they entered in great numbers, eventually finding their way, by 1870, to Albany. For some years William Tweed wielded great power in the state legislature. Of its fewer than thirty members, nine were native

Irishmen, the parents of another eight had been born in Ireland, and three had other Irish family connections.[41]

Tweed's power extended into the streets of the city, where his Irish backers formed the largest group of municipal workers. In 1871 Tweed introduced in the state legislature a new charter for New York City which was opposed by a group of anti-Irish dissidents calling themselves the "Young Democrats." Hoping to curb Tweed's control of the party, the group planned a coup. With the help of the Metropolitan Police, however, Tweed was able to prevent the meeting at which the takeover was to occur, an indication not only of his influence on the police force but of the large number of Irish who marched in its ranks. Other powerful forces were at work as well, led by wealthy reformers who, stimulated to action by disclosures in the Republican *New York Times* of massive fraud and financial misdealings within the city government, now sought to oust Tweed and restore fiscal responsibility. Unfortunately, any threat to Tweed was seen by the Irish political bloc as a threat to them.

By the time the July 1871 observance of the Battle of the Boyne arrived, the city's Irish were already roiling. In January their rival political factions, Catholic and Protestant, had vied for the honor of welcoming five Fenian prisoners recently released from English jails. Among the five were Jeremiah O'Donovan Rossa, who within a few years would command the distinction of being Ireland's most public, and most radical, exile, and John Devoy, the lifelong Irish freedom fighter. Devoy was a longtime associate of another exiled Fenian, John Boyle O'Reilly. The city's contending Irish sectarians were each eager to convey the rebels to the parade and festivities that awaited them. So fierce was the competition between the Tammany Catholics and the Orangemen that the exiles, who were interested only in gaining support for Ireland's cause, eschewed all convoys, turned away offers of swank hotels to stay at the less prestigious Sweeney's Hotel, and publicly chastised the New York Irish for their disunion.[42]

Spring brought its own troubles. In May there had been labor unrest, with Irish workers striking for pay increases. By July the city's Irish on both sides of the religious fence were smarting with the memory of the previous year's riot. The Catholics sought to have the mayor issue an order restraining the Orangemen from parading, but Hall chose to hide behind his superintendent of police and had him issue the ban. This cowardliness, as well as the ban itself, stirred the non-Irish of the city to public outcry. In an effort to quiet things, Governor Hoffman issued a proclamation sanctioning the observance.

Resentment at this edict coming from the governor they had elected spilled over into the streets as gangs of Irish laborers set upon the marchers with results much as Whitman described them. At the height of the riot, with the procession of Orangemen determinedly advancing on their tormenters, a shot was fired from a nearby window, and the militia of the Eighty-fourth Regiment, called out by the governor, fired into the crowd killing and injuring scores of people. The count of dead and injured on this one July day was in the neighborhood of 165.[43] It was, the *Times* said, "a day never to be forgotten in the history of the City of New-York." Certainly it was a day to arouse memories of the previous decade's draft riot, another stain on the city's history in which the Irish had figured prominently. One account of the Orange Riots, published in 1873, evoked the draft riot by way of praising "the almost universal faithfulness of the Roman Catholic Irish police to their duty. In this [the Boyne Day riot], as well as in the draft riots, they have left a record of which any city might be proud."[44]

Such praise was a tribute to the members of a largely Irish police force that all but owed its existence to the need, real or perceived, to hold in check the city's Irish. In nineteenth-century New York, street riots were a form of public exhibition, an "acting out" of frustration and grievance and so much a part of the cityscape that Whitman includes "the fury of roused mobs" in his descant on the city in "Song of Myself." Riots, along with increased crime, created a need for a fully staffed municipal police force to replace the system of part-time wardens and watchers considered sufficient early in the century. For a time, after the police force was established, members of the city's governing body, the Common Council, were allowed to appoint men to serve two-year terms as police officers, thus initiating a political connection to law enforcement not easily corrected. In 1845 the Democrats then in power brought into existence a force of eight hundred paid police; by 1856 the city's "Civic Army," as it was called, numbered twelve hundred, but, fearful of such an army in their midst, citizens insisted they be unarmed and without uniforms.[45] Uniforms were introduced soon after, however, in the hope they would command respect from the roughs of the city. With the Democratic Party's continued hold on city politics, jobs on the police force became a part of the party's patronage offered most often to the Irish on whose support the party relied. Though there were times when they were accused of favoring their own, over the years the Irish police came to win the respect of most of the city's citizens.

Whitman, too, was impressed by New York's police and their actions in the Orange Riots. He wrote to Peter Doyle:

The N. Y. police looked & behaved splendidly — no fuss, few words, but *action* — great, brown, bearded, able, American looking fellows, (Irish stock, though, many of them) — I had great pleasure in looking on them — something new, to me, it quite set me up to see such chaps, all dusty & worn, looked like veterans —[46]

Similarly, to William O'Connor he commented:

the *Policemen* looked & behaved splendidly — I have been looking on them & been with them much, & am refreshed by their presence — it is something new — in some respects they afford the most encouraging sign I have got — brown, bearded, worn, resolute, American-looking men, dusty & sweaty — looked like veterans — the *stock* here even in these cities is in the main magnificent — the heads either shysters, villains or impotents —.[47]

Whitman appears to have been looking at the police from a dual perspective, both of which aided his newly acquired respect. For one thing, he associates them with veterans of the Civil War, a group he held in the highest regard and personal affection. In so doing, he sees, perhaps for the first time, beyond their ethnic "stock," viewing them not as Irishmen but as Americans — or at least as "American-looking."[48] From the vantage point of this new regard, he can clearly delineate them from the scurrilous politicians at whose behest they function. Indeed, most New Yorkers were beginning to see those at the head of the city's political organization, the Tweed Ring, in the same light as Whitman does here, as villains. Perhaps the only good thing to come out of the Orange Riots of 1870 and 1871 was the way in which they hastened a public recognition of rampant political infamy so that, amid mounting evidence of fraud and corruption, 1871 saw the end of the Tweed Ring and its hold on the city's politics.

What we cannot fail to notice in Whitman's account is the personal reaction he registers, the pleasure he derives from observing the police, an emotion which is "something new to me," he says. If we connect this to his comment on their "stock," an obvious reference to their Irish roots, we recognize an admission of a change of mind, perhaps even of heart, about the presumed character of these Irishmen.

The question of character was a subject on which most nineteenth-century New Yorkers held opinions, since character and its national determination had come very much to the foreground of public discourse, largely as the result of the great influx of Irish. At the time of Whitman's letters, the individual who most fully epitomized the adverse image of the Irish politician as possessed of incorrigibly low character was one of the villains to whom Whitman obliquely refers, Irish-born Richard Barrett Connolly, known as "Slippery Dick," who came to America in 1826 and rose to become comptroller of New York City in the years 1867 to 1871. Connolly was the principal factor in the downfall of the Tweed Ring because of financial malfeasance from which he personally profited, to the tune of some six million dollars he is believed to have taken with him when he fled the country to avoid a jail sentence. Amid the general blatancy of the Ring members' wrongdoing, Connolly stood out for what was described as his low cunning, his greed, and the way in which he had distinguished himself in the course of his political rise by a shrewd use of his ethnicity to further his career.[49]

Connolly moved through the ranks, keeping pace with the political advancements being made by New York's Irish. In 1839 he was elected to the Tammany Society and worked his way up. He latched on to the campaign of the former Democratic United States Senator Fernando Wood when Wood sought Irish support for his bid for mayor of New York in 1854. So fully was Connolly later identified with the city's Irish that when Whitman wrote his 1871 letter to O'Connor, contrasting the upright behavior of the New York police with the chicanery of their leaders, he may well have had in mind the Irish-born Connolly. Whitman wrote his letter on July 14, just six days after the New York Times (its owner having refused a bribe from Boss Tweed not to publish) had begun printing the full record of Connolly's impropriety.

Whitman's improved perception of Irish police may also have been helped by his deep attachment to Peter Doyle and his family. Pete's brother, Francis, was a police officer in Washington, D.C. In May 1871, before leaving Washington for New York, Whitman had prepared an editorial defending Francis Doyle against newspaper claims of brutality in the arrest of a young boy on theft charges. Evidently the newspaper had taken up the case as something of a cause, for Whitman refers to a persistence in reportage that "amounts to persecution." The reprimand by Doyle's superiors is enough, he claimed, to bring the matter to an end, but Whitman could not resist adding his own admonition, that the attempt to make "martyrs and heroes of the steadily increasing swarms of juvenile thieves and vagabonds who infest the streets of Washington" is a disservice to the citizenry. As to Francis Doyle, he is described as "a little stern perhaps" but the bearer of "an excellent reputation" who "served the Union cause, as soldier or sailor, all through the war."[50] The article remained in Whitman's notebook, unpublished, perhaps at the request of the officer himself or of his family, who may have wished to avoid exacerbating the situation. Before the year was out Francis Doyle was dead of a gunshot wound inflicted by Maria Shea (known as the "Queen of Louse Alley") when he attempted to recover articles she had stolen. Whitman attended Doyle's funeral on New Year's Eve 1871 and must have found it a sad ending to a year that had seen the Irish caught up in too many instances of violence in American streets.[51]

The larger issue in the Whitman letters is his changed attitude toward the Irish in general. No longer the "coarse, blustering rowdies," as he described the union organizers he had once condemned, the Irish had come to mean to him such beloved friends as Peter Doyle and William Douglas O'Connor. If the events of that year moved Whitman to recall earlier ones involving New York's Irish, he could not have failed to note the distance he had covered in his personal reactions to this immigrant group. It was a leap shared by many Americans, for whom the Civil War and the heroic participation of thousands of Irish-born immigrants proved a turning point in attitudes. But despite his changed attitude, there is little reason to believe Whitman would not have continued to justify his intent, if not his rhetoric, in the *New York Aurora* in 1842 when he publicly reviled the Irish and took on no less a figure than the Reverend John Hughes, bishop (later the first archbishop) of New York. His intention would have been the same in 1871, for the one constant in Whitman's attitude toward the Irish is revealed in his description to Peter Doyle of a segment of the Boyne Day rioting, "the Irish lower orders (catholic)." It was their allegiance to Roman Catholicism, rather than the Irish themselves, that Whitman could not accept, for he viewed their church not only as undemocratic but as antidemocratic. When he could dissociate the Irish from their religion he found much about them to his liking, even identifying his poetic persona with them in *Leaves of Grass*. Privately, as in the cases of Doyle and O'Connor, he could love them above all others. But an Irish friend's Catholicism could remain a stumbling block, so much so that, as shall be seen in the case of John Boyle O'Reilly, Whitman felt forced to deny its existence.

Whitman's furious and unguarded attack on New York's Catholic Irish in 1842 might be offered as evidence of strong anti-Irish feelings had it not occurred when he was still quite young and opinionated, if it did not also suggest the matter was part of the ongoing viciousness common to the city's newspaper business, and, most significantly, if it did not reveal cultural influences he could hardly be expected to have withstood. Recent verifications of Whitman's journalism and the availability of the full texts of his *Aurora* editorials are helpful in understanding the matter.[52] Coupled with a historical background on the public school issue and placed within a biographical framework, they allow a more complete narrative to emerge.

When the twenty-three-year-old Whitman joined the staff of the *Aurora* in 1842, first as the writer of a series of articles and then as editor, the two-penny daily was one of many newspapers produced in New York City. Among the others were such popular papers as James Gordon Bennett's *Herald* and a relative newcomer, Horace Greeley's *Tribune*. Most of the newspapers of the time aligned themselves with a political party, and the *Aurora* was mildly Democratic, though it concentrated more on the city's social scene than on its politics. As editor, Whitman would alter this. He was no novice to the field, having already racked up at least ten years' experience on Long Island papers — the *Patriot*, a Democratic organ; the Whig *Star*; and the self-proclaimed *Democrat*. For one year, 1838–1839, he was owner, editor, and printer of his own paper, the *Long Islander*, produced near his birthplace in Huntington. In Manhattan he had worked on weeklies, Park Benjamin's *New World* and the somewhat idiosyncratically named *Brother Jonathan*. The jingoistic but literarily discriminating *Democratic Review*, owned by John Louis O'Sullivan, published some of Whitman's early short stories and poetry. In his late years Whitman recalled O'Sullivan as "a handsome, generous fellow. He treated me well."[53] To be treated well in the rough and tumble world of New York journalism of the time was not a small matter, but neither was Whitman's move into the heady atmosphere of the democratic crusade spearheaded by O'Sullivan and the *Democratic Review*.

John L. O'Sullivan was not typical of any of the Irish who came to America either in the prefamine or the famine years. While most Irishmen who arrived in the decade he did, the 1820s, were Ulster Protestants who fell into the broad category of artisans and craftworkers, the O'Sullivan family could boast an assortment of men who made their living and their mark as soldiers and rebels, fighting in various European countries (most often on the losing side) generally, though not always, in opposition to England. John Louis was born on a British warship off the coast of Gibraltar in 1813 and was brought to New York in 1827. Though baptized a Catholic, he was an Episcopalian for most of his life, before returning to the Catholicism of his family.[54]

O'Sullivan's true religion was democracy, which he believed was the future of all countries and the world's most needed form of political advance. Despite his own scholarly achievements, he eschewed the fields of teaching and the law to enter the world of newspaper and magazine writing. Early work in New York City led to the launching of a paper in Washington, D.C., in 1835. O'Sullivan decided to use its location in the nation's capital and its favored position with the newly elected Martin Van Buren to turn it into a national journal of literature and politics intended to further the advance of democracy and of the Democratic Party. O'Sullivan quickly gathered into his fold some of the country's outstanding writers and thinkers by promising them a truly democratic forum in which they might express any political idea, while he as editor would uphold the party line. In practice, the latter consideration pretty much limited the published materials to those written from a Democratic perspective, but the magazine also had a strong literary goal, which was to present the very best that a democratic society could offer. While the New England writers, with the exception of Nathaniel Hawthorne, generally sniffed at his invitation to write for the *Review*, O'Sullivan was really interested in the kinds of materials that were more likely to emanate from such democratic — and Democratic — centers as New York City. In 1841 he moved the *Democratic Review* to Manhattan. By then he was a member of the New York state legislature, and the magazine's ties to the Democratic Party were stronger than ever.

In addition to the party's aims, O'Sullivan hoped to advance those of the Young America movement, which in these, its early years, were principally literary and cultural. Young America had no real connection to the Young Ireland movement of the 1840s, but it shared a common nationalistic fervor, which in Ireland, of course, took the form of promoting Irish culture over the claims of the dominant English culture. O'Sullivan and the Young America group promoted the development of an American culture that would reflect the working-class interests and attitudes most evident in cities such as New York. Small wonder that Whitman felt himself to have been well treated by O'Sullivan, for Whitman's social, cultural, and political views accorded with his. In fact, Whitman's first entry in the *Democratic*

Review, "Death in the School-Room (A Fact)" in 1841, not only denounced corporal punishment of children but probably also was intended to support O'Sullivan's stand in the state legislature against capital punishment.

Whitman had already been initiated into the turbulent world of politics, both through his experiences with newspapers that served as party organs and via his own involvement as an appointed Democratic electioneer on behalf of Van Buren. In the 1840 presidential campaign he took part in political debates and gave speeches for the party and its candidate, achieving some local recognition though his oratorical skills were somewhat lacking.[55] He was also quite familiar with Tammany Hall and its political objectives. The Tammany Society, originally a fraternal group named for a Native American chieftain, had its origins in late-eighteenth-century Enlightenment ideals, which quickly became Jeffersonian principles. Its benevolence toward the indigent and the working poor of the city led to support from that quarter for Tammany's later political aspirations. In the 1820s the society offered membership to the Irish, and a decade later they and it were dedicated Democrats. By 1840, when the society supported Van Buren for president, its political influence reached deep and wide in the city, where it had become synonymous with the Democratic Party. Whitman's electioneering for Van Buren in that campaign brought him into close contact with Tammany. In 1877 he remembered learning much about Thomas Paine from a personal acquaintance of the great infidel, Tammany member Colonel John Fellows. It was, he recalled, "some thirty-five years ago, in New York city, at Tammany hall, of which place I was then a frequenter."[56] That would have been around 1842, about the same time he went to the *Aurora*. By then Whitman's philosophical and political ideas had been shaped by an early exposure, via his father's liberalism, to such socialistic and anticlerical reformers as Robert Owen and Frances Wright. His later absorption of firsthand accounts of one of his father's heroes, Thomas Paine, well may have served to fuel the anger evident in his *Aurora* editorials when Irish Catholics became a dominating influence on Tammany and the Democratic Party. At the time, Catholicism was antithetical to those who believed, as did Whitman and his father, in individual liberty and freedom of thought.

Given his political background, it is not surprising that the new editor of the *Aurora* would move the paper into the political sphere. Nor is it surprising that the issue that would capture his attention more than any other would be one having to do not only with Catholicism but with education. The classroom and schoolteaching were also a part of the young Whitman's recent past, and he had many strong opinions on the subject. His role as schoolteacher had come about not by his own choosing. When the great fire of August 1835 swept through the printing district of New York, only two of the city's six large morning newspapers survived the flames. Along with the print houses and newspapers lost in the fire went the jobs of many, like Whitman, who were employed within its precincts. Having attained the position of printer only a short time earlier in that year, Whitman's was a case of last hired, first to go, and he had reluctantly turned to schoolteaching. It was an alternative he preferred to working with his housewright father, but it thrust him back to Long Island which, after his years of city life, he found irritating. Letters to a sympathetic friend describing his torments at Woodbury, Long Island, in the years 1840 and 1841, though written partly in jest, reveal his dissatisfaction with life as a country school teacher forced to sleep in the homes of his pupils and partake of such rural pleasures as "huckleberry pic-nics."[57] Despite this dissatisfaction, Whitman took seriously the whole subject of education and later wrote articles and editorials advocating better education of teachers and improved methods of instruction. His very popular short story "Death in the School-Room (A Fact)" was written while he was teaching on Long Island, the year before his involvement in the Bishop Hughes school affair.[58]

While Whitman was still teaching on Long Island in 1840, New York City's Bishop John Hughes approached the city's Public School Society seeking funds for Catholic schools. The society was a private philanthropic agency instituted in 1805 to administer school funds drawn from the state budget and allocated by the city's Common Council. Since the hundred or so city schools were not part of the state's district school system, the society was also charged with providing general supervision of the city's schools. Attendance at city schools was not mandated by law, which meant that thousands of children did not attend any school and thus received no education. When the bishop informed the Whig governor William Seward that many Catholic children were kept from school or were sent to church schools by parents who saw it as a matter of conscience, the governor was genuinely, as well as politically, motivated to do something. He proposed reforms that would make the city's schools, including the eight church-funded Catholic schools educating approximately three thousand children, part of the state system and allow for the establishment of additional public schools that would satisfy the desires of Catholic parents.[59]

The reason why many Catholic parents felt conscience bound to keep their children from the public schools had to do with the generally accepted Protestant culture that permeated the schools, including hymns, readings without interpretation from the King James Bible (Catholics believed the Scriptures needed to be interpreted by clergy), textbooks that presented history from a Protestant viewpoint, and many teachers and supervisors who looked down upon their "unenlightened" Catholic charges. Perhaps the most blatantly offensive textbook was the widely employed *The Irish Heart* which, using poor imitations of an Irish brogue, presented Irish characters who in every way justified the claim of the book's preface: Irish emigration was making America "the common sewer of Ireland."[60]

Since the Irish made up the city's dominant Roman Catholic group and had the formidable Bishop Hughes as their leader, they became the center of the storm of protest that developed over the school fund issue. The protest began when, on the strength of the governor's proposals, Hughes went to the Common Council seeking funding for his schools. The Democratic-controlled council reacted by accusing Seward of trying to win Irish Catholic votes, which, through Tammany Hall, the Democrats were able to command. While the council considered Hughes's request, the Presbyterian Church and the Jewish community let the council know that they, too, would be looking for their share of the public funds; they were soon followed by the Baptists, Methodist Episcopalians, and Dutch Reformed. With this kind of stimulus, the council took a hard look at earlier state legislation (specifically the 1824 law nullifying the 1813 statute that had allowed sectarian schools to partake of public funds) before denying the Catholic request in January 1841. It concluded that Catholics had a right to send their children to Catholic schools, but Catholic schools did not have a right to public funds. At this Hughes went into high gear, issuing letters to the general public in which he argued the Catholic position and using the pages of the Catholic weekly newspaper, the *New York Freeman's Journal*, to advance his cause.

Irish-born John Hughes, who became bishop of New York in 1842, was not a careful and reasoned contender but an emotional one, and he saw injustice to his parishoners in this and many other aspects of the city's political life. His response to the council's decision was that since the state legislature had given the council and, through the council, the Public School Society, the right to administer state funds, only the legislature could rule on the matter. Hughes was counting on Seward to wield influence in Albany.

The Catholics presented their petition to the legislature, which turned it over to the state's highest educational officer, John C. Spencer. Spencer eventually recommended that the state district school system be extended to include New York City. Under this plan the districts would choose their own representatives to administer the district school, thus ethnic and religious concerns would be addressed on a local level. Hughes was delighted with this recommendation. It was submitted to the legislature for action but was delayed largely because of complaints from the Public School Society, which feared its own imminent demise under the new system. The nativists also began to rumble their displeasure, and with what seemed like a strong negative reaction to the proposal — and with an election looming in November — both the Whig and Democratic parties turned against the Catholics. Hughes took a desperate measure and offered a slate of independent candidates under the banner of Carroll Hall. His aim was really to push the Democrats into endorsing the Catholic position on the school issue, but they failed to give in. As a result, the Carroll Hall candidates, all of whom were elected, split the Democratic vote, allowing the Whigs to take City Hall. Only those Democrats who had not had Catholic backing were defeated, which proved Hughes's point to the party. At the state level the Whigs lost control of both houses as well as numerous other posts and began to fear both the power of Hughes's leadership and the Catholic vote.

The Democrats were equally fearful of losing the Catholics, and the Democratic majority in the state legislature soon was ready to pass whatever school bill would placate them. Seward first proposed Spencer's plan but, seeking a compromise, altered it to provide for the continuation of the Public School Society. Hughes gathered over twelve thousand signatures on a petition backing the governor's plan and presented it to the State Assembly in January 1842. The Public School Society, still fighting to retain control, asked for a delay and for an investigatory committee of state and city education officials. The committee, under the leadership of Assemblyman William Maclay, reported to the assembly that the Public School Society was not doing a good job of educating children, or of gaining the trust of parents, or of handling school funds. The assembly then engaged in a general debate of the bill and began writing rules of organization by which the new district schools would operate. March 1842 was the crucial time when New York City was engulfed in turmoil over this matter, and it was then the new editor of the *Aurora* entered the picture.

Whitman began by pointing out his familiarity and experience with the state district schools; he also claimed to have over the previous six months visited every public school in the city. He promised that the *Aurora*'s position would be based on "wholesome judgement of the city's truest advantage."[61] The paper's position proved to be squarely in favor of the Public School Society, which the editor claimed was educating all the city's children with no prejudice. He provided details of enrollments in various schools, including percentages of Catholic students, adding that there were many Catholic teachers. The following week Whitman began his attack on Bishop Hughes: the petitions Hughes had garnered did not contain legitimate signatures; on his instructions Catholics kept their children out of school when state officials visited in order to support his case; and, getting to the heart of the matter, "this cunning, flexible, serpent tongued priest has had the insolence to appear in the political forum."[62] Whitman continued to write editorials on the subject, questioning the wisdom of the state legislators who he claimed lacked experience to judge the matter, insisting that Hughes controlled Catholic politicians by the threat of excommunication, blaming priests for stirring up Catholic parents who were otherwise satisfied with the schools, and pointing out the intelligence and decorum of female students at a public school in Five Points, one of the worst Irish neighborhoods.

On St. Patrick's Day his editorial was headed, "Insult to American Citizenship!" It dealt with a rally held at City Hall Park the day before by supporters of the Public School Society and claimed the rally was overrun by its opponents using the rowdiest of mob tactics. Whitman describes them as "foreigners," "filthy wretches," "blear-eyed and bloated offscourings from the stews, blind alleys and rear lanes," who broke up the meeting with "howlings in their hideous native tongue." Priests were there, he says, "sly, false, deceitful villains" who encouraged the mob. He calls on citizens to rise up against the "hypocritical scoundrel Hughes, and his minions."[63] The following day Whitman published extracts from a letter he had received that defended Hughes, but he claimed his paper would continue to fight religious "fanaticism."[64]

With this diatribe Whitman had moved dangerously close to the position of the Native American Party, though when charged with this he protested it was not so. As he would later do on the question of slavery, Whitman tried to find a midpoint between what he saw as the extremes of nativism and a surrender to the demands of "foreigners" in the country's midst. Just four years later, in June 1846, he would editorialize in the *Brooklyn Daily Eagle* against the antiforeigner position of the Native American Party by pointing out the simple facts of available land in "the New World" as opposed to the old. Then, using Ireland to make his point,

There is too much mankind, and too little earth.—What horrors are every month to be seen in Ireland from Bantry Bay to the Giant's Causeway! What wretchedness in the hovels of the poor peasants! What grief and hunger have reigned among her people ever since Castlereagh [Viscount Robert Stewart] and Pitt [British prime minister] consummated the atrocity of "the Union!"[65]

On March 24, 1842, however, his *Aurora* editorial began to widen the focus of his attack in ways that need to be taken into consideration. He points out the bind in which Tammany finds itself for its heavy reliance on the Irish vote, which now places Tammany in Hughes's hands. He also attacks the party organ, the *New Era*, and its editor, Levi Slamm, for having gone over to the side of the Catholics.

With this piece Whitman appears to have begun a not-so-subtle campaign to discredit the *New Era* and, by suggesting the need for a "truly American" paper to represent the party, to posit the *Aurora* as a suitable replacement.[66] Whitman's attention to the school bill had been dwindling because for a time it appeared the bill would not become law. Instead, he stepped up his attack on the *New Era*, claiming it hoped to dictate to the Democratic Party its own support of foreigners, "a large portion of whom are now in open rebellion." Later in the month he would remind his readers of the party's already expressed dissatisfaction with its journalistic organ and asserted the Democratic Party will "*never*" be ruled by "foreign priests" and the *New Era*.[67] On March 29 he reviewed "The New York Press," evaluating each newspaper, and proclaimed the *Aurora* "by far the best newspaper in the town." Obviously hoping to displace the *New Era*, on the following day Whitman offered a definition of his paper's position relative to nativism, a position he no doubt believed would bring it into line with the Democratic Party. Claiming it is not "antiforeigners," the paper is, he says, pro-America in that it sees this republic as possessing the capacities for solving the problem of how far humans can evolve in self-perfection and self-government.[68] This definition, really of his own beliefs, is not to be discounted, for it reveals a genuine concern of Whitman's that remained with him throughout his life.

With an April 12 election looming that involved all the seats on the city's Common Council, the Democrats held an inconclusive strategy meeting at Tammany Hall on April 5. The next day Whitman implored the party not to follow the dictates of the *New Era* and its Irish Catholic cohorts but to stand by its democratic principles.[69] Hughes, however, was not waiting for the party to make up its mind. Once again he declared an independent Carroll Hall ticket of nominees for city offices but conceded the ticket would be withdrawn if the Maclay bill was passed. Whitman pleaded in the *Aurora* with the state Democrats to stand firm against these tactics, but the party was too fearful of losing the city's Irish vote to heed such pleas. After numerous amendments the legislature passed a school bill that did not allow public funding of religious schools but did proscribe all sectarianism in the public schools and made the city schools part of the state system with a board of education to oversee them. The school bill was passed (by a vote of 13 to 12 when New York City Democratic Senator John Scott, who opposed it, deliberately avoided the roll call), and the Carroll Hill candidates returned to the Democratic fold. The *Aurora* editor was so disgusted by his party's capitulation that he strongly urged Democrats not to vote for either party in the city election. Robert Morris, the Democratic mayor, was reelected, and the Whigs, who gained control of the Common Council, joined forces with the Native American Party to urge a repeal of the new school law. Whitman vented his fury crying, "Has it come to be, that *Irishman* is a better title to office, here, than *American?*" He warned that the Catholics would continue to press their advantage, which Tammany, having gone this far, would not be able to withstand.[70] His final word on the subject was titled "Americanism," where he firmly repudiated the doctrines of the Native American Party but confessed a desire to see Americans remain free of foreign influences whether from within or without the country.[71]

While Whitman's attacks on Bishop Hughes and Irish Catholics are highly offensive to readers today, they were exceeded by editors in other city papers, especially by James Gordon Bennett of the *Herald*, who engaged in personal vituperation bordering on mania and who believed Hughes was attempting to organize an Irish political party. The highly respected *Evening Post* warned Catholics against "priestly influence in the sphere of politics," and the Whig *Tribune* branded the actions of the Catholics "cowardice, insult and treachery."[72] All of these papers and their editors, including Whitman, were deeply concerned for a basic principle of democracy at stake in this issue, the separation of church and state, which they believed would have been compromised by the use of public funds to teach religion in the schools.[73] The matter of "priestly influence in the sphere of politics" was one that Americans eventually came to understand as a legitimate right of clergy in a democracy, but at the time it was frightening. Most important, what the Protestant majority, including Whitman, had to learn to accept was the justice of demands by minorities for full inclusion in the political process, not just — as was the case with the Democratic Party — to provide dependable votes. American history, of course, reveals that succeeding generations of varying majorities have had to learn to accept this idea, that it is part of the process of democratization and is perhaps most common to the urban experience.

Clear from Whitman's *Aurora* editorials is his genuine fear of the spread of ideas that bound the individual to religious beliefs and hierarchical institutions, such as the Roman Catholic Church, which he believed subverted the principle of self-determination underlying democracy. The Irish immigrant played into this fear only insofar as he or she refused to break free of the religious bond. Whitman's views were shared even by some of Hughes's supporters, among them Horace Greeley and New England's most conspicious convert to Roman Catholicism, Orestes A. Brownson. A decade later Brownson reached the conclusion that the Irish gave Catholicism a bad name and that anti-Catholic bias was really predicated on hatred of what Irish Catholics represented to the general public.[74] Unlike Brownson, whose spiritual journey took him through at least four religious affiliations, Whitman's appreciation of formalized religion was never to go beyond his admiration for the Quaker orator Elias Hicks. In notes written in the 1860s he seems to be attempting to modify his reactions to religious practices he had earlier condemned and to see them as part of a developmental process of which he no longer complains:

> Those stages, all over the world leaving their memories and inheritances in all the continents — how credulous! how childlike and simple! the priests revered — the bloody rites, the mummer-

ies and all the puerile and bad things. . . . Of present and past, I do *not* blame them for doing what they have done, and are doing — I applaud them that they have done so well.[75]

In 1842, however, when he saw the highly political Catholic immigrants rallying to their priests' cries, he clearly feared the worst for the future of the Republic. It was a reaction in which he was far from alone. Newspapers such as the *Aurora* reflected more than the thoughts and attitudes of their writers, they reflected the popular society within which they found an audience. The language Whitman employed was that of his readers, and the image his words evoked was one already familiar enough to be recognizable to them. His horror at the mix of Irish Catholicism and politics and his descriptions of the Irish as subhuman violent rioters point to the figure of "Paddy," invented by antebellum Americans faced with an influx of immigrants unlike any that preceded them. Whitman's characterization of the Irish as disturbers of peaceful political meetings goes right to the heart of the fear that gave rise to the stereotype: the perception of the Irish as politically subversive and, in their Roman Catholicism, a fundamental threat to democracy. One study of the stereotypical Paddy distinguishes between its two principal icons: extrinsic and intrinsic characteristics. Extrinsic characteristics, those that are manifest and demonstrable — having to do with inherited qualities and physical traits, economic conditions, religious and political convictions, and such behavorial dispositions as violence and "rowdiness"— constituted the popular image of Paddy in the 1840s and 1850s. This was a calamitous move away from an earlier perception that defined the Irish by intrinsic characteristics pertaining more to intellect, morality, and a love of freedom. The usual year of demarcation between the two is 1845, the year of the Irish famine; however, in New York City, where Irish immigration was heavy even prior to the famine, the change occurred a few years earlier, which places it at about the time of the 1842 public school debate.[76] In fact, we find Whitman using the word "Paddies" that year in the *Aurora.*

What occasioned the use of this particular ethnic slur was a bloody street fight that escalated into the kind of mob behavior so easily ignited in New York's troubled neighborhoods and just as easily turned into rioting. On the afternoon of the April 1842 city elections a band of Protestant Irish, nativists, and other anti-Irish Democrats, all of whom felt themselves to have been ignored by their party in favor of the Irish Catholics, descended upon a Catholic neighborhood and beat its inhabitants fiercely. The Catholics retreated but regrouped a few hours later, and the fighting resumed. Mayor Robert H. Morris and the police came to restore peace, but by some accounts the police did more harm to the Catholics than had their opponents. More and more combatants joined the action. When the Catholics retreated to their homes, they were followed by members of the Spartan Band (the principal instigators of the day's battles) who invaded the Irish Sixth Ward, even entering private homes and destroying the first floor of the Sixth Ward Hotel where a polling place was still open. The Spartans next headed for the bishop's residence behind St. Patrick's Cathedral on Mulberry Street. Hughes was not at home, so the mob vented its anger on the first floor of the building by smashing windows and threatening to burn the residence, a threat they might have made good but for the arrival of police.

Whitman commented editorially on the disturbances a number of times in the next few days, casually remarking, with regard to the damage to the bishop's residence, "Had it been the reverend hypocrite's head, instead of his windows, we could hardly find it in our soul to be sorrowful."[77] The following day he visited the Sixth Ward Hotel and, while admitting some destruction to property and individuals, denied it was extensive and accused the Catholics of having started "the whole rumpus, merely to generate sympathy for their cause, and to make capital of."[78] He also accused the "bog trotters" of having roamed the streets on election day seeking trouble and "grossly insulting" Americans. Even before the election day riot Whitman had briefly noted a "great fight" between some Sixth Ward Irish and members of "Mike Walsh's Spartans." "The Spartans routed the Paddies in magnificent style," Whitman reported, adding, "We like this young Walsh, and his society."[79]

The Spartan Band was led by Mike Walsh, a Protestant Irishman and friend of Whitman, who also wrote for the *Aurora* on occasion and who later would go far in Democratic politics. At this point he and his friend "Yankee" Sullivan were street brawlers and rioters, the very things that should have qualified them as Paddies, but because they were Protestants and, like Whitman, disaffected Democratic Party members, their behavior was excusable in his eyes.

Despite the disappointments he had experienced in 1842, Whitman regained his faith in the Democratic Party and proved himself so loyal to it that four years later he was rewarded with the editorship of the *Brooklyn Eagle*. One of his first pieces bears out his earlier contention in the *Aurora* that he was not a nativist. In the first week of March 1846 Whitman wrote in the *Eagle* of visiting New York docks where he saw ships at anchor that had weathered the cruel winter storms in the Atlantic the preceding months. The "dangers and escapes" these ships had endured were not lost on him, and he marveled at the condition of one, "[H]er spars, sails, and rigging are actually *drooping*." Two weeks later he was present when a Liverpool packet arrived, "her decks covered with emigrants." He was glad on their account that after their stormy passage the weather was fine, so that their impressions "of the strange land they had chosen for their home" might be sunny ones. The immigrants were, he says, "a robust good looking set, mostly Hibernians and, spite of Nativism, we sent them a hearty welcome to our republic, and a wish that they might indeed find 'better times a-coming!'"[80]

These are the same sorts of emigrants Herman Melville described in *Redburn* (1849), where his young sailor makes his first transatlantic voyage from New York to Liverpool and back. On the return trip the ship transports a number of emigrants, most of whom are leaving Ireland. While the conditions of their passage are stringent, it is clear from Melville's description, as well as Whitman's, that the "coffin ships" with their cargoes of starved and disease-ridden refugees had not yet begun to arrive in New York, so that Whitman could plausibly imagine the immigrants concerned only for good weather. It was no doubt the later arrivals of starved and sickened souls who moved him to write, in *Leaves of Grass*, of the sacredness of every individual, "no matter who, / Is it a slave? Is it one of the dullfaced immigrants just landed on the wharf? / Each belongs here or anywhere just as much as the welloff. . . . just as much as you."

Not yet aware in 1846 of the desperation that in many cases impelled the immigrants, what Whitman welcomed was a desire for political freedom that he read into the act of Irish emigration. A few months later this understanding of their situation was altered by his reading of a report on the Irish Coercion Bill of 1846 against which Daniel O'Connell fought a final battle before his death the following year. The copy was provided for him by one of the members of the Laborers' Association, several of whom earlier had taken him to task for his criticism of their association. The report proved something of a revelation to Whitman, who claimed never to "have realized the wrongs and destitution of Ireland so vividly" before reading it. "What a black and dreary narrative it furnishes," he exclaims, "of a nation having the truest and fullest resources, both in the natural talent of its citizens, and in the facilities of the country — and yet all crushed for the want of a judicious and liberal government!"[81]

It is obvious that Whitman saw signs of inherent good character in the Irish, so when he pointed to them as a stumbling block to the possibility presented by democracy for a human evolution into a more perfect form he was pointing to an extrinsic quality not rooted in character but in behavior, specifically the seeming refusal of the Irish to participate in this evolutionary process. This apparent refusal was especially frustrating to those who shared Whitman's more liberal view that a free society could not compel the individual; thus the Irishman who remained unwilling to change must be allowed to flourish in what Americans such as Whitman believed to be willful ignorance. To them the Paddy demonstrated not an inherent lack of character and intelligence but a determined preference for ignorance by clinging to his Roman Catholic faith, obeying its clergy, and maintaining a belligerent form of sectarian and political activity.

Distinctions such as those Whitman made between Paddies and the type of Irishman suggested by the nickname "Yankee" Sullivan (with the fusion that would later give rise to the hyphenated American) were of the kind that had transformed the earlier image of the Irish, and its generalized ethnic application, to more specific differentiations between Ireland-born long-term residents, recent immigrants, and Irish Americans. The distinctions would also explain Whitman's disavowal of the Native American Party, for, as he insisted, he was not antiforeigner and would not exclude any from the blessings of liberty and democracy. But he did expect the foreigner, once admitted, to seize the opportunity to improve his or her character and condition. An undated notebook entry gives evidence of Whitman preparing a speech, perhaps intended for a gathering of nativists, which expressed his feelings: "It is mentioned that the Irish and German and other foreigners mix in our politics. — Gentlemen with perfect respect I say you can think what you choose about this: — It is a credit to men and no disgrace to them to take an eager interest in politics."[82] A similar note finds Whitman addressing his imagined audience as "Proud sirs!" and mockingly adopting their tone in mimicry of their patronizing attitudes: "How those niggers smell! — How dare that Paddy ride in the same omnibus with me?"[83] Apparent contradictions fall away when these varied statements are viewed as part of the process of developing a wholistic concept of democracy and as part of Whitman's attempt to satisfy himself as to the role of the immigrant in its achievement.

Perhaps the opportunity he received to live away from New York for a time helped to enlarge Whitman's vision. When he lost his editorship of the *Brooklyn Eagle* in 1848, Whitman left New York to work on the *New Orleans Daily Crescent*. There he produced a series of character sketches drawn from that city's exotic types, one of them an Irishman named Patrick, but no Paddy. "Patrick McDray" is a sketch of a "hardy-looking Hibernian" who by dint of his industry in the hauling of goods to and from the levees has raised himself to the position of, as the fictitious name suggests, independent drayman, working the docks and streets of the South's most important port city. Whitman's Patrick may have been one of the Irish laborers who had earlier dug the canals young Jeff Whitman admired in the city. Many of the draymen had made their first mark in New Orleans as laborers on the canals before moving into the carting business, where they quickly pushed aside the blacks who previously had done this work.[84] Though some in the city complained of an Irish recklessness on the roads, Whitman is openly admiring of "Pat's" industry and the eagerness with which, once landed in "our rightful land," he has improved, so that he is now "*Mr.* Patrick McDray, who owns his own team and drives it like a gentleman."[85] The emphasis on McDray's title indicates Whitman's desire to suggest what Paddy might become in America — a capitalistic owner of his own business and worthy of being called "Mister." Unstated is the fact of slavery, which supported the economy into which Patrick McDray has bought himself a place.

In striking contrast to the portrait of the fictitious Patrick McDray is Whitman's description, for a later New York magazine article, of George Law, an Irish American who, though born to poverty, became very successful in the shipping industry and who, in developing political aspirations, showed contempt for the poor. Whitman's article, titled "Street Yarn," depicts Law as

> A big, heavy, overgrown man, with a face like a raw beef-steak, little piggy eyes, queer, dry, straight, harsh, coarse hair, "of a speckled color," made up of brownish red and gray, rather dirty clothes, and quite dirty, yellow dogskin gloves. He goes rolling along in an elephantine style, and for fear of being trod on, probably, people get out of the way. That is George Law, who never will be President.[86]

The political reference that concludes the sketch is specific to Law's thwarted presidential aspirations in 1853, but in a more general way it makes the point, even in this highly unflattering portrait, that his political failure is attributable to his character, not to his Irish ancestry.[87]

There were few questions of more general interest to antebellum America than character. The possibility held out by democracy for character formation and reformation led the states and their citizenry, especially in the North, into all manner of reform movements and attempts at social engineering. In the more high-minded New England states such movements were truly reformist, but in New York City they often took a political bent. Such was the case with the temperance movement, to which Whitman briefly lent himself out of a need for money. After leaving the *Aurora* Whitman accepted seventy-five dollars from Park Benjamin, owner of the *New World*, to produce a novel to be published as a supplement to the newspaper. Thus was born *Franklin Evans; or The Inebriate, A Tale of the Times*, a temperance novel. Whitman later offered a few different versions of its creation, one being that he wrote it while under the influence of rum, but he was clearly embarrassed by the novel and always insisted it was done for the money. Part of his embarrassment may have been for *Evans*'s purple prose (though it sold well both in the newspaper and in a subsequent book publication), but it may also have had to do with the politics surrounding New York's temperance movement at the time. Though the Washington Temperance Society was nationwide, temperance became a political issue in nineteenth-century New York State when, under the guise of reform interests, the Republicans attempted to pass legislation that would regulate the sale of liquor and limit the number of licensed saloons. This was aimed at New York City, where Democratic political power was closely tied to the high number of Irish saloon owners. By the mid-1850s nearly 15 percent of those Democratic officeholders whose occupations are known were saloon keepers.[88] The Tammany Society and the Democratic Party frequently held meetings in saloons, especially in Irish wards, where recruits were sought from among the ever-increasing numbers of newly arrived immigrants. Often, in return for the use of their premises for such purposes, saloon keepers were made ward captains and eventually became nominees for political office. Organizations such as the Washingtonians, which later published Whitman's novel, became part of the campaign to limit alcohol because their interests dovetailed with those of the Republican Party. In the 1840s they even made inroads among city firemen who, often in large numbers, took the pledge in Protestant churches.[89] In the *New*

York Aurora in March 1842 Whitman reported that the Washingtonians led a procession of New York City firemen past City Hall, followed by "an immense number of citizens, formerly intemperate men, but now worthy members of society."[90] The Republican effort to legislate the sale of liquor in saloons failed, at least in part, because of the opposition mounted by such New York Democratic worthies as Mike Walsh and "Yankee" Sullivan. While Whitman was writing *Franklin Evans* and Protestant churches were pledging firemen to temperance, Sullivan was opening his saloon, the Sawdust House, to firemen in Engine Company 27, who made it their headquarters.[91]

Reformers who did not commit themselves to specific areas, such as temperance or the penitentiary movement, often brought to bear on the subject of character reformation advances being made in science, especially in the field of what later was called eugenics. Whitman's interest in character formation as it pertained to the development of a society made up of morally superior individuals inevitably led him to considerations of the nature/nurture theme, which would have had particular application to immigrants. Embedded in this general theme were such questions as, Was it enough for individuals to be transplanted to a democratic soil? Could their characters be freshly nurtured and perfected simply by partaking of freedom, or were their characters already determined by nature and their native environments? If the latter, could their children overcome this inheritance to become the kinds of perfect Americans Whitman describes in "Starting from Paumanok": "A new race, dominating previous ones and grander far."

One of the places Whitman looked for answers to questions such as these was in the writings of German philosophers (which he read in translation), whose arguments often were predicated on physiological principles.[92] From them and from such American homespun theorists as Oscar Fowler he pieced together his own notions of progressive science and fashioned a hope for a future democracy based on a race of healthy, wholesome individuals capable of acting freely in a free society. As did many Americans in the 1840s and 1850s, Whitman looked to such contemporary sciences as phrenology and physiognomy for an understanding of the interplay of eugenics and character. These two closely related fields claimed to offer much needed assistance in determining the character of individuals and were taken very seriously in their time.

Because such theories supported the general reform movement alive in America throughout much of the nineteenth century, they were believed to have application beyond mere self-improvement. That Americans more than those in other nations felt the need to understand the connections between character and environment can be directly laid to the freedom afforded individuals in the United States and to the presence within the country of peoples from various national backgrounds. One instance of this was the concern focused on the freedom the country offered to take advantage of others, either in such entertaining ways as those of P. T. Barnum or in the criminal intentions of a confidence man. This freedom lent an urgency, especially in large cities, to the search for some obvious way of gauging the character of another — perhaps by observing head formations or facial characteristics. While the immigrant also could have benefited from such useful knowledge, it was more often the native born who sought ways to anticipate the probable outcome of encounters with the foreigner. Beyond this lay a more far-reaching concern for the influence on democracy of the "racial" characteristics, as they were then termed, of ethnic Americans.

Originating in Germany, phrenology came to the United States via the lectures of Johann Spurzheim. It enjoyed enormous success in the 1840s, with thousands flocking to learn its principles. In essence, it promised to provide information about individuals by means of craniology, measuring the skull, and then, by charting the skull's formation and contours, drawing conclusions about the brain, which was believed to be the principal factor in determining character. Whitman was introduced to this methodology in 1846 when he heard a lecture in New York by Orson Fowler, who with his brother, Lorenzo, formed a team that expounded the "science" and made it popular through lectures, publications, and private readings of heads. Fowler did not claim that character traits were permanently set by the brain's formations but that through learning what portions of the brain were most developed one could encourage desirable traits by exercising that capacity and repressing less desirable traits. Though Whitman dismissed Fowler's assertions of phrenology's total creditability, he saw a sufficient amount of truth in it to have his head read in July 1848 by Lorenzo Fowler, a reading that indicated he was high in self-esteem, caution, combativeness, and in both amativeness, that is, love for the opposite sex, and adhesiveness, the capacity for same-sex love.[93] For many years Whitman attempted to improve himself by either enlarging or "depressing," as he called it, some of these capacities, most notably by depressing his tendency toward adhesiveness when he felt it leading him too strongly.[94]

Physiognomy, an outgrowth of phrenology, was a simpler method of determining character, for it depended on observation and interpretation of facial features and expressions. Here one sees the potential for racial stereotyping reaching beyond that offered by phrenology. Phrenology demanded the use of measuring tools and charts, but anyone could engage in physiognomy merely by observing the faces of others. One of the poems (later called "Faces") in Whitman's first edition of *Leaves of Grass* draws its inspiration from this system, though it does not include references to specifically racial features. Such racial characteristics as flat noses, slanted eyes, high or low cheekbones and foreheads, and lip size could all be interpreted by the physiognomist in ways that developed a hierarchy of national groups. The simian-faced cartoon depictions of Irish males that became popular in New York newspapers and elsewhere left little doubt of where the Irish fit in this hierarchy.[95]

Orson Fowler took up physiognomy along with phrenology but, recognizing its limitations, moved beyond it to observations of the entire body in what was called physiology. Not surprisingly, the taller Anglo-American stature was privileged over that of other ethnic groups, and from this was drawn a conclusion of national and moral superiority. Again, reference to depictions of the Irish stereotype reveals Paddy's diminished physical stature. Obviously, the physical condition and appearance of many Irish were more attributable to poverty than to ethnicity, but such distinctions were easily blurred under the dictates of pseudoscience.

The influence on Whitman of these theories is clear, not only in his own adoption of phrenology as a self-directed discipline but also in his insistence on physiology via his body-based poetry. In an 1868 poem, "One's-Self I Sing," he makes it clear that he has moved beyond the exclusive tenets of phrenology and physiognomy and has taken up physiology: "Of physiology from top to toe I sing, / Not physiognomy alone nor brain alone is worthy for the Muse, I say the Form complete is worthier far." What this meant to his developing thoughts about the various ethnic groups arriving in the United States, the Irish in particular, is not certain, but the indications are that even before this he had become more of what we today would term a behavioralist, one who observes and values behavior over appearance or psychological characteristics as an indicator of character. The 1848 character sketch of the New Orleans drayman is a brief portrait of individualized character demonstrated in the behavior of one Irish immigrant. From it, as well as from other indications of approval of Irish individuals, it is possible to detect a movement away from his earlier fear that the Irish posed a threat to democracy.

As is often the case with Whitman, one finds the softening of attitude related to the female, either within his own personality or in those of others. If we return to the partially quoted stanza from "One's-Self I Sing" and complete it, we find the claim, "The Female equally with the Male I sing." But even prior to this Whitman had extolled the female and included the Irish female. The most sympathetic depiction of the Irish Whitman ever penned was of Irish women, though it never got beyond the pages of his notebooks. In a lengthy sketch probably intended for a newspaper and written sometime around 1850 or earlier but never published, Whitman presents a composite picture of Irish immigrant women seeking employment as servants, the occupation with which they became all but synonymous. Seeing in domestic service an opportunity to better themselves while living within the security of a middle-class home, Irish women — whose migration was not so often famine-driven as it was a desire for gainful employment — were happy to take positions that were scorned by American women. In the 1840s and 1850s when Whitman wrote his account, an estimated 80 percent of women employed as servants in New York City were Irish born.[96] Because of their vast numbers, they could only expect to earn from four to seven dollars per month in the city, though elsewhere in the country they commanded more.[97] If wages were lower, some compensation was found in the freedom with which the women could leave houses where they were made to work too hard or for too many hours and seek better positions. The demand for "help" was great, and since women in other immigrant groups sought marriage at an early age, the Irish women, who in general preferred to remain single and maintain their independence, quickly learned to advertise their availability once they had acquired some experience.

Whitman's article is titled "Wants," which refers to newspaper advertisements placed by those Irish women who had been in service already but were looking for new places and could afford to pay for such an ad. Whitman reminds us, however, that at the offices of the "Irish Emigrant Society" can be seen the women "just from Ireland" in their thick woolen capes on the warmest days, their worn leghorn hats, and heavy, "well-nailed" shoes, seeking entry into this occupation. The Irish Emigrant Society was founded in 1841 under the auspices of Bishop John Hughes, but in 1847 Republicans in Albany created a Board of Commissioners of Emigration. It is not clear from his notes to which of these organizations Whitman is referring, but he displays sympathy for the women, and their countrymen, for what he refers to as the inevitable consequences to the individual of despotic government. He paints a vivid picture of

> portions of the men and women of that land literally starving to death every year — the immense produce of their naturally fertile island, monopolized in the hands of a few, and mostly sent to foreign markets, while they emaciate and die . . . how can one help feeling a deep sympathy for these poor men and women, ignorant and awkward as they are?[98]

Directing the reader's attention to the society's offices, he describes low basement rooms crowded with Irish women arrayed on long benches, "perpetually standing or seated in that way, waiting for some master or mistress to come along and give them a 'call.'" Mike Walsh, by then a Democratic state assemblyman, similarly complained of the state-controlled Board of Commissioners of Emigration claiming that, at its behest, respectable Irish females were "put to sit on benches, shivering and shaking like so many aspen leaves."[99] Walsh's complaint may have been made mainly for political purposes, but Whitman's indicates a true feeling for the women subjected to public display: "To the Irish girl, out of a situation, the Intelligence Office is a place of public seeing and being seen." Seldom do we find, even among the sentimental writings of those who commiserated with the plight of the immigrant, such a sensitive awareness of the objectification endured by a lower-class immigrant group, especially its women. Indeed, Whitman offers here a Foucauldian insight into the hierarchy implicit in the act of looking, or gazing, at another.

Later Whitman displayed a similar sympathy for females engaged in prostitution, an occupation that included a disproportionate number of Irish, an unhappy consequence of the large number of unattached Irish females in the city.[100] In this case, his sympathy may have stemmed from a connection close to home, for the wife of his brother Andrew, Nancy McClure Whitman, was Irish and was suspected of playing the prostitute even while married.[101] After her husband's death in 1863 she took to the streets openly, and Walt's mother wrote to him that Nancy "goes it yet in the street," which eventually led to the birth of illegitimate twins.[102] Despite the disgrace that his mother felt so keenly, Whitman continued to send loving greetings to Nancy in his letters home and remembered her in his will.

Though Irish women did not suffer from the same negative stereotyping as did Irish men, that is, "Bridget" was never so grossly defamed as Paddy, Whitman seems spontaneously to direct toward the waiting, exhibited women at the emigrant office the kind of sympathetic scrutiny with which he endeavored to see all individuals once he had assumed his poetic persona. A semblance of the Irish female servant might have been included, along with her hod-carrier male compatriot, in "A Song for Occupations" had Whitman followed an outline he sketched for the poem that included a reference to the servant girl. Under the proposed title "America," he noted that here, as in no other country, "all forms of practical labour is [*sic*] recognized as honorable. . . . The healthy, fine-formed girl who waits upon the wealthy lady, not less than the wealthy lady—He who carries bricks and mortar to the mason, not less than the mason."[103] In the final version only the hod-carrier remained, but the image of the waiting women in the emigrant office may have remained a part of his consciousness. Not that this would prevent him from enjoying, along with many of the Irish servants themselves, a good Bridget joke. Much later in his life, in July 1888 when he was living in Camden, New Jersey, he had as his housekeeper Mary Davis. Her hesitation at going to see the fireworks for fear of a fire in her absence caused Whitman to tell her,

> That is very funny, Mary—very funny. It makes me think of a story I once heard of a Bridget whose mistress found her weeping bitterly before a roaring big fireplace. "What is the matter with you, Bridget?" asked the mistress, and Bridget, still weeping, said: "O mum, it's just this way: I might be after marrying Pat and we might have three or four children around and Oh the brats might fall into the fire and be burned to death!" That seems like you, Mary—anticipating trouble.[104]

Whitman's easy familiarity with his housekeeper may not have extended to the Irish women who came to help her. These women commanded, and received, the kind of respect they no doubt felt was their due, especially from the poet of democracy. In 1888 he discussed with his friend Horace Traubel the way of life Englishmen enjoyed with "wives, sisters, mothers—veritable and abiding providences," who, along with a "watchful valet," freed them from the details of daily life and made it possible for the men to achieve "a wealth of performance." Fortunately, he went on, in America there were no such persons waiting on the men, and they had to learn to care for themselves. He then recalled an incident involving his English artist friend Herbert Gilchrist, when Gilchrist and the American William Sidney Morse were both executing likenesses of Whitman at the house in Camden. Morse one day was blackening his shoes, and Gilchrist remarked that the Irishwoman who was that day working at the house should be asked to do the task. Whitman remembered, "I put in, that if we dared do such a thing the woman would probably up and curse us and leave the house." Gilchrist's explanation was that at home in England "the girl they had would feel hurt if not allowed to shine his boots"—to which Whitman says he could only reply that "this was democratic America—another state of society—in respects, another age, etc." Traubel then voiced his preference "for the independent instinct of the Irish woman," with which Whitman heartily concurred: "Yes—so do I: I abate nothing of my democratic sympathies."[105]

In his poetic persona Whitman foreswore partialities by making the conscious choice to represent all aspects of American society and to bridge the two worlds developing along the country's economic lines. In New York this consciousness of two cities, represented by its wealthy and by its poor, largely immigrant population, manifested itself at about midcentury in a number of books and articles emphasizing the contrast. Notable among these were Matthew Hale Smith's *Sunshine and Shadow in New York* (1868) and George G. Foster's *New York by Gas-Light* (1850). By 1860 the concern reached *Harper's Weekly* in Winslow Homer's engraving *The Two Great Classes of Society*. Whitman was a Bowery habitué, where the working class went to play in beer gardens, theaters, and dance halls. Thanks to his working-class attitudes, he would have been fully aware of the social division occurring in the city even without the protestations of his Irish friend Mike Walsh, who, now far removed from the days of his leadership of the Spartan Band, had become increasingly more socialistic though still a member of the Democratic Party. Drawing his support from the lower level of the city's workers, Walsh, who earlier had attacked both the Democratic Party and Tammany for their attempts to win over members of the city's banking and business industries, took up the most radical of labor reform measures, eventually opposing not just unfair practices but the capitalist system itself. Though Protestant, he led the attack on Trinity Church which, using its original 1705 land grant from England's Queen Anne as a base, had amassed enormous wealth. Walsh refused to honor the fenced-in privacy of the church's adjoining park and encouraged workers in the vicinity to do the same.[106] In addition to Trinity Church, Walsh singled out John Jacob Astor as the symbol of what he termed a "legalized system of plunder," by which the labor of a working man, his own property, was stolen.[107] Many of these attacks were made in speeches that helped elect Walsh to the state assembly in 1846, where he served two terms. Whitman also made a dig at Astor in the *Eagle* in April of that year with a two-line comment: "J. J. Astor has given $500 to the Fund for Firemen's widows and orphans. How on earth could he spare it?"[108] The year before Whitman had also aimed a blow at Astor in his essay "Tear Down and Build Over Again," where he deplored the American tendency to tear down buildings and erect new ones every few years. Arguing for the preservation of those edifices and places imbued with cultural significance, he avers, "There are those who would go farther to view even Charlotte Temple's grave, than Mr. Astor's stupid-looking house on Broadway." To such as these, he argues, "greatness and goodness are things intrinsic," adding, "[C]an Irishmen forget where their Emmet lies buried, though it should be marked by no grave-stone, and the proudest columns loom up everywhere around?"[109]

Walsh's attack on John Jacob Astor may have awakened in Whitman's mind a memory he would later include in *Specimen Days*, how as a teenager, in about 1832, he once saw the elderly Astor carried from his home to be placed in his sleigh. He remembered the old man "swathed in rich furs, with a great ermine cap on his head, led and assisted, almost carried, down the steps of his high front stoop (a dozen friends and servants, emulous, carefully holding, guiding him) and then lifted and tuck'd in a gorgeous sleigh, envelop'd in other furs."[110] The description emphasizes the enormous privilege of Astor's life and, if Whitman's remembrance of the year as 1832 is correct, underscores as well the contrast between this privilege and the suffering that was soon to descend on thousands of the city's poor in the ensuing cholera epidemic. In a report of Astor's death in the *New Orleans Daily Crescent*, Whitman says he recalls seeing the old man "two winters since," which, if the same incident, would obviate a cholera connection. But in this account he draws a direct parallel between the old man's condition, "bent down with age and sickness . . . entirely unable to help himself," and that of Astor's groom, "a hearty young Irishman, with perhaps not two dollars in his pocket [who] looked with pity upon the great millionaire!"[111]

Whitman neither attained nor desired Walsh's degree of radicalism, and indeed the two men later separated over the Free Soil issue. When Walsh was imprisoned for libel in 1846, however, Whitman used his position as editor of the *Eagle* to point out that an "intelligent majority of all parties" believed six months in the penitentiary too severe and that the governor "could not do a more commendable act, in its way, than to remit the sentence of Mike Walsh."[112] Walsh and Whitman were close enough friends to lend credence to the speculation that it was Whitman who wrote Walsh's obituary in the *Brooklyn Daily Times* on March 18, 1859, where Walsh's talents were honestly evaluated.

While the politics of a Mike Walsh were held suspect by many New Yorkers, the familiar figure of Paddy was making its way into popular culture and, in its stage manifestations, helping to ameliorate suspicions of the Irish. In the 1840s and 1850s Whitman went often enough to New York's theaters to be aware of the stage Irishmen whose descriptions were most often summed up in the word "unlucky." Usually displaying wit, charm, and a good-natured, rustic disposition, the stage Irishman was a confused, unlucky blunderer in an unfamiliar American setting.[113]

The stage "blunderer" is traceable to Thomas Sheridan's *The Brave Irishman: A Farce* (1754), though Sheridan actually attempts an examination of the prevailing English conception of the Irishman as a characteristically blundering fool, a conception similarly questioned by Richard Lovell Edgeworth and Maria Edgeworth in *Essay on Irish Bulls* (1802).[114] In his American stage appearances the Irish blunderer was not considered responsible for his poor condition in life and was laughed at with a high degree of pity. When the blunderer persisted in his ignorance, however, refusing the advice of others, he often brought disaster upon himself and them, a dramatic outcome that could engender anxiety in an audience. Thus, even through such popular forms as the theater, the stereotype of Paddy could be a double-edged sword as a comic figure turned swiftly into an impediment to democracy.[115]

New York's theater scene was also the setting for an incident that reinforced another image of the Irish, as fiercely violent. The Irish formed a large part of the mob that rioted on May 10, 1849, when the English actor William Macready appeared at one of Whitman's favorite theaters, the Astor Place Opera House, on the same evening that Edwin Forrest—"The *American* Tragedian"—appeared at the Broadway Theatre. Nationalism and hatred of England raised the level of passion far beyond what the matter called for, and twenty-two people died in the melee. Late in his life Whitman remembered the date of the riot and that he was at that time publishing the *Freeman*. He recalled attending both theaters, the Broadway and the Astor Place, and listed Macready and Forrest among those he had seen perform, recalling Forrest in specific roles "as Metamora or Damon or Brutus."[116] Whitman also saw the very popular Charlotte Cushman as Lady Gay Spanker in *London Assurance*, a comedy hit written by Irish playwright Dion Boucicault, and may have seen the foremost Irish comic, John Brougham, who performed at the Park Theater in the 1840s and 1850s.[117] Brougham frequently performed one-man shows in which he impersonated famous Irish orators such as Daniel O'Connell, a type of performance that would have attracted Whitman, who at this time had longings of his own for a career as an orator. In addition to his stage roles, Brougham was also a playwright, rivaling Boucicault in the number of his works.[118] Not to be forgotten is Whitman's fondness for Gerald Griffin's Irish novel, *The Collegians*, which surely would have led him to see Boucicault's stage adaptation, *The Colleen Bawn*.

The city also offered instances where image and reality intertwined to lend credence to popular conceptions of the Irish. The "Bowery b'hoys," a city phenomena, were visible on the streets of New York as well as on its theater stages, so that one image fed into the other, erasing the line between them. Mike Walsh was a leader of the b'hoys, who owed their name to the Irish brogue of so many of their number and who were city roughs sufficiently distinctive to create a culture of their own. The b'hoys were working class, many of them mechanics (including carpenters, cabinetmakers, and shipwrights), most of them Irish, who by this time made up approximately half of the city's mechanics and thus were distinguished from the lower-class Irish who ran with gangs such as the Dead Rabbits.[119] When later reminiscing about his early days in New York, Whitman remembered the kinds of laborers who were b'hoys, "the young shipbuilders, cartmen, butchers, firemen," and their stage re-creations, "the old-time 'soap-lock'" (referring to the slicked-down hairstyle preferred by the b'hoys), "or exaggerated 'Mose' or 'Sikesey,' of [Francis S.] Chanfrau's plays," and how the originals would be present in the audiences for these performances.[120]

So attracted was Whitman to the b'hoys in their dandified regalia and their streetwise manner (one thinks of the figure cut in twentieth-century films by the Irish American movie star James Cagney) that he openly identified with them on more than one occasion. First he adopted the name "Mose Velsor," a combination of his Velsor ancestry and a popular b'hoy name, for some of his newspaper articles. Later in *Leaves of Grass*, he presented a word picture of a b'hoy and referred to him fondly as "The boy I love."[121] It is small wonder that at least one critic of the first *Leaves*, in the *New York Examiner* of January 19, 1882, spoke of him as "the 'Bowery Bhoy' in literature."

Blended into the mixture that included the b'hoys were other groups with whom Whitman associated, in fancy though not in fact. The general category of "roughs," the city's workers, among whom Whitman proudly numbered himself, always included the Irish. Another group that would have included at least some of the city's more prosperous Irish who had arrived in the early years of the century was loosely referred to as "loafers," young men whose pose assumed a blasé attitude of studied nonchalance. Their stance seems to have been an attempt to outwardly convey a deliberate rejection of the city's business-engendered exertions in the pursuit of wealth and advancement. The attitude is demonstrated in the engraving Whitman chose as a frontispiece for the first edition of *Leaves of Grass*, where he appears loosely attired and with one finger hooked casually into a hip pocket. The easy, swinging gait he adopted at about this time and even the way in which he seems at times to have encouraged those opinions that — despite his steady employment in a variety of trades — labeled him "lazy," point to his desire to be thought of as one of the city's loafers.

We know little of the events of Whitman's life in the years just prior to the first edition of *Leaves of Grass*, but he tells us that its "gestation-years" were not spent in withdrawn composition but rather "in the way of first merging one self in all the living flood and practicality and fervency of that period," including "all the scenes, sights and people of the great cities of New York and Brooklyn," Broadway, the Bowery, shipyards, and all the life in and around New York.[122] This suggests Whitman was aware of all that was happening in the cities of Brooklyn and New York, much of which had to do in one way or another with the Irish. Among the events was the particular upsurge of nativism in these years, which found a focus in the rivalry between two of the city's "roughs," "Butcher Bill" Poole, a member of the Native American Party, and the Irish-born prizefighter John Morrisey, a Democrat from the Irish Sixth Ward.[123] In 1854 these two held a boxing match in the open air of a New York dock, with Poole the winner. In February of the following year some of Morrisey's followers shot Poole in a Broadway saloon. When he died two weeks later (his last words reputedly being, "I die a true American!"), his funeral became a full-scale event, with a procession led by a fifty-two-piece band and thousands of mourners.[124] Horace Greeley warned in the *Tribune* that such demonstrations encouraged young men "to prefer idleness, riot, vice, crime to labor, steadiness, respectability, and virtue," but such public mourning, like the riots that occurred throughout the century, was part of the street theatrics of New York City life.[125] Morrisey went on to become the proprietor of a successful gambling enterprise, a state senator, and a United States congressman.

The recent Irish immigrants made up a large part of those to whom Greeley referred, the city's street gangs, including the Plug Uglies, the Dead Rabbits, and the Rabbits' enemies, the Roach Guards. By 1855 it was estimated that at least thirty thousand men in the city owed allegiance to the gang leaders, who in turn owed allegiance either to Tammany Hall or to the Native American Party (and the Know-Nothing movement).[126] At elections the gangs were employed by rival political factions to disrupt voting and to vote often for the party paying them. The Bowery Boys (not the b'hoys) were most often aligned with the Native American Party, while the Dead Rabbits are said to have played a particularly large role in securing the mayoralty for Fernando Wood in 1854.

The Irish were also the major constituency of the large crowds that ran alongside the fire engines, simultaneously lending aid and bringing added confusion to the scene of a fire. For many years the city firemen were volunteers (numbering 1,661 in 1844), headed by a few paid supervisors.[127] As they increasingly sought the votes of the city's Irishmen, the Democrats opened the ranks of volunteers to them. Later, when the Irish had gained considerable political power, they moved into the newly created uniformed ranks of city firemen. Long before either of these were open to them, however, they formed a major part of an unofficial auxiliary to the volunteers which became infamous. Called the "fireboys," they were as much feared as they were appreciated. Though they made themselves essential by their assistance in times of great disasters, such as the fire in 1835 that destroyed the printing district where Whitman worked, they often hampered the activities of the legitimate firemen and volunteers and certainly did much to impede traffic when whole swarms of them would take off in the direction of a fire. Drawn for the most part from the street gangs that infested the oldest of the city's wards, the "fireboys" made looting a part of the city's fire-fighting history.

The Irish entered the volunteer ranks of the fire department in such large numbers that soon firemen were referring to extinguishing a fire as "painting it green."[128] With the Irish now officially in place, singing while fighting fires quickly became part of the city scene. James Hurley, known as the "Sweet Singer of the Dry Dock," would sing an Irish ballad with the refrain "Shule, shule, shule agra" ('Walk, walk, walk my love') to encourage the firefighters.[129] Whitman also sang the song of the New York firemen, beginning with the earliest version of what was later the "Song of Myself," where he offers a graphic depiction of their labor: "The ring of alarm-bells . . . the cry of fire. . . . the whirr of swift-streaking engines and hose-carts with premonitory tinkles and colored lights" and enters into their danger:

I am the mashed fireman with breastbone broken. . . . tumbling
        walls buried me in their debris,
Heat and smoke I inspired. . . . I heard the yelling shouts of my
        comrades,
I heard the distant click of their picks and shovels;
They have cleared the beams away. . . . they tenderly lift me
        forth,
I lie in the night air in my red shirt. . . . the pervading hush is for
        my sake,
Painless after all I lie, exhausted but not so unhappy,
White and beautiful are the faces around me. . . . the heads are
        bared of their firecaps,
The kneeling crowd fades with the light of the torches.[130]

When not fighting fires the Irish were especially adroit at many of the activities in which firemen engaged, such as engine races that pitted their company engines against each other or the turning of their water hoses on rival companies. The company engines had names, and the companies often were referred to by the engine's name. The fire engine belonging to Engine Company 44 at Houston Street was named Live Oak.[131] Whitman's "I Saw in Louisiana a Live-Oak Growing," which speaks of his loneliness in New Orleans while far from his New York friends, may have been prompted by his learning the name of the tree, a name which perhaps reminded him of home. One of the most noted engines was the "Washington," or "Lady Washington," of Engine Company 40 housed in Mulberry Street. Among the firemen assigned to the "Washington" was Moses Humphreys, model for the stage character "Mose, the Fireman." The company's rival was Engine Company 15 to which the actor Frank Chaufrau belonged. In 1842 the two companies engaged in playful battle until Engine 40 surrendered; it is believed that on this occasion Chaufrau conceived the idea for his stage creation, "Mose." Despite its popularity, his impersonation did not win the hearts of all. *America's Own, or the Fireman's Journal* took the actor to task, praising his ability but adding, "The effect of this character upon the juveniles who visit the theater is plainly visible, as they take every opportunity to imitate the character. Its effects on the Fire Department are serious, in the estimation of those who are not acquainted with its members, as they set every fireman down as a 'Mose,' degrading to youth."[132]

With or without the help of Chanfrau's "Mose," New York's firemen became a sort of easy reference to indicate that which was unruly and wild. It was this wildness that Ralph Waldo Emerson meant to convey, no doubt, by his comment (reported to Whitman by John Trowbridge in 1856) that there were "few who wrote English greatly—'there is also Walt Whitman, but he belongs yet to the fire clubs, and has not got into the parlors.'"[133] The remark stemmed from Emerson's visit to Whitman, believed to have been in the winter of 1855, when the two had dinner in a New York hotel. After dinner Whitman took his guest to "a noisy fire-engine society," which has been identified as Firemen's Hall, a Mercer Street social club for New York firemen.[134] It is probably safe to speculate that there were a good many Irish about, which would have contributed considerably to Emerson's estimate of Whitman.

On another occasion when Emerson was briefly in the city before going on to a speaking engagement in Newark, New Jersey, he called on Whitman at his home in Brooklyn. The year would have been 1856 or 1857, not long after the publication of *English Traits* (1856), where Emerson had said of Ireland that while it enjoyed the same climate and soil as in England, it had "less food, no right relation to the land, political dependence, small tenantry and an inferior or misplaced race."[135] The two walked three miles to the Astor House, on

Broadway in Manhattan, where the Bostonian was staying. The failure of a waiter to admit Whitman to Emerson's room while the latter went to check on railroad schedules to Newark caused Emerson to become annoyed, though Whitman assured him the man had only done his duty.

At dinner they fell into serious discussion, of the kind Whitman described as "hot, stormy (for us)," over the question of national character. Emerson, fresh from his published celebration of the English, confided, "I like the English — I do not like the Scotch so well: and as for the Irish —." "Here," Whitman recalled,

"he suddenly stopped . . . I didn't know what had happened. A young waiter who had been standing back of us left the room. Emerson looked at me quietly and said: "I was going to say more — more about the Irish: but it suddenly struck me that the young man there was himself Irish and might not find what I was going to say pleasant."

"It was thoroughly characteristic — just like him," Whitman concluded, "like his consideration, courtesy, unfailing tact."[136] Curiously, when Emerson met Thomas Carlyle in 1847, he was reminded, probably by the Scotsman's speech, of his Irish gardener, Hugh Whelan, at home in Concord.[137] One wonders if he told this to Carlyle.

The Irish figured in other aspects of the life of the city as Whitman knew it in the 1840s and 1850s. He may have been aware of the dance contest that took place in 1844 between a black man, William Henry ("Juba") Lane, and the Irish dancer "Master" John Diamond. Baseball, a sport Whitman enjoyed watching, had its fair share of Irish players. As Ed Folsom has reminded us, baseball, as we know it, was invented in New York City in 1845 with the Knickerbocker Club and not as myth would have it in rural, upstate Cooperstown, New York.[138] Teams consisted of working men, often from one occupation, so that those Irish who were established as mechanics, masons, or other laborers were prominent on teams as well as among the spectators. A *Brooklyn Daily Times* account, identified as Whitman's, of a ball game played in June 1858 between the Putnams and the Atlantics, Long Island's (Brooklyn's geographical location) champion team, is complete with box scores and names of players. The Atlantics boasted two O'Briens and one man with a surname that said it all, Ireland.[139]

Most certainly Whitman was familiar with one segment of the population of Brooklyn and New York, the newsboys, large numbers of whom were Irish. The newsboys slept in the corner of the press room and, at about 1:00 A.M. when the papers were printed, leaped to their feet and headed for the distributor to purchase their evening's supply of papers to be hawked on the street corners.[140] Distributors paid about $1.75 per hundred papers and sold them to the newsboys for $2.00. According to one account, the most successful distributors in the city were Irishmen who had started as newsboys and moved up, such men as Mark Maguire, Mike Madden, Tommy Ryan, and Pat Lyons.[141]

These names are so similar to others that appear in Whitman's notebooks for 1861–1862 that the unidentified entries may well have included newsboys. Certainly they include numerous Irish among the long lists of names, mostly of men he met in his city rounds. Little can be made, in the way of critical interpretation, of these unexplained lists. Perhaps the most suggestive comment appeared in Paul Zweig's 1984 study of Whitman, where Zweig addressed the subject directly by raising the question, "Were these men Whitman's lovers?" and offering by way of answer a nearly incredulous, "Possibly, but so many?"[142] The response is incredulous in more than one sense, for while Zweig seems to find the possibility hard to believe, given the sheer numbers involved, a reader aware of the lifestyle that prevailed in New York City's gay scene precisely at the time of Zweig's writing, and chronicled in Randy Shilts's *And the Band Played On* (1987), wonders at his disbelief. More recently, Whitman biographer Gary Schmidgall has set forth his belief that Whitman was actively gay in the years these notebook entries were made, which, if true, would strongly suggest a more than passing interest in "Tom Kinney," "James Doyle" (described by Whitman as a "plumpish young fellow, always smiling"), Pete Calhoun, and Neil McBride, a "young Irishman I met at the corner of Raymond & Myrtle Ave."[143] Doubtless there are others included, whose names are not so obviously Irish. All, however, seem to have been part of the democratic comradeship, described in terms of "adhesiveness," which was the overriding desideratum of the 1860 *Leaves of Grass*.[144]

One notebook entry lists the nicknames of various omnibus drivers, including "Graball," who was actually Patrick McMakin.[145] In similar, though longer, lists made about 1857 the men are often identified as "Irish" or of "Irish descent," sometimes with annotations such as "Tom Riley (handsome Irish fighter)," "Bill (23) round faced, blue eyes, light Irish skin," and "Tom Harvey (5th av.) smallish, timidish, Irish." That Whitman found Irish men attractive is clear from such notes as "John Kiernan (loafer young saucy looking pretty goodlooking)" and "Patrick Corr 26 (Irish boy good looking)."[146] As late as 1888, when he was sixty-nine years old, Whitman still found Irish men attractive. In the summer of that year the journalist Richard Harding Davis came to see him in Camden. Whitman did not realize who he was until Traubel identified the young man as the son of author Rebecca Harding Davis. Whitman was surprised, telling Trauble, "I thought him an Irish boy: I liked him — he was so candid, so interesting. Such tall, wholesome looking fellows are rare among American youngsters."[147]

Quite often Whitman's notations of young men he met include references to occupations — policeman, prizefighter, fireman, stage driver. The last of these, the stage drivers, played an important role in his New York life. While his later relationship with the Washington streetcar conductor Peter Doyle was exceptional, perhaps even unique, Pete was of a type that Whitman had always been drawn to. There were many Irishmen like him on the horsecars in New York and on the ferries that moved between Manhattan and Brooklyn, the kinds of young laboring men Whitman made his friends and in whom he took such genuine interest as to further their neglected education by teaching them himself. So fully did he share their hardships that if they were injured — as they often were on the dangerously crowded streets of Manhattan — or ill he would regularly visit them in the hospital.

It is clear from his own identifications that many of these stage drivers were Irish. In *Specimen Days* he recalls the Broadway omnibuses and their drivers, among them "Pete Callahan," and "Patsy Dee," and his notebooks bear such entries as "James McOwen Nov 22 '62 Irish, Broadway & 42 st. talk about the drivers & $2 a day — and being more square & respectable."[148] Others may be listed as well, though hidden beneath their familiar names, for if sober, honest, "square and respectable," Irish immigrants and Irish Americans could find a place for themselves as drivers in what was semiskilled work of a more permanent kind than the day labor to which many Irish were restricted. If allowed to imagine the possibility of it being an Irish stage driver involved in the street incident Whitman noted in the spring of 1862, one might have three Irish or Irish American representatives caught up in what was probably a familiar city scenario of the time. The entry reads:

Occurred on Thursday about sundown April 10th stage 436 Knickerbocker policeman 1726 (Macarthy) outrageous conduct of policeman — pulling the driver down from his stage, tearing the clothes off his back — and then going up to the stables, and taking him off to the station house, and locking him up all night — Brought before [Police] Justice [Michael] Connolly next morning, he was discharged, even on the policeman's own statement. Most of the Broadway squad of policemen are very well behaved to drivers (although there are exceptions). But new police occasionally detailed for some special occasion to Broadway are apt to be very insolent and unreasonable.[149]

While the police may indeed have been "insolent and unreasonable" on occasion, it is to the credit of Irish policemen that arrest records indicate they enforced the law without regard for national background and did not hesitate to arrest offenders with Irish surnames. In street riots where Irish mobs dominated, the Irish policemen acted with no regard for ethnicity.[150]

Whitman's later reminiscenses of the city drivers were of those years in New York when all his experiences were being stored up, part of "the gestation of 'Leaves of Grass,'" as he put it.[151] These experiences surface in the first edition of *Leaves* in the poem later to be known as "Song of Myself," where they are part of the cityscape Whitman draws: "The heavy omnibus, the driver with his interrogating thumb, the clank of the shod horses on the granite floor." The "interrogating thumb" is explained in his "Broadway, the Magnificent!" where he describes the drivers in their boxes set high up on the front of the coaches, looking for passengers and urging them to board by crooking a thumb.[152] In the same edition of *Leaves*, in a poem later to be titled "To Think of Time," the funeral of "an old stagedriver" is depicted, including the touching gesture of laying the driver's whip on the coffin as it is lowered into the grave. The driver is memorialized in words that well might apply to any one of the city's Irish drivers:

He was a goodfellow,
Freemouthed, quicktempered, not badlooking, able to take his
    own part,
Witty, sensitive to a slight, ready with life or death for a friend,
Fond of women, . . . played some . . . eat hearty and drank
    hearty,

> Had known what it was to be flush . . . grew lowspirited toward
> the last . . . sickened . . . was helped by a contribution,
> Died aged forty-one years . . . and that was his funeral.[153]

Though the omnibuses were still to be found on city streets in 1881 when he was writing his remembrances, Whitman acknowledged that "the flush days of the old Broadway stages, characteristic and copious, are over." The loss was part of the transition from private to public transportation in New York and other American cities, brought about by the need for large numbers of workers to travel to work. Until about 1825 horse-drawn carriages, or stages, offered for hire by individuals were the only method of transport other than walking, and though these carriages were plentiful along Broadway, they were expensive and limited in their capacity. Following the success of omnibuses in Paris, New York granted a license to Abraham Brower in 1826 to operate a transport service along Broadway, which offered inexpensive rides (about ten cents per ride) to twelve passengers at a time. The idea caught on so quickly that by 1846, 255 of these vehicles were licensed and crowding the streets; just seven years later there were twenty-two companies operating 683 cars.[154] In 1862 Whitman went to hear a lecture on the Paris "omnibusses" and took notes that no doubt were intended for an article that was never written.[155] About the same time he began a sketch of himself, "the pet and pride of the Broadway stage-drivers," atop a Fifth Avenue omnibus.[156]

Whitman consistently blurred the distinction between stages and omnibuses, but the explanation for this probably lies in the reminiscenses of another New Yorker, Dr. D. B. St. John Roosa, of the medical staff at New York Hospital, who knew Whitman from his regular hospital visits to sick and injured stage drivers in 1860 and 1861. Roosa claimed that "the real New Yorker never said omnibus," prefering to speak of them as "stages."[157]

Omnibuses provided a rough ride over cobblestone streets and were often slowed by both the difficulties under the horses' feet and the jostling of drivers for places in the crowds. In his fondness Whitman makes them sound like a bunch of jolly goodfellows, but omnibus drivers were noted for their rudeness to paying customers. The "largely animal" qualities that Whitman ascribes to them became part of their legendry, though few riders seem to have found them as endearing as did Whitman. George C. Foster describes the drivers as unheeding of passenger safety, to say nothing of comfort, and quite willing to move at snail's pace to attract aboard potential fares still on foot, only to attempt breakneck speeds (where traffic would allow) once the car was full.[158] Whitman's late-life remembrances of the stage drivers were that

> as a rule [they were] strong men mentally as well as physically. Some were educated, some not; but those who were competent to drive a stage for a length of time on such a street as Broadway, New York, for instance, were men of character and individuality. It took much skill to tool a bus or stage on Broadway. Usually they were intelligent and up with current gossip and news, and were rugged types.

The popularity of the drivers was such, Whitman adds, that people vied to sit beside them on the box where they perched, "gave them money, cigars, clothes, theater and opera tickets, and favored them in many ways."[159]

This felicitous association between public and drivers changed as the century progressed. A comprehensive survey of New York published in 1873 claims the job of streetcar driver (referring to the street railway, which was then the public transport) was most often politically obtained, and the result was a brutal treatment of passengers by men who were simply "ruffians."[160] By the 1870s the Irish were well established in the city's political life and heavily represented among the drivers of the streetcars Whitman rode when visiting Brooklyn and New York, but he has not left us his opinions of them or of the city politics that favored them.

The involvement of the Irish in high-level city politics was initially solidified when the Irish helped elect Mayor Fernando Wood in 1854, the year before the first *Leaves of Grass*. Earlier, when serving as congressman, Wood had been especially mindful of the Irish by seeking help for Irish political prisoners in England.[161] This was not forgotten by the city's Irish when he ran for mayor on the Democratic ticket. New York State, however, was controlled by the Republicans, and two years after his election Wood found himself stripped of a good deal of power by the Republican regime in Albany, which instituted a new municipal charter for New York. By its terms municipal agencies were reshuffled along with their executive controls, and the mayor lost command of the fire and health departments as well as the board of education. The charter also took away the mayor's patronage privileges with the school system and the police department, the two largest employers in the city.[162] The Municipal Police, with a force of two thousand, whose badges and copper-buttoned jackets were the closest thing to a uniform New Yorkers would countenance, had been one place where Wood was able to show his appreciation for Irish support. When the state assembly passed the Metropolitan Police Act, which established a state-adminstered police force, the Municipal Police were no longer empowered to maintain order in the city. Throughout the spring of 1857 matters grew increasingly tense, with both police groups claiming jurisdiction over the city's police stations. On June 16 the contending forces (the state's Metropolitans in their uniform frock coats and plug hats) joined in battle at City Hall in what quickly was termed a "police riot."

While the largely Irish Municipal Police were thus engaged, the city's largely Irish street gangs saw an advantage. Noting the preoccupation of the police, the Dead Rabbits set upon their rivals, the Roach Guards, with clubs, sticks, and revolvers. When police did attempt to quell the resulting melee they were attacked by both gangs, and it took the Seventy-first Regiment of the militia to beat back the mob. This gang eruption was instrumental in bringing Mayor Wood to the point of relinquishing his hold on the Municipal Police but had no lasting effect on the continued existence of gangs in the city. Though Wood temporarily surrendered, he appealed the case and was upheld.

On the day of the police riot Whitman wrote in his notebook, "The Mayor this forenoon issued an order to the various Captains, directing them to call in the men at 4 o clock this afternoon and have them deliver up the city property — the Captains to hold on to the Station Houses till the further action of the Common Council."[163] This was followed by two brief entries concerning possible poetic themes, and then, "for a Great City . . . A city may have great temples, avenues, etc., but in its common people, their personality, heroism, ruggedness beauty & strength," and finally, "The greater the reform, the greater the personality that is needed."[164] Whitman seems to have been ruminating, perhaps moved to do so by the events in the city, on the need for reform of individuals along the lines of those ideas he would later develop in *Democratic Vistas*, where he drew the intersecting lines between the highest individual development and the advancement of democracy. But the notes seem also to echo lines from his 1856 "Song of the Broad-Axe," where Section 5, which presents the conditions for "a great city," is introduced in the preceding section by the simple qualifier, "A great city is that which has the greatest men and women." The thought, set down in the notes and expressed in the poem, bears remembering, for it will recur near the end of this study when we shall find the "defiant deed" of rebellion called for in the poem enacted in the streets of Dublin.

In *Democratic Vistas* Whitman attempted to limn a model of the kind of character he envisioned evolving in the New World under a democratic dispensation. Eugenics would play a role since parentage, he believed, was important to the physical development of this model: "a clear-blooded, strong-fibred physique, is indispensable." Following this such matters as were vital to the health of the city and its peoples are addressed, "the questions of food, drink, air, exercise, assimilation, digestion, can never be intermitted." Finally, echoing many of the entries in his notebooks, some of which singled out the manly beauties of the Irish, he describes an ideal character,

> a well-begotten selfhood — in youth, fresh, ardent, emotional, aspiring, full of adventure; at maturity, brave, perceptive, under control, neither too talkative nor too reticent, neither flippant nor sombre; of the bodily figure, the movements easy, the complexion showing the best blood, somewhat flush'd, breast expanded, an erect attitude, a voice whose sound outvies music, eyes of calm and steady gaze, yet capable also of flashing — and a general presence that holds its own in the company of the highest.[165]

Whitman's admiration for New York's police forces, expressed in his 1871 letters to Doyle and O'Connor, does not come near equating them with this ideal, but the obvious pleasure he derived from observing the policemen — many of them Irish or, as he says, of "Irish stock" — and his declaration that they are "in the main magnificent" register the mental distance he had traveled from his earliest published references to the Irish at the time of the 1842 public school controversy. Most significant in tracing this distance is his language, principally for the way it departs from that used thirty years earlier in the *Aurora*. Always of importance, language is particularly so when used to describe an individual or group seen as "other." As Dale T. Knobel points out, in the language used to describe the Irish in antebellum America (which would include Whitman's in the *Aurora* editorials) can be found the key to the stereotypical Paddy that developed.[166] Whitman's 1871 consignment of the Roman Catholic rioters to the "lower order" is a clear indication of his still strong anti-Catholic feelings, but the precise language, the phrase "lower order," is used to assure his Irish friends, Doyle and O'Connor, that he does not refer to *all* Irish and to underscore his admiration that these particular lower-order specimens had become, perhaps because of their being policemen, "American-looking." By "American-looking" may be understood not just the appearance of the policemen but their acquired perceptions, their new, American way of looking at and understanding events, which wins Whitman's approval. Brief though the reference is, it suggests his recognition of an assimilation of American values by members of a previously scorned ethnic group, which offers Whitman a prospect more promising than the view of America he expounds that same year in *Democratic Vistas*.

Though Whitman published *Democratic Vistas* in 1871, he had been writing it from about 1869 and thinking about it for much longer. Perhaps because it was so long generating, or perhaps because it is a composite of previously written essays, the work itself is difficult to follow; then, too, Whitman as a writer of prose often seems to share his poetic persona's cavalier attitude toward self-contradiction. In this work he simultaneously clings to the idea of democracy as the world's last best hope and denounces the American society that has developed in democracy. He claims to have a wondrous view of an ideal democracy rooted in comradeship, but it is a distant, futuristic vision, and the present masses that he sees before him are far from achieving his ideal.

How to achieve the vision is the basic question underlying all of *Democratic Vistas*. At one point Whitman says that after an absence he is "now again (September 1870) in New York city and Brooklyn, on a few weeks' vacation."[167] While walking about the cities he feels that "not Nature alone is great," but, in the profusion of city life, "the work of man too is equally great." Yet still missing, he believes, are individuals worthy of what nature and people have produced in this country, and he proceeds to a discussion of what he has introduced as the major consideration of his *Vistas*, "the important question of character, of an American stock personality, with literatures and arts for outlets and return expressions, and, of course, to correspond, within outlines common to all."[168]

This question of "an American stock personality," referred to a number of times in *Democratic Vistas*, was one that absorbed Whitman in the post–Civil War years, when Reconstruction policies and the teeming immigrant populations seemed to him double threats to the future of the Republic. The question of individual character was directly tied, in Whitman's mind, to the survival of democracy and to its future course and seems to have awakened in him some of the same fears he had known in the days when Bishop Hughes and his constituents were demanding to be recognized. The old questions arose: How was the ideal democracy to be realized with these disparate and ill-prepared peoples as its constituents? How best to meld them into the fusion of individual with society that he believed right and necessary?

One way might have been to adopt the authoritarian model of certain European countries and institutions, to accept the Carlylean sneer at the "swarmery" of the masses. In Boston, an Irishman Whitman would not come to know for another decade, John Boyle O'Reilly, editor of that city's influential Catholic newspaper, the *Pilot*, wrote a lengthy editorial condemning both sectarian groups of Irish involved in the 1871 New York riot. He had done the same thing the year before, but this time the editor felt condemnation was not enough. Though O'Reilly had too much respect for his fellow Irish to consider their actions, even though riotous, "swarmery," he believed something definitive had to be done to forestall further riots. The Irish on both sides might agree never to parade "for Irish political objects" or, and this he believed to be the better solution, the one that "must come in the end, when America, tired out and indignant with her squabbling population, puts her foot down with a will and tells them all—Germans, French, Irish, Oranges—'You have had enough now. There is only ONE flag to be raised in future in this country and that flag is the Stars and Stripes.'"[169]

This would have been one way of handling the problem, but it was not the one Whitman would have urged. Despite his fears, his answer to the problem as set forth in *Democratic Vistas* amounts to a reiteration of his abiding faith in a gradual process by which individual character would be shaped by the democratic environment, while itself contributing to that environment. Ultimately, the individual would fuse with the masses in a manner similar to the way individual states fused with the union of states. Looking to "the elements of the American masses" for renewed faith that this fusion was possible and would occur, Whitman seems to have recognized in the "American-looking" New York Irish policemen, so respectable in their uniforms and having proven themselves responsible citizens, a validization of the democratic process as legitimate, for all its urbanity, as that which Frederick Jackson Turner later attributed to the frontier experience.

Of course, it was the police uniforms that reminded Whitman of the war, which had served to shape the "outline common to all" by bringing New York's Irish into the American mainstream of the city they had made their own. But in these particular Irish faces above the copper-buttoned uniforms, Whitman appears to have glimpsed the working out of American democracy he had long believed in, for here was Paddy rising above the sectarianism of a few hundred years and on his way to becoming what Whitman called "an American stock personality."

4

BOSTON, 1860

"I rose this morning early
to get betimes
in Boston town . . ."
"Boston Ballad"

In February 1860, with no apparent instigation on his part, Walt Whitman received a letter from the Boston publishers Charles Eldridge and William Thayer proclaiming, "We want to be the publishers of Walt Whitman's poems."[1] The tone of the letter was exciting, with a kind of electric quality about it that appealed to Whitman. The writers, both still in their twenties, claimed to have read *Leaves of Grass* at its first publication when they were clerks in the firm they now owned; they declared it "a true poem and writ by a *true* man." Whitman had an idea from the letter just how effective they might be in their advertising of books, for the writers declared, "We are young men. We 'celebrate' ourselves by acts. Try us. You can do us good. We can do you good — pecuniarily."[2] Thayer later claimed to have been the sole writer of the letter, executed with his partner's approval. So proud was he of it that in his unpublished autobiography he says Whitman later showed the letter to Emerson, who expressed his delight that Boston had such a free press in the hands of such capable young men.

The previous editions of *Leaves of Grass*, in 1855 and 1856, had been self-publications printed by Rome Brothers in Brooklyn, with the first edition distributed by Fowler and Wells of New York and the second by the author. As Thayer later explained it, because Fowler and Wells "could not endure the assaults of the critics, and some of the sentiments of the book were not acceptable to some readers," they had notified Whitman of their intention "to discontinue selling the book." Without saying how they learned of this, Thayer continues,

My partner and myself were indignant, and by letter informed the "Good Grey Poet" that there was one free press at least, that one controlled by Thayer and Eldridge, which was freely offered to him. The result was the publication of a superb edition of the book under Whitman's personal supervision. It did not sell rapidly but the demand was moderately steady and showed a gradual enlargement all the time we had control of business. Our motto was to stimulate home talent, and encourage young authors.[3]

Whitman had hoped to find a publisher for another edition of *Leaves* and had been actively seeking publication outlets for individual poems preparatory to the event. Now, suddenly, the opportunity presented itself, along with an invitation to come to Boston and oversee the edition himself. These, then, were the circumstances that brought Whitman, for the first time, to the city that was not only the intellectual and cultural capital of the nation but the city with the second largest Irish population in America. More significantly, it brought him into a hotbed of antislavery activity supported by the intellectual transcendentalist faction to whom, on this matter, the Boston Irish were adamantly opposed. Predicting which of the two groups Whitman would side with seems not to be difficult, given his desire to continue to impress Emerson and his eagerness to publish another edition of *Leaves*; but, as it turned out, Whitman's working-class attitudes overrode all other considerations, and while he was not openly supportive of the Irish point of view, it becomes clear that he shared their sentiments.

Thayer and Eldridge were very much involved in Boston's rampant radicalism, especially abolitionism, which they hoped to advance through their publications. They were full of plans and enthusiasm, "go-ahead fellows," as Whitman described them, of the sort he had been hoping to find. With the exception of some copyrights and stereotype plates acquired at the time they purchased the publishing house, all of their publishing ventures, other than *Leaves of Grass*, were in the antislavery cause. Among these was to be a novel, "an *American* Novel," as Eldridge emphasized to the neophyte novelist chosen to produce this marvel, William Douglas O'Connor, who signed a contract with the firm in the same month as Whitman.[4] O'Connor's book proved to be *Harrington: A Story of True Love*, a romance about a slave who escapes the South and makes his way to Boston, only to find there conditions of gross inequality. Through this plot device O'Connor managed to rebuke both North and South for mistreatment of blacks. It was an even-handed yet bold attack aimed at the very seat of abolitionism and was typical of O'Connor, a fiery young Irishman who was to play a significant role in Whitman's life. Unfortunately, according to Thayer, *Harrington* did not sell well. A Boston review referred to it and *Leaves of Grass* as mere "sensation books," which the reviewer claimed were "now the rage." *Harrington* was dismissed by this critic as "absolutely sickening" for its "manworship" (its glorification of Phillips, Garrison, Parker, and other abolitionists) and *Leaves* as "the veriest trash ever written, and vulgar and disgusting to the last degree."[5] Despite poor reviews and low sales, Thayer claimed in his autobiography that the firm realized a "profit of $17,000 in the first year," out of which they had to pay all their expenses, including $800 for stereotype plates for *Leaves of Grass*. There were other expenses, as well, which may have contributed to the firm's bankruptcy in 1861 and which perhaps were not manifest in its account books. Thayer and Eldridge were part of a band of what Thayer called "fighting Abolitionists," who "formed a little society in the back part of our store where we had concealed, but ready for use, pistols and ammunition, knives and bludgeons. Our members wore around the collar a narrow black ribbon as a distinguishing mark. We knew each other as 'Black Strings.'"[6]

As part of their activities in this society, Thayer and Eldridge put up money to help finance an expedition into Virginia led by the Reverend Thomas Wentworth Higginson. The object was to rescue two of radical abolitionist John Brown's coconspirators, Aaron Stevens and Albert Hazlett, who, along with Brown, had been condemned to death but were being held in a Virginia prison; Brown himself was hanged in early December 1859. Late in January 1860, Higginson went to Harrisburg, Pennsylvania, where he was to meet Charles Tidd, the one member of Brown's band who was still free. Higginson recruited journalist Richard J. Hinton to this effort and, according to Thayer's account, Thayer went along and delivered "first class burglar's tools" to Tidd, though, he insists, Tidd was "no thief." The attempted rescue, which cost nearly two thousand dollars, failed, and Hazlett and Stevens went to the gallows.[7] On February 10, 1860, Thayer, back once more in his publishing house and perhaps still excited from his adventure, wrote his invitational letter to Whitman.

Three other titles issued by Eldridge and Thayer before their firm succumbed to financial disaster were all by the same author, James Redpath, a Scotsman by birth who would later become a staunch advocate of the Irish National Land League. Redpath had come to the United States in 1850 and settled in Michigan. As a correspondent for the *New York Tribune* he met and quickly became a partisan of John Brown. In 1856 Redpath had attached himself to Brown's band of followers in Missouri, where they were fighting "Border Ruffians" who were attempting to make Kansas a slave state. Though Brown was widely believed to have been responsible at that time for the deaths of five men in Kansas, he was not prosecuted and came to Boston in 1857, where he became a favorite of Emerson, Thoreau, and just about everyone in their Concord and Boston coterie.[8] It was at this time that some of the country's outstanding abolitionists, including Theodore Parker, William Lloyd Garrison, and Wendell Phillips, became Brown's ardent supporters, raising both sympathy and funds for his cause. The uses to which these funds were put, to purchase weapons and ammunition, were known to some but not all of the New England abolitionists.[9] Brown eventually made his way to Virginia and in October 1859 seized the federal armory at Harpers Ferry, from which point he hoped to lead an armed attack on the South and free its slaves. Captured and hanged, Brown became a martyr to the abolitionist cause. Redpath's *The Public Life of Captain John Brown*, an abolitionist hagiography, was followed by *Echoes of Harper's Ferry* and *Southern Notes for Northern Circulation*, all from Thayer and Eldridge.

Also attached to John Brown's Kansas camp was Richard J. Hinton, another New York journalist and a friend of Redpath. Hinton went to Kansas as correspondent for both the *Chicago Tribune* and the *Boston Traveller* and thereafter was heavily involved in abolitionist activities, even serving for a time as bodyguard for Wendell Phillips and eventually writing *John Brown and His Men* (1894). In the Civil War Hinton served as an officer with the Second Kansas Colored Volunteers. He and Whitman met first in Boston and then again in a Washington hospital after Hinton was wounded.[10] In 1862 Hinton formed the Kansas Emancipation League, which raised funds for slaves who fled to Kansas in the first year of the war, and after the war he edited papers in New York, Washington, and San Francisco.[11]

Hinton claimed to have been the one who brought Whitman to the attention of Thayer and Eldridge and this may be the case, but there is evidence of an awareness of Whitman's poetry among New England abolitionists as early as 1850.[12] In a letter to the *Boston Transcript* dated May 17, 1850, William Lloyd Garrison defended himself against a charge of blasphemy and ended by quoting nineteen lines from a Whitman poem, "Blood-Money," without identifying the author. Depending on his source, it is possible that he did not know who the author was, for though the name "Walter Whitman" had appeared in the *New York Tribune* in March, the only identification when it was reprinted in the *Evening Post* in April was "Paumanok."[13] "Blood-Money" was a product of Whitman's heartfelt fury at what he considered Daniel Webster's act of betrayal in lending his support to the slavery compromise with the Southern states.[14] Other examples of Whitman's explosive anger had already appeared in print, each more bitter than the last, until he abandoned the divisive political arena for the more reconciling poetical stance he assumed in the 1855 *Leaves of Grass*. It is this renunciation of extremism that makes all the more ironic the circumstances that led him to be involved in the highly political, even radical, world of Boston abolitionism.

Whitman's political disillusionment came about gradually. Despite his anger in 1842 at its capture by the New York Irish, he had continued his support of the Democratic Party both in his personal politics and in his public statements in newspapers.[15] Eventually, however, slavery was the issue that caused him to break with the party. Not that he was an abolitionist, for this seemed to him too radical a stance; rather, he took the Free Soil position arrived at via his belief that the Wilmot Proviso would ameliorate the vexing situation by preventing the spread of slavery into territory gained from Mexico and in new states to be formed in the West. In large part Whitman's opposition to the extension of slavery was predicated on his support of the white laboring class, which, like many white Northerners, he felt needed to be protected from slave labor in the newly opened West and, in the Northern cities, from the competition posed by freed blacks if slavery were abolished. Even without such competition, Whitman saw new conditions arising in the industrial and capitalistic cities, creating a wage slavery to which the workers were bound. Complicating this situation even further were the masses of emigrants willing to work at anything for any wage and thus lowering the standard of living for all workers.

Years earlier Whitman had advocated in the *Brooklyn Eagle* some organized means of transporting at least some of the two thousand or so emigrants arriving daily in New York to "the 'far west'" where they could settle down "in an agricultural way." He acknowledged, however, that such a plan would have to offer advantage "to all parties."[16] Much later, in 1878, the Irish Catholic Colonization Society of America attempted just such a system of transport, but it failed, as

Whitman had surmised such schemes would, because of a lack of interest "to all parties." Not only did the potential settlers cling to their familiar city life, but the potential contributors preferred to support the National Land League and gave their money for the purchase of land for Irish peasants rather than helping to settle Irish emigrants as landowners in the American West.[17]

Whitman's Free Soil position eventually brought him into conflict not only with the Democratic Party but also with the Irish American politician who was in all likelihood instrumental in securing for him the editorship of the *Eagle*. The man was Henry Murphy, whom Whitman had met years earlier at his first job in a newspaper office. When Whitman was twelve he was apprenticed as a printer's devil to William Hartshorne and learned to set type in the basement of the Fulton Street building that housed the *Long Island Patriot*, the official organ for the Kings County Democratic Party. Whitman learned there not only how to set type but how to be a good Democrat. Among the many local party hopefuls who visited the premises of the "Pat," as it was called (not an Irish reference, but short for *Patriot*), was Henry C. Murphy, born in Brooklyn of Irish parents, a young man then in his teens who was studying law and who sometimes wrote for the paper. In later years Whitman remembered playing pranks with Murphy, but the young Irishman had serious objectives. He became a ward leader, then Democratic boss of Kings County, later a member of Congress, and eventually was appointed ambassador to the Hague. It was while he was county political boss that he controlled the *Eagle*, and, since Whitman had proven his party loyalty, Murphy no doubt helped him attain the editorial post.

That loyalty was severely tested, however, by the slavery issue. Among Whitman's editorials for the *Daily Eagle*, written between March 1846 and January 1848, only one addresses the subject of slavery, and it limits itself to a condemnation of the international slave trade, while avoiding the subject of slavery as an economic system within the United States.[18] What we do find, however, is a review of a lecture on the latter subject given at the Brooklyn Institute by a Unitarian minister, the Irish-born Reverend Henry Giles, an abolitionist who sufficiently tempered his message to allow Whitman to applaud its humanitarianism.[19] While it is clear that Whitman was horrified at the evils of the slave trade, he was equally horrified at the extremism of most abolitionists. For one thing, he viewed them as obstacles in the gradual progress of democracy, which he fully trusted would prove the instrument by which manumission would occur and slavery disappear from the United States. Much closer to his interests was the condition of the American laboring class, but it was precisely because of this that Whitman felt the slavery issue pressing on him, as it was on everyone in the nation. In the summer of 1846, when Whitman was writing of the need to speed the immigrants westward, Congressman David Wilmot of Pennsylvania proposed legislation that would exclude slavery from any land taken from Mexico. President Polk thought the idea preposterous, but there were many like Whitman who saw the Wilmot Proviso as the compromise they had been seeking. The young editor threw his full support behind the proviso, continuing to do so even after the Democratic Party split over it, with the majority rejecting it.

Whitman's friend Henry Murphy, then in Congress, opposed Wilmot. It must have been particularly galling to him not to have the support of his county's party newspaper, all the more so if indeed he had helped put its editor in that post. The party pressured the paper's owner, Isaac Van Anden, to dismiss Whitman, and it is almost certain that Murphy was one of those applying pressure. Whitman seems not to have held a grudge, however, for his later remembrances of Murphy were of good times shared at the "Pat" office and on clambakes. He even lauded Murphy's skills as a historian by pointing out the settlement of a minor point of Brooklyn history thanks to Murphy's scholarship.[20]

When Whitman lost the editorship of the *Brooklyn Eagle* he did a six-month stint on a New Orleans newspaper, then returned to Brooklyn. Back in New York, he became involved with the political splinter group the Barnburners (people who, it was said, would burn down the entire Democratic Party to rid it of those they detested), then joined the Free Soil Party, which in 1848 was supporting Martin Van Buren against the Democratic candidate for president, Lewis Cass. Whitman started a newspaper that was intended to be the Free Soil organ, the *Freeman*. Unfortunately, the paper's first issue was its last, for the print shop burned in a fire that appears not to have been deliberately set. When the Whig candidate, Zachary Taylor, won the election, Whitman turned away from politics to the role of worker-poet, opening a combination bookstore and print shop in Brooklyn.

Though he had removed himself from active participation in politics, the Compromise of 1850 drew from Whitman a deliberately insulting lyric, "Song for Certain Congressmen," published in the *New York Evening Post*. This was followed by "Blood-Money," a scathing poetic comparison of the betrayal of Jesus by Judas Iscariot to the betrayal by those, such as Daniel Webster, who argued for passage of the Fugitive Slave bill.[21] When William Lloyd Garrison quoted the poem in 1850 as part of his defense against a charge of blasphemy leveled by an anonymous writer to the *Boston Transcript*, he claimed not to know what his attacker, "Sigma," meant by the accusation. It is fairly clear, however, that the objection was to a particular rhetorical device widely employed by abolitionist speakers and writers, the application of scripture to secular, political circumstances.[22] In "Blood-Money" Whitman wrote, "Again goes one, saying, / What will ye give me, and I will deliver this man unto you? / And they make the covenant, and pay the pieces of silver."[23] The poem's biblical rhetoric would have made Whitman appear, once he had been identified as its author, to be fully party to the abolitionist cause, an assumption furthered by the appearance of still another caustic poem in the *New York Tribune* of June 14, 1850, "The House of Friends," which revealed Whitman's bitterness at the involvement in the Compromise of 1850 of some trusted Northern politicians.

From that time until the publication of the first *Leaves of Grass* Whitman worked at printing and house building, only occasionally publishing articles in New York newspapers. In the summer of 1856, when Richard Hinton was in Kansas with John Brown, Whitman issued a tract titled "The Eighteenth Presidency!" in which he bitterly denounced President Franklin Pierce and all those in the federal government who supported the proslavery movement in Kansas.[24] This and the publication of *Leaves of Grass* must have made it seem to Hinton and his friends Eldridge and Thayer that in Walt Whitman they had found not only a poet radical enough in his rejection of traditional poetic form but a voice defiant enough of slavery to warrant his inclusion in their publication plans.

Ten lines alone of the longest of the twelve poems (later called "Song of Myself") in the 1855 *Leaves of Grass* would in themselves have seemed to put Whitman in the abolitionist camp, lines that tell of a runaway slave who appears at the door of the poem's persona. The slave, "limpsey and weak," is taken in, bathed and clothed, his wounds attended, and a clean bed provided. During the week they spent together before the slave continued north the narrator claims, "I had him sit next me at table . . . my firelock leaned in the corner."[25] The reference to the firearm ready to defend the fugitive suggests sympathy with the abolitionist cause and is intensified later in the poem by the persona's identification with the "Hell and despair" of a "hounded slave":

> I am the hounded slave. . . . I wince at the bite of the dogs,
> Hell and despair are upon me. . . . crack and again crack the
> marksmen,
> I clutch the rails of the fence. . . . my gore dribs thinned with the
> ooze of my skin,
> I fall on the weeds and stones,
> The riders spur their unwilling horses and haul close.
> They taunt my dizzy ears. . . . they beat me violently over the
> head with their whip-stocks.[26]

But there was even more to catch the attention of Thayer and Eldridge. Among the twelve poems in *Leaves*, one would have been of particular interest to them, the one that in the 1860 Boston edition would be titled "A Boston Ballad." Here Whitman registered his disgust at the capture and trial in Boston in 1854 of Anthony Burns, a slave who had escaped his Virginia owner only to come afoul of the Fugitive Slave Law, which demanded his trial and return to slavery. In 1854 the slavery issue moved explosively onto the national scene, and for that reason the Burns case received wide attention. This and events such as the hanging of John Brown were effective in winning many to the abolitionist cause who had not to that time felt deeply about slavery. Final arguments in the Burns case were offered on May 31, Whitman's thirty-fifth birthday, and the coincidence may have in some way personalized the issue, making the impression of gross injustice all the greater for him.

The poem supposes the presence of its narrator, Jonathan, in Boston on the day Burns is marched through the streets to the ship that will return him to Virginia and slavery. At first Jonathan mistakes the gathered crowd as spectators at a parade and eagerly finds himself a good vantage point, only to see pass before him a company of phantoms in Revolutionary War attire. Ultimately, Jonathan seeks to banish them in favor of a more fitting observer to the shameful spectacle that plays out before him, the specter of England's George III. He cries out to this imagined royal apparition with bitter irony, "You have got your revenge, old buster—the crown is come to its own, and more than its own." Small wonder, on this evidence, that Whitman seemed an obvious candidate for inclusion in a catalog of abolitionist publications.

A series of letters between New York and Boston, following the initial invitation, had established the terms of Whitman's contract with his publishers. By mid-March 1860, manuscript in hand, the poet was in Boston ready to begin work on the third edition of *Leaves of Grass*. He settled into a boardinghouse, and, almost immediately, Emerson came to call, renewing the friendship begun in 1855 when Concord's most eminent citizen traveled to Brooklyn to meet the poet whose work he had hailed with the words, "I greet you at the beginning of a great career."[27] Henry David Thoreau and Bronson Alcott were also eager to renew acquaintances begun in Brooklyn, and there were new friends, his publishers, Thayer and Eldridge, William Douglas O'Connor ("personally and intellectually the most attractive man I had ever met," Whitman said of him), James Redpath, and later, John Townsend Trowbridge, a journalist and novelist who was not part of the abolitionist group.[28]

In this regard Trowbridge was in a decided minority, however, for Whitman found that the transcendentalists in Concord and Boston were almost entirely absorbed in antislavery ideology. Indeed, on April 4, 1860, Whitman was a silent spectator in Boston's courthouse when the young schoolteacher and ardent abolitionist Franklin B. Sanborn (then head of the Concord Academy where Henry David Thoreau had once taught) was tried for his involvement as one of six secret conveyors of funds to John Brown for the Harpers Ferry attack.

In such an atmosphere as Boston offered at the time, justice was swift, and Sanborn was acquitted the same day. But he loved to tell the story of his arrest and trial and in later years found a number of opportunities to do so, each time bringing Whitman's name into the account. One of these provides as vivid an image of the poet as does the photograph taken of him in the same year. Sanborn tells of closely watching those who were the principal actors in his trial, adding:

> I suddenly became aware of another face, no less remarkable, in the court-room. It was Whitman's, — he sat on a high seat near the door, wearing his loose jacket and open shirt collar, over which poured the fullness of his beard, while above that the large and singular blue eyes, under heavy arching brows, wandered over the assembly, as some stately creature of the fields turns his eyes slowly about him in the presence of many men.[29]

From John Trowbridge we have another description, also in the spring of 1860, of Whitman at work in the offices of Thayer and Eldridge: "We found a large, gray-haired and gray-bearded, plainly dressed man, reading proof-sheets at a desk in a little dingy office. . . . The man was Whitman, and the proofs were those of his new edition."[30]

Whitman observed a great deal of Boston in his short stay, and, typically for him, it was mostly the life of the city as he encountered it in its streets and thoroughfares. One of the things he noted was that there were fewer blacks seen in Boston than in New York but that here they were of "a superior order" and were treated with no distinction, being seated and served in restaurants, employed as clerks in the state house, and, in nearby Worcester, even serving on juries.[31] This is in obvious contrast to the widespread exclusion of blacks from the city's white society as described by William Douglas O'Connor in his novel *Harrington*. Jerome Loving has noted the similarity between the situation in which O'Connor's fictional Harrington finds himself and that of the actual slave Anthony Burns. Loving points to O'Connor's eloquence in picturing the poor conditions of Boston's blacks — their exclusion from meaningful work, from public schools, from places of assembly and entertainment, even from decent housing.[32] Whitman noted a different scene, however. The difference in perspective between Whitman and O'Connor, rather than the accuracy of either, is significant, for it forecasts opposing viewpoints on blacks that would shadow their relationship for years. O'Connor's total dedication to what was then called "the Negro cause" commands respect, but Whitman's conservatism, which kept him from committing to the abolitionist enthusiasm of his new friends, had the remarkable effect of leading him to a place where he could reject all exclusive points of view in favor of the attempt at reconciliation evident in *Leaves of Grass*. The persona he adopted there, expressed most often by the first-person singular that pervades the poetry, had become the means by which the poet identified with all conditions and all opinions, and he was not about to abandon it for Boston's sake.

To fully appreciate the source of the difference between Whitman and the circle of abolitionists who met in the back room of Thayer and Eldridge, it is helpful to review briefly some of the political tangle in New York which Whitman had turned his back on a few years earlier. The origin of the tangle lay in the public school controversy of 1842, which was a bitter experience for Whitman. In the wake of the controversy two factions arose within the Democratic Party, the Barnburners, who were radical Democrats opposed to the extension of slavery and with whom Whitman sided, and the Hunkers, conservative Democrats, many of them Irish officeholders, who opposed any agitation of the slavery question and who sided with the slave states. The quarrel between the two groups involved city, state, and eventually national politics, with Tammany Hall supporting the position of the Southern states until the firing on Fort Sumter.

Whitman's fellow Barnburners became Free Soilers after being all but run out of Tammany Hall by the Hunkers, but to gain political office they formed a fusion with the Hunkers to choose nominees for state offices. Some Hunkers, among them Mike Walsh and James T. Brady, formed a Democratic-Republican Executive Committee to oppose the fusion. The committee succeeded in splitting the fusion, and out of it came two more groups, each claiming to uphold the original Tammany Society principles. One group was led by Fernando Wood, suspected of being a Hunker but who did not want to risk losing votes by openly opposing the Barnburners. As a result of his careful manipulations, Wood, whom Whitman heartily despised and whom the city's Irish strongly supported, became mayor of New York in 1854 and was reelected in 1856. The other group was an outgrowth of the Democratic-Republican Executive Committee and was the first body in the North to denounce the Wilmot Proviso, which Whitman strongly supported. The consequences of the proviso's failure included Bloody Kansas, the organization of the Republican Party, and the decline of the Democratic Party. With this confusion of orchestrated and plastic political belief behind him, it is small wonder that Whitman refused to be won over into the radical camp of abolitionism. But he was not disinclined to have an abolitionist publishing firm produce *Leaves of Grass*.

The Boston that Whitman arrived in was a city of great tension, most of it arising from the slavery issue and a good deal of it from the antagonism between the city's Yankee Protestants and Irish Catholics. Strong anti-Catholic feelings in Boston dated to the time of the Know-Nothings in 1854. At that time Catholics were so suspect that a "Nunnery" Committee was formed by the city's Know-Nothing government, and an investigation was launched into Catholic girls' schools run by nuns. When the lines were drawn nationally over the issues of slavery, Kansas, and the emergence of the Republican Party, the situation in Boston was exacerbated by anti-Catholicism and the Irish adherence to the Democratic Party.

The Boston Irish remained at the bottom of the economic scale in 1860, still working as low-paid laborers, dockhands, cartmen, truckmen, domestics, and in whatever other occupations were open to them. The situation here was very different from that in New York; in Boston the Irish were not only seen as dirty and ignorant but as a moral danger to the Protestant City on a Hill. Strong elements of the Puritan ideal of a sanctified community were yet in place, translated into the language of transcendentalism by some, by others into the ethical Christianity of Unitarianism. The Irish presented a threat to both. Without such leveling influences as theater, where the comic Paddy, though an offensive stereotype, could at least assume less villainous proportions, Boston continued to emphasize the least favorable aspects of the immigrant Irish. Among the abolitionists this sometimes reached a level of demonization because of the Irish refusal to support their cause.

Once in Boston, Whitman found there was considerable pressure exerted in the effort to get him to throw himself into the abolitionist cause, pressure that he adamantly withstood. Judging by his comments in later years, however, the differences between him and his new friends had more to do with the degree of importance each side attached to the subject. Late in his life he admitted his inability to fully share the abolitionist fervor of his friends:

> All my friends are more ardent in some respects than I am: for instance, I was never as much of an abolitionist as [Frederick] Marvin, [William Douglas] O'Connor, and some of the others. [Wendell] Phillips—all of them—all of them—thought slavery the one crying sin of the universe. I didn't—though I, too, thought it a crying sin. Phillips was true blue—I looked at him with a sort of awe: I never could lose the sense of other evils in this evil—I saw other evils that cried to me in perhaps a louder voice: the labor evil, now, to speak of only one, which to this day has been steadily growing worse, worse, worse. I did not quarrel with their main contention but with the emphasis with which they asserted their particular idea. Some of the fellows were almost as hot with me as with slavery just because I wouldn't go into tantrums on the subject: they said I might just as well be on the other side—which was, of course, not true.[33]

A fact of Boston life that Whitman did not comment on in 1860 was the large number of Irish living and working in the city, though he could not have failed to see them operating the "carts, drays, trucks, express wagons, . . . vehicles of all sorts" that he noted on Commercial Street.[34] Of a total population of 138,788 in 1850, the Irish in Boston numbered 46,000. Because they wielded little or no political power, historical accounts of the slavery issue in and around Boston have focused on the educated, white, Protestant faction and seldom register the Irish point of view.[35] This deficiency also reflects certain contemporary attitudes, such as the failure of white Protestants of the time to comment on Irish exploitation in the mills and factories of New England while attacking Southern slavery. Even Whitman's "Boston Ballad" can be seen as something of a case in point. Though Anthony Burns does not appear in the poem, being made invisible by the events real and imagined of the narrative, Albert J. Von Frank has made us aware of another missing figure, missing not only from Whitman's poem but from most accounts of the Burns trial — the Irishman James Batchelder, an assistant to the United States marshal in Boston who the abolitionists killed in an unsuccessful attempt to rescue Burns from jail.[36]

Batchelder, born in Ireland, was twenty-four when he died. He had been a truckman at the Boston Custom House, but at the moment of his death he was volunteering his services along with a number of other laborers like himself, most of them Irish or Italian. They were all dependent for employment on the local Democratic Party machine headed by Mayor J. V. C. Smith. On May 26, 1854, a crowd of some five hundred people gathered at the courthouse, the door was rammed, and a small band led by the Reverend Thomas Wentworth Higginson forced their way into the upper passageway, where they hoped to remove Burns from the premises and to safety. Batchelder placed himself squarely in the passageway and was stabbed in the groin, dying within minutes.[37]

When Batchelder placed his body in the path of the determined abolitionists, he acted out an Irish opposition to New England Protestantism's antislavery stance that had begun more than a decade earlier. The spur to this resistance originated not in New England but in Ireland, in the form of an 1841 petition carrying sixty thousand signatures of Irishmen urging the Irish in America to take a public stand against slavery. Behind this lay a series of exchanges between Ireland and the worldwide antislavery movement involving the great Irish freedom fighter Daniel O'Connell. Bolstered by Ireland's long antislavery tradition and by the plaudits of American abolitionists, O'Connell denounced slavery in America and did not hesitate to publicly revile the nation that allowed it to continue.

In 1840 the World Anti-Slavery Convention brought to London Wendell Phillips, William Lloyd Garrison, and other leaders of the American abolitionist movement. From England they journeyed to Ireland to meet with their counterparts there, and in 1841 a statement titled *Address from the People of Ireland to their Countrymen and Countrywomen in America* was written jointly by the Americans and Irish. The two Irish authors were Richard Allen and Richard Davis Webb, both prominent members of the movement in Ireland. As shall be seen in a later chapter, Whitman subsequently corresponded with Alfred Webb, Richard's son.

The *Address* called upon all Irish in America to join the abolitionists, "the only consistent advocates of liberty," and "to cling by them" thereby doing "honor to the name of Ireland" in America.[38] First presented in Boston at an 1842 abolitionist meeting, the petition was reported in Garrison's *Liberator* on January 30, 1842, as having been enthusiastically received by an audience of four thousand people, including a good number of Irish, and to have met with no resistance. This complacencey was short-lived, however, for the Irish in America were not inclined to put themselves in a position of seeming to condemn the nation where they felt themselves to be only shakily established, nor did they wish to be drawn into a conflict where they would be expected to flout its laws. Further, and perhaps most important, as Noel Ignatiev has shown, the Irish needed to adopt a strategy "to secure an advantage in a competitive society," and the refusal of the abolitionist cause was part of their strategy.[39]

The first outspoken rebuf of the *Address* came from New York and from the person with the greatest influence on America's Irish, Whitman's soon-to-be nemesis Bishop John J. Hughes. This was in January 1842, the same year in which Whitman would use the editorial pages of the *Aurora* to attack the bishop over the matter of public funding of Catholic schools. Since the *Aurora* was a newspaper that concerned itself almost exclusively with the New York scene, its editor had little occasion to express views on the national question of slavery, so if the incidents surrounding the Irish *Address* made any impression on Whitman we have no way of knowing. Whitman briefly addressed the slavery issue only once in the *Aurora*, in April 1842, ostensibly at the instigation of a New York Irishman.

About the time that O'Connell in Ireland was beginning to feel himself squeezed between opposition from Americans in the Southern states to his Repeal movement and pressure from abolitionists in the North to demand more forcefully an Irish American condemnation of slavery, an editorial titled "Black and White Slaves" appeared in the *Aurora*. It began by describing a lithograph received "from A. Donnelly, 19½ Courtlandt Street" (the lithographer whose studio was at that address) and inscribed with the words Whitman uses as his title. The print, produced in 1841, offered representations of two supposed localities, one in England and the other in America. The first was the destitute family of a laborer, with the wife, Whitman says, "lying dead upon a heap of straw, an infant endeavoring to draw moisture from her breast, two or three famished children near by," and the laborer seated helplessly on a low stool with three other children clinging to him. A "fat, pompous, lordly parish officer" looms above them, issuing his command, "Come, pack off to the work house; that's the only fit place for you!" The second scene depicted what Whitman called "domestic life at the south. A gentleman and lady, with two children, come to pay a call at the shanty of a family of their slaves. Everything bears the impress of cheerfulness and content." Whitman draws from these contrasting scenes a simple moral: "It would be well if the English abolitionists were to reflect upon [their laboring class]" rather than becoming "sentimental" about American "negroes" whose condition is superior to that of "nine-tenths of the population" in England. "Let our transatlantic neighbors take the beam out of their own eyes — and then they can reasonably find fault with the mote in ours," he admonishes before concluding with a slap at the institutions that "make Britain but one vast poor house."[40]

The lithograph and others like it were numerous at the time and followed closely the line of attack taken by such Southern writers as George Fitzhugh in his *Cannibals All! or, Slaves Without Masters* (1857). The book was an outgrowth of Fitzhugh's earlier attempts to show the exploitation of workers in Great Britain as a greater and more oppressive form of slavery than chattel slavery. What was not said of such lithographs as the one Whitman describes was that they might very well be representations of Irish workers forced off their own land and caught up in the industrial mills of northern England, where they suffered poverty and sickness and often were evicted again. The deflection of attention toward England apparent in Whitman's editorial shows him siding in 1842 not only with the Southern states but with Irish Americans who resented as much as he what was seen as the "meddling" of Europe — especially England but, after the 1841 *Address,* also Ireland — in matters pertaining to the United States. Later, in 1847, when as editor of the *Brooklyn Daily Eagle* he expressed his opinions on slavery in the context of support for the Wilmot Proviso, Whitman echoed this earlier objection to European meddling by scrupulously acknowledging the right of Southern states not to be interfered with.

Bishop Hughes attacked the *Address* in the *Liberator* on March 25, 1842, first by casting doubt on its authenticity — in other words, by fostering suspicion of the Protestant abolitionists who had presented it — and second by denouncing, should the petition prove true, all such foreign attempts to sway "naturalized Irishmen or others" on any question "appertaining to the foreign or domestic policy of the United States."[41] Irish newspapers in Boston, New York, and Philadelphia took up the bishop's outrage and urged readers not to succumb to foreign appeals for support of a movement of radicals who would threaten the union of states. The *Boston Pilot,* the country's leading Catholic newspaper, hammered the final nail in the coffin of the *Address* by claiming the abolitionist movement was a plot instigated by England to threaten national security here.[42]

The shadow of England and its power hovered over many of the proclamations and denunciations coming from both sides. In Ireland O'Connell, who was nearing the end of his career, hoped to have the backing, if only the moral support, of the Boston abolitionists in his drive for repeal of the Act of Union. In the United States, Irish American supporters of O'Connell's repeal attempt opened themselves to suspicion when they accepted as their national leader Robert Tyler, son of the slaveholding president. Further damage to their cause came when they received the financial support of slaveholding Irish in the South. Compounding these issues were the unavoidable feelings of distrust bred by religious differences, which made Irish Catholics unwilling to align themselves with the Protestant establishment in America. The situation proved hopeless; O'Connell eventually disavowed the *Address,* and the abolitionists lost all hope of rallying the Irish to their cause.

While distrust of England's intentions and of rival religious institutions figured largely in all of this, there was also the matter of an almost palpable tension between the Irish and the New England abolitionists, the result of the vast difference in their comparative social status. Many of the same individuals who lionized Frederick Douglass and were willing, at the dictates of what they termed a higher law, to violently oppose the law of the land for the sake of Anthony Burns had no sympathy for the Irish truckman James Batchelder who was acting according to his own principles. While attempting to establish Whitman's attitudes toward the Irish, it is instructive to also take into account those expressed by others of his time, including some who were prominent in the abolitionist movement. For instance, letters that passed between Wendell Phillips and his wife reveal patronizing attitudes toward the Irish and the couple's actual discomfort when in the presence of those same Irish they were seeking to enlist to their cause.[43] Theodore Parker, the fiery supporter of John Brown's radicalism, was known to have frankly declared his aversion to the Irish and, in an 1850 article for the *Massachusetts Quarterly Review* entitled "The Causes of the Present Condition of Ireland," referred to them as "an ignorant, idle, turbulent, and vicious population" whose slavish condition could not be solely laid to English rule.[44] Just a year earlier Parker had published the "Moral Condition of Boston" and, after describing the Irish in much the same terms, put them on the level of wild animals: "Of course they will violate our laws, these wild bisons leaping over the fences which easily restrain the civilized domestic cattle."[45] On the Sunday following Batchelder's murder, Parker reminded his audience that the Irishman was a volunteer in the service of the marshal and that "he liked the business of enslaving a man, and has gone to render an account to God for his gratuitous work."[46]

Orestes A. Brownson, the peripatetic believer in a succession of philosophies and religions, finally settled in the Roman Catholic Church in 1844, only to find himself uneasily yoked there with the Irish. He joined them in accusing Daniel O'Connell of seeking to undermine American institutions when O'Connell attacked slavery, but when nativism became a forceful reaction to the postfamine waves of Irish immigration, Brownson took it upon himself as a native New Englander (born in Vermont) to serve as mediator between the two groups. However, in the pages of his *Quarterly Review*, most issues of which he wrote entirely, he spoke almost exclusively to his fellow (Irish) Catholics, admonishing them on how to become better Americans. In July 1854 Brownson wrote an article for the *Review* entitled "Native Americanism" and laid to Irish Catholics full responsibility for anti-Catholic and nativist feelings because of their "Irish clannishness" and their resistance to the dominant Anglo-Saxon culture of America.[47] Though he held the Irish responsible, Brownson also claimed to discern England's treachery and hatred for Catholicism behind the nativist agitation and even professed a belief that the Free Soil movement was of the same instigation. In his opposition to the Free Soilers, Brownson was joined by the Protestant Irish socialist, by then a senator from New York, Mike Walsh, who was also a fervid denouncer of the abolitionists. Privately Brownson was no different from most of the New Englanders; to Charles Montalembert, leader of the Catholic liberals in France, he wrote (in an un-Christian manner on, of all days, Christmas) of the Irish as "the most drunken, fighting, thieving, lying and lascivious class in the population."[48]

While there is no direct evidence of it, Whitman may have been aware of all these undercurrents of class consciousness circulating beneath the surface of the abolitionist movement. Perhaps there is a hint of this awareness in a comment he once made about William Douglas O'Connor's having learned the art of skillful argumentation "in the anti-slavery school—whether for good or bad I do not know—learned it all there, in the clash of classes—won his spurs in the struggles of the abolition period."[49] As both an Irish Catholic (though not a practicing Catholic) and an abolitionist, O'Connor may have found himself at times in an uncomfortable position among New Englanders on both sides of the issue. Elitist attitudes also came between the working-class Whitman and many of the upper-class New Englanders, and he would continue to feel the effects and complain of them throughout his life. As late as 1881, when Whitman was again in Boston, Bronson Alcott (who always seemed to appreciate Whitman's prose more than his poetry) declared him "too brawny and broad to be either high or deep, and [one who] must rank with the sensuous school of thought and style."[50] Even Emerson, as we have seen, was not immune to this class consciousness and on occasion allowed it to shadow his feelings toward Whitman despite his admiration.

The Irish remained a special case, and after the famine had brought them to the United States in greater numbers than had been believed possible for cities such as Boston and New York to absorb, it was felt necessary to distinguish and articulate the traits and characteristics that many Americans came to believe were innate contributing factors to their impoverished condition. Alcoholism, as might be imagined, was one of the principal factors pointed to by the Protestant New Englanders, many of whom totally abstained from drinking alcohol. Here, too, the Irish in America had failed the Boston abolitionists. In 1849 when the abolitionists brought to the

United States the famous Irish temperance lecturer Father Theobald Mathew, in hopes he would have as profound an effect on the Irish here as he did in Ireland, their plans were thwarted by Boston's Bishop John B. Fitzpatrick, who opposed such meetings because of their Protestant sponsorship and strongly discouraged Irish Catholics from attending.[51] Mathew himself proved a further irritant and raised the abolitionists' ire when he refused to observe the polarities of North and South and took his message to the Southern states.

Alcohol and the domination of priests aside, New Englanders still found it hard not to believe that the Irish were the cause of their own destitution. Thoreau, an inveterate expounder on all that came within his view, has left a number of comments on the Irish, some of which are more damning than others. As is widely known, the cabin Thoreau built at Walden for his two-year experiment in economical living was made from the lumber of a shanty belonging to the Irishman James Collins, who had worked on the Fitchburg Railroad. After Collins and his family moved on, Thoreau took the dwelling apart, piece by piece, laying the pieces out to dry in the sun. While he was thus occupied, he tells us in *Walden*, a neighbor, "Seeley, an Irishman," pocketed the still usable hardware and, "there being a dearth of work, as he said," remained "to represent spectatordom" while Thoreau worked.[52]

Two years before Thoreau went to live at Walden, Nathaniel Hawthorne, while walking in the vicinity of Walden Pond, had come upon "a little hamlet of huts or shanties, inhabited by the Irish people who are at work upon the rail-road," perhaps the very place where Collins had lived. Hawthorne was moved by the scene, by "the shouts and laughter of children, who play about like the sunbeams that come down through the branches." While the children played, the women were washing clothes, and he could see the fruit of their labor all about, "long lines of white clothes are extended from tree to tree." So natural did the people seem in this setting that, Hawthorne says, "Their presence did not shock me, any more than if I had merely discovered a squirrel's nest in a tree."[53]

From Thoreau we have quite a different response. Caught in a sudden storm late in the summer of 1845, Thoreau came upon a shanty in the woods near Walden Pond. At first he thought it uninhabited but within were neighbors, "John Field, an Irishman, and his wife, and several children," the youngest of whom he describes as a "cone-headed infant . . . John Field's poor starveling brat."[54] With a schoolteacher's manner and using himself as exemplum, Thoreau set about trying to instruct Field in living a life of simplicity and thereby improving his status. Neither Field nor his wife could understand the method, and Thoreau concluded that John Field was "born to be poor, with his inherited Irish poverty or poor life, his Adam's grandmother and boggy ways, not to rise in this world, he nor his posterity, till their wading webbed bog-trotting feet get *talaria* [wings] to their heels."[55] Though Thoreau was often very harsh in his judgments of the Irish, he once wrote, "The simple honesty of the Irish pleases me."[56] Simple honesty could not undo his horror at the effects of alcohol, however, and he says of another Irish neighbor, the former soldier Hugh Quoil, that though he had fought at Waterloo he "now awaits his future in an old ruin in Walden woods" convulsed by delirium tremens.[57] The unfortunate Quoil sold rum to other Irishmen on Sundays, Thoreau says, and eventually drifted away, never to be seen again by his Concord neighbors.

In October 1849 Thoreau walked the beach at Cohasset, Massachusetts, viewing the wreck of an emigrant-laden brig, the *St. John*, which foundered on its journey from Ireland. The remains of the known passengers were in boxes marked with chalk; others, like the swollen and mangled body of a drowned young woman — whose death brought no further comment from the Concordian than that she "probably had intended to go out to service in some American family" — lay beneath hastily thrown cloths.[58] While he seems not to have been much moved by this experience, Thoreau initially was quite affected in January 1852 by the sight of a small Irish boy, John Riordan, whose mother had patched his ragged clothes with "countless" pieces taken from an old pair of Thoreau's trousers. The misery of the child, who lacked proper outer garments in the cold and snow, caused Thoreau to feel guilt "that his little fingers and toes should feel cold while I am warm." In February he carried a new cloak to the child, noting in his journal, "These Irish are not succeeding so ill after all. The little boy goes to the primary school and proves a forward boy there."[59]

Pronouncements such as those of Parker and Thoreau on the nature and destiny of the Irish were attempts to locate character in ethnicity, an intellectual activity that much preoccupied native-born American intellectuals in the years before the Civil War. This was especially the case in the Northern states, where populations included large numbers of people of varying national origins, and became of even greater importance in those places where, it seemed, the Irish threatened soon to outnumber the natives. Though there were exceptions (Harriet Beecher Stowe's *Uncle Tom's Cabin* notably), this character study did not generally extend toward blacks, who were seldom seen as anything more than victims whose characters were fashioned by that status and by their acceptance of Christianity. Though both of these conditions had been imposed upon them, they were viewed nonetheless as a saving grace. Furthermore, blacks were clearly of a different race, not even to be thought of at this point as part of the future "race" that would emerge in the United States. In trying to determine what that future race would consist of, factors such as ethnicity, religion, national origin, even social and economic conditions, all came under consideration to varying degrees. Of the immigrant groups the Irish, by sheer weight of numbers, were the objects of the greatest scrutiny and of attempts to evaluate their worth as future Americans. Most of these attempts were at best condescending, at worst condemnatory or expressive of the same kind of resignation Thoreau felt in contemplating his Irish neighbor's future. Of the more condescending type one might take as an example the Reverend Thomas Wentworth Higginson's comments, made more than thirty years after he led the mob that killed James Batchelder: "The Irish race has its characteristic faults, partly the result of temperament partly of oppression; but I maintain that a due proportion of Irish admixture will help, not hinder American society: through the sunny nature of the race, its humor, its physical courage, its warmth of heart, and its strong domestic affections."[60]

As for Thoreau, despite such moments of hope as he may have felt for little John Riordan beginning primary school, his sense of resignation comes through clearly in a pessimistic poem that appears in his journal, the first stanza of which conveyed his belief in the futility of education for such a child:

I am the little Irish boy
　That lives in the shanty
I am four years old today
　And shall soon be one and twenty
　I shall grow up
　And be a great man
　And shovel all day
　As hard as I can.[61]

Standing somewhat aside from the usual evaluations of Irish character are those of Margaret Fuller, an eminent figure among the Concord transcendentalists and close friend of Emerson. In December 1844 Fuller came to New York to write for Horace Greeley's *Tribune*. She wrote book reviews and articles on feminism, philosophy, philanthropy, and just about anything that interested her and might prove of interest to her readers. On June 28, 1845, she wrote "The Irish Character," lauding the Irish, especially the immigrant women, for their devotion to family. As to the future of the Irish in America, Fuller believed it to be bound up in the future of America:

> When we consider all the fire which glows so untamably in Irish veins, the character of her people, considering the circumstances, almost miraculous in its goodness, we cannot forbear, notwithstanding all the temporary ills they aid in here, to give them a welcome to our shores. Those ills we need not enumerate; they are known to all, and we rank among them what others would not, that by their ready service to do all the hard work, they make it easier for the rest of the population to grow effeminate, and help the country to grow too fast. But that is her destiny, to grow too fast: there is no use talking against it.[62]

Fuller attributes their personal flaws to the Irish having been for so long an oppressed race, and though she is dismayed by their "extreme ignorance, their blind devotion to their priesthood, their compliancy in the hands of demagogues," she concludes that "we must regard them as most valuable elements in the new race," by which she means the race of future Americans.[63]

Fuller's prediction for the future of the Roman Catholic Church in America is particularly interesting for its speculation, "if there be Catholicism still, it will be under Protestant influences, as begins to be the case in Germany. It will be, not Roman, but American Catholicism where [the power of the church] must vanish in the free and searching air of a new era."[64] Expectations such as these did not fade easily. Eight months before his death in 1892, Whitman reviled the Catholic Church and Pope Leo XIII, whose teachings on social issues he viewed as "trying to make [the Church] consist with the fact of America," something Whitman believed could not be done because America "says *no* to Catholicism."[65] Clearly it was their religion, rather than the Irish themselves, that was objectionable even to their supporters, and viewpoints such as Fuller's, freely and publicly declared without either malice or intended condescension, cast greater light on Whitman's attitudes if only by indicating that they were far from exceptional.

Fuller's article drew hostile comments from her readers, who must have been mostly women with complaints of Irish domestic help. Typically, for Fuller, she responded by writing another column in which she contrasted the blessings of liberty enjoyed by Americans with the feudal conditions still prevailing in Ireland under England's rule. She offers precepts for Americans in their contacts with the Irish, to exercise patience and expect no gratitude in return, and urges consideration for the needs of the Irish servant who, though domiciled under their roof, was ignored by the household members. In applauding Fuller, however, one must not lose sight of the fact that her expressions of genuine concern were written prior to 1847, when the immigrant Irish, though numerous, had not yet reached their full swell. By the time she was again in Boston that city, which had been receiving four thousand or five thousand Irish a year, had seen thirty-seven thousand enter in the year 1847 alone.[66] Indeed, Henry David Thoreau saw the Irish as "naturalizing themselves" (by which he meant both in the political and philosophical sense) at so rapid a rate that they "threaten at last to displace the Yankees, as the latter have the Indians."[67]

Margaret Fuller's views on the Irish can be judged enlightened when compared to those of most of her New England peers, yet even here questions of race intrude, an indication of the "ethnological" thinking of the time, which a decade later would allow the Irish to be viewed as a separate race. That Whitman partook of this ethnological reasoning is indicated by his ready use, as late as 1871, of the word "stock" in referring to the Irish background of New York City policemen. There is also an unpublished Whitman manuscript, probably dating to late 1867, titled "Of the black question," which appears to be a refutation of Carlyle's objections to black suffrage using the ethnological argument that blacks would disappear from human history through the working of nature.[68] Dale T. Knobel points out that by 1860 the Irish had been given special status by most Anglo-Americans "as an 'alien' race," a status recognized by the 1860 report of the United States Bureau of the Census, which subdivided white inhabitants as "native," "foreign," and "Irish."[69]

Among the general population of Anglo-Americans it had come to be accepted that the deficiencies of Irish character were "the cause rather than the consequence of their particular Old World condition."[70] This conclusion was arrived at largely because of the social problems presented by the postfamine immigrants who were in such wretched condition that it was hard for Americans to believe they had not always been so. But in part it was also because the Irish opposed abolition. Their opposition was viewed, correctly, as an action taken to protect their status, such as it was, in their new country, but it was also seen as a callous indifference to the suffering of slaves and an open hostility toward blacks whose competition they feared. The latter belief lingered for many years. Looking back on the time of slavery in his autobiography, Frederick Douglass spoke of the Irish having been taught "to despise the Negro . . . [and] to believe that he eats the bread that belongs to them."[71] Irish opposition to abolition was also viewed, incorrectly, as proof of either an inability or an unwillingness to act in a democratic fashion. This was especially the case in Boston, where the abolitionists sought to swell their numbers by gaining Irish adherents and condemned them for their opposition by claiming they feared to break ranks with the Catholic clergy. As has been pointed out by all who have chronicled the history of the Irish in America, only their widescale participation in the Civil War (which they saw as a defense of the union of states, not as a war to free the slaves) brought them out of the disrepute into which they had fallen, a disrepute which in Boston was deepened by the abolitionist controversy.

Where Whitman stood on much of this is hard to tell, since for the most part he maintained the observer's role to the activities of his Boston friends, much as Franklin Sanborn described him as an observer at Sanborn's trial. A Free Soiler rather than an abolitionist, he continued to see the opening West as a place for the white worker to stake a claim in America, and there is no mention of a freed slave in his "Pioneers! O Pioneers!" In 1879 Whitman traveled to Kansas for the commemoration of its having become a territory twenty-five years earlier. While there he made contact with former abolitionists he had known, some of whom, including Richard Hinton, had taken part in the struggle to make Kansas a free state. The trip was made at the suggestion of a newspaper friend, Colonel John W. Forney, and was paid for by Forney's Philadelphia publisher.[72] There is little reason to think that Whitman would have made the journey under other circumstances, and he made no public reference to the "Exodus" into Kansas taking place in the same year when thousands of freed blacks fled the South. Publicly Whitman maintained silence on the abolitionist movement until 1891 when, in *Goodbye My Fancy*, he included his tribute to William Douglas O'Connor, which was originally printed as the preface to a collection of three of O'Connor's tales. There he tells of his Boston meeting with the twenty-nine year-old who was, "a thorough-going anti-slavery believer, speaker and writer, (doctrinaire,) and though I took a fancy to him from the first, I remember I fear'd his ardent abolitionism — was afraid it would probably keep us apart. (I was a decided and out-spoken anti-slavery believer myself, then and always; but shy'd from the extremists, the red-hot fellows of those times)."[73]

In 1888, when Traubel queried him as to "what had been his emotional experience at the time of the execution of John Brown," Whitman replied, "not enough to take away my appetite — to spoil my supper." Asked further, "Did your friends understand this at the time?" he responded, "Some of them — yes: some of them thought I was hard-hearted." His brother George, he claimed, had "thought [the hanging] a martyrdom," as did he, "but not the only one: I am never convinced by the formal martyrdoms alone: I see martyrdoms wherever I go."[74]

Whitman seems to have been echoing Emerson in this claim to "see martyrdoms wherever I go," for until the Fugitive Slave Law brought slavery into Boston, Emerson had begged off total commitment to the abolitionist cause by claiming he had other slaves to free. Indeed he had, especially among the white population, and he conscientiously went about the matter of freeing their minds of engrained habits of conventional thinking. As a result many were able to question governmental definitions of "free" and "slave" and when necessary to upset concepts of justice that, in practice, served to promote injustice.[75] Whitman seems to have been of the same mind as Emerson in this regard, for in his late years when asked if he had ever associated himself with "that radical crowd" (the Boston abolitionists), he responded, "No: but that wasn't because they were too radical: it was because they were not radical enough."[76] In a similar vein, he once was asked if he had withheld himself from what he termed the "fervid dead-earnestness" of his friend William O'Connor on the antislavery issue out of sympathy with Emerson's challenge to the movement's "one virtue," exclusivity. Whitman demurred: "I don't know that it was for Emerson's reason or for any conscious reason: I felt, I feel, that the cosmos includes Emperors as well as Presidents, good as well as bad."[77]

The Irish dissented from the abolitionist cause for reasons that seemed to them good and sufficient. Whitman may not have shared those reasons fully but did so at least to the extent of his intuitive belief that no cause was demonstrably wholly and entirely right. Whether or not he included the plight of Irish immigrants among those martyrdoms he claimed to see at every hand can only be gauged by such unpublished writings as his sensitive comments on the condition of Irish women kept on view at the hiring office in New York (see chapter 1) and such generalized sympathetic identifications as appear in his poetry. There is some evidence, however, that Whitman may have understood the position of the Irish in their antiabolitionist stand. In 1888 he looked back on his early life, probably to the time of writing "Blood-Money" and "A Song for Certain Congressmen," when, he said, he was "very bigoted in my anti-slavery, anti-capital-punishment and so on, so on, but I have always had a latent toleration for the people who choose the reactionary course," because, he claimed, he was at heart "not a *revolutionaire* [but] an evolutionist."[78]

This "evolutionist" posture was his late-life designation for that middle ground, ceded by most of his contemporaries in the 1840s and 1850s, on which he wrote *Leaves of Grass*. The position was deliberately chosen as his response to the prewar polarization of American society, with its lines drawn between nativist and immigrant, black and white, and the sectarianism of party politics and regional interests. The role of the reconciler was his attempt, as Betsy Erkkila has said, to "collapse the distinctions of race, class, and gender" which he saw fragmenting America.[79] Surely Martin Klammer is correct in stating that skin color was the greatest barrier to realizing this collapse, greater than religion or social and economic status, and that in pursuing it Whitman's adoption of the slave persona, in the "hounded slave" portion of "Song of Myself," is the single most "transcendent" identification he could have made.[80] Yet the very fact that Whitman could willingly assume this role put him at the opposite end of the spectrum from the Irish of his time, who were struggling to remove themselves from just such an identification, of black with Irish, imposed upon them not only by white Americans but by blacks as well. Evidence of the latter can be found in the angry words of Frederick Douglass, who claimed that in the pre–Civil War years blacks in the North were hourly

elbowed out of some employment to make room for some newly-arrived emigrant from the Emerald Isle, whose hunger and color entitle him to special favor. These white men are becoming house-servants, cooks, stewards, waiters, and flunkies. For aught I see they adjust themselves to their stations with all proper humility. If they cannot rise to the dignity of white men, they show that they can fall to the degradation of black men.[81]

Even at the end of the century Douglass contended the need for a recognition of the rights of blacks by asserting, "Fellow-citizens! We want no black Ireland in America. We want no aggrieved class in America."[82]

On this question of a "black Irish race" in America Whitman, if he ever contemplated it, was silent. If conclusions may be drawn from his silence it would appear, especially in view of his own unwillingness to join the abolitionist movement, that Whitman did not see the refusal of the Irish to do so as proof of their inability to embrace democratic principles. While his primary reason for shunning the abolitionists was his fear of national disunion, he also shared the protectionist, working-class attitudes that motivated the Irish and overrode other considerations. Never again after the New York City public school controversy did Whitman publicly, or privately so far as is known, utter any anti-Irish sentiments that could be said to even approach those of many of the New England transcendentalists. Like most Americans of his time, his principal requirement of the Irish, that is, the Irish Catholics, was not that they take up this or that cause, only that they "improve" their character by abandoning their religion or, at the very least, their clergy and its influence on their lives. It was not, however, a requirement the Irish Catholics in America were willing to meet, not even as part of a strategy of acceptance.

5

WASHINGTON, D.C.

"I dream'd that was the new city of Friends . . ."
"I Dream'd In a Dream"

Walt Whitman came to the nation's capital driven by the necessity of war, as were many other Americans in the years 1861 to 1865. He came not in a uniform or carrying a government-issued rifle but with empty pockets and a fearful heart. It was December of 1862, his brother George's name had appeared (though misspelled) on a list of those wounded at the battle of Fredricksburg. Whitman left New York immediately, had his pocket picked while changing trains in Philadelphia, and arrived in Washington, D.C., with no means of obtaining food or transportation. He walked from hospital to hospital looking for George and knocked on office doors seeking information about him but got nowhere — until two friends from his Boston days came to his rescue. William Douglas O'Connor was now clerking at the Light-House Board in Washington, and Charles Eldridge, one of Whitman's former publishers, was assistant to the Army Paymaster. Between them they provided money and assistance in getting to Falmouth, Virginia, where George's Fifty-first New York Regiment was bivouacked. As it turned out, George's wound was only superficial, and in a short time he returned to active duty. Whitman, however, had seen in the army hospitals piles of amputated limbs and the mangled bodies of suffering men — and had noted the scarcity of help for the surgeons and medical staff. He wrote to his mother that he would be remaining in Washington for a time. Except for visits, he never returned to his Brooklyn home. His subsequent wartime experiences, relative to the Irish, were such that they occasioned a mixture of emotions, strong positive feelings based on personal relationships and negative responses to the public emphasis on the idea of the "fighting Irish" as a major constituency of the Northern armies.

In the time between his visit to Boston in 1860 and his arrival in Washington two years later, Whitman had seen the publication of the third (the Boston) edition of *Leaves of Grass* and admitted, "I am very, very much satisfied." Once back in New York he also had tried unsuccessfully to help Henry Clapp save his *Saturday Press* from foundering. Clapp had been a good friend and had kept Whitman's name and poetry alive in the pages of his journal even when the reviews were bad. "Out of the Cradle Endlessly Rocking" made its first appearance (as "A Child's Reminiscence") in the December 1859 issue of the *Press*, and when William Douglas O'Connor met Whitman a few months later he was filled with awe to be in the presence of the author of a piece that showed such "reach of spiritual sight [and] depth of feeling."[1] Thayer and Eldridge, responding to Whitman's request, had tendered Clapp some money (perhaps an advance on Whitman's expected royalties), but it was to no avail. When the war broke out the Boston publishers lost monies owed them in the South, and not long after they, too, were bankrupt.

Whitman kept busy writing poems that were published in newspapers and enjoyed himself many nights at Pfaff's, a New York restaurant and café on Broadway near Bleecker Street, frequented by a crowd of bohemians. Years later, in the summer of 1881, Whitman went back to visit Pfaff's, then located at Twenty-fourth Street, and breakfasted with the proprietor, Charles Pfaff. The two reminisced about the old days, in 1859 and 1860, and drank a champagne toast to old friends, most of whom were dead.[2] Among those Whitman recalled was an Irish author, Fitz-James O'Brien, a writer of short stories well thought of in his time, though no longer read.

O'Brien was a native of Limerick, Ireland, born in 1828; he was educated at Trinity College and, having squandered an inheritance, came to the United States about 1852. A dandy, he was proud of his good looks and good clothes, but in 1858 his nose was badly broken in a fight. He was rather delightfully described by the editor and critic William Winter as having "a bluff and breezy manner of speech, tending at times to a joyous turbulence."[3] O'Brien wrote stories and poems, some of which appeared in *Harper's*, and a number of plays, one of which, the comedy *A Gentleman from Ireland*, was performed in New York. His stories were of the sort written by Edgar Allan Poe and owe little to his Irish background. At some point O'Brien became enamoured of the actress Matilda Heron and followed her to Boston, where she was appearing in *Camille*. She seems to have abandoned him to his luck, however, and he fell on hard times. In 1861 he joined the Seventh Regiment of the New York National Guard and was shot in February 1862. His wound became badly infected, leading to the condition known as lockjaw, or tetanus; he lingered until October when he died in a Virginia hospital.[4]

No doubt because O'Brien's work was well received at the time, Whitman thought him a reliable enough critic to have asked the Irishman for an opinion of his own poems. In February 1857 he queried O'Brien as to what was most lacking in their composition, to which O'Brien responded *"euphony*— your poems seem to me to be full of the raw material of poems, but crude, and wanting finish and rhythms."[5] When Whitman noted this exchange to himself, he added that when asking others the same question, "the answer has been — 'You have too much procreation.'" Obviously the Irishman had the good sense not to raise that objection.

In the years before the war Whitman not only spent pleasant evenings at Pfaff's but also continued to attend opera performances, a practice he had begun some time in the 1840s. It chanced that he was returning home from a performance of Gaetano Donizetti's *Linda di Chamounix* at the New York Academy of Music on the night of April 13, 1861, when he heard the newsboys' shouts of the firing on Fort Sumter. That September, after the disastrous Union defeat at Bull Run, he read a draft of a new poem to his friends at Pfaff's, a war cry called "Beat! Beat! Drums," which, probably because of its timely subject matter, appeared simultaneously in the *New York Leader* and *Harper's Weekly*.

While welcoming Whitman to its ranks, the *Leader* had absorbed some of the writers formerly associated with the defunct *Saturday Press*, among them Ada Clare and Henry Clapp. Its editor, Charles G. Halpine, had emigrated from Ireland in 1851, and so Whitman's "City Photographs" series, recounting hospital visits to injured New York stage drivers, many of whom were Irish, quite naturally found a place in the *Leader*. Halpine, soon to be in uniform himself, no doubt saw that Whitman's latest poem fell nicely into line with the general efforts being made by newspapers and periodicals to rouse their readers to the Union cause.

On November 2 another poem, "Old Ireland," also appeared in the *New York Leader*. Since it is one of Whitman's lesser known works and is germane to this study, the poem appears here in its entirety.

For hence amid an isle of wondrous beauty,
Crouching over a grave an ancient sorrowful mother,
Once a queen, now lean and tatter'd seated on the ground,
Her old white hair drooping dishevel'd round her shoulders,

At her feet fallen an unused royal harp,
Long silent, she too long silent, mourning her shrouded hope
    and heir,
Of all the earth her heart most full of sorrow because most full
    of love.
Yet a word ancient mother,
You need crouch there no longer on the cold ground with
    forehead between your knees,
O you need not sit there veil'd in your old white hair so
    dishevel'd,
For know you the one you mourn is not in that grave,
It was an illusion, the son you love was not really dead,
The Lord is not dead, he is risen again young and strong in
    another country,
Even while you wept there by your fallen harp by the grave,
What you wept for was translated, pass'd from the grave,
The winds favor'd and the sea sail'd it,
And now with rosy and new blood,
Moves to-day in a new country.[6]

Though Whitman later would write poems similarly addressed to countries other than his own, such as France and Brazil, "Old Ireland" is distinguished from these both by its imagery and content. The poet addresses Ireland in terms of its antiquity and, by reference to a "royal harp," invokes its bardic age. Just a few years earlier, sometime between 1856 and 1858, Whitman had penned a note to himself about the mythical bard Ossian, "The Irish swear that Ossian belongs to them — that he was born, lived, and wrote in Ireland."[7] The note may indicate his awareness of protests made by defenders of Irish culture, such as Thomas Davis, poet and leader of Ireland's Young Ireland movement, which made wide use of Ossianic national symbols, the shamrock and bardic harp.

The protests were against claims made by the Scottish poet James Macpherson who in 1762 published what he said were translations of third-century Scottish poems supposed to have been written earlier than any known Irish bardic poems. While Macpherson's were actually of his own fashioning, the Oisin (which Macpherson rendered as "Ossian") ballads belonged to a Scots-Irish tradition; since their subjects were Irish, however, objections were raised to the claims of a Scottish translation. To one who had set for himself, as Whitman had, the goal of becoming his country's bard, all such claims were significant, as were the bardic symbols, so that in referencing the harp he is honoring Ireland's ancient Celtic culture and its poets. The dominant image of the poem, the mother/country, is one used by poets everywhere, including the Irish poet Thomas Moore, whose works were well known and loved in Whitman's time, both in Ireland and in the United States. Whitman read Moore, along with Scott and Burns, throughout his lifetime, claiming in his old age that he went to them "again and again in certain humors: they are very consoling."[8] In Whitman's poems the mother/country image appears again in "Thou Mother with Thy Equal Brood," where the individual states in America are equally protected and nurtured by the "Mother of All," the democratic union. Yeats and the literary revivalists later used such female personifications of Ireland as Deirdre of the Sorrows or Cathleen ni Hulihan, figuring Ireland as a poor old woman who will be returned to queenly status only when she finds gallant warriors, as those in the days of Gaelic Ireland, to exert her claims. These personifications drew on a type of medieval Irish poem, called the *Aisling*, a dream vision form similar to that found in Chaucer's *House of Fame*. While Whitman's maternal image seems now a cliché and the observation a generalization, it is also a truism that Whitman could offer no greater respect than to depict Ireland, or any country, in terms of the maternal, so highly did he revere motherhood. In "The Return of the Heroes," written in 1867, the image expands so that "the Mother of All" is Nature herself (as nineteenth-century American writers invariably used the word, capitalized and female) who oversees all — the returning Civil War soldiers, the harvesting of her bounties across a still unified nation, and the silent march of the war's spectral dead. By conjoining the themes of war and plenitude, the poem presents what seems at once a complementary and an opposing image to that drawn in "Old Ireland."

In its content "Old Ireland" goes beyond anything Whitman wrote about any country and its people (other than the United States) and may indicate his recognition of Ireland as the source of the largest immigrant population in America. The poet clearly grasps, at this point, the horror of the situation that has driven the wholesale emigration from Ireland, conveying it by reference to the grave over which crouches the sorrowing mother/country, mourning her loss of future generations. He proclaims a message of hope expressed in terms of resurrection that (presciently, if one thinks of the Easter Rising of 1916) evoke the promise of Easter, "The Lord is not dead, he is risen again young and strong in another country." The "country," however, is not that realm of the resurrected Lord but America, to which the future of Ireland has been "translated, pass'd from the grave," by wind and sea—almost as if Whitman were imaging, in "The winds favor'd and the sea sail'd it," the Irish adage of the famine years that spoke of emigration as "hope from the sea."

The final two lines of "Old Ireland," as they appeared in *Drum-Taps* in 1865 and in all subsequent editions of *Leaves of Grass*, simply affirm what has gone before by contrasting the improved physical appearance of the immigrant Irish in their "new country" with the poem's earlier images, of death, a grave, and a "shrouded hope." When the poem first appeared in the *New York Leader*, however, the final line read, "Moves to-day an armed man in a new country." The editors of *Leaves of Grass, Comprehensive Reader's Edition* explain the original final line as follows, "The Fenian Brotherhood, an Irish-American revolutionary society, was founded in the United States in 1858."[9] To be more specific, the Fenian Brotherhood was founded in New York City on March 17, 1858, and organized the following year.[10] A historian of the brotherhood (named for legendary warriors of Irish myth, the Fianna) describes it as "an organized body of men devoted to a system of political, financial, and military action on the part of the Irishmen of America, aiding and co-operating with an allied body of revolutionists in the British Isles, for the purpose of gaining the independence of Ireland."[11] Whitman's original 1861 reference to the immigrant Irishman as "an armed man in a new country" well may have been an appeal to the Fenians, who at the time were being actively solicited for service in the Union army with such slogans as, "You have fought nobly for the Harp and Shamrock, fight now for the Stars and Stripes."[12] If Whitman indeed sought to enlist the Fenians in the Northern cause, he may have felt differently after witnessing the widespread glorification of Irish soldiers and their bravery that became part of New York's wartime ethos.

If we accept that Whitman was appealing to the Fenians, it may be worth considering another, though more tenuous, suggestion in the poem's title. "Old Ireland" might be construed as a rejection of the Young Ireland movement, begun in Ireland in 1846 because of disappointment with Daniel O'Connell's nonviolent Repeal movement. Members of Young Ireland had viewed with alarm the emigration of thousands from their homeland as a weakening of any possible military attempt at independence. A brief, unsuccessful revolutionary attempt by Young Ireland in 1848 had been quickly put down, and the movement died an ignominious death, its leaders either transported to Australia or escaped to America. Whitman's "Old Ireland," which sees emigration as having been the only hope for Ireland's youth, can be read as a refutation of the Young Ireland argument, a refutation supported by the fact that when the rebels who participated in the 1848 uprising had fled to New York they found many among the immigrant Irish who were eager to join them in establishing the Fenian Brotherhood.[13] Still, even such a speculation as this, that Whitman may have been discrediting Young Ireland, pales in light of his 1856 poem later called "To a Foil'd European Revolutionaire." Surely the support offered there to revolutionaries everywhere by "the sworn poet of every dauntless rebel the world over" was as much directed to the foiled revolutionaries of Young Ireland as to any.

The Fenian Brotherhood of 1858 planned to spread across the United States, drawing into membership Irish Americans who would be willing to train and arm themselves, with the prospect of returning to Ireland to effect a revolution. Irish militia companies were formed in New York State and elsewhere, but before much could be accomplished in the way of training the Civil War broke out, and the Irish were caught up in its fury. Something of the bitterness felt by these volunteers and conscripts at finding themselves in a war not truly their own comes through in the rhyme attributed to the Irish fighting men:

War battered dogs are we
Gnawing a naked bone
Fighters in every war and clime
For every cause but our own.[14]

What became a long, delaying interval for Fenianism proved ultimately to be a time of great advancement for the Irish in America, for they entered the Union army in numbers upwards of 140,000 and won for their people a larger measure of respect from Americans than they had ever enjoyed. It is, then, not unlikely that the final line of "Old Ireland," as Whitman originally wrote it in 1861, was intended as a rallying cry aimed specifically at the Irish; his possible reasons for changing the line will be discussed later in this chapter.

Since the general reaction to the Fenian Brotherhood in New York newspapers had been negative, placement in the *Leader* of a poem suggesting that the brotherhood of militant Irishmen now be viewed as potential armed forces in the Union cause would have shone a more positive light on that organization. This speculation is supported by the fact that the Irish immigrant editor of the *Leader*, Charles Halpine, used his paper to propagandize for support of the war and would have welcomed such a suggestion. Halpine, the son of an Episcopal priest, was a longtime Tammany Hall activist and commanded a wide readership among the city's Irish. He joined the Sixty-ninth Regiment, New York's Irish regiment, shortly after the outbreak of the war and, after serving as an officer with the regiment, was stationed in New York.[15] Though in later editions of *Leaves of Grass* it was moved to the "Autumn Rivulets" section, the fact that "Old Ireland" became part of *Drum-Taps* when that collection of Civil War poems was first published in 1865 would indicate that Whitman saw it as related to the Civil War.

Once Whitman had decided to remain in Washington his most pressing needs were for work and a place to live. Through the good offices of "Charley" Eldridge he obtained work as a copyist in the office of Major Lyman S. Hapgood, Army Paymaster. There he also wrote letters for the *New York Leader* and the *Brooklyn Standard*, written in the style of a war correspondent but focusing on the activities of New York regiments. Afternoons he spent visiting the army hospitals in and around Washington. Turning to another friend, William Douglas O'Connor, now married to Ellen (Nellie) Tarr, he accepted the couple's invitation to rent a hall room in the same boarding-house, at 394 L Street, where they and their young daughter occupied rooms. In this way he was able to take dinner and breakfast with them and keep his expenses low. Whitman had intended to continue this arrangement for only two weeks or so, but, at the insistence of his friends, he remained for months before moving to another boarding-house. The landlord at 394 L Street was, like O'Connor, an Irishman, by the name of Quinn. Ellen O'Connor later remembered Quinn as a very mean man whom Whitman once observed cheating someone. Whitman reprimanded him, though without raising his voice: "I can hear his voice now," she recalled, "very gentle, but very firm and ringing."[16] Whitman also remembered Quinn as "a mean Irishman" but added, "I do not intend by that to reflect on Irishmen in general — to say that Irishmen are mean — but rather to indicate that Irishmen are so rarely mean that when you meet one of the real stripe, he seems to make up for all the rest!"[17]

"So rarely mean" certainly implies that on the whole Whitman's encounters with the Irish were favorable. Clearly, if we were to judge by his praise of William Douglas O'Connor we would have to say they were more than favorable, for in the plethora of compliments with which Whitman surrounded almost every mention of O'Connor's name — with repeated references to his Irish ancestry — there lies the strongest clue to the poet's appreciation of what he took to be peculiarly Irish qualities. The story of the friendship between these two men has filled two books thus far and countless additional pages. To Whitman, O'Connor was a chivalrous knight of old, a friend of his soul, and an Irish bard. He appears to have been the first person with whom Whitman could fully share his poetic intentions, which were nothing less than the revolutionizing in form and content of American poetry.

William Douglas O'Connor was a native of Roxbury, Massachusetts, born there in 1832 to an English mother and Irish father. His father, Peter D. O'Connor, was a laborer who, having left Ireland at an early age, was among the earlier wave of immigrants to America in the nineteenth century. William left home when still a child to live and work on his own. His formal education was scant, but he made excellent use of the Boston Mercantile Library Association so that he later was better read, especially in the literature of the English Renaissance, than most of his contemporaries. As a young man he turned his artistic skills to the daguerreotypist trade, in Providence, Rhode Island, and continued to write and publish poetry and short fiction in that city as he had done in Boston.

O'Connor's first notable story was called "What Cheer?" and appeared in *Putnam's Monthly* in July 1855. It is a highly moralistic tale in which a young student despairs of the world and decides to kill himself by drinking laudanum. At the moment of drinking he is arrested by a scream from another part of the building where he resides. With the aid of a local restauranteur he investigates and finds a woman in a desperate situation, impoverished, with young children, and having just found her husband dead, a suicide by the very means the student had intended for himself. The moral is quickly obvious, as the student realizes he has been self-absorbed and uncaring of others around him. Of no small interest is the fact that the poor family the student has ignored is Irish, the husband described by the restauranteur as "A cussed Irishman, of course. Gets drink somehow; dunno how, for he aint in work. Licks his wife, just for rum an' ugliness, an' drives the children out o'doors."[18]

O'Connor presents both a practical and a philosophical explanation for the condition of the "cussed Irishman." The restauranteur admits his anger at the man's behavior, but when he puts himself "in the man's boots" he realizes the cause: "he got seventy-five cents a day for totin' brick an' mortar up a ladder, from mornin' to night. That's four dollars an' a half a week, ye know, an' will you have it now, or wait till ye get it, 's the principle, you understand, with the man that hires him." The omniscient narrator offers a more deterministic, New England puritanical, view, describing the dead man as "a poor, ignorant, besotted, brutalized Irish laborer," the result of previous generations "making him all he was, and never to rise above that level, but to sink lower and lower forever."

The story suggests a division within O'Connor as to the root cause of Paddy's condition, whether the result of circumstances, in America as in Ireland, of which he is the victim, or the result of generations of poverty and ignorance, which can only breed more of the same. Born in New England and possessed of superior intelligence, O'Connor cannot have found it easy to identify with the immigrants all around him, despite having been forced by the circumstance of his own impoverished childhood into something near their level of existence. While he devoted much to the abolitionist cause, there is no evidence that O'Connor ever took up the cause of the Irish immigrants. In 1853 he returned to Boston and went to work on a periodical, the *Commonwealth*, whose offices served as a gathering place for Boston's abolitionists. O'Connor quickly fell in with the movement, and a year later he met Ellen Tarr, who worked for William Lloyd Garrison's abolitionist paper, the *Liberator*. Two years later they married, and O'Connor took an editorial position at the Philadelphia weekly the *Saturday Evening Post*.

While working in Philadelphia O'Connor, who had become something of an authority on Elizabethan literature, took up the cause of Delia Bacon, a Massachusetts woman who claimed descendency from Sir Francis Bacon, the real author, she argued, of Shakespeare's plays.[19] O'Connor became convinced of the accuracy of this argument, and late in his life he ardently defended an Irish immigrant, Ignatius Donnelly, whose study, *The Great Cryptogram: Francis Bacon's Cipher in the So-Called Shakespeare Plays*, was published in 1888. Almost entirely out of respect for the judgment of his good friend O'Connor (for he claimed not to be convinced of the argument nor to have read all of Donnelly's book), Whitman wrote "Shakspere-Bacon's Cipher," a short poem in which he diverts the question of the disputed authorship to his belief that in every aspect of nature "A mystic cipher waits infolded."[20] Throughout his lifetime, however,

O'Connor was not to be dissuaded on the subject and frequently tried to convince others, drawing on what Whitman saw as his Irish intensity to ignite his rhetoric. One friend of the Washington days remarked, "O'Connor was a man of unfailing eloquence, whom it was always delightful to listen to, even when the rush of his enthusiasm carried him beyond the bounds of discretion, as it did in the Bacon-Shakespeare business."[21]

O'Connor remained with the *Post* until 1860, when the new publishing firm of Thayer and Eldridge coaxed him into returning to Boston to write a romance that would advance the abolitionist cause. There he met the poet whose work he had admired since the first publication of *Leaves of Grass* in 1855.

"Did you take to him from the first?" Whitman once was asked of his meeting with O'Connor. "Yes, without a suspicion of uncertainty," he replied, "he was so bright, magnetic, vital, elemental: I think the thing was mutual — was instant on both sides."[22] O'Connor was twenty-eight, Whitman forty-one, but the attraction clearly was mutual. O'Connor wrote of the older man, "it is health and happiness to be near him; he is so large and strong — so pure, proud and tender"; Whitman said of the younger man, "he was a gallant, handsome, gay-hearted, fine-voiced, glowing-eyed man; lithe-moving on his feet, of healthy and magnetic atmosphere and presence."[23] For Whitman the best was yet to come, since he found in this charismatic young Irishman an intellectual companion who responded to *Leaves of Grass* with mind and heart and who would prove himself one of the poet's most faithful friends.

O'Connor appealed to Whitman on just about every level. Whitman found him physically attractive, "one of the most graceful of men: agile, easy: yet also virile, vigorous, enough." The movements of his friend's body as he walked on the street Whitman could only compare to those of "a beautiful deer . . . his bearing was so superbly free and defiant."[24] As to his intellect, Whitman declared him the most brilliant of all the men the poet knew. "For brilliant mental equipment O'Connor is the pride of the flock," he declared. "He has an essentially honest mind: is possessed of the most severe literary integrity: his learning is vast. . . . William can see truth at a glance — can instantly probe to the heart of experience, fact."[25] Much of what he found admirable in his friend he attributed to his Irish nature, especially his eloquence and wit. From all accounts, O'Connor undoubtedly was a first-class speaker, one who had developed a technique of public address that involved, among other things, a pacing of his address designed to hold an audience. In describing it Whitman once was reminded of an Irish adage:

William was even — his passion, fire, always lasted. As the Irish coachman said, hearing complaints during the trip that he was slow, "I'm giving him wind, so he may go in style!" — the last half hour being to him the important stretch. . . . When William gets started, he's for a great way — goes on and on, almost with increasing power. Yes, he's the Irish canter.[26]

In the final years of his life Whitman sometimes devised descriptive comparisons of his friends when discussing them with Horace Traubel, so that the young man might better grasp the individual personalities of the men who had earlier surrounded the poet. Thus Whitman, in one such comparison, claimed: "[Richard Maurice] Bucke is of course not subject to the flights we learn to look for in O'Connor: the soarings, the brilliant sparkle of satire and wit — the Irish — in William is rich in color — is mad with irresistible, indestructible life."[27] But on another occasion he placed O'Connor in a singular position among all his friends: "I know of no one — have never met any man or woman, not a single person — in whom there was such a vigor, such a depth and fervent innate power, and at the same time such an exquisite sense of literary and art form."[28]

In the summer of 1863 the pleasant arrangement at the L Street boardinghouse came to an end with the removal of the O'Connors to a larger apartment. Since their new quarters were nearby, Whitman continued to take many of his meals with the family and spent at least Sunday evenings with them, if not other evenings as well. He was not the only one to do this, for a circle of friends formed around the O'Connors that included at least three more comrades from the Boston days: Charles Eldridge, Richard Hinton, and John Trowbridge. John Burroughs also joined the group in 1865 and thereafter remained one of Whitman's closest friends; it is from Burroughs we learn that one of the favorite haunts in Washington for the circle of friends was Harvey's, where they ate oysters while perched at a counter on high stools.[29]

Intellectual discussions were the order of the gatherings at the O'Connors', and the subject matter ranged widely over literature, politics, philosophy, and, inevitably, the war. Unlike the quiet observing manner Whitman seems to have maintained while in Boston, he freely participated in these discussions. O'Connor's eloquence, however, made him the dominant speaker in the group. As to his manner of argument, Whitman once remarked, "William's onslaught is terrifying—it always means business. He never charges the enemy with an apology on his lance. That is the idea—he is fiercely in earnest: nothing can stand against him: when he comes along God help you if you don't get out of his road." But O'Connor seems also to have been subject to chimerical changes in temperament, which may actually have been the result of a manic-depressive disorder that Whitman confused with his friend's Irish ancestry, seeing his "constitutional melancholy, his Irish bardic nature" as explanation for the extremes to which he was often led.[30]

His friend's fierce earnestness became public when, in 1865, Whitman was dismissed from his government position. In that year Whitman had moved from the Paymaster's Office to the Indian Affairs Bureau of the Department of the Interior, where he was a clerk for Secretary of the Interior James Harlan. The reasons for the dismissal appear to have been many but apparently included Harlan's personal objection to his clerk's poetry.[31] Whitman was then preparing another edition of *Leaves of Grass* and kept in his office desk a copy of the 1860 edition as his working blueprint. The book came into Harlan's hands, and he found the poems offensive enough to use them as at least partial excuse for the dismissal. Whitman was given another post the same day, in the Attorney General's office, but O'Connor was incensed at what he perceived as a disgraceful offense to freedom of thought and expression. The result of his indignation was the now famous defense of Whitman, *The Good Gray Poet*, published nine weeks later. In this pamphlet polemic O'Connor, fully aware that he was risking his own government position, brought to bear all of those argumentative skills Whitman and the other friends were so keenly aware of—the passion, fire, and earnestness that made O'Connor unique among them. Though at times he allows himself to be carried away to such a degree that he weakens his argument, one cannot fail to be impressed by the erudition of his defense and the sincere adulation of the poet that infuses it. Reading it one must agree with Whitman, who said of O'Connor, "he is a withering fire to his enemies and a sustaining fire to his friends."[32]

Overlooked perhaps even by Whitman at the time was the extent to which his friend's Irish background may have made him such a firebrand, especially in defense of the poet, for it was in large part O'Connor's finely honed sense of political oppression that led him to react as he did. Centuries of subjugation by a tyrannous government may have been as much a part of his psychological makeup as of any among the Irish in America and elsewhere. That an attempted suppression of literature by a government officer (for such was O'Connor's interpretation of the dismissal) should occur in a democratic country was intolerable, and O'Connor responded in the only way he knew, by blasting both the individual offender and his compatriots in general for a lack of appreciation of the "Good Gray Poet." Not until a year before his own death did Whitman indicate his grasp of what may have been the true source of O'Connor's rage. To Traubel he confided, "O'Connor is distinguished first of all by an abysmic flavor — an Irish bardic ardor centered in him out of six generations of patriotism, national aspirations. It made a vast heart."[33]

A large part of O'Connor's defense of Whitman was based on the poet's unselfish visitation of the wounded in military hospitals begun almost immediately after his decision, in 1862, to remain in Washington. Initially a hospital visitor who brought fruit, reading materials, tobacco, and other items to the patients, Whitman progressed to writing letters for them — and often to inform parents of their deaths — and eventually to actual nursing duties such as cleansing wounds and changing dressings.[34] The poems included in *Drum-Taps* faithfully recorded his experiences in the hospitals, as did his letters, especially those written to his mother, and *Specimen Days*, his prose autobiographical account of some of the events of his life. The letters and the long lists of soldiers' names entered in his notebooks reveal the presence in these hospitals of Irish and Irish American soldiers from all parts of the country. One of the most touching accounts in *Specimen Days*, however, concerns a young soldier who came from Ireland specifically to volunteer his services. His name was Thomas Haley of Company M, Fourth New York Cavalry, "a regular Irish boy, a fine specimen of youthful physical manliness — shot through the lungs — inevitably dying — came over to this country from Ireland to enlist — has not a single friend or acquaintance here," Whitman wrote.[35]

Whitman saw Tom Haley when he was first brought to the hospital (apparently Campbell Hospital in Washington) on June 15, 1863, and did not believe the young man could live twelve hours. At the time of writing, Whitman says, "He lies there with his frame exposed above the waist, all naked, for coolness, a fine built man, the tan not yet bleach'd from his cheeks and neck." The wounded youth slept most of the time, but when awake he was "like some frighten'd, shy animal." Whitman sat beside Haley in silence, observing his breathing and the beauty of his youth, "so handsome, athletic, with profuse beautiful shining hair." At one point Haley awoke and turned on Whitman "a long steady look," then sighing, returned to sleep. "Little he knew," Whitman says, "poor death-stricken boy, the heart of the stranger that hover'd near."

Unlike Thomas Haley, who came directly from Ireland, approximately a third of the 140,000 Irish who served in the Civil War were from the New York area.[36] Among the first to enlist, they had responded to the call for volunteers out of a devotion to their adopted country and to the idea of the union of states. Still conservative on the question of slavery, they did not see themselves as volunteering for the purpose of abolishing slavery; in fact, many were still sympathetic to the Southern states. The majority of the New York Irish volunteers served in all-Irish units, such as the Seventy-fifth Regiment, the "Irish Rifles," and in the famous Sixty-ninth Regiment under its commander, Michael Corcoran, an 1849 immigrant who had been a leader of the Fenians.

The Sixty-ninth Regiment was a militia unit prior to the war, with Corcoran at its head. In October 1860 the Prince of Wales visited New York, and Corcoran refused to have his unit march in the welcoming parade. He was placed in court martial, and the trial was still under way when the war started. At that point he issued a highly effective call for Irishmen to volunteer, and the charges against him were dropped. On the matter of the visit of the prince, Whitman disagreed with the city's Irish, and in "Year of Meteors," a poetic retrospective of the year 1859–1860, he sings of the occasion:

And you would I sing, fair stripling! welcome
    to you from me, young prince of England!
(Remember you surging Manhattan's crowds as
    you pass'd with your cortege of nobles?
There in the crowds stood I, and singled you
    out with attachment;). . . .[37]

Corcoran was taken prisoner at the first battle of Bull Run, but by then the Sixty-ninth Regiment was part of the Irish Brigade formed by Thomas Francis Meagher. Meagher had been exiled from his homeland and sent by the British to Van Diemen's Land (Tasmania) for his part in the 1848 uprising; he escaped and made his way to New York where he founded a weekly newspaper, *Irish News*.[38] Throughout the four years of the war Meagher was variously seen as hero or as drunkard, but he managed to generate a tremendous amount of excitement and garnered great public adulation for the Sixty-ninth. A full-scale parade and ceremony attended the departure of the regiment from New York, and a similar, though far more somber, observance greeted the return of their vastly diminished numbers after Bull Run.

It should be recalled that in September 1861 when Whitman published his battle call, "Beat! Beat! Drums!," it was as part of a general rallying effort that followed the defeat at Bull Run. The ranks of the Sixty-ninth Regiment were so ravaged there that their return to the city was for the purpose of recruitment. Not long after this event Whitman would have been made personally aware of the enormity of the contribution made by the men of the Sixty-ninth, for it was at the battle of Fredricksburg where his brother George was wounded that the regiment was next engaged and where it won its fame, not only for the losses that nearly wiped out the regiment but also for bravery of such magnitude that some of the best-remembered Irish heroism in the war was displayed there. The New York newspapers made much of this, especially of Meagher's report that, of his 1,200 men who went into battle at Fredricksburg, only 280 remained alive the following day.[39] Robert E. Lee is said to have hailed the Irish brigade at Fredricksburg with the words, "Never were men so brave. They ennobled their race by their splendid gallantry."[40]

The Fifty-first New York Regiment had also suffered losses at Fredricksburg, sixty-nine infantry men and six officers killed or wounded. At the end of the first year of the war the regiment had only three hundred of its original thousand men.[41] Whitman may have chafed at the amount of publicity accorded the Irish Brigade, perhaps feeling that other fighting units and their men were being slighted. Because of his brother's assignment to the Fifty-first New York Regiment, Whitman took a special interest in it when sending news articles home. In June 1864, having been ill and told by the doctors to remain away from the hospitals until he felt better, Whitman returned home despite his fears that George might be injured while he was away. By midsummer he felt well enough to visit the New York hospitals where the war wounded were tended, and late in the summer he and his mother attended the funerals of two of George's friends killed in battle. In October he published "Fifty-First New York City Veterans," a brief history of George's regiment, in the *New York Times*. It recounted the movements of the regiment from the time it left New York in October 1861, and may have been born of a desire to offset the publicity garnered by the Sixty-ninth Regiment, or at least of the hope of providing a balance to it.[42]

Whitman lacked the ability, and no doubt the desire, to produce the kind of humorous writing about the war that contributed to the image of the Irish volunteer as a good-natured hero who, despite his troubles, found much about the army that was laughable. It was, in fact, just such a hero as this who captivated many New Yorkers. Charles Halpine, with whom we may assume Whitman had friendly relations when Halpine was editor of the *Leader*, chronicled the adventures of a fictional New York Irishman, "Private Miles O'Reilly of the Forty-seventh New York Volunteers," in the pages of the *Irish-American*. Because of its comic appeal, the series commanded a wide readership, and the newspaper proudly boasted that only the president was better known than O'Reilly. Halpine collected the O'Reilly pieces in *The Life and Adventures, Songs, Services and Speeches of Private Miles O'Reilly* and, amusingly, described his hero as possessing "the usual strong type of Irish forehead — the perceptive bumps, immediately above the eyes being extremely prominent."[43] The description, with its snide allusion to phrenology, indicates an awareness of the way in which this pseudoscience of head bumps frequently was turned against the Irish.

In 1864, when Halpine was stationed in New York, he joined in the city's ceremonious welcome of the furloughed Sixty-ninth Regiment and in April of that year published a poem celebrating its third anniversary. Whitman's October 23, 1864, *New York Times* article on his brother's Fifty-first Regiment may have been spurred by Halpine's effort. Even the fact of its appearance in the *Times* is significant, since that paper had earlier indicated its displeasure at the way in which the Sixty-ninth Regiment held itself to be exceptional. That Whitman may have felt a sense of rivalry existing between the Irish units and others, such as the Fifty-first, is borne out by an undated note he wrote about the war memoranda he intended to produce after the war. Forgetting, perhaps, Tom Haley, who came from Ireland to fight and eventually die in the war, Whitman reminded himself to

make a *fuller* point that the armies were composed mainly of American born & raised men. The New England States, the west, the Middle States, Michigan, Wisconsin, Illinois, agricultural New York & were all native born & made the main bulk of the soldiery. A far larger percentage of the Union soldiery than is generally supposed, came from the Southern & Border states. There were several whole regiments from those States, and squads and individuals from them were sprinkled all through. There were several Irish and German regiments, mostly from the great cities; they did good service,—fought well—but in comparison with the great military bulk-volume, they were only drops in the bucket.[44]

In *Democratic Vistas* Whitman distinguishes the valor of "the American born populace" that sprang with alacrity to fight the war and seems to set them off from the European-born by pointing out that the Americans were "the peaceablest . . . race in the world" and the "least fitted to submit to the irksomeness and exasperation of regimental discipline."[45] Correctives such as these hint strongly at a fear Whitman no doubt shared with other Republicans, that the Irish would try to build a political power base for the Democratic Party on the role they had played in the war. This also may have been the reason why, when Whitman included "Old Ireland" in *Drum-Taps*, he deleted the reference to the Irish immigrant as "an armed man in a new country," in hopes of downplaying the role of the Irish in the war.

Another possible contributing factor to the deletion cannot be ignored, however—the four days of antidraft rioting that took place in New York in July 1863, largely at the instigation of the city's Irish. As already noted, the Irish had been quick to volunteer their services to the Union cause. Though some conservative Irish, especially those who had business interests in the South, were among those Northerners of every background who opposed the war, the greater majority of the Irish population in New York quickly responded to the call for volunteers. Like Whitman's brother George, many of them initially signed up for a three-month enlistment but then reenlisted for the duration of the war. Despite this, the Irish eschewed the politics of Lincoln and remained loyal to the Democratic Party throughout the war and after it. Their feelings were well expressed by Halpine in one stanza of his "Song of National Democracy":

> To the tenets of Douglas we tenderly cling,
> Warm hearts to the cause of our country we bring;
> To the flag we are pledged—all its foes we abhor—
> And we ain't for the "nigger" but are for the war.[46]

They may have clung to Douglas's Democratic principles, but the city's most influential Irish newspaper, the *Irish-American*, consistently urged its readers' loyalty to the president. This kind of support was severely tested, however, by Lincoln's proclamation of the emancipation of slaves, which raised for the Irish laborer the specter of a mass influx into the North of competitive black workers. The willingness of blacks to take the place of striking Irish workers and the eagerness with which employers replaced striking workers with blacks were fresh in the minds of the city's Irish, many of whom still labored at the lowest economic end of the workforce.

The breaking point for New York's Irish, in their support of Lincoln and the war, came with the passage of the Conscription Act in March 1863. The act exempted those who could either pay three hundred dollars or provide a substitute, which to the low-paid Irish seemed grossly discriminating. Whitman and his mother worried that his brother Jeff would be drafted, and Walt wrote his mother that there seemed no way to avoid it but to borrow the money needed to buy Jeff's way out.[47] Jeff's presence and financial support were vital to Louisa Whitman, especially since another of her sons, Andrew, had been discharged, presumably for poor health, and was at the time seriously ill (he died in December 1863); but there were many in the city with equal need who had no place to turn for such a loan.

Like most of those who were away at war, Whitman learned of the New York City draft riots from the newspapers. On July 15 he wrote to his mother from Washington, "So the mob has risen at last in New York—I have been expecting it, but as the day for the draft had arrived and every thing was so quiet, I supposed all might go on smoothly—but it seems the passions of the people were only sleeping, and have burst forth with terrible fury, and they have destroyed life and property." The feeling in Washington, he told Louisa, was "savage and hot as fire against New York, (the mob—'*copperhead mob*' the papers here call it)," and he heard everywhere, even in the hospitals, "threats of ordering up the gunboats, cannonading the city, shooting down the mob, hanging them in a body, etc."[48]

Initially, Whitman's reaction to this fury was, as he said, "partly amused, partly scornful," but on reflection he quickly changed his mind. As he wrote his mother in the same letter, "we are in the midst of strange and terrible times—one is pulled a dozen different ways in his mind." The fact that he had been expecting some sort of riotous reaction to the draft, even welcomed it—as his words "at last" would indicate—and that he was relieved when the conscription was temporarily suspended in the city (for, as he said, "the deeper they go in with the draft, the more trouble it is likely to make") suggests Whitman's sympathies remained with the rioters even after he had overcome his first enthusiasm. His feelings appear to have been partially shared by his brother Jeff, who on July 19 wrote him an account of the events that began, "We have passed through a wonderful week for our New York. A week that I think will eventually be productive of great good to our country, but had at a fearful cost."[49] Jeff believed the news reports of the riot were exaggerated but that the number of deaths was underreported. He offers a figure of four hundred rioters killed, though of the five hundred or so deaths recorded historically, most were not rioters.

The week that Jeff referred to began when the first names, twelve hundred of them, were drawn for the draft on Saturday, July 11, 1863. It was an unfortunate choice of date for its proximity to the annual Boyne Day reminder, on July 12, of the great defeat of Ireland's Catholic forces by William of Orange. Sunday was a day of rest for the laborers, which allowed them ample time to attend to the publication in the Sunday newspapers of the names selected for conscription. When the majority of names proved to be those of mechanics and laborers, among whom the Irish numbered predominantly, it seemed that history was repeating itself in a new form of oppression, and so the rioting began. Jeff Whitman felt so bitterly toward the Irish for their participation in the riots ("I'm perfectly rabid on an Irishman") that he feared not enough of them had been killed by the army troops sent to quell the insurrection, and his brother George, writing from Kentucky where he was part of the Union troops, wished more of the rioters had been killed.[50] While Walt quickly corrected his initial reaction to the riots, he gave no indication that he held the Irish responsible for the uprising, nor, on the other hand, does he seem to have believed that they were being unduly singled out for conscription.

The riots began on Monday, July 13, when Boyne Day, having fallen on a Sunday, was observed, though not with the Orange parades that the city would come to know in later years. Rioting did not begin, as might have been expected, in the poorest districts of the city. Rather it was the industrial workers, painters, carpenters, bricklayers, and stonecutters who began the first acts of defiance, and in this fact lies the reason for the support of the action by Jeff and Walt Whitman, who were themselves of the laboring class. Inevitably, because unchecked, the rioting spread and drew in the criminal or near criminal elements who took advantage of the situation to loot and burn the homes and businesses of prosperous Republicans. Later in the week most of the rioters' anger was directed at blacks, and murder was added to crimes against property. Police forces in the city, whom Jeff Whitman claimed "covered themselves with glory" in the riot, were insufficient to quell the uprising, and Union troops stationed nearby had to be brought in. The affair brought no small condemnation of the city's Irish from New York's mayor George Opdyke, who promptly vetoed a bill that would have enabled many of those called up for the army to pay their way out of the draft. As it turned out, news of the bravery of the Irish volunteers and the heavy losses sustained by the Sixty-ninth Regiment at Gettysburg only a week before the riot began quickly pushed the lurid riot stories off the front pages.[51]

Among those who had supported the Conscription Act and who helped to quell the riots was Whitman's one-time enemy, now Archbishop John Hughes. Hughes followed the official line of his church, which was to support the Union but to refrain from taking a stand on the issue of slavery. Abolitionists, of course, saw this as tantamount to a proslavery stand and as the principal reason why the Irish refused to support their cause and the draft. Partly because of the position of the Catholic Church on slavery, many New Yorkers disapproved of the use of priests as chaplains in the Irish regiments. The archbishop protested, and the disapproval was overcome. Whitman, who to that point probably had had very little contact with Roman Catholic priests, met a number of these chaplains while in Washington and, as with so many of his wartime experiences, these connections somewhat changed his opinion, though his 1870 essay "Democracy" has him calling for a "divine Literatus" to replace the priest, by which he means the clergy of all religions. Years later he told Horace Traubel,

> When I was in Washington it was surprising how many Catholic priests I came to know — how many took the trouble to get acquainted with me — on what good terms we kept with each other. I think we were unified on the strength of the deeply religious, deeply adoring, spirit that was patent behind our differences of technology, theology — our differences of lingo, name.[52]

Though one cannot know if the clergyman in an anecdote Traubel reports was Catholic or Protestant, he tells us that Whitman had an unpleasant encounter with a "distinguished Irish clergyman" who came to visit in Camden, New Jersey. On entering, the clergyman immediately put the elderly poet off by announcing that he "had travelled three thousand miles to question Whitman about certain philosophies in 'Leaves of Grass.'" Whitman was offended (probably by his tone), and the interview was "ridiculously brief."[53] Though in this instance it appears to have been the man, not his church, that offended, Whitman generally found some aspects of Catholicism offputting, the grandeur of its cathedrals, for one, especially St. Peter's in Rome which sinned, he thought, by its one defect, "it lacks simplicity." Expounding on this to Traubel, he reverted to his days in the Civil War:

> I could tell you of a wonderful experience . . . of an incident in which all the integers were simple — were more directly related to life. It was in Washington, during the war, in one of the wards of a hospital — a poor room, with cheaper furniture than this one you see in my parlor . . . a three legged stool for an altarpiece — no light but the light of a candle: then a priest came and administered the sacrament to a poor soldier. . . . I stood aside and watched, aroused in places to sympathy, though mainly impressed by the spectacular features of the event — by its human emotional features.[54]

Just as Whitman changed his attitude with regard to Catholic priests as a result of the war, so, too, did many in the North change their still-lingering negative attitudes toward the Irish because of their eagerness and bravery in defending the Union. But the South also had brave Irishmen who fought and died for its cause, though often, as in the North, poverty or conscription was the goad. Whitman came in contact with many Southern soldiers in the hospitals, never allowing their place of origin or their political sympathies to interfere with his dedication to their recovery and their comfort. Sometime in the winter months of early 1865 he met a young Irish American, Peter George Doyle of Richmond, Virginia, who had served eighteen months in the Confederate army. In September 1862 he had fought at Antietam, where George Whitman's Fifty-first Regiment took heavy losses and where 506 of the Irish Brigade's 3,000 men were killed or wounded. The meeting between the poet and the former soldier was pure happenstance, but it would bring Whitman many years of happiness.

For all their sorrow and despair, the war years also brought great joy to Whitman, for he found in tending the wounded an outlet for those tender nurturing instincts that were so vital a part of his personality.

His contacts with the young and not-so-young soldiers brought him friendships that were, for the most part, as intense as they were fleeting. But as is so often the case with those who find themselves thrown together to share brief times of pain, loneliness, and uncertainty, relationships developed that could not be continued beyond the national emergency. "Many a soldier's kiss dwells on these bearded lips," Whitman later wrote of those days, but the kisses faded either into death or distance, and letters written in peacetime went unanswered or brought responses that told of new lives, with wives and children.[55] The one great difference was his wartime friendship with Peter Doyle, "Pete the Great," as Whitman dubbed him, the young Irishman who did not drift away until circumstances forced him to and who never forgot the man whose love he understood, if not always his poetry.

Peter George Doyle, born in Limerick, Ireland, on June 3, 1843, to Peter and Catherine Nash Doyle, came to the United States with his mother and three brothers in 1852.[56] The Doyle family settled in Virginia, where Peter later became a machinist and possibly a cooper, that is, a barrel maker. When the Civil War began he joined the Confederate army to serve in a Richmond light artillery unit, one of ten enlisted men who were natives of Ireland.[57] His company saw action at Richmond, Manassas, and Antietam, where Doyle was wounded and sent to a hospital in Richmond. There he entered a petition seeking discharge on the grounds that he was "not a Citizen of the Confederate States" having been born in Ireland.[58] Further, he claimed to have lived in Washington, D.C., from the time of his arrival in America and that he had been conscripted in Virginia when he went there seeking employment. A few days after entering this petition he attached an addendum stating his intention to return to Ireland as soon as possible. Doyle was discharged on November 7, 1862, and years later was a member of the United Confederate Veterans.[59] A month after his discharge his company was involved in the battle at Fredericksburg, where George Whitman sustained the wound that brought his brother Walt south.

The addendum to Doyle's petition for discharge was probably made at the urging of Confederate army officers, who sought assurances of foreigners seeking a way out of the army that they would leave the country. When Doyle did not leave, he was arrested four months later for desertion and returned to his company. Wounded, hospitalized, and released, Doyle never returned to duty. On his way north he was captured and imprisoned in Washington. A short time later he and some others in like situations were freed after swearing not to aid the Southern cause.

Once free, Doyle remained in Washington with some family members, one of whom was his older brother, Francis, a police officer killed in the line of duty in 1871. Pete worked at the navy yard along with many other Irishmen and took a second job as a conductor on the Washington and Georgetown Railroad Company. His horsecar route may well have been along the length of Pennsylvania Avenue since most of the sixty-car operation covered that thoroughfare. On a stormy night in 1865 Doyle had but one passenger in his car, Walt Whitman. Though in later describing their meeting Doyle misremembered the year, he was clear in his remembrance of their shared emotion:

> You ask where I first met him? It is a curious story. We felt to each other at once. I was a conductor. The night was very stormy,— and he had been over to see [John] Burroughs before he came down to take the car—the storm was awful. Walt had his blanket—it was thrown round his shoulders—he seemed like an old sea-captain. He was the only passenger, it was a lonely night, so I thought I would go in and talk with him. Something in me made me do it and something in him drew me that way. He used to say there was something in me had the same effect on him. Anyway, I went into the car. We were familiar at once—I put my hand on his knee—we understood. He did not get out at the end of the trip—in fact went all the way back with me. I think the year of this was 1866. From that time on we were the biggest sort of friends.[60]

Being "the biggest sort of friends" included taking long walks of five or ten miles in Washington and out into the countryside, something Whitman did not do with the unathletic William Douglas O'Connor.[61] The major difference between Whitman's two Irish friends was not that O'Connor was highly intelligent and Doyle barely literate but that O'Connor was insistent on proving himself right in most discussions; Doyle, on the other hand, was happy to listen quietly as Whitman explained things or just to join the older man in comfortable silence. A frequent rider on Pete's car line later recollected seeing the two together often and commented on the lack of conversation between them, adding, "perhaps because the young Apollo was generally as uninformed as he was handsome."[62] Pete recalled other things, however, Walt "always whistling or singing," reciting poetry, "especially Shakespeare," humming or shouting in the woods.[63]

Whitman's remembrance of Pete was as "a rare man: knowing nothing of books, knowing everything of life: a great big hearty full-blooded everyday divinely generous working man: a hail fellow well met . . . Pete fascinates you by the very earthiness of his nobility."[64] Clearly, Peter Doyle was, in Whitman's mind, the epitome of the working class, with all its values rolled up in this one Irish mechanic. So important did Whitman consider Pete to an understanding of his poetry that at one point he claimed it was necessary to include their friendship in order to "get the ensemble of 'Leaves of Grass.'"[65]

During the next few years Whitman and Doyle continued together as much as possible. Though they often talked of living together this was not possible, as Pete was supporting his widowed mother; he stayed on with her, and Whitman lived in boardinghouses. Whitman's affection for the young Irishman was such that he was miserable when the often taciturn Doyle seemed not to return his love. In July 1870 Pete must have seemed especially distant, for Whitman chastised himself in a note, "Depress the adhesive nature / It is in excess — making life a torment," and again, "REMEMBER WHERE I AM MOST WEAK, & most lacking. Yet always preserve a kind spirit & demeanor to 16. BUT PURSUE HER NO MORE."[66] Whitman used "16" as the code reference for Pete, based on the numerical placement of his initials in the alphabet, and "HER" was his later substitution for the original "HIM."[67] His feelings changed, however, when, on the night before Whitman left for Brooklyn to visit his mother, he and Pete said a tender farewell on a Washington street corner. From Brooklyn Whitman wrote how comforted he was by that leave-taking: "I never dreamed that you made so much of having me with you, nor that you could feel so downcast at losing me." Then, acknowledging his need, he adds, "I foolishly thought it was all on the other side. . . . I now see clearly, that was all wrong."[68]

It was the following year, in July 1871, when Whitman was again in New York, that he wrote to Doyle and O'Connor about the Irish rioting in the city. Then, a year later came a break with O'Connor; the following year, 1873, Whitman suffered a stroke, which initiated a series of strokes that eventually took him away from Washington and from Pete. Whitman went to live with his brother George and George's wife in Camden, New Jersey, later buying his own home in that community where he died. Pete changed jobs to work on the railroads and managed to see Whitman only now and then. In 1875 Whitman visited him in Washington for two weeks. For a time they exchanged letters, then postcards. When Whitman was able to get about again (with the help of a cane Pete gave him), he began giving lectures on Lincoln's assassination. He made vivid the event by using the firsthand account provided by Doyle, who was present in Ford Theater, heard the shot, and saw Booth jump to the stage and fall before crying out "something," which Doyle said, "I could not hear for the hub-bub," before disappearing from view.[69] Doyle attended some of these lectures, which afforded them brief reunions.

Two years before his own death Whitman was startled one day by a newspaper headline, "The Death of Peter Doyle." Although it referred to a different Peter Doyle, it "knocked the breath out of me," he told Horace Traubel, and he then went on to remember "Pete — a rebel — not old — big — sturdy — a man, every inch of him!"[70] But toward the end of Whitman's life there was almost no contact between them, something which Pete later explained as his fault. When the old poet was ill and needed care, Pete felt he wanted to nurse him, he told a friend, because "we loved each other deeply," but he knew "there were things preventing that" and so stayed away.[71] He came for the poet's burial, however, and remained in touch with some of Whitman's friends. It is from one of them we know that Peter Doyle "never swerved from him" (Whitman) and, from another, that the two were so closely associated in the minds of Whitman's friends that when Pete died in 1907 it was "almost like losing Walt anew."[72]

One thing Whitman shared with the Irish in America was their joint participation in the Civil War, and like them he took from that experience both good and bad. For him it was the goodness of personal relationships that enriched his life, mixed with a somewhat grudging attitude that too much attention had been paid to the wartime exploits of this one immigrant group. But while the Irish gained from their participation in the war greater and greater strength in the American society, Whitman was noticeably weakened, physically, by it. The great, robust physique that was frequently commented on by others seemed to leave him from that time, to be replaced by an even greater sensitivity of mind and heart due, in no small measure, to "the dear love of comrades" he had known in the war years.

6

BOSTON, 1881

"I hear it was charged against me . . ."

The Civil War took its toll on Whitman, physically and emotionally, as it did on many who found themselves drawn into it in one way or another. But like the Irish, he came out of it better off in some ways, especially for the friendships he had formed and the depth of emotion he had found himself capable of expressing in actions and in poetry. His poetry was deepened by the war experiences, and *Drum-Taps* showed a gravity that had not been evident in his work before. The war over, Whitman stayed on in Washington during the Reconstruction period, still working in the Treasury Department. There were, now and then, new contacts with Irish people, both in the United States and abroad. While some of these were minor and of little consequence, there was one new friendship, with the Boston-based Fenian hero John Boyle O'Reilly, which meant a great deal to both men and which has not to this point been sufficiently examined. Unfortunately, the beginning of one Irish friendship roughly paralleled the loss of another, with William Douglas O'Connor.

Before O'Reilly came on the scene, however, there were other Irish contacts. One was with Louis Fitzgerald Tasistro, an Irishman of so many talents that Whitman's admiration led him to solicit donations of money for the man when he came on hard times.

Born in Ireland in 1808, Tasistro came to the United States as a young man. In the 1840s he was a journalist, novelist, travel writer, actor, and lecturer. In New York he was known for his portrayals of Shakespearean roles, especially Othello and Macbeth. He toured the South appearing in plays and wrote two volumes on the southern states; later he lectured in New York, wrote for a Boston weekly, and published a novel. At some time prior to the Civil War he was a translator for the State Department, then returned to the New York stage. Whitman may have known him in New York, though it seems more likely that they met when Tasistro was teaching languages in Washington and perhaps working in a government office. On April 26, 1872, the *Washington Daily Morning Chronicle* carried a letter from Walt Whitman seeking "pecuniary assistance for a man of genius, whose name, twenty or thirty years ago, was one of the bright stars." Now, at the age of seventy, Whitman says, he is "stranded, without a dollar, lingering, disabled by injuries, and down with obstinate, long-protracted ailments, starving, slowly dying, in this city."[1]

Contributions did arrive, in the amount of $122, to which Whitman added $10 before turning the money over to Tasistro. After Whitman left Washington the following year he continued to ask after the Irishman in many of his letters to Peter Doyle; later he inserted into his notebook the notice of Tasistro's death, adding in his own hand, "died Sunday May 2 — 1886."[2] Given the number of Irishmen Whitman may have met through Doyle in Washington, there is no reason beyond a tempting speculation to connect Tasistro with the badly stained letter from Doyle to Whitman dated January 18, 1878, which reads in part, "the little Irishman that was here this winter! you remember him."[3] Whoever the Irishman was, Whitman probably remembered him.

In 1872 we also find Whitman writing to Alfred Webb of Dublin, Ireland, in response to a letter received offering hospitality, no doubt in Webb's home at 77 Middle Abbey Street. Webb was the son of the Irish Quaker and abolitionist Richard Davis Webb, one of the authors of the 1841 *Address* from the people of Ireland urging Irish in America to denounce slavery. The letter, never previously published, reads:

December 5, 1872
Alfred Webb:
Dear Sir:

I must write just a line of thanks for your hospitable offer — and for all the cordial letter to me, which has just come to hand.

I am still working here at my daily work — keep well — entertain some (but not fully definite) prospects for public readings or lectures in the future.

I send respects and love to my friends in Ireland — affectionately including yourself and wife. Shall be glad to get the letter on Froude (that new Quiscotte [*sic*]) — and always to hear from you.

Walt Whitman
Solicitor's Office Treasury
Washington, D.C.
U.S. America[4]

The greeting "love to my friends in Ireland" would have been directed to the group of Whitman enthusiasts at Trinity College, Dublin. Most prominent among them was Edward Dowden, who in 1871 had published an impressive article (discussed in a later chapter), "The Poetry of Democracy: Walt Whitman," in the *Westminster Review*. The "new Quiscotte," as the letter makes clear, is the English historian James Anthony Froude, who in 1872 had published the first volume of his four-volume study, *The English in Ireland* (1872–1874).

Froude was the most widely read historian of his time, controversial for the undisguised biases he betrayed but with a narrative style highly prized by those of a strong literary bent. He was an avid disciple of Carlyle, whom he joined in an admiration of force as a determinant of right. On this ground Froude argued against conciliation between England and Ireland and believed that so long as a people were unable to successfully take their independence by force, they must forfeit the right to self-government. It is clear that Carlyle's defense of Cromwell's conquest of Ireland, in his editing of *Oliver Cromwell's Letters and Speeches, With Elucidations* (1845), considerably influenced Froude's account of the English in Ireland, nor did his opinions change over time. In 1889 he published a novel set in eighteenth-century Ireland, *The Two Chiefs of Dunboy*, where, as Oscar Wilde wrote, "Mr. Froude admits the martyrdom of Ireland, but regrets that the martyrdom was not completely carried out."[5]

In October and November 1872 Froude came to New York, where he gave a series of five lectures on Irish history based on his study. Scribners, his American publishers, honored him with a dinner at Delmonico's restaurant on October 15. Among the guests were Ralph Waldo Emerson, Henry Ward Beecher, William Cullen Bryant, and Thomas Wentworth Higginson. Letters of regret at their inability to attend were read from the aging Henry Wadsworth Longfellow and John Greenleaf Whittier. Speakers at this grand occasion included Emerson, Bryant, and Higginson.[6] Despite the laudatory reception, Froude found considerable opposition in New York to his theories on the Irish. In truth, he was a man of conflicted emotions about Ireland and its people. Having spent a good deal of time in that country, he genuinely liked the Irish but simply did not believe them capable of governing themselves. New York, the seat of Irish immigration, could not be expected to welcome such sentiments. The public received him politely, but Froude was unable to convince New Yorkers that England was not responsible for Ireland's woes. On the matter of Irish character Froude was of the same opinion as many of the New Englanders who had come to welcome him, for according to the *Tribune*, he found "the misfortunes of Ireland rather due to the congenital qualities of the race than to wrongs inflicted by their conquerors."[7] The *New York Times* on October 26, 1872, in commenting on the lectures, claimed Froude had drawn an unfair picture of England's treatment of Ireland but quoted Emerson on Froude's "faculty of seeing wholes and the faculty of seeing and saying particulars" and offered high praise for the historian's ability to "paint pictures in words."

Whitman was living in Washington at the time and, so far as we know, did not attend any of the lectures. It seems safe to assume that he was not invited to the dinner reception. In "Our Eminent Visitors," the opening piece in *November Boughs* (1888), he includes a long quotation on the American reception of Froude, supposedly taken from the *London Times*. The piece is critical of the eminent Americans who hailed the historian, claiming they are no more representative of the masses of Americans than Froude may be said to be the ambassador of his people. Froude is characterized as a "master of a charming style" who can take a single subject and present it as a living figure. "But," the article continues, "the movements of a nation, *the voiceless purpose of a people which cannot put its own thoughts into words, yet acts upon them in each successive generation*—these things do not lie within his grasp."[8]

Whitman uses the article as a springboard to the point he will make, that there is, similarly, "such a thing as the distinctive genius of our democratic New World . . . not specially literary or intellectual." It is for this reason, he implies, that the Boston literati, in applauding Froude, have missed the point, though "the intelligent reader," as he describes the average American, would not.[9]

A search of the *London Times, New York Times,* and *Irish Times* failed to produce the quoted material. It is possible that the piece is actually from "the letter on Froude" that Whitman refers to in his letter to Webb, which may have been sent to one of these papers by Webb but not published. If Webb sent Whitman a copy of the letter, Whitman no doubt copied it for himself thinking it had been published. It is clear from the quotation as it appears in "Eminent Visitors" that Whitman has copied it, for the spelling is not English: "honor'd" is spelled without a "u," and Whitman's distinctive elipsed past tense appears in a number of words. The underscoring of some of the words, no doubt done by Whitman's hand, makes them stand out in direct support of his argument, that there is a collective spirit that guides and moves a people but which is not expressed in the works of the "literary classes and educators" as represented by the guests at Delmonico's. Though Whitman read and approved of Froude's biographies of Carlyle and Julius Caesar (claiming for the former the one thing that had damned its author in the eyes of many, that it was "true"), the inclusion of these comments in "Eminent Visitors" strongly suggests his disapproval both of the interpretation of Irish history Froude had come to America to expound and of the distinguished American literary people who had honored him for it.[10]

Contributing to Whitman's feeling, perhaps, was the memory of what Boston's *Literary World* of June 3, 1882, had said of *Leaves of Grass* when it was being suppressed: "We felt at the time that it was a grave error in taste, policy, and good morals for a respectable house like that of James R. Osgood & Co. to put its imprint on a book containing such downright indecencies as this of Whitman's." Whatever the emotions that drove the argument, there is present beneath its surface an interesting self-alignment in which Whitman distances himself from "the full-dress coteries of the Atlantic cities" and places himself on the side of the Irish. That he should choose to make this the lead essay in *November Boughs* in 1888, when Ireland's demand for Home Rule dominated British politics, seems a pointed indication of where Whitman stood on "the Irish question." Privately he had no reservations on the subject. In January 1889 he was asked by Horace Traubel how he stood on Home Rule. "Home Rule? I want home rule for everybody — every section: home rule: for races, persons: liberty, freedom: as little politics as possible: as little: as much goodwill, as much fraternity, as possible: that's how it presents itself to me."[11]

The tenor of Whitman's 1872 reply to Alfred Webb's letter suggests this was the first communication to pass between the two men. Later, in February 1876, Webb ordered some books from Whitman, and there were other letters as well, which have been lost.[12] Even if this was the first contact between them, it is quite possible that Webb's name was known to Whitman through the latter's connections to Bostonian abolitionists. Alfred Webb (1824–1904) was originally a printer in his father's Dublin printing business. He later wrote travel articles for periodicals and in 1878 published *Compendium of Irish Biography*. In the 1890s he was a member of Parliament. Webb's father, Richard Davis Webb, was a Quaker who played an active role as a temperance and antislavery reformer. In this role he became one of the authors of the 1841 *Address* to Irish Americans and editor of the London *Anti-Slavery Advocate*. Later he was a member of the Central Relief Committee, which carried out the Quakers' program of famine relief. Like a number of American abolitionists, he wrote a biography of John Brown, *The Life and Letters of Captain John Brown*, published in London in 1861. When Frederick Douglass toured England, Ireland, and Scotland from August 1845 to April 1847, Richard Webb was his host in Ireland. The elder Webb died in 1872, after which Alfred and his wife visited the United States, arriving in New York and going on to Boston where, while staying with Garrison in Roxbury, they heard Douglass speak at the Colored Republican convention at Faneuil Hall.

In the 1880s Webb was an important figure in the Irish struggle for land ownership and served as treasurer for the Irish National Land League. The Irish revolutionary Micheal Davitt described him as "in many ways a safeguard, in all the movements he has been connected with," and hailed him for his show of "courage and a public spirit on many an occasion."[13] In that decade of intense activity Webb and John Boyle O'Reilly worked toward the same end of land reform in Ireland, with O'Reilly acting for a time as Webb's American counterpart in his duties as treasurer of the American Land League.

Webb may have become aware of Whitman through Dowden's 1871 article or even earlier through the publication in England of William Michael Rossetti's *Poems of Walt Whitman* (1868), but even without these, his Boston connections were sufficient to bring the poet to Webb's attention. Later, of course, O'Reilly would prove a point of contact between them, as would James Redpath, the former abolitionist and disciple of John Brown who had become one of Whitman's close friends in 1860 when they were mutually involved with the Boston publishing firm of Thayer and Eldridge. Later the editor of the *North American Review*, Redpath had further proven himself Whitman's friend on a number of occasions by obtaining for him writing commissions and even making cash gifts, which Whitman later claimed "saved me from bankruptcy."[14] During the Civil War Redpath, then a Boston publisher, had raised money in that city to support Whitman's hospital work, and Whitman had hoped Redpath would publish his book of war memoranda, a project to which Redpath could not commit for financial reasons.

Though born a Scot, Redpath increasingly associated himself with the Irish cause and in 1880 went to Ireland to report for the *New York Herald* on the National Land League. Just as years earlier he had moved from reporting on John Brown's abolitionist activities to being a partisan, Redpath quickly became a propagandist for the Irish cause, for which he lectured widely in Ireland and America. It was Redpath who made the term "boycotting" part of the public discourse in describing the policy of social ostracism applied to those estate managers who, like the English captain John Boycott, profited by acquiring land from which Irish tenants had been evicted.[15] Whitman's comments on Redpath reveal much about the latter's personality. He was, the poet told Trauble, not just loyal but "militantly so: he was a perpetual challenge."[16] Of his involvement with the Irish cause of independence Whitman said, "He is a vehement Home Ruler: fiery, flaming: is an Irish sympathizer of the intensest sort."[17] After Redpath's death in 1891 Whitman told Traubel that, like "the typical New England woman . . . James had views — that was one of his drawbacks." He concluded however that, "in spite of everything, he was a noble man — believed something — was no liar or coward."[18]

Like Redpath, William Douglas O'Connor's abolitionist activities also had been replaced after the war by another cause, his almost unceasing efforts to gain Whitman the worldwide recognition O'Connor believed he deserved. After publishing *The Good Gray Poet* in 1866 O'Connor had made numerous attempts, some more successful than others, to bring to public attention the fourth edition of *Leaves of Grass*, published in 1867, and the 1871 prose volume *Democratic Vistas*. In 1868 O'Connor had published a short story in *Putnam's Monthly Magazine* titled "The Carpenter," which offered a Christ-like fictional representation of the poet. Despite the parallel the story suggests, O'Connor insisted he was not a disciple of Whitman's but his "champion."[19] However he chose to characterize the relationship, it came to a sudden, explosive halt in 1872.

The approximate time of the argument has been variously placed as in the summer or in December of the year. The exact time matters little, for the cause lay in the passage two years earlier of the Fifteenth Amendment, which gave blacks the right to vote.[20] O'Connor, as might be expected on the basis of his abolitionist record, was totally in favor of the amendment, while Whitman, as might also be expected, was not. It was as simple, and as momentous, as that. The argument took place at O'Connor's home and seems to have been a matter of things being allowed to go beyond their usual level of containment, at which point Whitman left without resolving the disagreement. John Burroughs later described O'Connor as having become enraged at Whitman's comments about "the unfitness of the negroes for voting." As Burroughs said, the two were in the habit of "goring each other in argument like two bulls," but for O'Connor this was too sensitive a topic to withstand much goring.[21] Whitman wanted to put the matter behind them quickly and offered his hand the following day, but O'Connor refused. Much later, when Whitman spoke of the quarrel with Traubel, he admitted to having been "repelled" by O'Connor's "moral devotion" to the "Negro cause," adding, "There has come to me some self-regret — some suspicion that I was extreme, at least too lethargic, in my withdrawals from William's magnificent enthusiasm."[22] But on another, similar occasion he said something about O'Connor's style of arguing that also must be taken into account, especially in view of the latter's refusal to accept Whitman's apology: "I often thought William carried his opposition too far — drove with too deadly a determination — told him so. He would take a poor devil — shake him like a cat a rat. But often he would go on when there was no necessity — when in fact he should have stopped."[23]

A ten-year silence ensued, though Whitman maintained contact with Nellie O'Connor, which allowed each man to remain aware of the other's situation. Despite this, when Whitman had a stroke the following year, 1873, and Nellie was one of those who came to his aid, there was no word from William. Peter Doyle was still an important part of Whitman's life, however, and his comradely presence filled much of the void left by O'Connor's departure. The remainder of the decade brought great changes for Whitman, his removal to Camden, New Jersey, to the home of his brother George and his wife, and the loss of his government post because of his illness. But there were some welcome events as well: the publication of a Centennial volume of *Leaves of Grass*; a lengthy stay in the United States by a new friend from England, Anne Gilchrist; his first trip to the great American West in 1879; and a trip to Canada the following year to visit another new friend, Dr. Richard Maurice Bucke.

Bucke was the head of a mental hospital in London, Ontario, and Whitman struck up a number of happy acquaintances with the attendants and workers at the site. One of these was his "Irish friend" Richard Flynn, a twenty-four-year-old gardener, "a modest, reticent sort of fellow, disinclined to self," as Whitman described him.[24] Claiming Flynn was "in some respects the grandest man I have personally come in contact with," Whitman later recalled how he had "praised him once or twice up there, and he resented it — did not like it at all — sort of drew himself up — so I did not venture often on that line."[25] According to the poet, Flynn's manner of response to his praise was to point out that "he was only working, only making a living, though it was true he loved his work!"[26] Whitman liked the sound of Richard Flynn's name, which he said came "easy from the tongue! I like to run it over, it trips along so easily!"[27] In August 1889 Whitman had the pleasure of seeing Flynn again when the Irishman, who was visiting in Philadelphia, came and stayed the night before returning to Canada. Whitman found him "very quiet" but was glad of the visit.[28] Pleasant though this association may have been, Whitman was soon to make the acquaintance of another Irishman whose friendship would mean far more.

In February 1881 Whitman received an invitation to come to Boston to deliver the lecture on Abraham Lincoln that he had given with some success in New York the previous spring. The invitation was from a literary club, the St. Botolph Club of Boston, inaugurated on January 3. Whitman's appearance was to be the first big venture of the club, which modeled itself on New York's Century Club and included among its 260 original members the city's leading authors and other outstanding people.

Whitman's account in *Specimen Days* of his 1881 journey to Boston affords an excellent glimpse into the "wonders" of rail travel in what is today known as the northeast Metropolitan Corridor. The journey was accomplished by means of a daily through train from Washington to Boston, which he boarded in the evening in Philadelphia. In his sleeping car he slumbered soundly through New Jersey to New York and was only half conscious of the midnight steamer that took him from Jersey City around the Battery to the New Haven railroad that brought him into Boston in the morning. A chance meeting with a fellow traveler resulted in a safe passage through the depot crowds and the favor of a cab ride to his hotel.[29] At the end of this (to us) arduous journey, Whitman was back in Boston twenty-one years after his first visit.

The St. Botolph Club was wealthy enough to have from the outset its own building, the principal gathering room of which was the scene for Whitman's address. He later described the occasion to Traubel:

The St. Botolph high jinks came off in the Hawthorne Rooms — a hall a good deal like our Morgan's Hall [Philadelphia] yet handsomer — more fitted for culture, refinement, well-dressed ladies, and all that. It was crowded, crowded — people standing — as if all the town who frequented places of that kind came out. It was the best woman audience I ever addressed. These particular women were of the large sort — came because they were sympathetically, emotionally, moved to it, not because it was the thing to do.[30]

The occasion was a great success, for Whitman and for the club, and seemed to make the poet more acceptable in the eyes of many who for almost thirty years had looked askance at his work. Whitman also had an opportunity to meet a number of younger club members who were more immediately receptive to his poetry. Outstanding among these was an Irishman who was very active not only in the St. Botolph Club but in almost every aspect of Boston life, the editor and, with Boston's archbishop, the Reverend John J. Williams, part owner of the *Boston Pilot*, John Boyle O'Reilly.[31] O'Reilly was one of the founders of an earlier literary club, the Papyrus Club. This, a far less formal group than the St. Botolph Club, had its roots in a gathering of journalists who had come together at the Parker House in 1872 to honor Henry M. Stanley, the *New York Herald* reporter recently returned from Africa and his successful search for the missionary explorer, Dr. David Livingston. O'Reilly had delivered the welcoming speech for Stanley and then led the after-meeting dinner at a chop house, which became the setting for the founding of the Papyrus Club.

The Papyrus Club, while not on a level with the later St. Botolph Club, was a kind of high-class version of the bohemian group that used to meet at Pfaff's when Whitman was a young New Yorker. (Unlike Pfaff's, however, no women were included except on special occasions.) In fact, one or two of the old Pfaffians, notably William Dean Howells and Thomas Bailey Aldrich, had moved up into more polite society and were soon Papyrians.[32] They were not the only ones moving up socially; there was no one among them making greater strides of upward mobility than John Boyle O'Reilly. While much has been written of O'Reilly's remarkable life, his friendship with Whitman has not been fully examined; in light of Whitman's deep affection for his other close Irish friends, Doyle and O'Connor, it is important to place this friendship in that same perspective and question its depth, extent, and relative significance.

"If you take a pinch of the best Irish salt you get the best salt of the earth," Whitman once said of John Boyle O'Reilly and William Douglas O'Connor, though he was still estranged from O'Connor at the time of his first meeting with O'Reilly.[33] Perhaps it was because he missed O'Connor that he took so readily to this new Irish friend, though by all accounts it was virtually impossible not to like O'Reilly. But, as Whitman said, O'Reilly and O'Connor were as "like as two peas in some ways," since both were of the "tempest class. Ardent Irish natures — clean, clear, afire with ideals of justice — willing, eager, anytime to live or die for justice."[34] O'Reilly he proclaimed "a brave man among brave men . . . staunch with the staunchest: he is a man of whom we can be sure: his whole life has been a life of loyalty — to persons, to causes, nobly most of all to his own principles."[35] Lest this and similar comments be construed as Whitmanian hyperbole, it should be noted that Michael Davitt similarly described O'Reilly as "handsome and brave, gifted in rarest qualities of mind and heart . . . a personification of all the manly virtues" and as someone whom it was impossible to know without being his friend.[36]

O'Reilly, who remained Whitman's friend until his untimely death in 1890 at the age of forty-six, was a native of Drogheda, Ireland, on the Boyne River, not far from the site of the battle commemorated so many years later by the Orange Day parades in Boston and New York. With little future in Ireland, the young man had gone to live with his aunt and uncle in Preston, England, where he joined the English army. In 1863 he returned to Ireland as a trooper in the Tenth Hussars, though he was now full of republican ideals and eager to fight for a free Ireland. Recruited to the Fenians by the revolutionary John Devoy, O'Reilly joined a band of conspirators secreted within the ranks of the unit. Devoy was arrested in 1865, along with Jeremiah O'Donovan Rossa; O'Reilly and others in the Hussars were arrested a year later. Devoy and Rossa served time in prison in Millbank, England; O'Reilly, after having his death sentence commuted, was sent to the infamous prison colony in Fremantle, Australia.

A daring escape, of the type that one imagines only to find in adventure stories, brought O'Reilly to America in 1869, in time to accompany the second ill-fated Fenian invasion of Canada a year later as a reporter for the *Pilot*, then the official organ of the Archdiocese of Boston. Once before, in 1866, the Fenians had invaded Canada in the wild hope of holding it captive until England would accept their offer to exchange it for Ireland. Though it lingered on in the hopes of some, the failure of the 1870 campaign was the final blow to American Fenianism.

O'Reilly's fellow Fenians, Devoy and Rossa, were released from prison in 1871. The tumult that accompanied their arrival in New

York in January and the rivalry it stirred among contending Irish forces in the city were, as has been pointed out (in chapter 1), contributing factors to the rioting on Boyne Day in July of that year, when Whitman was visiting the city. By that time O'Reilly was editing the *Pilot*, where he roundly condemned the riots, sparing neither Catholic nor Protestant in his scathing criticism of Irish disunity.[37] In his maturity and as a result of his years of prison hardship, O'Reilly had become a conservative fighter for liberty, eager to succeed in America and do all he could for Ireland by legitimate and lawful means. He was a staunch Catholic, one of Boston's outstanding citizens, a novelist and poet, and the best of the *Pilot*'s editors to his time. Dating as it did to 1829, the *Pilot* had come to wield a nationwide influence on Irish Catholics and was considered the country's outstanding Catholic publication. O'Reilly brought to its pages a greater consciousness of poetry and literature. Oscar Wilde's first appearance in print in America was in the *Pilot*, and, after learning of William Butler Yeats from former Fenian John O'Leary, O'Reilly published the young Irishman's poetry before he was known in America and but little known in Ireland.[38]

O'Reilly was a strong advocate of all things Irish, especially Irish literature. In May 1879 he was one of the principal promoters of a festival to honor the centennial of Thomas Moore's birth, at which Oliver Wendell Holmes read a poem. O'Reilly's poetry was well received in his time, and Massachusetts honored him by commissioning him to write poems for such occasions as the dedication of Plymouth Rock, the unveiling of the Crispus Attucks monument, and the memorial to Wendell Phillips held in 1884. Implicit in these commissions — astonishing when one considers that Longfellow, Holmes, and Whittier were all residents in the Boston area — is a recognition of O'Reilly as a model immigrant, and thus worthy of the Plymouth Rock commission, and as a strong supporter of "Negro" rights in a state that once had considered all Catholic Irish the enemies of blacks. O'Reilly, of course, had arrived in the country after the Civil War and thus was not caught up in the abolitionist controversy, but in fighting for the political and civil rights of the Boston Irish he never failed to make abundantly clear his belief that what he argued for were human rights not to be denied to blacks.[39]

Perhaps O'Reilly's most impressive accomplishment was his ability to gain access to Brahmin Boston, an "ascendency" he worked hard to achieve and, having done so, of which he was very proud. He once wrote to an admiring critic expressing his delight at having his poetry recognized by a member of the Boston literati. Claiming to be even more of a Brahmin than they, he enthused tellingly, "Truly, if I were not the editor of the *Pilot* . . . you would never think me such a terrific Papist and paddy."[40] He had reason to be pleased, for despite his immigrant background he counted among his friends such luminaries as Holmes, Whittier, Emerson, and, not so surprising given his support of blacks, Thomas Wentworth Higginson and Wendell Phillips. One of the few old-time Bostonians O'Reilly did not get on with was his fellow Roman Catholic Orestes A. Brownson, and there were times when the two crossed swords in print over matters of both theology and politics.[41]

When the St. Botolph Club was formed in January 1881, with O'Reilly as one of its organizers, its first ranks were made up of these same Boston luminaries. Very quickly it expanded to include the leading members of Boston's publishing houses, among them Benjamin Ticknor and James R. Osgood. And so it happened that John Boyle O'Reilly suggested to Osgood that he contact Whitman about publishing *Leaves of Grass*, a suggestion that had serious consequences.

In 1895, three years after Whitman's death, Horace Traubel wrote an article in *The Conservator* detailing the scandal that surrounded the 1881 edition of *Leaves of Grass*. Returning to the starting point, he told how "[i]n the early part of May, 1881, John Boyle O'Reilly, a personal friend and admirer of Whitman, wrote to him, saying that Osgood wished to see the copy of the new edition of 'Leaves of Grass' which Whitman contemplated bringing out." On May 8, 1881, he related, Whitman wrote on the back of the O'Reilly letter the following:

MY DEAR MR. OSGOOD

I write in answer to the note on the other side from my dear friend O'Reilly. My plan is to have all my poems down to date, comprised in one volume under the name "Leaves of Grass." I think it will have to be in brevier (or bourgeois) solid [type]. I want it plain, but as fine a specimen in type, paper, ink, binding and as bookmaking can produce. A book of about 400 pages to sell at $3. Not for luxury however but for solid wear, reading, use. The text will be about the same as hitherto, occasional slight revisions simplifications in punctuations and a more satisfactory consecutive order — some new pieces (20 or 30 pages) — *Fair warning one point, the sexuality odes about which the original row was started and kept up so long are all retained and must go in the same as ever* [emphasis added by Traubel].

Should you upon this outline wish to see the copy I will place it in your hands.[42]

Of the emphasized words, Traubel says they "are the keynote of this matter," confirming that "Whitman was approached first on the subject of the publication by Osgood through O'Reilly and that he was absolutely fair and explicit at the outset about the 'sexuality odes.'"[43]

All of this was intended to make clear that Osgood was at fault for capitulating to the Massachusetts district attorney by halting publication of the book when it was deemed obscene. Once this was established, Traubel believed, Whitman could be exonerated for removing his book from Osgood and having it published elsewhere. Since Traubel's account of it, the story of the suppression of the 1881 edition of *Leaves of Grass* has been told many times in many places; its relevance here is to point out the roles played by two of Whitman's Irish friends, John Boyle O'Reilly and William Douglas O'Connor.

O'Reilly's role appears to have been mainly to establish a contact between a fellow club member and a poet whose work he greatly admired. In addition to being a member of the St. Botolph Club, Osgood was one of the city's, and the country's, most respected publishers. When he acted on O'Reilly's suggestion and approached Whitman about *Leaves of Grass* there may have been, on Whitman's part, some feeling of vindication, since it was Osgood who had published Emerson's anthology of favorite poetry, *Parnassus* (1874), in which no poem of Whitman's appeared.

His caveat concerning "the sexuality odes" having been accepted, a contract was drawn up, and Whitman returned to Boston in September 1881. With more time to spend than when he had been there for the Lincoln lecture, Whitman had a chance to see something of the city. With the help of maps published two years earlier, which featured balloon views of the area from Boston Harbor to Provincetown, he was ready to renew his 1860 acquaintance with Boston.[44] He found it changed in some ways, though not so changed as most other parts of the country in the post–Civil War years. Boston was a larger city than it had been twenty-one years earlier, for it had recently absorbed a number of neighborhoods, some of them decidedly ethnic (including Roxbury, where O'Connor was born), but with the Irish still the major ethnic group. Whitman was impressed by the city's geographic growth, finding himself reminded by it of the revelations of archaelogical excavations that reveal stages of urban development.[45] For the most part, however, Boston was still staid, still bound by its puritanical mores and, paradoxically, liberalized by them as well in its reformist tendencies. The old literary figures were fading, a sad fact especially noticeable in Emerson's case. Whitman was invited to Concord (where he was not welcome in 1860) to dine at the home of Franklin B. Sanborn. Emerson and his wife were among the guests, and Whitman was greatly moved at Emerson's physical decline. While in Concord he also visited the graves of Thoreau and Hawthorne in Sleepy Hollow cemetery. In Boston Whitman took up his favorite pursuits: walks along the main streets, streetcar rides to South Boston and to the harbor, and observations of people and places, some of which he noted in writing. Obviously surprised at one segment of its immigrant population, he wrote: "In Boston there is quite an irruption of Chinese, mostly running launderies. You see their signs . . . every few blocks." He also noted a Chinese professor in Cambridge,"dressed in his native costume, walking about the streets."[46]

As in 1860, he makes no specific comment on the Boston Irish, whose very ubiquity seems to have made them invisible as a group to his eyes. However, on a piece of letterhead for Osgood and Company Whitman lists the names of various drivers, conductors, and newsboys whom he met on his excursions. They include an "Edward Kelley, boy of 9 or 10 I met on the Boat June 30"; "Denny M'Carty" [*sic*] and "Collins Donne" (Dunne?) are listed as Harvard Square drivers.[47] Though Whitman may not have noticed, the Irish as a group were not so invisible in the life of the city as they had been in the days before the war, when James Batchelder's death at the hands of an abolitionist mob could be all but overlooked in the turmoil surrounding the return to slavery of Anthony Burns. The Irish population had continued to grow, with the most recent arrivals always crowded into the worst areas of the city, but second-generation Irish had moved up socially and economically — and, as in New York, had gained in political power, with ward leaders following the familiar path into local politics.

Whitman took a room at the Hotel Waterson on a quiet street near the more fashionable Revere House. The firm of Osgood and Company was at 211 Tremont Street, not far from Scollay Square where most of the streetcars stopped. Middays he spent in the Common enjoying the air and the surrounding activity.[48] His publisher sent its work to Rand and Avery, one of New England's largest book and job printing houses. There, in a small office room, Whitman spent part of every day setting the book and reading copy more closely for errors, he told Traubel, than he had done with any previous editions.[49] It was there that O'Reilly came to tell him stories of his days with the Fenians, his trial for treason, and his imprisonment in Australia. Whitman remembered the first time O'Reilly spoke to him of his prison life: "He was all alive with the most vivid indignation — he was a great storm out somewhere, a great sea pushing up the shore."[50]

Whitman claimed to have had "wonderful talks with him there in Boston" while preparing the third edition of *Leaves*, for O'Reilly, he says, came every day to see him.[51] O'Reilly, a very sociable person, surely would have entertained Whitman during his Boston stay. On August 30 he was forced to withdraw a theater invitation because of family obligations but took the occasion to return an article that has been tentatively identified as Whitman's *New York Tribune* piece "Custer's Last Rally," on the painting by John Mulvaney.[52] The identification can be considered conclusive when all the facts are put in place.

John Mulvaney was born in Dublin in 1844 and came to the United States in 1856 after studying in Germany. In the early 1870s Mulvaney had become enamored of the American West and began to collect and study western materials. For the Custer painting, which took two years to complete, he visited the battleground, consulted army officers and the Sioux, and studied every detail of the scene.[53] The painting, seventeen by twenty feet, was completed in Boston in June 1881 and shipped to New York for exhibition without a public viewing in Boston.

The *Boston Pilot* for June 18 described the painting's subject and gave a brief account of the artist's life. On July 2 the *Pilot* reprinted a review of the painting from the *Boston Transcript* of June 30 based on a private showing to Boston art critics prior to the painting's transfer to New York. The reviewer claimed that "Mulvaney's Irish-American nationality has aptly fitted him for such an essay as a grand national and historical painting. The Irish passion for the heroism of combat and the intense Americanism cultivated in Western life since his return from Munich . . . have been brought to the compositon of his masterpiece." Whitman saw the painting in New York before leaving the city for Boston and wrote his reactions for the *New York Tribune* of August 15. O'Reilly naturally was eager to know what Whitman thought of his countryman's work, especially since Whitman had talked with Mulvaney about exhibiting the painting abroad. Whitman had advised showing it in Paris, which would have been a bold stroke in view of the French preeminence in historical paintings, but instead the painting was shown in Munich in 1886. While Whitman was more than enthusiastic about the work, claiming it needed to be seen again and again to be fully appreciated, he made no reference in print to the artist's national origins, which no doubt disappointed O'Reilly. Despite this lack O'Reilly republished the *Tribune* article in the September 3 *Pilot*, after which he apparently sent it back to Whitman.

Whitman returned to Camden, and the sixth edition of *Leaves of Grass* was published in November 1881. One evening in that same month Whitman penned a strange memorandum to himself as he crossed and recrossed the Delaware River between Camden and Philadelphia. Perhaps with the remembrance of time spent with O'Reilly and with conversations they may have had about Irish literature fresh in his mind, Whitman found the night to be nothing short of "Ossianic," and quoted freely from James Macpherson's "Fingal" and "Dar-Thula," works that appeared as part of *Poems of Ossian* (1762). The night sky was filled with clouds that shaped and reshaped, "throwing an inky pall on everything," he wrote, and on this "real Ossianic night — amid the whirl, absent or dead friends, the old, the past, somehow tenderly suggested — while the Gael-strains chant themselves from the mists."[54] Clearly the spell of the supposed Irish bard was upon him.

The reviews of the latest *Leaves of Grass*, though mixed, were generally good. One anonymous review in the New York *Critic* contained both commentary and language that distinguish it from others and suggest an Irish hand. Acknowledging the moral objections of many to Whitman's work, the reviewer allows that it "must be confessed that . . . the doctrines taught by Whitman might readily be construed [as excuses] for foul living." Despite Whitman's "frank sensuality," the reviewer argues for the purity of the poet's private discourse, ending with, "he does not soil his conversation with lewdness." Turning to more literary matters, the reviewer makes a comparison not found in most critiques of Whitman's work, not even those that link him to such early traditions as the Greek and Hebrew. Whitman's "crowded adjectives" are said to be "like the medieval writers of Irish, those extraordinary poets who sang the old Irish heroes and their own contemporaries, the chiefs of their clans." "No Irishman of today," the reviewer continues, "has written a nobler lament for Ireland, or a more hopeful, or a more truthful, than has Walt Whitman."

At another point this anonymous admirer of *Leaves* makes an observation unique among reviewers of the time:

> A cardinal sin in the eyes of most critics is the use of French, Spanish, and American-Spanish words which are scattered here and there. . . . He [Whitman] shows crudely the American way of incorporating into the language a handy or a high-sounding word without elaborate examination of its original meaning, just as we absorb the different nationalities that crowd over from Europe.[55]

The sensitivity displayed here to America's absorption and assimilation of language and of immigrant populations suggests a reader peculiarly attentive to such matters, while the particular attention called to Whitman as an inheritor of the Irish bardic tradition also suggests one whose ear is culturally attuned to that tradition. Could the reviewer have been John Boyle O'Reilly?

It would not be surprising to find O'Reilly writing anonymously in order to protect himself and the Catholic *Pilot* from possible attack for defending the book's "frank sensuality." Assurances given of the purity of Whitman's "private discourse" indicate someone who had frequent conversations with him, and the writer's earnest guarantee displays a rather middle-class concern for the mores of proper Bostonians — both Yankee Protestants and Irish Catholics. Further, such words as "confessed" and "doctrines" reveal a tendency toward the theological turn of phrase, perhaps made habitual by occupation, while the praise for the unnamed "Old Ireland" as superior to anything done by a contemporary Irish poet suggests the modesty of O'Reilly, Boston's premiere "Irish" poet.[56] Even the admission the reviewer makes, that Whitman had not achieved recognition from the working class whose champion he claims to be, that he has in fact remained "caviare to the multitude," exhibits a greater awareness of this group than most reviewers for literary magazines could claim. It was, however, the kind of awareness that the editor of the country's most influential Catholic newspaper — with its largely working-class readership — would be likely to possess.

Perhaps it was in part the reviews of the 1881 *Leaves*, with their unanimous acknowledgment of Whitman's frankness in matters sexual, that caused the problems of the following year. In March 1882 James R. Osgood received a letter from Boston district attorney Oliver Stevens notifying him that the book fell within the statutory definition of obscene literature and suggesting its immediate withdrawal. Though Stevens did not reveal it, he had received complaints from the New England Society for the Suppression of Vice, one of the organizations that had started up in various parts of the country in response to the efforts of New York's antivice zealot Anthony Comstock. Osgood requested Whitman's permission to temporarily withdraw the book and make emendations. Whitman agreed to some changes, suggesting word alterations in three of the poems, "Spontaneous Me," "A Woman Waits for Me," and "I Sing the Body Electric." He was stunned when Osgood sent him a list of the district attorney's requirements for continued publication: some 150 lines to be altered or dropped, plus the excision of three poems, "To a Common Prostitute," "A Woman Waits for Me," and, most surprisingly, "The Dalliance of the Eagles."

Infuriated, Whitman refused; the contract was voided and the book's plates returned to him. Subsequently, Whitman placed the book with the firm of Rees Welsh and Company in Philadelphia, succeeded later by David McKay, who was just starting his own publishing firm. When the book reappeared it sold three thousand copies the first day. Clearly, notoriety paid off, and Whitman, who had remained sanguine throughout the commotion, was more than satisfied. As he later remarked, "what radical Massachusetts was too good to do conservative Pennsylvania was bad enough to do, and we were safe."[57]

He and the book were "safe," as he claimed, but there were others who were grossly insulted by the Boston district attorney's offense. One was Richard Maurice Bucke, who also suffered the loss of a publisher as a result of the scandal. Osgood had agreed to publish his biographical study of Whitman, but that, too, came to an end with the voiding of Whitman's contract. (Bucke's *Walt Whitman* was published by David McKay in 1883.) In preparing his biography Bucke had asked O'Connor for permission to include the text of *The Good Gray Poet* and had requested of him a prefatory letter. O'Connor, still working in Washington and in poor health, responded with a lengthy critique of Whitman's *Leaves*, its purpose and accomplishment, which Bucke printed in its entirety. When Bucke informed O'Connor of the action of the Boston district attorney, O'Connor flew into a rage and attempted to take the matter up with the United States attorney general who, as it turned out, had no jurisdiction in the matter. O'Connor then wrote to Whitman, reestablishing a connection that had remained closed for ten years. Offering no comment on what had gone wrong between them, Whitman sent O'Connor the information requested — details of his association with Osgood — and waited to see what would follow.

Bucke had already attacked Oliver Stevens in a letter to the editor of the *Springfield* (Massachusetts) *Republican* on May 23, 1882. The day before, the *New York Tribune* published the facts of the case with no additional commentary. But neither of these sources could be expected to deliver the fire of a William Douglas O'Connor. On May 25 it erupted, when "the noble O'Connor" rose to the occasion in a *Tribune* article titled simply "Suppressing Walt Whitman."[58] O'Connor accused Osgood of failing to stand up to Stevens and of failing to live up to his contract with Whitman. He blamed Stevens for manipulating the law to his own purposes and compared him to the seventeenth-century Puritan divine Cotton Mather. Defending Whitman against the Massachusetts authorities, he reiterated the recently deceased Emerson's endorsement of the 1855 *Leaves of Grass*. Emerson had died on April 27, 1882, and thus was spared the rehashing of his approval and disapproval of *Leaves* that followed.[59]

Ultimately, George Chainey, a former Baptist minister in Boston, broke the ban. Chainey had his own newspaper, where he published his lectures. In a sermon-lecture titled "Keep Off the Grass," he defended Whitman against the district attorney and read the poem "To a Common Prostitute." Chainey faced possible prosecution if, after publishing the text of the poem as part of the printed lecture, he sent it through the mail. His plan was to print the poem and mail it separately, but he first sought the approval of the Boston postmaster. That official deferred to Stevens, however, which angered Chainey. Chainey then wrote to O'Connor, who appealed to the acting postmaster general, James M. Marr. In July Marr ruled against the Boston postmaster, which effectively cleared Whitman's book of the obscenity charge.

O'Connor came through once again with the fierceness that had so endeared him to Whitman years earlier and which Whitman saw as part of his being Irish. Their friendship rekindled, it remained unshaken until O'Connor's death in 1889 after a long and paralyzing illness.[60] But because O'Connor's combativeness seemed to Whitman to derive from his Irishness, he came to expect the same trait in others of Irish background. Such stereotypical thinking is suggested by Whitman's remarks about a young man he added to his coterie of admirers in the winter of 1880–1881, William Sloane Kennedy, whose Irish ancestry remains buried in his name.

Born in Ohio to parents who were native Americans with strong Protestant roots (his father was a Presbyterian minister), the thirty-year-old Kennedy was working in Philadelphia for the *Saturday Evening Post* when he met Whitman. A Yale graduate, he had spent two years at the Harvard Divinity School before deciding not to follow in his father's footsteps. Whitman seems to have been impressed by his training in classical studies and wrote to his friend John Burroughs that young Kennedy "has *the fever called literature* and I shouldn't wonder if he was in for it, for life."[61]

Despite his classical education, Kennedy found himself balking at the sex poems in *Leaves of Grass* and said so in an article he published early in 1881.[62] A few years later, when Kennedy had lost some of his original ardor for the poet, Whitman commented on the change he noticed in Kennedy's letters: "He used to write martial letters — warlike letters," Whitman complained, "was up in arms about things. . . . When Kennedy was passing through the early stages of his faith in the Leaves — the first fervors of conversion — he made Whitman the password: opposed to Walt Whitman opposed to me — that sort of chip-on-the-shoulder business."[63] Though Kennedy eventually came to terms with his reservations about the sex poems, the objections raised in his 1881 article appear as a harbinger of things to come in Boston the following year.[64]

There is no evidence of O'Reilly's reaction to the suppression of the 1881 *Leaves of Grass*; he seems to have maintained silence on the subject throughout. Among the many speculations Whitman and O'Connor entertained as to who may have raised the initial objection to the edition and brought it to the attention of Oliver Stevens, neither O'Reilly nor Boston's archbishop Williams was ever mentioned. Certainly O'Reilly had not hesitated to herald the book in the *Pilot*. He appears to have been elated at the prospect of a second Boston edition of *Leaves*, for on August 27, 1881, a week after Whitman's arrival in the city, the *Pilot* declared: "Walt Whitman's poems will soon have the recognition of a well-known publishing house. James R. Osgood will publish 'Leaves of Grass' without any expurgations, the author having made that a condition of his contract." In November, when the edition was published, the first page of the *Pilot* offered "The Dead Mocking-Bird" (actually "Out of the Cradle Endlessly Rocking") "By Walt Whitman," with the notice that it was "From Osgood's Complete Edition of His poems just Published."

On December 10 O'Reilly reviewed the new edition, claiming it was "literally the expressed soul of the man [Whitman]. . . . We may dislike part of it, but it is not the dislike we feel for a failure in art." Indeed, O'Reilly insists there is "no art in the book any more than there is in a mountain, a tree, or a wide countryside." Those things charged against the book as "impure," he points out, are "not prurient, though they are naked." While raising no objection to this, O'Reilly faults what he calls the book's vagueness and lack of structure: "the outreach is large but it never rests. There is no plan in the poet's mind. He is always generalizing," defects which the reviewer "deplores." O'Reilly then makes the rather startling but insightful comment, "A democratic poet, he has not studied democracy," explaining, "In fact, Whitman is only an observer, a seer of the symbolism of things." Returning to the matter of the "so-called impurity of his volume," such objections, O'Reilly says, "we pass over in silence. It is a pity that anyone could say against Walt Whitman that he left a stain on the soul's page. He certainly is not guilty of the implied."

Had Archbishop Williams, O'Reilly's co-owner of the *Pilot*, raised an objection to Whitman's poems, it is unlikely this review would have appeared. Its appearance does not preclude, however, the possibility that O'Reilly authored the anonymous review in the *Critic* in the same month. In fact, the comment in the New York magazine concerning Whitman's rejection by the laboring class corresponds to the comment in the *Pilot*, that the poet is "only an observer" of the actuality of democracy, "a seer" of its "symbolism" rather than its poetic definer. The possibility remains that both are by the same reviewer.

O'Reilly's failure to come to Whitman's defense at the time of the suppression could indicate that he preferred to keep the *Pilot*'s name out of the fray, or — and this is the greater likelihood — that he was too involved in Irish politics at the time to take an active role. One of the more surprising examples of O'Reilly's social adroitness was his ability to maintain his credibility in both the Brahmin world of Boston literature and the world of Irish politics — and not just its politics but its radicalism. Though he resigned his membership in the Fenian Brotherhood in 1870, protesting the incompetence of its leaders, O'Reilly remained close to the rebel John Devoy. After Devoy came to America, O'Reilly aided him, as well as his successor in Ireland, Michael Davitt.

John Devoy, who had recruited O'Reilly to the Fenian cause, came to America in 1871 after his release from prison determined to wage from its shores the fight for Irish independence. He had hoped that after the Civil War America would aid Ireland in gaining its freedom.

Since that had not happened and the attempt to attack England via Canada had failed, Devoy hoped to raise both an army and money from Irish Americans to effect a revolution in Ireland. O'Reilly did not support Devoy's plan. He saw no reason why the Irish in America should make Ireland's independence their cause (and thereby lend credence to the general perception of them as a "foreign" faction), especially when there were still civil rights for Irish Americans to be won in the States. He warned Devoy not to be misled by the wild enthusiasm shown by New York's Irish because, he claimed, they did not represent Irish elsewhere in the country. Still, he did what he could for Devoy, though it was mostly in the form of advice on becoming successful in American busines, advice which held no interest for Devoy.[65]

O'Reilly did give his wholehearted support to Michael Davitt's National Land League, which, while not revolutionary in the way Devoy had hoped, was clearly the most radical effort — in its intent to effect land reform — yet undertaken by the Irish nationalists. As Davitt later explained, however, Ireland's agrarian agitation did not begin with the Land League in 1879 but was then nearly 250 years in existence, with "the undeniable wrong and oppression of landlordism, the offspring and agency of confiscation.[66] It was this wrong that the Irish National Land League attempted to address.

The league had two leaders, Davitt and Charles Stewart Parnell. Davitt was released from prison in 1877 after being sentenced in 1870 for supplying the Fenians with arms and came to America seeking aid from Irish Americans for general nationalist undertakings in Ireland; it was Devoy who pushed him to a greater radicalism by putting forward the notion of land reform. Parnell, a member of the British Parliament, was also an Irish landlord, a member of the Protestant ascendency, and originally a conservative in the matter of Irish nationalism. While the reasons for his conversion to a more revolutionary stance remain a mystery, historians speculate that his visit to America in 1871, when he was treated no better than the poor immigrant Irish, had much to do with it.[67] Converted to nationalism, Parnell always preferred to work within constitutional means to achieve political change. When Devoy decided to join with Parnell and work toward land reform and self-government along constitutional lines, the initiative was termed the "New Departure." John Boyle O'Reilly enthusiastically backed this program; however, in Ireland Michael Davitt began his own program of land reform, the Irish National Land League, and asked O'Reilly to rally the Irish in America to its financial support. In the spring of 1880, at a convention of delegates drawn from many states, the American Land League was formed to support the one in Ireland. O'Reilly was elected its temporary chairman. Davitt arrived from Ireland to join the convention on its second day of meetings, and, not many months later, Parnell became part of the American Land League and immediately undertook travel throughout America to raise funds for its support.

Parnell arrived in New York in December 1880. The Irishman's mission was to raise money to be used by the Land League for the purchase of Irish land from English landowners. O'Reilly was one of those delegated to meet Parnell in New York. In the *Pilot* on November 15, 1879, he had likened the cause to "that wild anti-slavery agitation which proposed that the United States should pay the Southern planters for their liberated slaves" but saw the current movement as having greater legitimacy since, he argued, England's claim, based on conquest, was less just. When Parnell was forced by political moves in England to return unexpectedly to Ireland, the American Land League swung into action, with O'Reilly as its treasurer. Parnell was arrested in Ireland and imprisoned in the autumn of 1881 for instituting a No Rent policy by which Irish tenant farmers refused to pay rent to English landowners. In the United States, the American Land League gained national attention, but internal divisions quickly developed, led in some instances by Catholic bishops who opposed the No Rent measure and in others by extremists who advocated terrorism, specifically by placing dynamite charges in public places in London.

O'Reilly fiercely fought out the complex land reform issues in the pages of the *Pilot*. Though never wavering in his support of Parnell, he eventually began to advocate a greater concentration on Home Rule than on land reform. In a carefully reasoned article in the January 1882 *American Catholic Quarterly Review*, he reviewed the aims of and the objections to land reform in Ireland, concluding that the Land League had made its point, that revolution was not the next step to be taken, and that Home Rule was the only sensible solution.[68] Despite these conclusions, in April of that same year O'Reilly attended a national meeting of the American Land League in Washington where he and other delegates adopted resolutions aimed at revitalizing the league, which was suffering from its internal divisions.

Parnell was released from prison a few weeks later after signing an agreement with the British government that would slow the land reform movement, but within days of his release two government officials were brutally murdered in Dublin's Phoenix Park, an act that jeopardized the entire movement. Parnell denounced the murders in an official message and cabled O'Reilly a copy for distribution throughout the United States. According to Davitt, Parnell also wired a copy to "Mr. Alfred Webb, of Dublin" (Whitman's correspondent) with instructions to print the message as a placard for distribution throughout Ireland.[69] A few years later Webb would be one of the Irish MPs who would vote to have Parnell removed as head of the Irish Party when personal scandal made his leadership ineffective.

These events surrounding Parnell and the land reform movement in Ireland and the United States occurred at the very time Whitman's book was suppressed in Boston. Two of the people Whitman might have counted on for support, John Boyle O'Reilly and James Redpath, were both so involved in these issues that neither came forward to object to the suppression. It is doubtful that Whitman was aware of the complexities of the land movement, for his comments to Traubel concerning the involvement of Redpath and O'Reilly in the Irish cause do not suggest it. On the other hand, we know that in 1881 O'Reilly introduced Whitman to Philip Bagenal when the Englishman was in Boston gathering information for his book *The American Irish* (1890) and that Bagenal states in his book that the leader of the Land League organization in the United States and editor of the *Boston Pilot* was the head of one of three schismatic political groups among the American Irish.[70] While this does not prove Whitman's knowledge of the extent of O'Reilly's involvement, it strongly suggests it.

In 1890, just months after O'Reilly's death, when Parnell became a figure of international notoriety because of the revelation of his long-time affair with a married woman, Whitman was at first so disgusted by the charges and by what he termed "the venom with which the papers pressure Parnell" that he refused to read the stories.[71] As the weeks went by and the accusations turned into a confrontation between Parnell and William Gladstone, Whitman concluded that Parnell had to forfeit his position as head of the Irish Party for the sake of the Irish cause. As he told Horace Traubel, "It is another item in the long list of evidences that the Irish are calculated to ruin all their own best prospects by division. The graceful manly thing for Parnell to do would be to step down — retire — erase himself. What is he? — only a person —*one* person; he is by no means the cause; the cause is bigger than any individual — separated from individuals."[72]

Whitman's final word on the matter was to explain to Traubel why he refused to comment on the personal aspects of the case: "It appeals to me on the part of the *cause*—before the consummation of whose hopes no individual should stand."[73] In 1891, at Parnell's death, he registered his sorrow by commenting that in such cases death often comes as a result of "excitement, worry—what is called failure. Death and defeat! It is tragic."[74]

Whitman's belief that there could be a cause larger than any one individual yet powerful enough to lead one to direct all of one's individuality to it actually described John Boyle O'Reilly, which may have especially endeared him to Whitman. Traubel tells us the poet was "immensely approbative of O'Reilly always" and in narrating one example of this approval provides a powerful impression of the two men. The passage is too long to reproduce in full but begins with Whitman telling Traubel (who never met O'Reilly) that O'Reilly's charm was the result of his "tremendous fiery personality" and that the Irishman—whom he says is not "the typical Irishman: rather, Spanish: poetic, ardent"—had endured experiences that were reflected not only in his speech and dress but "in his attitude of body and mind."

During their talks at the printer's offices, Whitman continues, O'Reilly provided him with glimpses of what he calls a "memorable life . . . full of drama" because the Irishman was a man "stepping out of a background of vital experience," which could not fail to arouse one's feelings. He then recounts one incident (not included in O'Reilly's autobiographical *Moondyne*) that O'Reilly had related of his prison days in Australia. When "the prisoners suffered from bad food or too little food" and O'Reilly was chosen to present a complaint, the official to whom he spoke gave no indication of having heard a word except to deal the young soldier a blow to the mouth that staggered him. The impact of this blow on Whitman's imagination was as sharp as to O'Reilly's face. Traubel says Whitman dropped back in his chair and closed his eyes, resuming a few minutes later with eyes flashing: "Think of it, Horace!— think of it! what must that have meant to O'Reilly: he was a mere boy, I should think: scarcely twenty or not more: noble, manly, confiding: think of it: try to comprehend it: what it must have aroused and entailed. . . . It is horrible! horrible!" What this story signified to Whitman and the reason for its great impact on him becomes clearer as he guides the young Traubel's apprehension of the horror he perceives in it. "Put these things together," Whitman says, "think of such men: the best sort of men:

the plain elect: all their young hopes of life scattered — the blessed joys of camaradarie all crushed out: power, brutality, everywhere to annul, to destroy: everything crushed out of a man but his resentments, the unutterable memories of barbarisms, the heart's uncompromising revolt."[75]

Evident in this reaction is Whitman's frequent outrage at authority perverted into raw power and exercised at the expense of the helpless, a reaction traceable to some of his earliest pieces of fiction, such as "Death in the School-Room" and "Wild Frank's Return," where young boys are tyrannized by male authority figures.[76] His response had been similar when years earlier he saw Union soldiers who had been starved as prisoners of war. Their treatment was evidence, he claimed, of an "indescribable meanness, tyranny, aggravating course of insults." Of the reported starvation of some fifty thousand prisoners Whitman said, "reader, did you ever try to realize what *starvation* actually is? . . . There are deeds, crimes, that may be forgiven, but this is not among them."[77] Beyond the general inhumanity of both, the link between this and O'Reilly's prison story is the example of actual or near starvation as a demonstration of tyranny, the very horror that had been perpetrated on Ireland by a tyrannous England, which Whitman no doubt saw symbolized in O'Reilly's tale.

Whitman's visceral reaction to O'Reilly's story points to the strong psychological bond between him and the Irish: their long history of rebellion, which made them so attractive. Whitman always believed himself to be a rebel against the norms and conventions of society, and the mental image of himself that he carried was one cast in the mold of the eternal insurgent and patriot. Offering himself as the spokesperson for revolutionaries everywhere was the generalized expression of this identification, and the quick, strong friendships with people such as O'Connor and O'Reilly were the personal realization of it. In part it led to stereotyping because, like other Americans of his time, most of his Irish contacts were with those who had either left Ireland as a result of persecution or been driven from it for resisting the persecutor. Whitman understood the Irish to be born fighters with a finely honed sense of injustice and bearing within themselves what he believed O'Reilly to have felt, "the heart's uncompromising revolt."

For all his approbation of O'Reilly, there was one thing for which Whitman faulted him. Late in 1888 he complained to Traubel of a falling off in what he termed O'Reilly's "noble" nature because of his increased political activities. Comparing him to President Grover Cleveland, Whitman claimed O'Reilly was "too much interested in the Irish vote."[78] Whitman was at the time incensed at Cleveland's dismissal of the British minister to the United States, Sir Lionel Sackville-West. The dismissal came about because of a letter written to the minister by George Osgoodby, a California fruit grower, who wrote under an assumed name and represented himself as a naturalized citizen of English birth. He pretended to seek the advice of the British minister in the matter of the upcoming presidential election, claiming that if Sackville-West favored the Democrat Cleveland, he would convey the message to others that a vote for Cleveland would be a service to England.

Sackville-West responded by giving his support to Cleveland, and Osgoodby immediately took the letters to the Republican supporters of candidate Benjamin Harrison. From there the letters went to the *Los Angeles Times* for publication. Irish Americans were infuriated at this evidence of British interference in an American election, and one of the first to wire the president urging the British minister's dismissal was John Boyle O'Reilly. A few days later O'Reilly followed up by going to Washington where he and an Irish American congressman met with Cleveland who, quickly perceiving the need to follow their advice, had Sackville-West sent home. Cleveland was accused by many, including Whitman, of seeking to placate Irish Americans by dismissing the British minister. Whitman called the move "a play to the Paddy O'Reillys and the McMullins" and, as we have seen, complained to Traubel of O'Reilly's interest in the Irish vote.[79]

Though Whitman did not acknowledge it, it is possible that he also resented O'Reilly's vigorous role in the Massachusetts electoral campaign of Whitman's detractor, the Reverend Thomas Wentworth Higginson. Again, at a more substantial level, he may also have viewed O'Reilly's constantly expanding field of labor as a detriment to his literary development. When O'Reilly's "Crispus Attucks" was published in the *Boston Transcript*, Whitman was disappointed with the poem. It was "strong," he told Traubel, "but to my ear it is rather the rhetoric, the rhetorical quality, which comes uppermost — most forces itself upon my attention."[80] In other words, Whitman found it more of a political than a poetic statement, a reflection perhaps of his lack of enthusiasm for the "Negro cause" to which O'Reilly, like O'Connor, lent full support, but also a fair critique of the poem's polemical tone.[81] Still, he found the poem "artistically fine, polished. It is like a big feast: the setting superb; everything there: not a good thing missing: finger-glasses, wines, fruits, pastries: yet I growl, yet I am not satisfied, yet I think of the ten cent dinners."[82] It is impossible to ignore the association Whitman makes here between O'Reilly's literary work and food. Perhaps Whitman believed his friend's insatiable desire to be involved in a multitude of activities, political and otherwise, was driven by some psychological need. O'Reilly did suffer from frequent exhaustion and insomnia, which is often a sign of depression, as well as from a restless need to be at the center of every activity, all of which Whitman may have intuitively attributed to an awareness, on his friend's part, of some inner vacuity, an emptiness Whitman saw reflected in the poem.

Whitman was partly correct in his complaint about his friend, for in the 1880s O'Reilly became increasingly active not only in the cause of Ireland's freedom but also in social reform in America, especially as it affected Boston's Irish Catholics. Actually, things had improved greatly for the Irish. The *Pilot* frequently noted how they were taken more seriously, with earlier associations to rioting, brawling, and drunkenness giving way to a greater respect because of their steady assimilation into American culture. Privately O'Reilly enthused that the Irish "are gradually and inevitably assimilating, by absorbing American principles from the physical, social and political air."[83] It was, of course, what Whitman had hoped for in *Democratic Vistas*, the fusion of the individual with the societal mass, forming, out of the disparate immigrant races, the new race of Americans. Despite this, O'Reilly, while not quite the politician Whitman may have thought him, was not one to allow positive tones to drown out the still discordant notes of inequality evident in the lives of Irish factory workers and others remaining on the low end of the economic scale. Nor was he content to see the assimilation of the Irish into the democratic mass without a concomitant greater participation in the governmental system: he regularly reported in the *Pilot* the number of Irish in the ranks of city workers at all levels, especially in the public school system.[84]

The amazing thing is that with his myriad activities Boyle O'Reilly yet found time for his literary work. He published an autobiographical novel, *Moondyne: A Story of Convict Life in Australia*, serially in the *Pilot* and later (1880) as a volume, and *The King's Men* (1884), a novel of an imagined future for Ireland written in collaboration with several other writers of his republican sympathies. Poetry was his principal ambition, however, and his poetic output was considerable though largely undistinguished in the judgment of those beyond his Boston circle. Joseph Pulitzer commissioned him to write a poem for the dedication of the Statue of Liberty. It was called, fittingly, "Liberty Lighting the World" but later was totally eclipsed by the poem by Emma Lazarus that now graces the monument. In a poem of the Civil War, "Fredericksburg—December 13, 1862," which, given its subject, could not have escaped Whitman's attention, he writes of Irish troops fighting on both sides, "green against green." Of Meagher's Sixty-ninth Regiment he says,

> Twelve hundred they came, and two hundred go back.
> Two hundred go back with the chivalrous story;
> The wild day is closed in the night's solemn shroud;
> A thousand lie dead, but their death was a glory
> That calls not for tears — the Green Badges are proud![85]

One of the poems most beloved by O'Reilly's Irish readers was "The Exile of the Gael," in which he seemed to recall his trial in England for treason:

> No treason we bring from Erin — not bring we shame nor guilt!
> The sword we hold may be broken, but we have not dropped
>   the hilt!
> The wreath we bear to Columbia is twisted of thorns, not bays;
> And the songs we sing are saddened by thoughts of desolate
>   days.
> But the hearts we bring for Freedom are washed in the surge of
>   tears;
> And we claim our right by a People's fight outliving a thousand
>   years![86]

In spring of the same year in which the Osgood edition of *Leaves* appeared, 1881, O'Reilly published his third book of poems, *Statues in the Block*, containing what he believed to be the "best things I have written."[87] A year earlier he had met Whitman for the first time, but he obviously had been reading him admiringly for some time. There are poems in *Statues* that show a definite Whitmanian style — lack of form, a similarity in subject matter, even a comparable diction. "From the Earth, a Cry" is the most obvious of these. It offers as its heading a list of historical events between the years 1870 and 1880 in which the lowly have been trampled by the mighty of the earth.

The poet invokes the downtrodden, in a Whitmanian voice, to heed the earth's cry and strike back:

Insects and vermin, ye, the starving and dangerous myriads,
List to the murmur that grows and growls! Come from your
    factories and mills,
Pale-faced girls and women with ragged and hard-eyed children,
Pour from your dens of toil and filth, out of the air of heaven —
Breathe it deep, and hearken! A Cry from the cloud or
    beyond it,
A Cry to the toilers to rise, to be high as the highest that rules
    them,
To own the earth in their lifetime and hand it down to their
    children![88]

It is interesting to note the difference in responses to poems such as this in reviews of *Statues* that appeared in a New York and a Boston newspaper. The *New York Herald* for April 3, 1881, praised the poems for adopting a Whitmanian formlessness but predicted that "petticoated Boston" would "frown down" at their "wildness; for it is ever so much too masculine." The *Boston Journal*, while not entirely fulfilling the *Herald*'s prediction, did not approve the lack of form but made more of another lack, the absence of O'Reilly's indignation at social ills which, when present, it claimed, caused his poems to "stir the blood of the reader as by the sound of trumpets."[89] Clearly, Boston preferred the rhetoric of O'Reilly the social reformer to his attempt at a Whitmanian poetic.

John Boyle O'Reilly died in the early hours of August 10, 1890, from an apparently accidental overdose of a chloroform-based sleeping potion taken during a bout of insomnia. Because of the relative frequency in the nineteenth century of such overmedication with chloroform (Charles Halpine died in a similar fashion when trying to alleviate the pain of severe arthritis), the death has been generally accepted as accidental.[90] His loss was a blow to thousands who had known and loved the man in any of the many facets of his life. There is every reason to believe that Oscar Wilde had O'Reilly in mind when he wrote, just a year before the latter's death:

An entirely new factor has appeared in the social development of the country, and this factor is the Irish-American, and his influence. To mature its powers, to concentrate its action, to learn the secret of its own strength and of England's weakness, the Celtic intellect has had to cross the Atlantic. At home it had but learned the pathetic weakness of nationality; in a strange land it realized what indomitable forces nationality possesses. What captivity was to the Jews, exile has been to the Irish. America and American influence has educated them. Their first practical leader is an Irish American.[91]

For Whitman news of the loss of "the noble O'Reilly" led to an evocation of his friend's physical charm, all "the handsome light and shadow of the man," his "dark hair and eyes," indicating the "Irish-Spanish mixture he was."[92] The *Pilot* wired requesting the poet's comments, but he found it difficult to comply and finally retreated behind the excuse that with so many others doing so it was not necessary for him to add his thoughts. But his thoughts and his heart were full. Not long before his death, O'Reilly had noted Whitman's seventy-first birthday in the *Pilot* of June 7, 1890.[93] With no equivocation and despite the notoriety attached to the 1881 edition of *Leaves of Grass*, he identified Whitman in the pages of the Catholic newspaper as "the greatest poet America has yet produced," adding, "He is known and honored in all lands as an illustrious American." "He has been faithful to us," was Whitman's comment when it appeared, and he seemed not to be able, publicly, to say more at O'Reilly's death.[94]

It is clear that O'Reilly never lost his love for Whitman and his poetry. In 1885 Whitman received a letter from him in which O'Reilly enclosed a grateful letter from I. G. Kelly, a friend of his to whom he appears to have presented a copy of *Leaves of Grass*.[95] O'Reilly wrote to Whitman that Kelly was "one of the ablest men I have ever known: and I send [the letter] to you as another little proof that Irishmen understand and honor you." He also mentions having been told that Whitman had been in Boston within the month (he had not) but "could not believe that you would have gone away without letting me have the pleasure of seeing you."[96] In the same year O'Reilly was among those who donated money to purchase a horse and phaeton for Whitman's use in getting about in Camden, and he was treasurer of the "cottage fund" started by the poet's Boston friends to build a summer cottage for him in southern New Jersey. Had Whitman felt that O'Reilly failed him in some way by not coming forward at the time of the suppression, he would surely have said so to Horace Traubel, but there was never anything but praise.

When Whitman found himself unmoved or unable to write about

O'Reilly's death, Traubel offered to fill at least some of the lack by publishing something in his monthly paper, the *Conservator*, which he did. He chose to comment jointly on two recent decedents, O'Reilly and John Henry Newman, using as his common denominator their Catholic faith, though he claimed that to see in them only their Catholicism was "to narrow their significance." Speaking of them as "poet and priest," Traubel does not seek to compare O'Reilly for genius to the scholarly, intellectual Newman, but he points out that the scholar was "distinctly inferior" to the poet "in those resources of democratic feeling which absorbed O'Reilly's life and gave throb and stir to his fearless verse."[97] Whether intended or not, Traubel seems to be offering an apologia for O'Reilly's Catholicism which he, and others, clearly wished the Irishman had abandoned. After its publication Traubel told Whitman that he had received some complaints about the piece from Catholics.[98] Whitman's response was an emphatic, "But O'Reilly was no Catholic!—it was not in him. I know he was in the formal sense — it was the thing to be, he was born to it — was in fact a Catholic as he was a Democrat, for reasons that did not run to the deep."[99] Whitman was not alone in his uneasiness, for similar reservations about O'Reilly's long continuation as editor of the Roman Catholic *Pilot* surfaced at his death. One in particular appeared in an article by Whitman's former advocate Benjamin R. Tucker, who wrote of O'Reilly, "The chief lesson of his life to me is the disastrous effect of religion upon one who by nature and training was unable to cast it off and yet was conscious that it terribly impeded him in his efforts to further that cause which every drop of blood in his veins was burning to serve,— the cause of human liberty."[100]

Whitman was indignant at this, claiming Tucker was wrong: "No, that is a mistake—I am not worried at all about Boyle's Catholicism—it was not a vital, so much as a technical thing with him — one of the technicalities."[101] Balancing what he termed "a Jesuitism . . . a mild conservatism" in O'Reilly was the Irishman's "hate of tyranny in all its forms." This loathing, he insisted, was born at the moment of the slap from the English officer (of which he reminded Traubel with a gesture of the back of his hand) and remained in O'Reilly as "hate of overbearingness, ill treatment, hate of formal superiority, sympathy for the masses," all of which, woven together, Whitman seems to have viewed as a counteragency to his friend's religion in determining the direction of O'Reilly's life. It seems fairly obvious, however, that the statement "I am not worried at all about

Boyle's Catholicism" is more an indication of Whitman's own need to deny that the man he so admired and respected could have persisted in his religious faith than it is a statement of fact about O'Reilly who, to all appearances, remained a sincere Catholic to his death.

With William Douglas O'Connor and John Boyle O'Reilly dead and Peter Doyle all but gone from Whitman's life, Whitman's Irish connections in the United States were narrowing. What remained now for him was the friendship of admirers in Ireland, some of whom came to call, some who would only write, but all of whom would express their love.

CAMDEN & EMINENT VISITORS

"Welcome to them each and all!"
"Our Eminent Visitors"

On the afternoon of January 18, 1882, the front door of the house at 431 Stevens Street, Camden, New Jersey, was opened either by the Irish maid or by the woman of the house, Louisa Whitman, sister-in-law of Walt Whitman. The visitors on the doorstep were expected, indeed had been invited, by the aging and infirm poet who sat waiting expectantly in the parlor. Because of his infirmity Whitman had declined an invitation from Mrs. George W. Childs and her publisher husband to dine at their Philadelphia home that evening. When the morning of the eighteenth found him in good health, however, Whitman had penned the brief invitation out of an eagerness to meet the man who was to be the guest of honor at the Childs's dinner. The note, written with unaccustomed formality, read:

> To Oscar Wilde & J. M. Stoddard 1.18.82
> Walt Whitman will be in from 2 till 3½ this afternoon
> & will be most happy to see Mr. Wilde & Mr. Stoddard.[1]

With this invitation Whitman opened the door to a new world of "lovers," as he often termed those who were perceptive enough to prove understanding readers of *Leaves of Grass*. Oscar Wilde was not only an aesthete, he was both writer and scholar and was connected to some of the foremost names in contemporary English literature. Once aware of Wilde's admiration and that of Edward Dowden, professor of literature at Trinity College, Dublin, Whitman eagerly, if somewhat bewilderingly, sought to embrace his new audience. In his declining years when ill health and infirmity prevented him from finding the easy companionship that in earlier times had been his, the New York firemen and the handsome Irish boys he had formerly noted in his daybooks were replaced by Trinity College undergraduates and their Anglo-Irish teachers. Not until after his death would he find lovers among the working-class Irish, so that the situation in Whitman's lifetime was the same in Ireland as in the United States, with the working class failing to heed his voice. But there were perils, as well, to be found within these new circles of scholarly lovers, some of which Whitman could not anticipate, perils that arose from fear and repression and which sometimes found expression in innuendo and half-truths.

Oscar Wilde's visit was a historic event, for it brought Whitman face to face for the first time with an admirer from Ireland. And what celebrity this admirer enjoyed! The personification of the aestheticism he had come to explain to Americans, Wilde was attired in his morning dress of brown velvet and brown trousers, suitably dressed to meet the "Good Gray Poet." He came in the company of Joseph Stoddart, a successful Philadelphia publisher who in a few years would become the editor of *Lippincott's Monthly Magazine*, one of the city's outstanding periodicals. Had the meeting occurred a hundred years later it would have been a media event, with full coverage resulting in the usual sixty-second soundbite on the evening news. As it was, just one reporter interviewed both principals, with the inevitable query put to each, "What did you think of him?" The twenty-six-year-old Wilde's response was to speak of Whitman as "the grand old man" and to refer to what the reporter (unhappily echoing the title of P. T. Barnum's autobiography) called the poet's "struggles and triumphs." Whitman said of Wilde, "He seemed to me like a great big, splendid boy." He certainly was.

Oscar Fingal O'Flahertie Wills Wilde was first introduced to Walt Whitman's poetry by his mother, probably through William Michael Rossetti's 1868 edition. For Americans, one of the more surprising things about Wilde — a man of many surprises — was not his soft-hued clothing, his knee breeches, or the long green fur-trimmed coat he wore almost everywhere but the fact that the mother of such a dandified young man, Lady Jane Francesca Wilde, had been an enthusiastic participant in the Young Ireland revolutionary movement of the 1840s. She was, in fact, the "Speranza" whose ardent poetry had helped inspire the nationalist movement in 1848. Speranza began her revolutionary career by attacking Ireland's advocate for independence, Daniel O'Connell, for his hesitancy to use force. Late in 1847 she published a poem called "The Lament," which bewailed O'Connell's refusal to take up arms and voiced suspicion of his reasons in lines such as:

He whose bosom once ranged with humanity—
Sunk to a time-serving, drivelling inanity—
God! why not spare our loved country the sight.
Was it the gold of the stranger that tempted him?[2]

Ballads and stirring anthems flowed from Speranza's pen, all on themes emphasizing English persecution, the deaths of Irish heroes, or the starvation of Ireland's people, and for these she won a place in the hearts of the people she sang. The future Lady Wilde did not limit her expression to lyric poetry, however. In 1848 when the Young Irelanders rose in rebellion, she wrote an unsigned article for the *Nation* that called for widespread popular support of the armed movement. The article was used as part of the evidence produced against the *Nation*'s editor, Charles Gavan Duffy. Duffy was also the editor of *The Spirit of the Nation* (1843), an anthology of poetry by Irish writers which for many years was the mainstay of Irish patriots and which had an American edition published in Boston in 1844. Speranza publicly acknowledged her authorship, but, because of the respectability of her middle-class family, no action was taken against her.[3]

When John Boyle O'Reilly produced his *Poetry and Songs of Ireland* (1887), he included some of Speranza's poems, and he and Oscar Wilde even discussed the possible publication of her poems in America. Wilde was enormously pleased at the suggestion, which never developed further, and wrote to O'Reilly, "I think my mother's work should make a great success here: it is so unlike the work of her degenerate artistic son. I know you think I am thrilled by nothing but a dado. You are quite wrong, but I shan't argue."[4] O'Reilly had already demonstrated his admiration for the poetry of Speranza's "degenerate artistic son" by introducing Wilde to America in the pages of the *Pilot*. In September 1876 he published "Graffiti D'Italia (Arona, Lago Maggiore)," which was later renamed "Rome Unvisited." Wilde wrote to express his gratitude to O'Reilly, adding, "I esteem it a great honour that the first American paper I appear in should be your admirable *Pilot*."[5]

Wilde's second encounter with the poetry of Walt Whitman was when he read it while at Oxford. Here again the edition would have been the selections made by William Michael Rossetti, who truly was the person responsible for bringing Whitman's poetry to the attention of most of the European literati. Rossetti was the brother of the

Pre-Raphaelite painter Dante Gabriel Rossetti. Along with Holman Hunt, John Everett Millais, and Thomas Woolner, Dante Gabriel Rossetti was part of the aesthetic movement of which Wilde became a principal proponent. Poetry, too, was a part of the movement, with the work of Algernon Charles Swinburne, an admirer of Whitman, as the prime example of the poetic aesthete. The Pre-Raphaelites promoted a return to paintings of a simpler Italian mode, before the advent of Raphael. Botticelli was their model, and until Edward Burne-Jones so exaggerated the mode as to make it almost a caricature of itself, the movement produced some beautiful pictures. "Beautiful" was the key word, for beauty, not utility, was the sole object of aestheticism, especially as it was defined by Wilde.

While Walter Pater was a major influence on aestheticism, the movement was closer to the fringes of early socialism and derived much of its emphasis from John Ruskin's concern for the declining importance of the worker in the country's increasing industrialization. As Wilde understood this concern, it did not lead in the direction of William Morris's return to craftsmanship but rather toward the belief that the worker should become an artist. For the enrichment of their own spirit, workers should surround themselves with things of grace. Stained glass, wrought iron, "bric-a-brac for the what-not," as the favored small figurines were sometimes ridiculed, and, most beloved by Wilde, blue china cups and saucers were among the items advocated for the workers' edification. For their decoration, nature's designs were highly prized, with flowers held in such esteem that Wilde's enthusiasm for calla lilies and sunflowers as motifs for clothing and house decoration led to all manner of derision when he came to the United States.

How Wilde happened to come to America had little to do with an appreciation of his aesthetics and everything to do with showmanship. Richard D'Oyly Carte, a London showman and producer of Gilbert and Sullivan plays, had a new work from the creators of *Trial by Jury* and *H.M.S. Pinafore*. Called *Patience*, it featured a character named "Bunthorne, the Fleshly Poet," who was patterned on Wilde and provided new hilarity for Londoners already regaled by the witticisms and affectations of the original. D'Oyly Carte knew that American producers would soon steal the music of his new show, as they had done with his previous hits, and would even produce it on their stages, as they also had done in that era before copyright protection. Rather than have this happen again, D'Oyly Carte planned to open his own production of *Patience* in New York, and to promote it he hoped to offer the genuine Bunthorne, Oscar Wilde, giving a series of lectures on aestheticism. Perhaps to the showman's surprise, Wilde (who had a promotional objective of his own — to find an American producer for his play *Vera*) accepted the offer and set sail for the United States in December 1881. America was about to welcome to its stages a character who, though modeled on an Irishman, was unlike any stage Irish it had seen hitherto and to its shores an Irishman unlike any it had thus far encountered.

He was, as Whitman said, "a great big splendid boy," for at twenty-six Wilde was all of six feet tall, with long hair of the sort worn in England by English boys of an earlier time and a large, pallid face. He affected a languid air and a graceful, mannered movement but was surprisingly strong. For all his mannerisms, he was splendid, for he was extremely intelligent, had a sharp wit to go with it, and was known to be extraordinarily kind, especially to those in the lower ranks of society.

The meeting between Wilde and Whitman was dutifully recorded by the sole reporter to cover the story, a journalist with the *Philadelphia Press* who came the same evening to interview Whitman. Whitman told the reporter that after a time spent in the parlor where they finished a bottle of wine and talked of London's literary people, he had taken Wilde to his "den" on the upper floor of the house. Whitman claimed they quickly became "on thee and thou terms," with Whitman assuming a first name basis with his guest who, laying his hand on the older poet's knee (as Peter Doyle had done the night they met), assured him, "I like that so much." Whitman believed Wilde had been glad to get away from his lecturing and from fashionable society to "spend a time with an 'old rough.'" He declared Wilde "genuine, honest, and manly," quite unlike the Wilde the public had thus far seen, and spoke of "his youthful health, enthusiasm, and buoyancy," all of which Whitman declared "refreshing." Whitman explained the disparity between this and Wilde's public image by saying, "I imagine that he laid aside any affectation he is said to have, and that I saw behind the scenes."[6] This has a strong ring of truth, for Wilde seems to have had such respect for Whitman that he would have considered it disingenuous to assume his studied manner in the older man's presence.

There had been talk between them of Wilde's aesthetic philosophy, concerning which Whitman had little to say other than to wish the young man well and offer him an encouraging "go ahead." Perhaps by way of illustrating his principles to Whitman, Wilde at one point exclaimed, "I can't listen to anyone unless he attracts me by a charming style or by beauty of theme." Whitman's reproof to this was, "Why, Oscar, it always seems to me that the fellow who makes a dead set at beauty by itself is in a bad way. My idea is that beauty is a result, not an abstraction."[7]

Whitman admired Tennyson's poetry and enjoyed an occasional exchange of letters with England's poet laureate, so it was probably with some hint of regret that he asked if Wilde and the other young literary lions of England were not going to "shove the established idols aside, Tennyson and the rest?" Wilde reassured him on this but pointed out that Tennyson had removed himself from "the living world" to dwell "apart from his time," whereas Wilde and his friends lived "in the very heart of today."[8] Wilde's belief that Whitman was similarly contemporaneous may have shaped the homage he paid him in O'Reilly's autograph book. Under Whitman's signature Wilde added the words, "The spirit who living blamelessly but dared to kiss the smitten mouth of his own century." It was a double allusion, Richard Ellmann points out, to Whitman and to himself, since Wilde had already used the phrase in his poem "Humanitad."[9] Ellmann sees the kiss alluded to in the inscription as the one Wilde later claimed Whitman had given him, but it is more likely a reference to Wilde's belief that Whitman had fulfilled the ideal expressed in "Humanitad," that passion can be diverted into art.

Pressed by the Philadelphia reporter as to Wilde's opinions of American poets, Whitman modestly acknowledged his guest's claim that in England it was generally believed America had only two poets, "Walt Whitman and Emerson." When Wilde had been asked this same question by reporters at the time of his arrival in Philadelphia he had given this response, adding that Longfellow, though admirable, had not produced anything genuinely American. Then, in what must have been a surprise to American readers, he revealed that his highest admiration was for Edgar Allan Poe, "this marvelous lord of rhythmic expression"; however, Poe was dead, he reminded the reporters, and so could not figure in his enumeration.[10] If Wilde confided this admiration for Poe to Whitman, he no doubt heard from him an account of Whitman's journey to Baltimore in 1875, where he was the sole representative of American literature present for the reburial of Poe's remains.[11]

In elaborating to reporters on his opinion of American poets, Wilde enthused about Whitman, saying, "There is something so Greek and sane about his poetry, it is so universal, so comprehensive.

It has all the pantheism of Goethe and Schiller."[12] Mention of "something so Greek" in Whitman's poetry, if made in their private conversation, may have either nettled the older man or at least have caused him to relate to Wilde the substance of letters he had received from John Addington Symonds, who seemed to have made a similar connection. Symonds, a classicist with a special interest in Greek and Roman forms of male friendship, had asked Whitman in 1872 for an elaboration of "Calamus," a group of poems dealing with what Whitman called "adhesiveness," or the love of men for men. Symonds knew, he claimed, what such love had been in the past and what it now was in the present (at which he adds the word "alas!"), but he could only "dimly discern" what Whitman was saying "it can and shall be" and so remained unsatisfied.[11] Whitman acknowledged the letter but ignored the request. There were other letters from Symonds that made no overt reference to "Calamus," but Whitman perceived the unasked question in each one, complaining to Traubel that "Symonds is still asking the same question."[13] Finally, in 1890 he would roundly reject the notion of erotic male love that Symonds inferred from the poems.

Though they were never close, Wilde was familiar with Symonds's work, having read his *Studies of the Greek Poets* while at Oxford, though it was with his tutor's disapproval.[14] Among the English writers and critics of the time, references to things "Greek" in literature were often coded references to homosexuality, a word that had not yet come into being. Wilde's use of the term to describe Whitman's poetry may indicate that he had already formed an opinion as to the poet's sexuality. One of Wilde's friends from his Oxford days was George Cecil Ives, a minor poet and author of works on the subject of deviance and the law who devoted his principal talent, as an organizer, to the cause of same-sex love and its societal acceptance. Ives was the founder of a secret society of such men, the Order of Chaeronea, and later a founding member of the British Society for the Study of Sex Psychology.[15] The Order of Chaeronea took its name from a battle place in Greek history where a band of young Theban men, sworn to mutual love and loyalty, were massacred. The order's symbol was a double wreath, the outer wreath supposedly of calamus, for Whitman's poems of male love.[16] According to Ives, Wilde is supposed to have told him that in their meeting Whitman spoke plainly of his (Whitman's) sexual preference for males and that in parting Whitman had kissed him on the lips.[17] Joseph Stoddart described to the *Press* reporter how Wilde had sat "on a little stool" at Whitman's feet, which seems to refer to their time together on the upper floor. If Stoddart, whom Whitman barely knew, was present in the "den" throughout the conversation (Whitman's later recollection was that he had left the house), it is highly unlikely that such an admission would have occurred at that time. Even if Stoddart was not present, it is not creditable that Whitman, who was so careful about his privacy, would have revealed himself to this stranger, Wilde, no matter how charming.

Richard Ellmann states, however, that there was a second visit in May, when Wilde came alone.[18] The claim is supported (though not by Ellmann) by a diary entry made by one of Wilde's dinner companions on the evening of May 10, 1882. According to this, Wilde had that afternoon returned to Camden, presenting himself at Whitman's address attired as an American cowboy.[19] It is, of course, quite possible that at the second visit Whitman confided something to Wilde that he never revealed to anyone else, not even to the trusted Horace Traubel. But it is also quite possible that Wilde, or Ives, in an effort to claim Whitman for the cause Ives was championing, elaborated upon the conversation. As to the kiss he said Whitman bestowed, there is no reason to doubt that it occurred; to the end of his days Whitman kissed his closest male friends and was pleased to do so. If, in fact, the parting occurred as Wilde averred, it must have seemed to him to be an enactment of the lines in one of the "Calamus" poems: "The one to remain hung on the other's neck and passionately kiss'd him, / While the one to depart tightly prest the one to remain in his arms."[20]

Though he probably was not privy to the upper-room conversation, Joseph Stoddart was present when the wine was proffered in the parlor, an elderberry wine made by Whitman's sister-in-law Louisa. Stoddart claimed Wilde downed "this not overpalatable drink as if it were the nectar of the gods." When Stoddart later asked if this had not been difficult, Wilde cut off any further critical comment with the remark, "If it had been vinegar, I would have drunk it all the same, for I have an admiration for that man which I can hardly express."[21] As a token of his admiration Wilde gave Whitman a copy of his poems bound in a cover of what was then called "Yale" blue. Whitman passed the book on to a young niece of Louisa Whitman, which may be an indication of the opinion he later voiced to Horace Traubel, that though Wilde wrote "exquisitely . . . there seems to be a little substance lacking."[22]

While traveling the country Wilde sent Whitman a photo of himself, one of many he had taken by the famous New York photographer Napoleon Sarony, who had photographed Whitman as well in 1878. When the Wilde photo arrived, Whitman wrote to his young friend Harry Stafford that it was a foot and a half long, "nearly full length, very good."[23] After Whitman's death the photo stood on the piano at George Whitman's home in Burlington, New Jersey. When Wilde fell into disgrace in 1895, George read the newspaper reports and inquired what had become of the photo. Reminded that it stood in the parlor, he banished it with the two-word edict, "Burn it."[24]

George was not the only one in the Whitman circle to react to the news of Wilde's trial. Daniel Brinton, a professor of linguistics and archaeology at the University of Pennsylvania and a close friend of Whitman, had met Wilde when he was in Philadelphia. At the time of Wilde's arrest, Brinton registered his surprise to Horace Traubel by referring to the meeting and remarking, "No trace of the disease then."[25] John Burroughs, the naturalist who wrote a biography of Whitman in 1896, had entertained the visiting Wilde at his home in Riverby, New York. He was, Burroughs wrote in 1906, "a splendid talker, and a handsome man, but a voluptuary. As he walked from you, there was something in the motion of his hips and back that was disagreeable."[26]

Though there may have been no overt references to his sexuality, there were obviously enough comments made about Wilde at the time of his American visit to cause Whitman to say somewhat defensively that he thought him "manly." A few years later he told Traubel, "Everybody's been so in the habit of looking at Wilde cross-eyed, sort of, that they have charged the defect of their vision up against Wilde as a weakness in his character."[27] Whitman would have been sensitive to this kind of biased viewing, for he, too, had been looked at "cross-eyed" by many for the open sexuality of his poetry. Indeed, just a few weeks after Wilde's visit the anti-Whitman bias would recur with the suppression in Boston of his latest edition of *Leaves of Grass*.

Whitman seems to have been conflicted in his feelings about Wilde, for despite his defense of the Irishman to Traubel on the occasion just noted, there was another in which he admitted to Traubel that Wilde "may have been some of him fraud at that time [when he visited] but was not all fraud." "He has extraordinary brilliancy of genius," he continued, "with perhaps rather too little root in eternal soils. Wilde gives up too much to the extrinsic decorative values in art."[28] Contributing to these conflicting thoughts, voiced in 1888, may have been the apprehension that Wilde's lack of roots in what Whitman believed to be "eternal soils" would render him incapable of withstanding such strong winds of opposition as those Whitman had had to endure, should they ever blow his way. Had he lived to see it, the American may have been surprised at the resources Wilde found within himself when the winds of opposition blew.

One amusing remnant of the eventful meeting in Camden remains as a literary footnote. The November 1882 issue of *Century Magazine* contained a poetic conjecture by Helen Gray Cone of what the encounter had been like, with the supposed words of each poet cast in a clever imitation of his own prosody. Entitled "Narcissus in Camden," it was subtitled "A Classical Dialogue of the Year 1882" and opened with Paumanokides (Whitman) offering a greeting:

Who may this be?
This young man clad unusually, with loose locks, languorous,
    glidingly toward me advancing,
Toward the ceiling of my chamber his orbic and expressive
    eye-balls uprolling,
As I have seen the green-necked wild-fowl the mallard in the
    thundering of the storm,
By the weedy shore of Paumanok my fish-shaped island.
Sit down, young man!
I do not know you, but I love you with burning intensity,
I am he that loves the young men, whosoever and wheresoever
    they are or may be hereafter, or may have been any time in
    the past,
Loves the eye-glassed literat, loves also and probably more the
    vender of clams, raucous-throated, monotonous-chanting,
Loves the Elevated Railroad employee of Mannahatta my city;
I suppress the rest of the list of the persons I love, solely because
    I love you,
Sit down *eleve*, I receive you!

To which Narcissus (Wilde) responds:

O clarion, from whose brazen throat
    Strange sounds across the seas are blown,
Where England, girt as with a moat,
    A strong sea-lion, sits alone!

A pilgrim from that white-cliffed shore,
    What joy, large flower of Western land!
To seek thy democratic door,
    With eager hand to clasp thy hand!

After three or four more such exhanges Narcissus bids farewell:

What more is left to say or do?
    Our minds have met; our hands must part,
I go to plant in pastures new
    The love of Beauty and of Art.
      I'll shortly start.
    One town is rather small for two
      Like me and you!

To this Paumanokides replies simply,

So long! [29]

Wilde continued his journey, arriving in Boston in late January. Two Irish friends awaited him; one, the playwright Dion Boucicault, was his friend from Dublin theater projects, the other, John Boyle O'Reilly, he knew only from correspondence. Though O'Reilly's newspaper, the *Pilot*, carried the news of the impending lecture, there is no evidence of the reaction of the Irish Catholic population to his presence in their city. But Boston's Yankee Protestants, especially among its very sizeable literary community, were all agog. The lecture hall was sold out for Wilde's January 31 appearance, with the front sixty rows occupied by Harvard students who made a grand entrance in fanciful "aesthetic" attire, including the inevitable lilies and sunflowers. While in the city Wilde visited with Oliver Wendell Holmes, John Greenleaf Whittier, and James Russell Lowell by invitation and with Henry Wadsworth Longfellow, it was reported, by dint of an unannounced arrival, which the old poet could not evade.[30] O'Reilly took him about the city, and Wilde enjoyed a Sunday luncheon with the family and friends of Julia Ward Howe, who had written the stirring anthem "The Battle Hymn of the Republic." It was this luncheon (and perhaps the fact that it occurred on a Sunday) that roused the Reverend Thomas Wentworth Higginson to fury.

Higginson had survived the glory days of abolitionism and the Civil War, acquitting himself with distinction in both these struggles, to become a writer in all literary forms but fiction and to be elected a member of the Massachusetts legislature. He continued his reformist efforts, still championing "the Negro," women's rights, and, in later years, the rights of immigrants. He wrote and edited numerous books, including the first editions of Emily Dickinson's poems, though this was after dismissing them some years before when Dickinson first approached him with her work. Higginson wrote literary and cultural criticism for such widely read periodicals as the *Nation* and more regional ones such as Boston's *Woman's Journal*. Never an admirer of Whitman's poetry, he had criticized *Drum-Taps* by censuring Whitman for not entering combat during the Civil War, choosing instead to serve in the hospitals. In 1881 Higginson found the latest edition of *Leaves of Grass* as "nauseating" as earlier ones.

But Higginson saved his strongest language for the visit of Oscar Wilde when he excoriated Bostonians, especially the city's women — "guardians of the public purity"—(with what seemed a pointed reference to Howe) for welcoming and entertaining in their homes a poet whose works he deemed "immoral." The Wilde poem that most scandalized Higginson and many other Americans was "Charmides," in which a young man sexually violates a marble statue of the chaste Athena and dies for having so profaned the goddess. The poem would have particularly shocked Americans who throughout the nineteenth century experienced a love affair of their own with the style of marble neoclassical sculpture best exemplified by the work of Hiram Powers. They had justified the public exhibition of such statuary, most often executed as nudes, by convincing themselves that the cool marble nullified all erotic suggestion.[31] Now here was Oscar Wilde with a poem that dismissed that rationale. This may have been the stimulus for the critic quoted by Higginson (who no doubt missed the humor) as having said that Wilde's poems "carry nudity to a point where it ceases to be a virtue." Higginson claimed that if "Charmides" were read aloud to mixed company not a woman would remain in the room to the end, yet the author was entertained in drawing rooms.

Not content to villify Wilde, Higginson widened his attack to include Whitman, perhaps linking the two because of Wilde's visit to Camden or because his anger at Boston for welcoming Wilde reminded him that Whitman had been published in that sacred city just the previous year. Lamenting what he says may have been a rash claim, "that the influence of women has purified English literature," Higginson protests, "When the poems of Wilde and Whitman lie in ladies' boudoirs, I see no evidence of the improvement." To Higginson's mind, both poets were guilty of a lack of delicacy for writing about sexual matters and nudity in a way that "a real man" never would. The subject of manliness led Higginson once again to thoughts of war and Whitman's alleged dereliction of "manly" duty. Wilde, too, was guilty on this score, according to the former army officer, for he was nothing like his mother, Lady Wilde, whose poems "upon the wrongs of Ireland are strong and fervid enough . . . to enlist an army." Now, when Ireland needs its best men, Higginson scolds, Wilde has chosen "to cross the Atlantic and pose in ladies' boudoirs or write prurient poems."[32] Higginson, no doubt unconscious of doing so, was contributing to the incipient notions of gender identification that in a decade or so would crystalize into categories of hetero- and homosexuality; to all appearances, however, he was quite consciously associating Whitman with Wilde in order to situate them both, in the minds of Americans, "beyond the Pale" (to use an appropriately Anglo-Irish boundary term) of acceptable behavior.[33]

Howe defended herself and Oscar Wilde in the *Boston Transcript* but said nothing of Whitman. Wilde triumphed in Boston despite the Reverend Higginson, whom he referred to as "this scribbling anonymuncule in grand old Massachusetts who scrawls and screams so glibly about what he cannot understand."[34] Later, Wilde recalled Boston as a place where English puritanism lingered on, though not, he hoped, for long.[35] Because Higginson's diatribe appeared early in February and the letter to John R. Osgood from the state district attorney declaring *Leaves of Grass* obscene was dated March 1, William Douglas O'Connor suspected, for a time, that Higginson was the source of the official complaint, but there is no evidence of this being so.[36] Nevertheless, O'Connor and Whitman had nothing but contempt for Higginson from that time forward. More than once Whitman shared his opinion of Higginson with Traubel, on one occasion saying he believed him one of "the good fellows who had an awful belief in respectability — an awful hunger to be gentlemen."[37] His comments to Traubel range from a short-tempered, "Oh! damn Higginson!" to "Higginson . . . has always been mere sugar and water. He lacks all else."[38] His most trenchant comment serves as a summing up of the matter to which nothing more need be added: "there are some who in the natural order couldn't accept Walt Whitman — couldn't appreciate the inmost purpose of his art: it is the absence of affinities." As an example he offers "Higginson, with his strict, straight, notions of literary propriety—I call them enemies, creatures natively antipathetic."[39]

In December 1881 Whitman wrote to Benjamin Ticknor to thank him for the suggestion he and O'Reilly had made, that Swinburne be asked to write a review of the latest edition of *Leaves of Grass*. While grateful, Whitman refused consent for such a request although, he wrote, he had sent Swinburne a copy of the book along with some clippings about it. No doubt he hoped this would prompt a review or an article without anyone having to ask for it. This evidence of O'Reilly's confidence that Swinburne would write approvingly of Whitman's latest book opens a door to the consideration of Swinburne's "defection," as it has been seen, from the ranks of Whitman loyalists. While belonging more properly to studies of Whitman's reception in England, Swinburne's change of heart has some bearing on the present discussion mainly for the possibility of Oscar Wilde's involvement in the alteration.[40]

Algernon Charles Swinburne was the principal poet of the aesthetic movement Wilde had come to expound to Americans. His most notable contribution to literature is his collection *Poems and Ballads*, the first series of which appeared in 1866. The book was attacked for what was perceived as its lewdness, but it was defended by William Michael Rossetti, who was soon to edit the English edition of selections from *Leaves of Grass*. In 1868 Swinburne produced a study of William Blake in which he claimed so great a likeness between Blake and Whitman as to substantiate a claim for "the transition of souls or transfusion of spirits." Though he acknowledged both poets had moments when they descended from their greatness and were "at times noisy and barren and loose," he concluded that no higher praise could be paid to either poet than the comparison of "breadth of outline and charm of colour" found in each.[41] Three years later, 1871, brought "To Walt Whitman in America" from *Songs before Sunrise*, where Swinburne hailed Whitman:

> O strong-winged soul with prophetic
>   Lips hot with the bloodbeats of song,
> With tremor of heartstrings magnetic,
>   With thoughts as thunders in throng,
> With consonant ardours of chords
> That pierce men's souls as with swords
>   And hale them hearing along.[42]

In 1872 Robert Buchanan, a Scottish novelist and critic who greatly admired Whitman, wrote an article, "The Fleshly School of Poetry," where he took issue with certain English poets, specifically Swinburne, for the sensuality of their works. Swinburne responded in "Under the Microscope" (1872) by pointing out the inconsistency in Buchanan's acceptance of Whitman while rejecting the same kind of sexual explicitness from English poets.[43] Dante Gabriel Rossetti also took up the defense of his fellow aesthete, but Buchanan demolished both their objections by proclaiming Rossetti and Swinburne mere "Singers," while Whitman was "a Bard." Buchanan's term "Fleshly Poets" resonated in Gilbert and Sullivan's character, "Bunthorne, the Fleshly Poet," and because Wilde was the most familiar figure of the type, Bunthorne was endowed with his characteristics.

When Wilde visited Whitman in 1882 the American poet was naturally eager to speak of Swinburne, who had not published any word of criticism of the *Leaves of Grass* Whitman had sent him. Whitman still may have hoped to prod Swinburne to respond by his gift of a photograph, which he sent via Wilde (not neglecting to make the same gift to Wilde), and by importuning the young Irishman to relay his good wishes. Wilde wrote immediately to Swinburne who, on February 2, 1882, acknowledged receipt of the letter. Swinburne asked to have Whitman assured, if the occasion arose, that "I have by no manner of means either forgotten him or relaxed my admiration of his noblest work." He also wished Whitman to know that he believed him to be at his best when he speaks "of great matters — liberty, for instance, and death." But, he adds, this does not mean he agrees with all of Whitman's theories or that he admires with equal measure all of his work, since that kind of admiration he considers insincere.[44]

Wilde sent Whitman a copy of Swinburne's letter, and Whitman heard nothing more of or from Swinburne. But in January 1884 William Michael Rossetti wrote to Edward Dowden that Swinburne had "considerably cooled about Whitman."[45] In January 1885 Edmund Gosse, a literary critic who would write an unflattering biography of Swinburne in 1917, called on Whitman to convey the good wishes of a number of English friends, including Swinburne. There was nothing in any of this to prepare Whitman for the article Swinburne published in the *Fortnightly Review* in 1887, "Whitmania." Here Swinburne managed to pull off quite a feat of criticism. Without recanting his earlier enthusiasm (which, it should be remembered, had been tempered by certain reservations), he deflated it, and Whitman, by claiming that as a poet "no amount of improvement that self-knowledge and self-culture" might afford could make up for the deficiences of what Swinburne termed "voluminous and incoherent effusions."[46] To his not unfamiliar complaints of lack of form, Swinburne added something new, however, having to do with Whitman's treatment of sexual matters. Such material was acceptable when done well, ran the essence of his argument, but, with reference to two of Whitman's more notable female poetic figures, Swinburne found his Eve "a drunken apple woman, indecently sprawling in the slush and garbage of the gutter amid the rotten refuse of her overturned fruit-stall," and his Venus "a Hottentot wench."[47]

While the Eve and Venus references caught the attention of readers and continue to be the most often quoted part of Swinburne's essay, the true topic, as its title makes clear, is not Whitman's poetry but "Whitmania," the uncritical adulation that Swinburne had very pointedly told Whitman, via Wilde, he considered insincere. Actually, Swinburne's use of the term "Whitmania" predates the essay. In a letter of December 1886 where he turned away the offer of a friend to provide him with Bucke's study of Whitman, Swinburne wrote, "I am by no means a Whitmaniac, though I still genuinely admire his best earlier work." He makes clear in the same letter that he considered "Whitmaniacs" to be Whitman's "indiscriminate admirers," of whom he had "almost wearied and sickened."[48]

The word "sickened" provides a clue to understanding why Swinburne devotes the opening paragraph of "Whitmania" to a medical description of what he views as a pathological devotion to Whitman on the part of (though he uses no names) people such as William Michael Rossetti, Robert Buchanan, John Addington Symonds, and perhaps Oscar Wilde. But here he is not so exculpatory of Whitman as he is in his letter, for he claims the poet has "inoculated" some English readers and writers with "the singular form of ethical and aesthetic rabies for which his name supplies the proper medical term of definition." He would not, he continues, have "thought it necessary to comment on the symptoms of a disorder which happily is not likely to become epidemic . . . had the sufferers not given such painfully singular signs of inability to realise a condition only too obvious to the compassionate bystander."[49]

One has to wonder why a literary critic would choose to employ medical tropes to describe an enthusiasm for a writer, even if he does not share that enthusiasm. It is true that the conceit he employed in

"Under the Microscope" was scientific, as he claimed to be accommodating himself to the world of science by bending his critical judgments to the classification of various species of writers.[50] It is also true that Peter Bayne, the Scottish writer and journalist, had delivered a vicious attack on Whitman in an 1875 issue of *Contemporary Review*, concluding with a warning of the deadly peril he saw, "that our literature may pass into conditions of horrible disease" if Whitman's example were to prevail.[51] But Swinburne's earlier conceit had remained only that, an unsustained premise for his essay, and twelve years had intervened since Bayne's article and his was no longer a voice to be quoted.

Terry L. Meyers has suggested that Swinburne's essay was "driven in part by homophobia," a suggestion he supports by examples of Swinburne drawing away from the overtly homosexual Symonds (whom Swinburne referred to after Symonds's death as "the late Mr. Soddington Symonds") and others whose homosexuality either had become known or was strongly suspected.[52] Swinburne's own sex life, in his earlier years, had involved various practices (especially flagellation), public disclosure of which he seems to have feared in the increasingly punitive English society of the 1880s and 1890s. The suggestion that begs to be made then is this: if, as George Ives claimed, Oscar Wilde returned from America in 1883 with the story of Walt Whitman having confided to him his homosexuality and if Wilde in turn confided this to others among the English literati or to Swinburne directly, the story could account for Swinburne's tightrope walk in "Whitmania."

It is clear that what Swinburne tries to do there is to balance his critical opinion of Whitman's work with his strange contention that Whitman's most vocal English admirers were in some mysterious way ill. Whitman is made the source of their disease, for he has "inoculated" them, and thus they have become victims of a "singular form of ethical and aesthetic rabies." Further, they have "symptoms of a disorder," and their shared enthusiasm is said to be "a condition only too obvious to the compassionate bystander."[53] In truth, it may have been the obviousness of homosexuality among the English adherents of Whitman that Swinburne feared.

Swinburne may have been aware, as was Symonds from his knowledge of Richard von Krafft-Ebing's *Psychopathia Sexualis* (1886), that the medical profession was already beginning to claim as a medical condition what Krafft-Ebing had labeled "homosexuality," proclaiming it a perversion of nature. This may account for the timidity with which Symonds protested Swinburne's article in the next *Fortnightly*, of September 1887, a timidity he attempted to explain away to William Sloane Kennedy as an attempt to keep a "very low" tone in order to win recognition of Whitman's merits.[54] Significantly, in his 1889 review of *November Boughs*, Wilde chose to quote portions of "A Backward Glance" where Whitman defends sexuality as a major theme of *Leaves of Grass*, "Literature is always calling in the doctor for consultation and confession, and always giving evasions and swathing suppressions in place of that 'heroic nudity' on which only a genuine diagnosis can be built."[55] In choosing to quote Whitman on this particular topic Wilde may have been rebutting Swinburne for his assumption of the role of medico-critic, while simultaneously attempting to set aside, via Whitman's own words, Swinburne's implications of pathology lurking behind poetic intensity.[56]

Whitman chose not to respond to Swinburne's article and even reproved some of his friends for their violent reactions to it. Ernest Rhys, the Welsh poet who made his home in London, claimed that when he visited Whitman during a lecture tour of the United States in 1888 the old poet dismissed Swinburne with the comment, "Ain't he the damndest simulacrum!" a telling thrust aimed at Swinburne's authenticity.[57] Traubel's account of Whitman's response to Swinburne's revised opinion goes considerably beyond this. According to Traubel, Whitman commented, "It's not necessary to believe Swinburne's original notion was dishonest, nor that the new view is: they stand for two Swinburnes: you can take your choice: one is as honest as the other: which do you choose?"[58] Whitman's understanding of Swinburne's divided mind may have derived from an intuitive, or experiential, understanding of a divided self, the kind that may have driven both himself and Swinburne into closeted retreat. But just as surely as Swinburne wished to distance himself from Whitman and his possible homosexuality, Whitman no doubt wished to distance himself from the aesthetic ideal the Europeans had established for homosexuality, an ideal so widely at variance from his own workingman and comrade model.

If we put the events surrounding the Swinburne essay in chronological order what emerges is the following: Wilde returned to England from his American trip late in 1883; in 1885 the Criminal Law Amendment in England made even private, consensual sex acts between males criminal; in 1886 Krafft-Ebing's study labeled homosexuality a perversion; in 1887 Swinburne published "Whitmania" against a backdrop of increasing homophobia and medicalization of same-sex love; in 1895 all of Swinburne's fears may have seemed justified when Wilde was found guilty of sodomy and sentenced to two years imprisonment.[59] While it cannot be said with certainty that Wilde was responsible for Swinburne's turning away from Whitman, one must consider the possibility that in seeking to convey a sense of shared intimacy with Whitman, perhaps even to elevate himself above others in the circle of Whitman admirers, he said enough to prompt Swinburne's public distancing of himself from further identification with the "Whitmaniacs." Swinburne's attempt at separation seems, in this light, somewhat desperate and suggests that Wilde, in the manner of an Irish prankster, may have manuevered him into wearing a green carnation.[60]

In 1875, when Oscar Wilde was twenty years old, he met the first of a number of women with whom he would fall in love before marrying Constance Lloyd. His first love was all of seventeen when they met; her name was Florence Balcombe, and she seemed to fall as much in love as he. Three years later, a few months after successfully completing his studies at Oxford, Wilde's hopes of marrying Balcombe were shattered by the announcement of her impending marriage to Abraham (Bram) Stoker, a civil servant who, while Wilde had been off at Oxford, had been living just blocks away from her in Dublin. Having recently made a move from civil service to management of a Dublin theater, Stoker was ready to marry. He and Florence were wed in December 1878 and entered upon a life centered on the stage. Wilde felt the rejection deeply and gave evidence of still having tender feelings for Florence in 1881, not long before leaving for America.[61]

Bram Stoker managed to turn a passion for theater into a livelihood when he became the touring manager and secretary for the famed English actor Henry Irving. Later, when Irving's career ended, Stoker pursued a literary career begun earlier with the publication of some stories and a novel, *Dracula* (1897). His *Personal Reminiscences of Henry Irving* (1906) told the story of his theatrical tours and *Famous Imposters* (1910) was a humorous exposé. A few mystery stories completed the roster of his works, but nothing he wrote came near the success of *Dracula*.

In March 1884, two years after Oscar Wilde's visit, Walt Whitman met Bram Stoker and Henry Irving at the home of Whitman's friend Thomas Donaldson. It was quite an important occasion for Stoker. For one thing, it brought together two of the men he most admired,

Irving and Whitman. But the occasion had for him a significance far beyond the scope of the moment, extending back to his days at Trinity College, Dublin, and his first reading of *Leaves of Grass*. A subsequent chapter, when our narrative moves to Ireland, will explore the Trinity-Whitman connection; for now it will suffice to say that Stoker was one of a circle of Whitman admirers there.

On February 14, 1876, at a meeting of Dublin's Fortnightly Club, Stoker defended Whitman against those who deplored and ridiculed him. The same night, unable to maintain a scholarly distance, he took his admiration to a personal level by writing to the poet. Enclosed was a draft of a letter written four years earlier. (Curiously, it was almost four years to the day, for the first was dated February 18, 1872.) He explains the long delay by saying he had learned after writing the draft "that you are addressed as *Mr.* Whitman," something he had not done in his impulsiveness, and so for this, and perhaps other unstated reasons, the letter had lain in his desk all this while.

In fact, Whitman cared not a whit for such formalities and welcomed the 1872 letter even more for its brashness, telling Traubel in 1889 that Stoker was "fresh, breezy, Irish." Again, as with his other Irish friends, there was this attraction to what he assumed to be the essence of "Irishness," a directness and frankness that greatly pleased Whitman. In his 1876 letter Stoker expressed sorrow at Whitman's poor health because, he says, "Many of us are hoping to see you in Ireland." It is regrettable that Whitman never had the opportunity to meet his Dublin supporters, for from all indications he would have found them and their Irish nature much to his liking.

Stoker's 1872 letter is remarkable for its profuse and uninhibited torrent of words that make no attempt to conceal the writer's emotions. Some have used the word "gushing" to describe it, but there is a suggestion of insincerity in that which is not evident in Stoker's letter. Stoker himself seems to have feared being perceived as insincere, however, for he repeatedly encourages his reader to stop reading the letter and simply "Put it in the fire if you like."[62]

Stoker supplies Whitman with a detailed description of his physical appearance, his disposition, his likes and dislikes. He tells the poet the varying circumstances under which he has read *Leaves*— late at night behind a locked door or at the seashore. In one of his more insightful comments, Stoker acknowledges Whitman's ability to create in his poems a perfect democracy by confiding that at times the poet's word or phrase "takes me away from the world around me and places me in an ideal land." In the Preface to *Leaves* one image struck Stoker especially and caused him to ponder it for hours, "the weather-beaten vessels entering new ports." The words must have suggested to his mind the emigration of thousands from his own country with America their destination, for he adds, "to you who sing of your own land of progress the words have a meaning that I can only imagine."

Readers today wonder how to interpret Stoker's letter. Are we to conclude that Stoker was, like John Addington Symonds, Oscar Wilde, and possibly Algernon Charles Swinburne, drawn to Whitman because of the Calamus pull exerted by the poet? If so, then we need nothing more than Stoker's closing remark to substantiate that conclusion: "I thank you for all the love and sympathy you have given me in common with my kind."[63] What Stoker at twenty-five considered to be his "kind" remains a mystery, though surely he betrays a sexual ambiguity when he tells Whitman, "How sweet a thing it is for a strong healthy man with a woman's eyes and a child's wishes to feel that he can speak so to a man who can be if he wishes father, and brother and wife to his soul." Whitman's comment on this, "How sweet, indeed! where there is love, why not? why not?" should not be snidely or even casually set aside, for where there was so obvious a love, why should he not have welcomed the spiritual bond being offered?[64]

If, however, not all the emphasis is placed on the closing comment and the entire letter taken into account, what seems to have compelled this impulsive outpouring is not entirely the evident sexual ambiguity but the need to communicate emotions and ideas not spoken in his everyday exchanges, not even with the "large number of acquaintances" and the "five or six friends" of whose existence Stoker informs Whitman. He has been, he says, "reared a conservative in a conservative country," which may be why he would "like to call [Whitman] Comrade and to talk to you as men who are not poets do not often talk." This, too, is part of the Calamus message, the comradeship that Whitman offers to those, like young Stoker, who cannot find their "kind" among the businessmen, the politicians, the engineers of their society. Stoker later found himself when he had entered the world of theater, and he seems to have gained a father figure in Henry Irving to provide much of what he had earlier hoped to find in Whitman. Of all the things Stoker pours out in the 1872 letter, he reveals what seems to be his greatest need when he writes, "You are a true man, and I would like to be one myself, and so I would be towards you as a brother and as a pupil to his master." Clearly, Bram Stoker was seeking what psychologists today call a male role model for the kind of man he wished to become.

Whitman understood this and told Traubel that he had accepted Stoker's letter at the time, and still did in 1889, as genuine. He also seems to have understood the reticence that had overcome Stoker's original impulse and caused the four-year delay, and so his reply was encouraging but not effusive. Whitman told Stoker he had been right in following his impulse and writing "so unconventionally, so fresh, so manly, and so affectionately."[65] He shared Stoker's hope they might someday meet, though he expressed doubt it would happen, and then moved on to speak of the books Stoker would be receiving soon. Young Stoker's reticence lingered on into adulthood, for in *Personal Reminiscenses of Henry Irving,* he speaks only of the second letter, with no mention of the original one sent four years after it was written. Of the second letter he says, "I poured out my heart. I had long wished to do so but was, somehow, ashamed or diffident — the qualities are much alike."[66]

Perhaps Whitman could understand Stoker because he had received other letters similar to his. There were, for example, the letters from Bernard O'Dowd (1866–1953), whose father was an Irish policeman. Born and raised in Melbourne, Australia, he started a Walt Whitman Society there. In young manhood when he was librarian of the state Supreme Court library, O'Dowd read Rossetti's edition and then the complete *Leaves of Grass.* He began at least one letter to Whitman, in 1889, before actually sending a letter in March 1890. In one of many such missives O'Dowd confessed, "I can hardly think it is not a dream that I am writing to Walt Whitman. Take our love, we have little more to give you, we can only try to spread to others the same great boon you have given to us."[67] O'Dowd went on to earn the title "Australia's poet of the dawn" for his long career as a writer of prose and poetry.[68]

There was also the letter Whitman received from Allen Upward, a young Englishman living in Dublin and working as a civil servant, as Stoker had before he moved into theater management. In March 1884 Upward sent Whitman a lengthy letter offering his deepest thoughts on life, love, death, and all the imponderables, to the contemplation of which he had been moved by reading *Leaves of Grass.* At one point he says, "I am an orator and a demagogue (I prefer the name demagogue for myself.) I have delivered speeches on behalf of free thought and democracy. I have gone, a Saxon, among the embittered children of Erin, and they will not report unfavorably of me." Elsewhere he confides, "I assure thee that I wrote letters at midnight to an imaginary friend!"[69]

Though he pretended to be "amaze[d]" by such letters, Whitman said to Traubel concerning Upward's, "This letter is very much like Stoker's in character," indicating his grasp of the same emotional need that underlay the two.[70] If Whitman had limited his appreciation of the Irish temperament (as he believed it to be) to the outgoing impetuosity of a William Douglas O'Connor or a John Boyle O'Reilly, he would not have understood Bram Stoker's need and his conflicted feelings at having confided it. But O'Connor and O'Reilly were not the only "Irishmen" Whitman had loved; there had been Peter Doyle, who despite the love he felt for Whitman could not express it as Whitman wished he would. While Whitman may have believed this reticence was part of being Irish, it was more likely to have been simply a part of Doyle's own nature, just as the desire for the approval of an older man was part of Stoker's. Thomas Donaldson, Whitman's friend and admirer who arranged the meeting between Whitman and Stoker, testifies, unwittingly no doubt, that Stoker became the "true man" that in the suppressed letter he had confided he hoped to be. Writing in 1896 Donaldson described him as, "Bram Stoker, born Abraham, and who should still be Abraham, because of manhood and breadth of humanity."[71]

Still another visitor came to Camden to share with Whitman something of Ireland. William Summers, a member of the British Parliament, junior whip of the Liberal Party, and a supporter of Home Rule for Ireland, arrived on September 26, 1888. He had been introduced to Whitman via a letter from Mary Costelloe, whom Whitman had known when she was Mary Whitall Smith of Germantown, Pennsylvania, daughter of Robert Pearsall Smith and Hannah Whitall Smith. Mary had married Frank Costelloe, an Irish barrister active in London politics and in the Liberal Party. In introducing Summers, Mary had assured Whitman he would provide "an interesting inside view of English political life."[72] As it turned out, Whitman was mostly interested in learning whether Gladstone really knew what it was Ireland needed and was not satisfied by what he heard.

We have two accounts of the meeting, one by Whitman and the other by Summers, but Whitman's is the more immediate to the event and thus deserving of first attention. On the evening following Summers's visit Whitman gleefully announced to Traubel that he had received that day "a real live member of parliament" who, he said, "made a grand show-up—had fine ways—was young, strong, optimistic." Then, getting to the heart of his concern,

> I have always seriously asked myself whether Gladstone knows anything about Ireland after all— is really bent upon any policy of benefit for Ireland: knows himself what he wants or Ireland needs. I thought to myself today: this is my oportunity—this is your opportunity, Walt Whitman — so I turned to Summers and put it directly to him — the straight question: told him my own suspicions —asked him as one of them, as coming in contact with the men right at their work—Do you, Summers, think better of this— know better?—and so on.[73]

Summers response was to the effect that Gladstone "realized" the condition of Ireland, knew that something had to be done, and was doing "what he could, what the moment suggested." Whitman found the answer unsatisfying though he acknowledged that, unless "he pleaded guilty and made a confession," it was no doubt the only one Summers could give. The next day he was more troubled by it, however, and spoke to Traubel of the response, calling it "that strange evasion . . . ending nowhere, leading to nothing."[74] He referred to Mary Costelloe's comment that Summers would give him "an inside view of English politics," adding that had he been well enough he might have availed himself of the chance, for Summers struck him as "a good believer, a sparkling lieutenant," and a person of value in his position.

A month later Mary Costelloe sent Whitman the account of Summers's visit that he had published in the Liberal newspaper, *Pall Mall Gazette*. She spoke of Summers, whom she confessed not to know very well, as possessed of a "first rate political ability, but extraordinarily lazy." "If he were more energetic," she contended, "he would rise to be one of the Liberal Leaders — but he has been cursed with a comfortable income and has never been forced to work." Since Frank Costelloe's ambition was to become one of the "Liberal Leaders," Mary and her husband were tireless workers in numerous socialist and philanthropic endeavors, so she forthrightly concludes, "The parable of the Camel and the Needle Eye is not confined to the Kingdom of Heaven."[75]

The *Gazette* story provides a thumbnail sketch of Whitman's life as told in his own words to Summers and then turns to talk of British politics and the Irish question in particular. Whitman indicates his lack of assurance that Gladstone knows just what should be done about Ireland, adding that it

> seems there was no "leaf, herb, or medicine" that would cure Ireland's disease. However, if I were a young man as you are, I would certainly throw myself into the conflict on the side of the Irish. I have many kind friends who write to me from Ireland in favour of Mr. Gladstone's policy; and my wish, my desire, my animus, would certainly be on the side of the just, wise, brave, and sensible Irish people. Still, as I said, I am puzzled. It seems as if nothing would help Ireland at all. The country appears to be under a spell — an incantation. For the last thousand years or so no good appears to have come out of anything on Irish soil.[76]

Summers wonders, "If that is the case, what is the reason? Is it the land, or the people, or the treatment to which the people have been subjected?" He reminds Whitman of his "Old Ireland," quoting the last ten lines of the poem and asking, "Do not the Irish prosper when they come to the new country?" Whitman agrees that they do, "especially in the matter of politics," which he describes as in this country meaning "getting anything from one to ten thousand a year, so that there is plenty of scope for the Irishman here."[77]

Whitman proclaimed the *Gazette* story accurate, that it stuck "pretty decently to the facts," so we may safely conclude that the conversation went much as reported.[78] It constitutes the only public, "on the record" statement of his support of Home Rule for Ireland.

Although the visitors who came to Camden from abroad are more prestigious, mention must be made of an Irish American visitor whom Whitman also welcomed there. In the spring of 1891, the year before Whitman died, a New York sculptor, William R. O'Donovan, came bearing a letter of introduction from George Childs. On the strength of this he won the poet's consent (though he was weary of being "scarified," as he called it) to pose for an uncommissioned bust O'Donovan hoped to create. William O'Donovan was born in Virginia to an Irish father and German mother. Like Peter Doyle, he had served in the Confederate army. When the war ended he made his way to New York, where he hoped to have a career as a sculptor. Though self-taught, O'Donovan was successful and achieved recognition for his realism and his portrait busts.

With no suitable room to be found in Camden, O'Donovan moved in with the artist Thomas Eakins at his Chestnut Street studio in Philadelphia, intending to ferry across the river for the sittings he would require of Whitman. Eakins had completed an oil portrait of Whitman in 1887 and had become the poet's friend. Since Eakins and O'Donovan were associates in some projects prior to the latter's arrival in Camden, it is possible that Eakins suggested the bust. O'Donovan proceeded with his work but came irregularly, made unscheduled trips home to New York, and to Whitman's surprise — since it seemed unrelated to the making of a bust — arrived one day to take a cast of his left hand.[79] Then he came on a few occasions with a photographer, Samuel Murray, to photograph Whitman. So many photographs were taken that Whitman complained to Traubel of the number, claiming it was "hell's times in all sorts of posishes [sic]."[80]

After a time Whitman began to lose patience, and confidence, in the sculptor. Instructing Traubel to go to Eakins's studio, he told him, "Take a squint — see what they are making of the critter there." Traubel was not impressed by what he saw and brought back a photo of the bust, still a work in progress. Whitman confided to his young friend his lack of faith in the sculptor's ability and in July received what must have seemed to him confirmation of his reservations. In a letter from New York O'Donovan enclosed clippings from a newspaper announcing, with an accompanying photograph, the unveiling by the sculptor of his statue of Archbishop John Hughes. One can imagine Whitman's reaction as he gazed on the sculpted likeness of the man he had so fiercely attacked fifty years before. He made no reference to the coincidence, however, commenting to Traubel only on the statue: "It has," he ruminated, "a recommendable faithfulness, I guess — is a figure in full canonicals — aprons, robes, all that — more or less after conventional modes. I hardly know what it leads me to: in part this — that he [O'Donovan] is not to catch 'Leaves of Grass.'"[81]

When the Whitman bust proved so poor a representation of its subject (Whitman considered it a perfect likeness — of the transcendentalist minister Theodore Parker!) that O'Donovan voluntarily took it apart to be completely refashioned, Whitman was not surprised.[82] He told Traubel he had sometime before lost confidence in O'Donovan and that the sculptor seemed now to have reached the same conclusion.[83] If one considers the statue of Archbishop Hughes, it is not hard to guess at what precise point in the process Whitman lost confidence.

In his essay "Our Eminent Visitors (Past, Present and Future)" in *November Boughs*, Whitman voiced a fervent welcome to the various guests who had recently come from Europe to the United States. "They do good," Whitman said of these visitors, "though quite certainly not in the ways attempted — which have, at times, something irresistibly comic." Had he Oscar Wilde in mind? Wilde is mentioned in the essay, along with James Anthony Froude, Henry Irving, and others, and while the poet admits it can be "farcical" to see "a worthy gentleman coming three or four thousand miles . . . to speak complacently . . . on matters of which he both entirely mistakes or knows nothing," he nonetheless welcomes and thanks these visitors, even emitting the hearty wish, "and may the procession continue!" For the most part, the procession of visitors who sought Whitman in his Camden retreat, whether in person or by letter, whether eminent or not, found in him a noble heart, for he truly meant it when in this essay he queried, "were they and we to come face to face, how is it possible but that the right understanding would ensue?"[84] Perhaps such a meeting would have prevented Swinburne from turning on Whitman as he did, but given the circumstances of English society at the time it is doubtful.

8

DUBLIN

"love to my friends in Ireland . . ."
Walt Whitman to Alfred Webb

Unfortunately, Walt Whitman never visited Dublin, though he was invited to do so by more than one of his admirers in that city. In 1872 Whitman's good friend John Burroughs wrote to William Michael Rossetti in London and to Edward Dowden at Trinity College, Dublin, suggesting that Whitman make a visit to their cities to offer public readings of his poems. Whitman was "stagnating for want of a change and some wholesome excitement," Burroughs wrote, lending firsthand testimony to the speculation that in this year the poet suffered a physical and emotional decline.

Burroughs saw the ocean voyage and meetings with foreign friends as just the answer. Rossetti seems to have been somewhat horrified at the idea of a public reading, claiming that there was no precedent in England for poets to do so, that actresses did this sort of thing, as did Dickens, who was "enormously popular," but, he pointed out, neither Whitman nor his poems had a following in London sufficient to secure an audience.[1] This response was a disappointment to Burroughs, for he knew there were others in England, besides Rossetti, with whom Whitman would have enjoyed visiting, most notably Tennyson, but also John Addington Symonds, Oscar Wilde, and Anne Gilchrist. After Rossetti's reaction Burroughs was hesitant to pursue the matter.

Edward Dowden's response, however, was quite different from Rossetti's: "the chance of getting Whitman over is one to be valued so much that whether he were to succeed as a reader or not we should be tempted to urge him to come," the young man enthused, adding a reference to his recent lecture on Whitman where the audience was carried away by his reading of the poems.[2] Bram Stoker also was eager to have Whitman come to Ireland and offered the hospitality of his home, as did Alfred Webb in his letter to the poet. With these assurances Whitman's mind was made up, and had his stroke not prevented it he might well have fulfilled the plans he made, not to read his poems but to lecture — on Lincoln, on the men who fought the Civil War, and on democracy.[3] Pleased though he was by the responses of his Irish friends, it was Dowden's proffered hospitality that probably meant the most, since Dowden had the prestige that attached to his profession and to his institution. To literary Americans, being a professor of literature at Trinity was almost as good as being at Oxford, and though he displayed open contempt for scholars, Whitman was delighted to win their appreciation. Dowden had offered his in 1871, though anonymously, in the pages of London's *Westminster Review*, and when his authorship was revealed to Whitman, the poet crowed to Horace Traubel: "Dowden is a confirmed scholar — the people who call my friends ignoramuses, unscholarly, off the streets, cannot quarrel with the equipment of Dowden. Dowden has all the points they insist upon — yet he can tolerate Walt Whitman."[4] What Whitman could not know was that in the formulation yet to be made as to what should constitute modern Irish poetry, the deciding voice would not be Dowden's but Yeats's, who would then represent his country's political writers.

Edward Dowden, born in 1843 of English parents in County Cork, Ireland, had become professor of English literature at Trinity College, Dublin, in 1867, just four years after completing his studies there. In the 1890s he was lecturer at Oxford and Cambridge universities. His *Shakespeare: A Critical Study of His Mind and Art* (1875) established the three time frames in which Shakespeare wrote his plays and remains his finest literary achievement. Among the modern poets, Dowden ranked highest Wordsworth, Shelley (of whom he wrote a book-length study), Browning, and Whitman. Like Robert Buchanan, he saw Swinburne's poems as sensuous, whereas he believed Whitman's contained a spirituality that moved them beyond the physical; like his countryman Standish James O'Grady, Dowden found in Whitman a joyousness born of hope. While they concurred in this and in other literary opinions, Dowden and O'Grady disagreed on a matter of great importance, the essential issue of Irish literature.

Dowden was Anglo-Irish, not only by birth but also in his political and literary opinions. The term "Anglo-Irish," used originally to indicate the English Protestant landowners who came into Ireland as "planters" (farmers) beginning in the mid-sixteenth century, also refers to the literature created by that class, as well as to writing in English by writers of Irish birth. (In recent years, Irish literature is considered literature written in English or Irish, and the word "Anglo" is no longer used.) A man of his class, Dowden supported the union of Ireland and England and would take no part in movements whose aim was Irish independence. His unionist stand led to his refusal to participate in the most important literary movement of his time and place, the Irish literary revival, though he greatly admired some of its outstanding figures.

An earlier Celtic revival dates to about 1762 when the Scotsman James Macpherson produced some bardic "translations," supposedly from Gaelic, the ancient language of Scottish and Irish peoples, including the poem *Fingal*, which he claimed had been written by the Gaelic bard Ossian. Whitman read Macpherson's poems of Ossian on the seashore of his native Long Island and was no doubt moved by them as he was by Scott's Border Minstrelsy. In November 1881, after returning from Boston, we find Whitman quoting from Ossian's poems, perhaps stirred to this remembrance by his enjoyment of the time he had spent in Boston with John Boyle O'Reilly.

The matter of language was of extreme importance to Irish culture and to the literary revivalists. With English the official language of Ireland while England was in power and therefore the language of politics for both unionists and nationalists, the Irish language lost ground. The language of instruction was English and the desire to emigrate to America encouraged English, so the Irish language was more and more restricted to rural areas in the west country. These Irish-speaking areas were especially hard hit by the famines of 1845–1849 because losses by death and emigration were high. As a result, the Irish language was near the point of extinction at midcentury.

Significant support for the Irish language and the literature it produced came from Sir Samuel Ferguson, a contemporary of the constitutional nationalist Daniel O'Connell, who was himself an Irish speaker. A Protestant from northern Ireland who was a nationalist culturally but a unionist politically, Ferguson did not agree with O'Connell's drive for independence because he feared Catholic domination and a decline into cultural insularity. In 1840, while O'Connell was absorbed in efforts for repeal of the Union and on the verge of becoming involved in the American abolitionist movement, Ferguson wrote an essay in the *Dublin University Magazine* that set forth his belief that Ireland must recover its lost heritage of language and literature. Toward that end he collected and published translations of early Irish poems, an important step in the movement toward cultural advance.

Thomas Davis, leader of the Young Ireland movement, also believed in the importance of Irish culture, and though he made it subordinate to the cause of nationalism, it was his hope that a shared culture would overcome geographic and religious divisions. Many years later William Kirkpatrick Magee said that Davis's "proposal to unite Ireland by means of a national culture which should ignore the 'religious question' was a little like proposing to act *Hamlet* without the Prince."[5] When O'Connell's constitutional movement declined, Davis and his colleagues attempted to use Irish songs and ballads as a means to radicalize the Irish people. Oscar Wilde's mother had lent her talents to the Young Irelanders as the songwriter and poet Speranza, and John Boyle O'Reilly was recruited to this cause, which led to his imprisonment, his escape to America, and his eventual friendship with Whitman. To this mix we now add the somewhat improbable combination of the unionist Edward Dowden, with his admiration for the American "poet of democracy," and the man who would become known as the father of the nationalistic Irish literary revival, Standish James O'Grady.

Chronology demands a pause in the story of Dowden and Whitman to establish O'Grady's claim to fatherhood of the nationalist literary movement. As a young man O'Grady chanced upon a history of Ireland by Sylvester O'Halloran, which traced the country's antiquity to a pre-Christian era. This led to further reading and eventually to his writing a two-volume *History of Ireland* (1878–1880), which revivified the historical material by the addition of redactions of Irish myths and legends, especially the narrative of the heroic Cuchulain. O'Grady's history and his *Early Bardic Literature* (1879) — later part of the second volume of the history — inspired some of the young Dublin intellectuals who would become important figures in the literary revival and whose influence would extend to the movement for a national literature headed by William Butler Yeats and Lady Isabella Augusta Gregory. We shall concern ourselves with O'Grady's response to Whitman shortly but must now return to Dowden's.

Within a year of reading Rossetti's edition of selections from *Leaves of Grass*, Dowden obtained a copy of the complete work and sought to place his article, titled "The Poetry of Democracy: Walt Whitman," in *Macmillan's Magazine*. The editor of *Macmillan's* had requested an article of him but on learning its subject rejected it.[6]

Dowden was not only professorial—indeed, he was Ireland's outstanding literary scholar—but evangelistic as well about literature. He began in May 1871 to bring Whitman to the attention of students by reading a paper to the members of Trinity's Philosophical Club, "Walt Whitman and the Poetry of Democracy."[7] His letters also show him eager to share his discovery of the American poet with his brother, John, and others.[8] He was frustrated in his publishing efforts, however, first by *Macmillan's* refusal and then by the withdrawal of a promise of publication in the *Contemporary Review* when the editors found his essay "too alarming."[9] Both refused because they objected to Whitman, not to Dowden. Bravely (there is no other word for it), he sent the article to the *Westminster Review*, one of the most prestigious English periodicals of its time, which in 1860 had dismissed Whitman as "a drunken Helot."[10] Perhaps because the article was by Dowden, or perhaps because in the intervening decade Whitman had not disappeared from the literary scene as it had hoped, the *Review* published the essay anonymously in its July 1871 issue.

This event brings us full circle to the discussion in chapter 1 of Whitman's summer vacation in Brooklyn and New York, when he wrote to Peter Doyle and William Douglas O'Connor about the Orange Riots in New York City. Earlier in the year his first prose volume, *Democratic Vistas*, had been published. In spring Whitman had been enormously cheered to receive from Algernon Charles Swinburne a copy of his new book, *Songs before Sunrise*, which included the homage "To Walt Whitman in America." This, of course, was prior to Swinburne's diagnosis of the disease "Whitmania." In January an article in the Oxford periodical *Dark Blue*, by English critic Roden Noel, bore a similar title to Dowden's, it being "Walt Whitman: The Poet of Modern Democracy." Clearly, the publication of *Democratic Vistas* had stirred a fresh examination of Whitman's poetry as an exemplification of the kind of poetry a democracy could be expected to produce. In essence, then, Dowden's article must be considered as much a political as a literary statement and thus bound to have resonances among the politicized writers of the Irish literary revival of the next two decades.

Dowden begins by establishing that the current critical mode connects literary and political history (though he speaks of the latter in broad terms), but it has failed to apply this methodology to an examination of American literature. A brief review of the major American writers leads him to suggest that the failure stems from the fact that most American literature is too similar to that of Europe to reflect a democratic influence. Interestingly, in light of what would become a dominant question in Ireland under Yeats's influence, Dowden points out that in Longfellow's novel *Kavanagh* (1849), one character demands "a national literature," to which another offers the reminder that "what is best in literature is not national but universal, and is the fruit of refinement and culture."[11] This was the crux of the controversy that would later develop between Dowden and Yeats in the matter of an Irish literature, with Yeats at first drawn to Whitman as a national poet but later rejecting his model and Dowden dismissing the whole idea of literary nationalism.

In discussing Whitman, Dowden does not advocate principles that should be sought in a poem produced in a democratic state; rather, he turns his attention toward the man who has announced himself "with a flourish of critical trumpets as Bard of America, and Bard of democracy" so that it then might be asked: What does a national bard say, and how does he or she say it? Such questions were already taking on grave import in Ireland, and Sir Samuel Ferguson, Standish James O'Grady, and James Clarence Mangan had each offered versions of what he believed exemplified the poetry of the country's ancient Gaelic bards. Soon the question of what constituted a modern national literature, a national poet, a national dramatist, would demand definitions that would embrace such issues as language (English or Gaelic?), subject matter (self or society?), form (ancient or modern?), and audience (nation or world?). While Ireland was not a democracy, having lost even its parliament, the whole topic of its developing a national literature late in the nineteenth century was shadowed by the presence in the world of a new form of government, democracy, which would offer a model different from hitherto existing models created by aristocracies. A crucial question was: If Ireland's literature chose to reject the aristocratic past, should it allow itself to be influenced by the present as represented by democracy?

Dowden had already expressed his welcome of the democratic influence on literature when he addressed the Trinity College Philosophical Club. Referring to a previous speaker's drumroll of literary giants, "Rousseau, Voltaire, Wordsworth, Byron, Coleridge, Shelley, Scott, Dickens, Eliot, Newman"—at which point he paused to note parenthetically, "alas, among them not one Irish name!"—Dowden claimed to have noticed behind these figures "a great shape looming and towering." "What was it?" he asks, then, responding to his own question, "To me it looked like a burly and benevolent giant — the giant Democracy . . . a giant whose horny hand I should like well to shake."[12]

In the essay on Whitman, Dowden first lays out the characteristics of literature created in aristocracies, then, using a broad concept of what he calls "democratic tendencies in art," as in Shelley, lays out the characteristics of a democratic literature. In formulating the latter, he owes much to Whitman's as yet unstated example. Turning then to *Leaves of Grass* as his example of democratic poetry, he finds the most obvious difference to be form, or rather the lack of it, and the appearance of a number of things proscribed in an aristocracy by the demand for an adherence to formal concerns. Further, in the poetry of aristocracy "the common people do not show themselves *en masse* except as they may follow in a patient herd" and, as individuals, are "never objects of equal interest with persons of elevated worldly station." With regard to form, "Walt Whitman can find no authority superior to himself, or rather to the rights of the subject which engages him."

Whatever may be considered formal in Whitman's poetry, Dowden claims, is dictated by the "principle of democracy upon which the democratic form of society is founded." Unlike the selectivity of aristocratic poetry, democratic poetry is inclusive, with all things being equal — "The difference between the President and the Broadway mason or hodman is inconsiderable"— differing only "by quality" (good or evil). Dowden defends Whitman's catalogs on the basis of this need to be democratically inclusive and his self-celebration as a celebration of that which he shares with his fellow Americans. Admitting that the poet speaks of things better left unsaid, he applauds the "conviction" that leads Whitman to include his poems of sexuality and sees the "Calamus" poems "revealing his heart in its weakness and its strength more than any others."

Considering these comments in light of questions having to do with the creation of Ireland's national literature, what we find is that Dowden sees the question of form subsumed into the question of subject matter: "Whitman can find no authority superior to . . . the subject which engages him," he claims, since his subject is individuals of great diversity but of equal interest as himself. The question of language is answered by democracy's acceptance of the past with which it claims kinship, and here Dowden quotes Whitman, "I conn'd old times; / I sat studying at the feet of the great masters: / Now, if eligible, O that the great masters might return and study me!"

As to audience, Dowden sees Whitman's faith in democracy leading from nationalism to his "vision of a common life of the whole human race." Democratic nationalism thus led outward, not into the narrow provincialism Dowden later feared would be the result of an Irish-centered literature.

Dowden's later objection to the writers of the Irish literary revival probably owed much to his expectations for the development of a modern aesthetic in literature that would correspond to what he termed in his essay on Whitman "the larger history of society and the general movement of civilizations, creeds, forms of national life and feeling." The general movement of civilization was toward democracy, he believed, that giant whose hand he wished to shake. The return to Irish myths and legends, to fairy stories and mysticism, that became a large part of the literary revival did not connect modern Ireland to its own time and thus could not claim Dowden's allegiance. In 1895 he would make his stand publicly and irrevocably against the revival by dismissing its aims as irrelevant to modern history.

Dowden's desire for a correspondence between literature and its historic and social milieu is apparent in one of the more interesting features of his essay, the cultural approach (as we now designate the mode) taken throughout, especially in his use of Alexis de Tocqueville's *Democracy in America* (1835–1940) to illuminate the democratic roots that underlie Whitman's thought and work. While he makes no mention of it, Dowden would have read Tocqueville's account of his visit, with Gustave de Beaumont, to Ireland in 1835. Beaumont's *Ireland: Social, Political and Religious* (1839) was an insightful work but, largely owing to Europe's greater interest in the New World's fledgling democratic society, never achieved the fame of Tocqueville's examination of America. In that examination Tocqueville structured his comments on democracy's effect on the writing of poetry along the same lines as Dowden's, that is, by comparing the poetry of aristocracy with what might be expected of a democratic poetry.

Tocqueville's belief was that democracy, by its distaste for the past and its concentration on equality — including the equality of the "ignorant, low, and enslaved"—would rob poetry of both the past and the present, leaving little as poetic subject matter.[13] In a democracy, where all are made insignificant by their commonality, no ideal conception can be made by the poet, he claims. Nonetheless, while he admits that "the Americans have no poets," he is not ready to allow "that they have no poetic ideas." These ideas he sees as fixed on their own trek across the American landscape — "drying swamps, turning the course of rivers, peopling solitudes, and subduing nature." Perhaps most pertinent to Dowden's application of Tocqueville's theories to Whitman's practice of poetry is the French aristocrat's assertion that the poetry of a democratic people "will not be fed with legends or the memorials of old traditions," nor will the democratic poet "attempt to people the universe with supernatural beings in whom his readers and his own fancy have ceased to believe."

This alone, had Dowden quoted it, would have been a rebuke of Ferguson, O'Grady, and Yeats, who sought to revive Irish legendry and heroic myths. Moreover, had he chosen to quote him, Tocqueville's final word on what he believed would be the subject of democratic poetry would have left little doubt that Whitman, alone in his country and in his time, fulfilled the prophecy:

> All these resources [of aristocratic poetry] fail him; but Man remains, and the poet needs no more. The destinies of mankind — man himself, taken aloof from his country and his age, and standing in the presence of Nature and of God, with his passions, his doubts, his rare propensities and inconceivable wretchedness — will become the chief, if not the sole, theme of poetry amongst these nations.

Tocqueville's enthusiasm for American democracy was tempered by his judicious common sense, especially with regard to the growing masses in America and the threatening potential for their forming a tyrannous majority. Like Tocqueville, Dowden points out, Whitman also sees the dark side of democracy, for evidence of which Dowden turns to *Democratic Vistas*. He quotes at length from that work, beginning at the point where Whitman says, "After an absence, I am now (September, 1870) again in New York City and Brooklyn, on a few weeks' vacation." Whitman goes on to decry the apparent lack of individuals worthy of the works of nature and of the people in these great cities, asking finally: "Is there a great moral and religious civilization — the only justification of a great material one?" But, as Dowden says, "in spite of all that he discerns of evil in democratic America, Whitman remains . . . a believer who does not waver in his democratic faith." Then, getting perhaps to the root of Whitman's distrust of religion and its institutions, he points out that this faith rebels at systems of religions and philosophies, for when one is possessed of faith in democracy and "a vision of a common life of the whole human race has filled the imagination . . . the mind seems to shrink in horror from the suspicion that the final purposes of God or nature, with respect to man, can be other than beneficent."

Perhaps it was statements such as this last one that made the article too dangerous, and after Dowden had rejections from two periodicals he sent the piece to William Michael Rossetti seeking comments and advice on publication. Rossetti responded positively but thought it unjust of Dowden to find fault with Whitman for what Dowden perceived as shortcomings in the poet's philosophy. In his essay Dowden quotes Whitman's Preface to *Leaves of Grass* that "the flawless triumph of art" occurs in literature when the poet speaks "with the perfect rectitude and insouciance of the movements of animals, and the unimpeachableness of the sentiment of trees in the woods, and grass by the roadside." While admitting to the "deep truth in this," Dowden argues "it must be added that, when the poet broods over his half-formed creation," giving it shape and form, "he does not forsake his instincts, but is obedient to them."[15]

Dowden, of course, was exercising critical judgment, but Rossetti found the criticism unfair; he pointed out to the young Irishman that Whitman was a "daemonic man" and therefore could only be expected to utter "his own vision of truth." Dowden defended himself by clearly stating what he perceived as an "error" in Whitman's theory: "That error, as it presents itself to me, is an exclusion of self-consciousness from Nature, and all that proceeds from self-consciousness; whereas Nature really includes self-consciousness." It was matters such as these that kept Dowden, the literary critic, from the kind of passionate commitment Whitman expected of his admirers. With no hesitation Dowden told Rossetti "what [he] would grow passionate for," a philosophy of nature that unites conscious activity with an unconscious energy to create the highest accomplishment in art and life.[16]

From the outset these reservations did not go unnoticed. In the same letter of July 14, 1871, in which Whitman gave William Douglas O'Connor his account of the Orange Riots and commented favorably on the New York police, he mentions the unsigned article in the *Westminster Review*, declaring it "rather quiet in tone, but essentially very favorable and appreciative."[17] The *Review* no doubt sent an advance copy of the July issue to Whitman, for it was too soon for him to have received the copy sent on July 9 by Rossetti. Had he received it and Rossetti's enclosing letter, he would have been especially delighted to inform O'Connor that Rossetti believed the writer of the piece to be the Irish scholar Edward Dowden.

Whitman wrote to Rossetti that he would like to know the author of the "profound and eloquent essay," saying he "was proud to be the subject of it."[18] Not long after, confirmation of the author's identity arrived in the form of Dowden's first letter to Whitman, dated July 23, 1871. Dowden half-apologized for the tone of his essay, explaining its low tone was deliberate and meant to counter the prejudices of some. To John Todhunter, another Whitman admirer at Trinity, Dowden later explained that his low tone was

> partly because for my own sake I have to assume a cool, somewhat nonchalant way of talking about things and people I love to any third person. It seems less inadequate than a middle way of praise and love would be; and to say the whole truth would be neither profitable nor possible. If A would very contentedly accept annihilation to do B a little good, A had better say something quite commonplace and usual. And in like manner I kept a prudent mask of common sense over my face (which in reality flushes, and pales more than a strong or sober person's might) while discoursing to the Fortnightly folk of Walt.[19]

The full-hearted outpouring to which Dowden here refers was of the type Whitman had come to expect from his "lovers," as he called his admirers, and would have better satisfied him than the cool tone and masked face, the latter even suggesting a reason for the anonymity maintained in publication.

Dowden's comments to Todhunter indicate his awareness of the political power of language, especially as he had let it be known that he considered Whitman the model of what a democratic system will produce as poetry. With his admiration for Whitman already cast in a political frame, he chooses to restrain his own enthusiasm and present his theme in the dispassionate language of reasoned discourse. It is, however, rather startling to see the possibility he suggests, that "A's" (Dowden's) reputation could suffer "annihilation" for "B's" (Whitman's) sake, and hence the advisability of holding back. The suggestion is made all the more startling by the postscript:

> The Clown, you know, brought in his "pretty worm of Nilus" under fig-leaves. So I with Walt — "Truly I have him; but I would not be the party that had you touch him, for his biting is immortal; those that do die of it, do seldom or never recover."

The allusion to act 5 of Shakespeare's *Antony and Cleopatra* is humorous, but lurking behind the humor is a suggestion of real danger to the scholarly reputations of these two Trinity College professors should they be too open in their admiration of Whitman. As it turned out, Dowden may have been prescient, for in 1882, after the sixth edition of *Leaves of Grass* had been suppressed in Boston, he presented a copy of *Leaves* to the Trinity College Library, which returned it because of objections raised by Joseph S. Galbraith, a Fellow of Trinity College.[20] The *New York Tribune* reported the story on August 15 of that year, and O'Connor wrote informing Whitman of the refusal, adding, "It was in Dublin, either at this College or the University, that Tyrrell lectured on you, glorifying the book they now proscribe. 'So runs the world away.'"[21] According to Bram Stoker, at about this time the college even threatened to withdraw its patronage from the local bookseller, named McGee, the only Dublin source from whom the complete *Leaves* could be had.[22] Dowden commented in his diary, "Better also withdraw Aeropagitica from the Course!"[23]

Stoker gives us a humorous glimpse of Trinity College students reacting to the notoriety that attached to *Leaves of Grass*: "Needless to say that amongst young men the objectionable passages were searched for and more noxious ones expected. For days we all talked of Walt Whitman and the new poetry with scorn — especially those of us who had not seen the book."[24] When Stoker did obtain a copy, from a student who felt he had had enough of "the damned thing," he immediately became "a lover of Walt Whitman." A few years later the librarian of the National Library of Ireland, William Archer, had to defend himself against an accusation of having prohibited reader access to *Leaves of Grass*, a charge he heatedly denied in the *Dublin University Review*.[25]

The story of the Trinity College Library suppression has one hopeful tag. By 1886 the Rossetti edition of *Poems of Walt Whitman*, which had done so much to win Whitman a following in the British Isles, was no longer in print. Richard William Colles (1862–1919), the Irish writer better known as Ramsay Colles, was bitterly disappointed to learn of this because he had lost his only copy. Taking it upon himself to write to the publisher and to Rossetti about the matter, Colles was instrumental in having another printing issued. In his reminiscenses he describes the volume as "a handsome edition in buckram."[26] Then, having heard that Whitman was in need, Colles wrote to him suggesting the raising of funds among Irish friends and admirers. Whitman replied that he would "accept anything which you and my Irish friends care to give" but pointed out that Dowden "must not be approached, as he has already been most generous." "Take leisure and ease about it," Whitman advised of the subscription effort, "and let it be large or small, or naught at all, if Destiny so decide."[27] Colles claimed to have written to many friends. When none responded, he sent two pounds, promising to make it an annual sum. Whitman chose to consider the gift as a book order and mailed off copies of *Leaves of Grass* and *Two Rivulets* for the sum, which Colles much appreciated; until the poet's death he continued to send two pounds annually with Whitman acknowledging each gift with books, so that at Whitman's death Colles sold the autographed volumes to the National Library of Ireland. He also sold copies of *Leaves* and *Specimen Days* to the provost of Trinity College, Dublin. It is to be hoped, given Dowden's futile attempt to do so, that the provost was able to place these in the college library, but Colles says nothing more on the matter.

Dowden did come in for harsh criticism from some quarters for his admiration of Whitman. In 1877 he published a book of critical essays, *Studies in Literature*, which included his essay on Whitman. A reviewer in the *Spectator* took him severely to task, warning that "some portion of the contempt" felt for "that shallow and bumptious writer [Whitman] must inevitably seem to recoil on his own exaggerated laudation of an author who is our special aversion."[28] *John Bull's* reviewer regretted finding "so accomplished a writer falling a victim to that absurd culture of Walt Whitman, which has, in certain quarters, almost assumed the dimensions of an unhealthy literary epidemic."[29] This sounds like a harbinger of Swinburne's language in "Whitmania" in the 1887 *Fortnightly Review* and might have had serious implications for Dowden had he been, in fact, part of the William Michael Rossetti group in London when Swinburne issued his rebuke. As it was, though Dowden played the role in Dublin that Rossetti played in London by promoting the sale of Whitman's books, he was far removed from the possibility of being included in Swinburne's diatribe.

Swinburne's objections to Whitman's delineations of the female (his Eve and Venus) also seem to have been anticipated at a meeting of the Fortnightly Club in Dublin when Dowden and Stoker were present. Dowden wrote to Whitman simply that the poet had been the subject of the meeting, but Stoker gives us a more detailed picture. The unidentified speaker of the evening is said to have been a man of some social standing in his county, a good scholar of the classics and of English literature, and a brilliant humorist. Apparently, he turned on Whitman's "Children of Adam" all of these attributes, delivering a clever but devastating attack that culminated with a challenge to readers to find in the entire collection "mention of one decent woman." Dowden then delivered what Stoker calls "an impassioned speech" (though Dowden, it will be recalled, claimed to Todhunter that he wore a "prudent mask" when addressing the club on Whitman) and took up the speaker's challenge by reading the lines from "Faces" that describe the Quaker mother.[30]

No doubt Whitman would have been pleased to hear Dowden's "impassioned speech," if such it was. He once told Traubel that "Dowden does not melt himself and melt me . . . he is more stiffly literary" but seems later to have come to an understanding of Dowden's position. In 1888 he may have been defining Dowden's method to himself as much as to Traubel when he said that Dowden "seems to maintain a fine balance: judicial—looking both sides, not hurrying to decisions." Then, perhaps at seeing a smile on Traubel's face, he hastened to add, "I know you may say I don't always talk like this: that I love O'Connor for doing exactly the opposite thing: so I do: I like William to do what he does, I like Dowden for doing what he must do."[31] At other times he pointed out that Dowden had "trained himself against effusiveness" and once claimed Dowden wrote in the manner of literary critics who say, "Keep your fires hot but don't keep them so hot they will burn you."[32]

A comparison of Whitman's reactions to the appraisals of Dowden and John Addington Symonds reveals something of the attraction he felt for the latter in spite of his professed annoyance at Symonds's persistent questioning of the "Calamus" poems. He told Traubel:

Dowden is not the very best but he is next to the very best. I suppose Symonds must always be first: his loyalty takes such an ardent personal form: it has not the literary tang, except incidentally. I never feel quite as close by when Dowden is around: there always seems to be something or other left between us—some qualifying no: with Symonds everything is down—we are face to face.[33]

Whitman liked Symonds's "ardent personal form," so long as it did not amount to what he considered an invasion of his privacy, at which point not *everything* was "down." Symonds tested Whitman's patience beyond the breaking point in 1890 by pressing for an explanation of "Calamus" that would support erotic same-sex love.

Whitman told him such a construction placed on the poems was "terrible" and, in an obvious attempt to distance himself from the issue of same-sex attachments, went on to make the extravagant claim of having fathered no less than six illegitimate children.[34] Dowden would never have crossed the line of privacy in such a way, but while Whitman valued this reticence he yet wished for a greater show of ardency, which he would soon attempt to provoke.

It was the latter part of August 1871 before Whitman responded to Dowden's letter admitting authorship of the *Westminster Review* piece. His response was a four-sentence acknowledgment of, but no comment on, the essay and some photographs. (After seeing the photos Dowden described Whitman as "an old man with a very beautiful face [who] looks older than he actually is.")[35] He did, however, ask to hear more of "Mr. Tyrrell" whom Dowden had mentioned.[36] Perhaps Whitman was more impressed by the fact that Robert Yelverton Tyrrell was, as Dowden had told him, a Fellow of Trinity College (an impressive title to the American's ears) and a Greek scholar who had given a public lecture in Dublin on Whitman. In February 1876 Dowden wrote to Whitman making reference to "Abraham Stoker, who writes to you," commenting, "He has told you perhaps of a very lively debate we had at our Fortnightly Club on The Genius of Walt Whitman last Monday evening Feb. 14th."[37] Dowden either believed Stoker had regular correspondence with Whitman or was referring to the letter Stoker wrote immediately after the meeting in which he enclosed his earlier, unposted letter written in 1872. Dowden describes the meeting, which opened with what he says was "a most savage, but ill-planned speech which consisted in the main of apt selections from L. of G. and Democratic Vistas."[38] To his surprise and satisfaction, "speaker after speaker [followed] on the Whitman side — a barrister, a young clergyman [Dowden's brother, John], a man in business, and others" all of whom defended the American poet. "The result was on the whole," Dowden concludes, "highly satisfactory," adding that it was "the second evening occupied by you during the present season."[39] Whitman's cause was clearly gaining adherents in Ireland.

Some of these adherents published homages to Whitman in a college literary magazine, *Kottabos*, edited by Tyrrell. These "Poems Written in Discipleship" include two "of the School of Walt Whitman" by John Todhunter. A footnote claims these are "in no sense parodies, but intend to be affectionate studies or sketches in the manner of some of the masters of song." "A Proem," however, can hardly be seen as anything but parody, affectionate though it no doubt was. Strangely, it moves from what appears to be burlesque,

> I am come — he you was inquiring for a moment ago.
> Did anyone tell you I was well and hearty, and without disease?
> I say to you I am on the contrary full of diseases — a lazar —
> I confess to you I have but just now risen from a sick bed:
> (But I am not for that reason to be shunted as of no account in
>   the world . . .

to an outright imitation of Whitman's poetic style:

> Sublime passion of death,
> O august solitudes of death, O aloneness of gradual dying!
> O shock of sudden changes, abrupt, dreadful, delirious,
> O rendering up of the self!
> . . . .
> I trust myself to you, O ages, to you, O non-existent divine
>   potentialities
> Of happiness, blissfulness, life-fulness — the serene something
>   beyond![40]

Todhunter, originally a medical doctor who turned to literature, later proved himself a better poet, though not a great one, in *The Banshee and Other Poems* (1889). When Yeats reviewed this book he pointed to the title poem, "The Banshee," calling it "a noble chant over the sorrows of Ireland" and claiming its "wild, irregular verses" were "something between Walt Whitman and the Scotch Ossian." While not much can be said of its debt to Ossian, the resemblance to Whitman's "Old Ireland" is unmistakeable. Todhunter images Ireland as an aged mother of many children "exiled and dead," whom the poet comforts in the final verse:

> Wail no more, lonely one, mother of exiles, wail no more,
> Banshee of the world — no more!
> Thy sorrows are the world's, thou art no more alone;
> Thy wrongs the world's.[41]

Also to be found in Trinity College's *Kottabos* is Thomas W. H. Rolleston, the student of Edward Dowden who would undertake a great effort at translation on Whitman's behalf. Here he is represented by his poem "On Walt Whitman's 'Leaves of Grass.'" There is no hint of parody or of imitation to be found, only a heartfelt admiration:

> Bring her no crowns of jewell'd gold —
> Such the Republic may not wear —
> Nor summer flowers whose leaves unfold
> Rich fragrance to the languid air!
> But thou hast woven a coronal
> More meet to deck her brows than all
> That ever rested there;
> Thy wreath of grass is fitter far
> Than fairest flowers or jewels are.[42]

Dowden had an opportunity to meet one of Whitman's closest friends in December 1871 when John Burroughs traveled to England and Ireland to meet Whitman's admirers. Burroughs described Dowden as "a grave, serious young man of English descent, but of Irish birth and brogue, and I like him immensely, and his wife — a cultivated, enthusastic Irish woman — also."[43] After reading the copy Burroughs sent him of his *Notes on Walt Whitman, As Poet and Person* (1867), Dowden fell into a disparagement of his own essay on Whitman, expressing the belief "that such an official, inhuman way of looking at Whitman . . . is little fruitful compared with the more personal relation which your book originates from. The vital nourishing contact with a great man is with his personality, not with the man 'attenuated to an aspect' (J. H. Newman's phrase)."[44] Burroughs kindly reminded the young man of his long association with Whitman, which allowed him a closer, more personal perspective.

When Dowden wrote again to Whitman in September 1871 he provided some details of the Dublin Whitmanites. They included his brother, John, a clergyman; Elizabeth West, one of his students who became his second wife; John Todhunter, author of the previously quoted poem in homage to Whitman and later of a *Study of Shelley* (1880), where he claims as the three great poets of democracy Shelley, Hugo, and Whitman; artist John Butler Yeats, father of the poet William and the painter Jack; Edwin Ellis, an artist like Yeats with whom he shared a London studio; John Nettleship, an artist and literary scholar; and Standish James O'Grady, whose name lives today mainly for his position as "the father of the Irish Literary Revival."[45]

O'Grady, whom Dowden once pronounced "an aristocratic-democrat or democratic-aristocrat" (he wasn't sure which) published an essay in 1875 that seemed to take its impetus from Dowden's comment on the hopefulness of Whitman's poetry, though its tone was lighter and more enthusiastic than Dowden's.[46] Titled "Walt Whitman: The Poet of Joy," the piece appeared in the *Gentleman's Magazine* in December 1875 under the name Arthur Clive. The essay declared Whitman a poet who brings "happiness and delight in this our sublunary existence." He is "unceasingly gay, and fresh, and racy," speaking of the common things of everyday life, "and yet he is always artistic."[47] Whitman responded warmly, telling Dowden the article "dwells on *what I like to have dwelt on*," and sent a photo of himself to Arthur Clive in care of the magazine.[48] He learned the author's true identity from William Michael Rossetti, but O'Grady himself did not write to Whitman until 1881.

In his essay O'Grady associated the "Calamus" poems with that "capacity for friendship of a most absorbing and passionate character [as the] Greeks were well acquainted with," but unlike Symonds he saw nothing in them to question. In 1890 O'Grady's essay came to hand in Whitman's Camden room, and the poet urged Traubel to read it if he had not already done so. By this time Whitman had found a point on which he disagreed with O'Grady: "One of his great points," he told Traubel, "is that Walt Whitman, though the poet of democracy, is received, can be received, only by the cultured few, an inner circle: that the masses can never be expected to compass him."[49]

This claim had been made by others, Edmund Clarence Stedman for one, and always caused Whitman to feel some resentment. Of O'Grady's assertion he said, "But I know, I see better than that the measure, capacity (if it has any at all) of 'Leaves of Grass.'"[50] His resentment at these claims, as well as at another of Stedman's that Whitman brought up at this time — that Whitman had "snubbed the collegiate"—was born of his conflicted desire to be approved both by the masses and by educated scholars while at the same time claiming to have no regard for the opinions of the latter. Perhaps it was this lack of regard for scholarship that prevented Whitman from reading O'Grady's *History of Ireland: Critical and Philosophical*, which the author sent him in 1881, the year of its publication. When O'Grady wrote to Whitman in October of that year he directed the American's attention to the work and, acknowledging Whitman's interest (expressed in *Democratic Vistas*) in the Niebelungen Saga, offered his belief that "Cuculain [*sic*] our primitive Irish hero" was the equal of any of the heroes of the Niebelungen Lied, "but English literature has the ear of the world and wilfully ignores everything of the kind."[51] He went on to mention his earlier two volumes of Irish history and his re-creation of the Cuchulain myth, then paid Whitman a high compliment, "I dare say like most men but for you I would have swung round to the theory of strong governments, an aristocratic ruling class, etc."[52] This was a memorable tribute coming as it did in the year that marks the start of the Irish literary revival, the span of which is generally accepted as 1881 to 1921.

Whitman's problem was that he did not understand this kind of national literary movement with its focus on the past rather than, as his had always been, on the future. Furthermore, he did not know how to "read" these erudite young Irishmen who, with their vast knowledge of literature and history, were so unlike the enthusiastic, often uneducated, Irish Americans and who did not succumb to discipleship.[53] He was unable to reconcile the classicism of the Irish scholars with their nationalism, their erudition with their ready acceptance of his "b'hoyism." To Traubel he confessed that such men surprised him — "almost upset my applecart," was his colloquialism — continuing, "it seems natural for men like O'Connor, like [Robert] Ingersoll, to like me: they are my own kind through and through: but those other fellows have been trained in other schools — as a rule we expect, in fact get, other things from them."[54]

There is no evidence that Whitman read the book O'Grady sent, and in 1888 when he turned over O'Grady's letter to Traubel neither of them seemed aware of the Irish writer's importance to the movement for a national Irish literature. "Where was Standish O'Grady now?" Traubel asked, "Did he get diverted?"[55] To Traubel anything other than the Whitman cause would be a "diversion." "Possibly," Whitman responded, adding, "he does not seem to have kept me on his list. The young fellows come — the old men go — often, often: they serve an apprenticeship with me, in their youth, when they are getting their roots well in the soil — then they die, maybe become professional, adopt institutions, find that Walt Whitman will no longer do."[56]

In this Whitman was partially correct, for O'Grady, and William Butler Yeats as well, did take him up in their youth and did draw inspiration from him; they did not, however, "adopt institutions" but strove instead to create national institutions based on Ireland's cultural past. As has already been pointed out, it was a struggle in which Edward Dowden refused to participate, despite his admiration for its foremost proponents. For Dowden there was no great change wrought by reading Whitman; at most, he turned Whitman to fit his own notion of a "democratic-aristocrat" who might combine the best of both systems.

It is regrettable that Whitman, who longed to wield a lasting effect on literary development, did not see the significance of O'Grady's tribute or catch the implication of his statement, "I find as I change I cannot so change as that I do not meet in you the expression of every changing ideal."[57] What Whitman could not accept was the note of finality in O'Grady's letter, which clearly signaled the writer's commitment to his national cause rather than to a Whitmanian discipleship: "Farewell," O'Grady wrote, "Know that there are many in the 'ancestor continents' of whom towards you might be said what was sung of our Irish hero Cuculain meeting his friend, 'He poured forth a torrent of friendly welcome and affection.'"[58]

A few years after writing this, the extent of Whitman's effect on O'Grady could be gauged by the political stance he took in *Toryism and the Tory Democracy* (1886). Here O'Grady backed the "Tory Democracy" advocated by Lord Randolph Churchill, who sought to displace English Toryism and supplant it with a movement that would bring together workers and capitalists who would, he hoped, prove a force against the landed aristocracy in both England and Ireland.

While O'Grady never became part of the Irish National Land League, he believed the landlord system in Ireland had outlived its time, except — and this was a big exception — if the landlord would be willing to return to his estate and employ Irishmen to work it. Under such a plan the landlord would be directly responsible for the well-being of these workers, who would in turn owe him loyalty. The model for this was a feudal one, which O'Grady freely acknowledged, and his advocacy of it thrust him into the rearmost ranks of the nationalist movement. Clearly his studies of ancient Ireland, while they had produced a literature that served its people, had also clouded his perspective. O'Grady faded from the public consciousness to such an extent that his work soon was little known in Ireland and almost not at all beyond its borders, making Whitman's and Traubel's ignorance of him understandable.

Another of Dowden's Dublin friends who shared his love of *Leaves of Grass* was Bertram Dobell, printer, bookseller, and general man of letters who at times helped Dowden with his research needs. In 1885 Dowden urged Dobell to reprint the essays on Whitman written by the English poet James Thomson.[59] *Walt Whitman: The Man and The Poet* did not appear until 1910 and then reprinted only part of what Thomson, best remembered as the author of "The City of Dreadful

Night," had written. The book consisted of two essays, one of which appeared in the *National Reformer* in 1874 and another from *Cope's Tobacco Plant* for 1881–1882. *Cope's* was discontinued before the entire series of essays appeared, and the remaining portions are lost. While Thomson concentrated on the man and his personality more than on the poetry, Dobell's preface directed attention to the latter.

After concluding that Whitman's outlook on life was "the kind of counsel needed by the average man to guide him through the trials, temptations, and perplexities of life," Dobell entered into a comparison of the poems of Whitman and the seventeenth-century poet Thomas Traherne, a study of whom he had recently completed.[60] The main point of his comparison is a rather shallow reference to their shared optimism: "Like Whitman, Traherne was a thorough optimist and could or would see nothing wrong in the constitution of the world."[61]

While this observation may seem facile, one cannot help but note the emphasis placed by a number of Whitman's early admirers in Ireland on his hopeful, optimistic, even joyful outlook. It seems to have answered a need (perhaps postfamine?) among them for something to offset the "doleful prophets," as O'Grady called Ruskin, Carlyle, and the romantic poets of England; in fact, Dowden, when he sought to encourage Whitman to visit Ireland in 1872, claimed, "We think that *you* are just the communicator of vitality and joy that *we* require." Indeed, a twentieth-century critic has identified Whitman's joyousness as rooted "in a world without tabus" and sees it as the principle informing what he believes to be Yeats's central debt to Whitman, his ability to write a poetry of the body that manages to include not only Whitman's joy and vitality but the sense of guilt Yeats could not throw off.[62]

It was not until January 1872 that Whitman saw fit to respond at length to Dowden's first letter, and when he did he attempted to lay the groundwork for what he was later able to make into a small international uproar. Whitman expressed his approval of the *Westminster Review* article and expounded upon its main point, *Leaves of Grass* as a model for a democratic poetry, by elaborating on it and defining *Leaves* as a "model or ideal . . . of a complete healthy, heroic, practical modern *Man* . . . a grander better son, brother, husband, father, friend, citizen than any yet."[63] Almost immediately after drawing this ideal figure, Whitman asks Dowden to be mindful of any occasion for publication that may arise; complains of the neglect he claims to suffer in the United States from "sneering" editors, publishers, critics, and an uncaring public, the opposition of "a large majority"; and insists that he was "turned out of a small government employment and deprived of his means of support by a Head of Department at Washington solely on account of having written his poems."[64] He writes this on the letterhead of the Solicitor's Office, Treasury Department, Washington, D.C., where he was then employed, perhaps unaware of the contradiction it implies and possibly hoping for a surge of anti-governmental anger of the type his friend William Douglas O'Connor had displayed at the time of the dismissal.[65] As Whitman already intuited, however, Dowden was a very different type; he was, in fact, an upholder of the English government who favored the continuance of the Anglo-Irish Union and not one to initiate the tumult Whitman seems to have been seeking.

Whitman had better luck in 1876 when he sent William Michael Rossetti the same request, along with a newspaper article that he had planted in the *West Jersey Press*. The article made the same claims of neglect Whitman earlier had directed to Dowden. Rossetti set about enlisting others in the cause, and together they wrote to London newspapers excoriating the American public for its shabby treatment of their national bard. When there were protests from some Americans and denials of Whitman's dire condition, Whitman backtracked by claiming he was able to support himself — or, as he put it, "keep the wolf from the door" — by the sale of his books, a statement that did much to improve their sale among his friends in Europe. In Dublin Dowden collected orders for books from among his literary friends, which he then relayed to Whitman in New Jersey. Between this source and the number of students to whom Dowden introduced *Leaves of Grass*, Whitman saw such an increase in orders from Ireland that he commented to Peter Doyle, "it is funny how many of my books are sent for from Ireland."[66]

A review of Whitman's actions about the time of this international furor indicates a degree of emotional instability, which he himself admitted at a later point. The year 1872, when he wrote the self-pitying letter to Dowden, a relative newcomer in his circle of friends, is the same year in which he broke with O'Connor — though each man seems to have borne a share of responsibility for that event. It was the year before Whitman's major stroke, which may explain his instability, for he was suffering from hypertension. Later, in 1888, he referred to his promulgation abroad of the belief that he was in penury. He indicated to Traubel his appreciation for what had been done by his friends in England (among whom he included Dowden) by saying that at such times "all the little irritations disappear in the stronger note of the affections."[67] Then he continued,

> When I look back over that period — well, it was all sad enough (glad enough, too): I was down, down, physically down, my outlook was clouded: the appearance of that English group seemed like a flash out of heaven. I never felt like reproaching anyone here — why should I? . . . The people here owed me nothing: why should I have presented a bill for goods the people did not order?[68]

One thing that resulted from the furor was Whitman's increased appreciation of Dowden. Years later he said of him to Traubel, "Dowden: dear man — truly steadfast through the thick and thin of my darker days: I have got to sort o' look to him for good will."[69] This feeling of gratitude was only surpassed, perhaps, by the deep emotion Whitman experienced at reading one of Dowden's earliest letters, written in 1871, the year of his *Westminster Review* article. Dowden concluded the letter by acknowledging not only the powerful attraction felt by Whitman's admirers but also the way in which the poet shunned robbing the mind "of its independence"; "you make no slaves, however many lovers," Dowden concluded. "Dowden has divined the whole secret," Whitman told Traubel, who was himself one of the "many lovers." "I have seen many defections," Whitman once told Traubel, perhaps with Swinburne in mind, "Dowden is still haunting the corridors."[70]

In 1882 Dowden reviewed *Specimen Days and Collect* in *Academy*, finding it "sweet and sane and nourishing."[71] His admiration for Whitman also led him to extend himself toward others elsewhere who shared it. He reviewed favorably Bucke's biography of Whitman, *Walt Whitman* (1883), and edited a portion of the "Contemporaneous Notices," "English Critics on Walt Whitman," which appeared in the Glasgow edition of Bucke's work in 1884. Ever true to his own lights, Dowden states at the outset of this survey that his estimate of "Whitman's position in literature" differs in important aspects from that of Bucke and points out that some of the writers who are quoted qualify their admiration for Whitman in ways, "sometimes gravely, sometimes smilingly expressed." In addition to the many laudatory excerpts, Dowden includes one from Peter Bayne's attack as well as some that reveal a lesser degree of scepticism. On the positive side, O'Grady, Todhunter, Rolleston, and Dowden are quoted, and reference is made to Tyrrell's public lecture in Dublin, the text of which was not available then, nor has it ever come to light. The only other Irish critic quoted seems to be Fitzgerald Molloy, from the essay "Walt Whitman" in *Modern Thought* for September 1882. As did other Irish critics, Molloy finds that "the most striking feature of his poems is the wonderful buoyant sense of delight he feels in all things — a healthy manly enjoyment of life and all that life holds."[72]

Among the students in whom Dowden inspired a love of Whitman was Thomas William Hazen Rolleston, whose poem in Whitman's honor appeared in *Kottabos* and who undertook a great project in the furtherance of Whitman's cause, a translation of *Leaves of Grass* into German. Rolleston founded and for a time edited the *Dublin University Review*; wrote poetry and a book of Irish myths and legends; published translations from Latin, Greek, and German; and in 1900 edited *A Treasury of Irish Poetry*. Though born in Ireland, he lived with his wife and children in Dresden, Germany, for a number of years, returning frequently to his Irish residence but for the most part behaving much like one of the Anglo-Irish absentee landlords. When he returned permanently to Ireland, he became active in the literary revival and considered Yeats a good friend.

Once introduced to *Leaves of Grass*, Rolleston developed a rich appreciation for the work and was delighted to meet a fellow enthusiast, Standish O'Grady. The two went hiking together, an occasion that called forth Rolleston's poem "March 24th 1881," in which he declared,

> —And ever as we went, there hover'd near us another spirit,
> sometimes unseen, oftener between us, holding a hand
> of each,
> For the power of the mountains was on us that day, and the
> power of the Sea, and of Walt Whitman, poet of
> comrades.[73]

Rolleston also introduced some of his friends to Whitman's poetry. One of these, John Fitzgerald Lee, a native of County Galway, was a Russian-language scholar living in Dresden where he had many friends who were Russian exiles. Lee wrote to Whitman in 1881 seeking permission to translate *Leaves of Grass* into Russian. Nothing came of the idea because Lee received a government appointment in London, taking him from the friends who would have assisted in the translation, but Whitman's enthusiastic endorsement produced a warm address to the Russian people, which he suggested Lee use as a preface.[74]

Another friend of Rolleston who became aware of Whitman while a student at Trinity was William Wilkins, author of *Songs of Study* (1881) and a contributor to *Kottabos*. Wilkins's poetry has long since faded from view, but it provides an instance of Rolleston's somewhat questionable literary judgment. In February 1882, after hearing from Whitman of his visit with Oscar Wilde, Rolleston wrote: "So you have had a visit from the Aesthete!"[75] He told Whitman of having met Wilde "once or twice" while at Trinity, where his "presences and talk exercised an extraordinary fascination" on him so that he felt he "would have done anything for him." But his poetry he found "entirely worthless — dead and artificial — not even good singing."[76] Rolleston then suggests Whitman look for the poetry of Wilkins, who he says "has only a limited range and he's not always sincere and is often affected" but who he insists finds "real dash and life about him and that a page of him is worth all Oscar Wilde's poetry put together."[77] After his one volume, Wilkins's poetic career seems to have met the same fate as Lee's Russian translation.

Shortly after his hiking trip with O'Grady, Rolleston initiated a correspondence with Whitman, and in September 1881 he wrote proposing a German translation. Seeing in this offer another opportunity to gain an international audience, Whitman gave his immediate approval but suggested that the text appear in both German and English. He later rescinded this, after hearing Rolleston's concern for the increased cost it would involve, but he insisted that the work be complete. This was not to be, however, for despite his earnest efforts and the assistance of a German collaborator, Karl Knortz, *Grashalme*, completed in 1884 but not published until 1889, was only a partial translation of *Leaves*. Rolleston also undertook at least one critical study of Whitman, in which he hailed him as "this Yankee the world-poet of the age" and which he delivered as a lecture in Dresden in 1883.[78]

Rolleston's letters to Whitman written from Ireland contain his reactions to events in that country, especially the activities of the Land League and its rent strike. In January 1881 he mentions the lack of agrarian violence in the country, which he attributes, negatively, to the iron rule of the Land League whose dictates he claims no one dares transgress on fear of death.[79] He sent Whitman a copy of a letter he had written to the Home Rule and Catholic newspaper, the *Freeman's Journal*, protesting the rent strike, and also a report of a speech by John Dillon, an Irish nationalist and officer in the league, advocating such strikes against any landowner who did not support the league's cause.[80] Rolleston assured Whitman that to his mind Michael Davitt, founder of the Land League, was an honorable man but was also "well-known to be a rebel," which Rolleston feared would ultimately undermine the league's objectives.[81] Whitman, reading these letters and their enclosures, would have been particularly interested because of John Boyle O'Reilly's heavy involvement in the American Land League, but there is no record of his reaction. Under the influence of William Butler Yeats and John O'Leary, Rolleston was soon to become more politically radical, evidently with Whitman quietly sharing his nationalistic sentiments.[82]

Whitman's extant letters to Rolleston do not touch on Irish matters, but in 1888 Traubel read aloud to him a Rolleston letter of November 1883 in which the young man asserted that if Whitman could but live for a time in Ireland "and see this sensitive, keen-sighted, but helpless nation dragged about in the clumsy lurches of English opportunism," he would wish the Irish "Godspeed." At this point Whitman interjected, "I do wish you, I did wish you, Godspeed, God knows, Rolleston: yes I did, do, out of my whole body and soul!" Traubel then read another letter, of August 1884, which confined itself to matters pertaining to the translation Rolleston was working on. After hearing it read, Whitman, who clearly connected the translation of his poems to the cause of worldwide republicanism, told Traubel, "Rolleston is a sort of republican: has no notion for kings: looks ahead: sees the Empire crumbling: all that. Then he is for a free Ireland: so am I and for a free every country. If I had my way I would break down the last barrier between nations — abolish the last separatist law."[83]

The more Rolleston advocated his country's cause, the more Whitman loved him for it and for demonstrating that kind of fire he had come to associate with the Irish and which he found so lacking in Dowden. "Rolleston has the Irish spirit," he told Traubel, "is fiery, strong, vehement, uncompromising."[84] But Rolleston had not always been so fiery. Because of his apprehension at the prospect of Roman Catholic dominance in an independent Ireland, Rolleston was initially hesitant to commit himself to the idea of independence, which, as he told Whitman in 1881, he believed an "undesirable" scheme. In June 1882, however, not long after the May 6 Phoenix Park murder of two government officials, he recanted, surprisingly, given the escalation of violence the murders evidenced. Claiming the nationalist movement had always commanded his "affection and interest," he saw in the murders a clear expression "of a national will" and was ready to commit himself to it and to endure those conflicts (between Catholics and Protestants) which he believed "inevitable" after separation in order to gain "a grander liberty and nationality." "I see that the English can *never* govern us," he states, "and do worst when they mean best."[85]

So far had Rolleston moved from his earlier hesitation that he expresses a longing for arms for Ireland (a hint at the provision of arms undertaken secretly by the Clan na Gael in America) so that Ireland might move against England while it was diverted by the pressures of occupying Egypt. Accepting the unlikelihood of such an armed uprising, he accedes to the idea of constitutional measures (Parnell's aim) as Ireland's only hope and in this regard states his apprehension that "nothing perhaps does us more harm than your dynamite party in America," a reference to the most militant wing of the American Land League under the leadership of Jeremiah O'Donovan Rossa, against whose influence O'Reilly and other moderates struggled.[86]

In 1885 Rolleston and his family moved to County Wicklow, Ireland, within easy reach of Dublin, as he told Whitman, adding that this was important to him, for "I am coming forward in the political line and belong to the Dublin Young Ireland Society."[87] Rolleston was especially impressed with the society's president, John O'Leary, a former Fenian who at about this time became mentor to the young William Butler Yeats.[88] O'Leary had been imprisoned along with Rossa for his part in the Fenian revolution of 1865. Released after six years, he was banned from Ireland for twenty years, at the conclusion of which he immediately returned from his exile in France to take up his nationalist activities. The twenty-year-old Yeats met him then and immediately came under the freedom fighter's spell, made all the more forceful by his thrusting white beard and piercing dark eyes. (John Butler Yeats made a powerful sketch of him and in 1904 a memorable portrait.) But O'Leary was more than a freedom fighter; he was a patriot who understood that the greater part of nationalism was the literature it produced, and it was he who moved Yeats to the decision to become a self-consciously Irish writer.

Yeats, Rolleston, Todhunter, Douglas Hyde, George Russell (who is better known as A.E.), Katharine Tynan, and others wrestled with the question of what it meant to be an "Irish" writer.[89] As Rolleston put it, it did not mean becoming "part of the main current of English literature," and it was not "trying to express the ideas and emotions current in England, handed down by the traditions of English literature and closely interwoven with the very texture of the English language." To the contrary, it was endeavoring "to take up the thread of another literature written in a far other tongue [and] full of conceptions strange to English literature."[90] Here was the root of what would prove a grave problem for the revivalists, the "otherness" of the Irish language and the peculiarity of Ireland's ancient literature. Ultimately, it would lead Yeats away from the nationalist cause to an ever deeper involvement in fairy tales, paganism, and, finally, magic and mysticism.

One of the first things the group of young nationalists did was to institute the *Dublin University Review*, begun in August 1885 with Rolleston as editor. The *Review* not only included pieces by Yeats and O'Grady but also offered the unusual combination of the unionist Dowden and the Land Leaguer Davitt. Rolleston claimed, in an 1885 letter to Whitman which enclosed the first issue of the *Review* (its cover emblazoned with an ancient Celtic design), that the periodical "aims at introducing Nationalist thought among the upper classes in Ireland."[91] It may have had even wider aims, for the issue included a favorable review by Rolleston of William Morris's *Chants for Socialists*, but its immediate concern was spelled out for Whitman by Rolleston: "We have to go forward very cautiously in this enterprise, political questions here are so fiercely debated, and at present we can only reconcile the landed interest and conservative element by opening our columns to both sides alike," which explains the presence among the pages of subsequent issues of articles by both Dowden and Davitt.[92]

Yeats began his examination of the question of nationalistic literature by turning to the writings of the Young Irelanders of the 1840s but could not overcome his critical sense that their literary abilities fell far short of their patriotism. An 1888 anthology, *Poems and Ballads of Young Ireland*, evoked the earlier movement by reference but actually served to introduce the new young poets of the Young Ireland of the 1880s. Yeats, Todhunter, and Rolleston were among the contributors, and despite the admiration of the latter two for Whitman, there was no manifestation of his influence in their poems. Rolleston provided the book's dedicatory poem, "To John O'Leary," which was the only work from these, his revival days, to be included in his late collection, *Sea Spray: Verses and Translations* (1909), where it was identified as the "Dedication of a Book of Irish Verses by various hands."

Dissatisfied with the literary example of Young Ireland, Yeats turned his attention to another generation of writers who had emphasized Irish culture, the generation of Sir Samuel Ferguson, William Allingham, and, later, Standish O'Grady. O'Grady's connection to Whitman has already been discussed and Ferguson's, via Yeats, will be shortly, but Allingham, whose poems recounted fairy stories of the Irish countryside, remains a shadowy footnote to a letter written to Whitman in 1865 by William Douglas O'Connor. At the time O'Connor was preparing his defense of Whitman, *The Good Gray Poet*, following the poet's dismissal from his government position for what his superior took as offensive material in *Leaves of Grass*. In his letter O'Connor thanks Whitman for sending an anonymous review of the 1856 *Leaves* that appeared in the *London Leader* of June 30, 1860, and adds, "I wonder if young William Allingham wrote it? The Leader is the paper he is on. He is a poet, you remember — one of the most promising of the young British choir. He is an Irishman and a reverent lover of Emerson's genius. I shouldn't wonder if he wrote this critique."[93]

O'Connor included a lengthy passage from the review in *The Good Gray Poet*, but nothing has been found to substantiate his speculation that Allingham was its author. In fact, it is unlikely, since Allingham, having gone to London in 1854 where he wrote for *Household Words* and the *Athaeneum*, left the city after only a few months and did not return, except for short visits, for several years. He wrote to Emerson, whose work he greatly admired, when Emerson was in England in 1847 and thereafter maintained a correspondence with him, though they did not meet until Emerson's third visit in 1872. Yeats had a sustained admiration for the Ulster-born Allingham's poetry (as did Tennyson), perhaps because he was introduced to his *Laurence Bloomfield in Ireland* by John O'Leary, though that long work dealing with Ireland's land problems did not so much impress him as did Allingham's poems about his native town of Ballyshannon. Still, his admiration did not blind him to Allingham's shortcomings. In 1892 he wrote of him that "he sang Ballyshannon and not Ireland" and that his vision never took in the wide sweep of humanity and nature. Yeats may have had Whitman in mind as he continued, "In greater poets everything has relation to the national life or to profound feeling; nothing is an isolated artistic moment; there is a unity everywhere, everything fulfills a purpose that is not its own; the hailstone is a journeyman of God, and the grass blade carries the universe upon its point."[94]

The death, in 1886, of Sir Samuel Ferguson, who had done much to spur the reclamation of Ireland's lost history, became the occasion for Yeats's first long prose work, a careful but spirited evaluation of the poet whose *Lays of the Western Gael* was published in 1865, the year of Yeats's birth. Ferguson had been only briefly influenced by the Young Ireland movement before returning to his unionist position, which in his later years won him a British knighthood. Yet because of his pioneering histories, Ferguson was crucial to the construct of a national poetry, which Yeats was struggling to define, and Yeats's essay proved to have a twofold purpose. Its primary aim was to celebrate the nationalism of a poet who had remained a unionist all his life but who had brought to the telling of Irish myths and legends "the supreme gifts of the story-teller — imagination enough to make history read like romance, and simplicity enough to make romance read like history."[95] Its second purpose was to attack the unionist literary critics and scholars of Trinity College, epitomized by Edward Dowden, whom he faulted for his failure to encourage Irish writers. This was the beginning of a controversy between Yeats and Dowden that continued for some ten years. Though it never prevented Dowden from appreciating Yeats as a poet, the controversy was fueled mainly by Dowden's refusal to take up the nationalist cause and support the literary revival.[96]

Yeats's essay on Ferguson appeared in the second issue of the *Dublin University Review*, November 1886, a copy of which Rolleston sent to Whitman. Whitman's prior reading of Ferguson's poetry would have predisposed him toward the article, which he later proclaimed "very fine" and which he marked profusely. What we know of his reading of Ferguson comes from the careful notes of Horace Traubel. In 1889 a conversation with Traubel about John Boyle O'Reilly caused Whitman to recall reading a Ferguson collection, probably his *Lays of the Western Gael*. Whitman told Traubel that he had found the poetry "deeply fascinating: there was something even wild, even barbaric, in it: it attracted me, fascinated me, like the border minstrelsy — Scott's — seeming to contain the same elements of virile emotionalism. You will find traces of this influence everywhere in the Irish character — especially in the strong fellows like Boyle."[97]

In 1889 Yeats was unknown in America beyond Boston, but Traubel, who professed no knowledge of Irish literature, believed Yeats's essay important enough to enter into the chronicle he was keeping all of its points that Whitman had marked before sending the *Review* on to William Douglas O'Connor as Whitman had asked. The passages, with Whitman's emphasis added, are as follows:

> To know the meaning and mission of any poet we must study his work as a whole.
>
> For in his works [Ferguson's] grow luxuriously those forms of fancy and of verbal felicity that are above all things portable; while the mighty heathen sought rather after breadth and golden severity, knowing well that *the merely pretty is contraband of art*. With him beauty lies in great masses — thought woven with thought — each line, the sustainer of his fellow. Take a beauty from that which surrounds it — its color is faded, its plumage is ruffled — it is dead.
>
> He is one of those who apply to all the moral obligations of life *the corrosive power of the intellect*.
>
> In thus describing these persons I have not sought to convey to my readers, for it were hopeless, *their fine momentum, the sign manual of the great writers*. I am in every way satisfied if I have made plain the personality of the work.
>
> Almost all the poetry of this age is written by students for students. But Ferguson's is truly bardic, appealing to all natures alike, to the great concourse of the people, for it has gone deeper than knowledge or fancy, deeper than the intelligence which knows of difference — of the good and the evil, of the foolish and the wise, of this one and of that — to the universal emotions that have not heard of aristocracies, down to where Brahma and India are not even names.
>
> Of all the many things the past bequeaths to the future, the greatest are great legends; they are the mothers of nations. I hold it the duty of every Irish reader to study those of his own country till they are familiar as his own hands, for in them is the Celtic heart. If you will do this you will perhaps be saved in their high companionship from that leprosy of the modern — *tepid emotions and many aims*. Many aims, where the greatest of the earth often owned but two — *two linked and arduous thoughts — fatherland and song*. For them the personal perplexities of life grew dim and there alone remained its noble sorrows and its noble joys.[98]

Looking at these passages out of their intended context provides little additional knowledge about Ferguson, but the emphasized words clearly show that Whitman agreed with Yeats. Of particular interest to him would have been the reference to the "truly" bardic poet as one whose appeal is universal, who speaks to the "great concourse of the people," a desideratum Whitman had long entertained. In fact, Whitman agreed with the entire thrust of the essay, telling Traubel, "anything which tends to keep art, books, writing, poetry, pictures, music, on the level where the people are, without untoward decoration, without haughty academic reserves, has your assent as well as mine, I know."[99] The mention of "haughty academic reserves" could not have been a conscious blow aimed at Dowden, for in his later years Whitman had learned to overlook Dowden's professorial reserve. Still, one wonders what he made of Yeats's open attack on Dowden for neglecting Ferguson in favor of "elaborate pages ... spent on the much bewritten George Eliot," especially since Whitman had been pleased not only by Eliot's writing but by her recognition of him.[100]

Whitman could not have known, in 1889, the extent of Yeats's commitment to the cause of a national literature nor the difficulty he found in defining what such a literature should be in the modern age. Clearly something more was needed than the kinds of claims Yeats would make in his 1893 edition of Blake's *Works*, that the great visionary poet was of Irish extraction and that it was possible to see in the extravagance of Blake's poetic imagination a resemblance to the bards of ancient Ireland. The desire to draw connections between Irish writers and the outstanding writers of other countries was strong, however, and Yeats's letters refer to Whitman's writings with a show of pride at learning that the American was a great admirer of Ferguson.[101] In a letter to someone unknown to him but whom a mutual friend had identified as a Whitman admirer, Yeats wrote in 1887, "To me also Whitman is the greatest teacher of these decades."[102] Precisely what he learned from Whitman is hard to say, though surely he must have found comfort in Whitman's assurances, in the Preface to the 1855 *Leaves of Grass*, that the English language was "the powerful language of resistance." Like many of Ireland's writers, Whitman was essentially a political poet, and like them he had fashioned his works by writing against a literary tradition inherited from England but with a keen appreciation of the underlying constitutional principles that informed the tradition. Had Yeats truly seen Whitman as one of the great teachers of his time, he might have drawn inspiration from Whitman's democratizing poetic style, but in fact he did not.

The stumbling block to Yeats's full acceptance of Whitman's example was the matter of audience. Whitman had concluded his 1855 Preface with a prophecy that forty years later remained unfulfilled:

"The proof of a poet is that his country absorbs him as affectionately as he has absorbed it." The need to find an audience was a crucial one for Yeats, for what purpose would be served by a national poet who failed to speak to the hearts of the nation's people? To speak *of* the nation's people was but one part of the poet's task, a part that Whitman had filled undeniably, as Yeats himself seemed to intimate in an 1892 letter (which seems to hint at Whitman's cradle image in "Out of the Cradle") to *United Ireland* when he claimed, "The cradles of the greatest writers are rocked among the scenes they are to celebrate."[103] But to have truly spoken *to* a nation's people, to have found in their acceptance that which was, in Whitman's own words, "the proof of a poet," was not something America's would-be bard could claim.

In part, Yeats's concern was rooted in what one commentator has called the "real debate of the revivalist generation," whether modern Ireland's literature should adopt a national or a cosmopolitan tone.[104] In 1893 the debate was fully articulated in a series of newspaper articles by Yeats, John Eglinton, George Russell, and William Larminie. The principal adversaries were Yeats and Eglinton, with Yeats defending the literary use of Celtic traditions against Eglinton's claim that such materials had no relevance in the contemporary life of the nation. These arguments inevitably involved the question of whether Irish writers should address a national or cosmopolitan audience, with Yeats in the nationalist role.

From his nationalist stance Yeats viewed Whitman as a failed national bard. In 1894 Yeats wrote in *United Ireland* of an American public "hounding [Whitman] from a Government post," and that "Walt Whitman, the most National of her [America's] poets, was so neglected and persecuted that he had, perhaps, fallen silent but for the admiration and help of a little group of Irish and English artists and men of letters."[105] None of this was true, of course, but Whitman had succeeded some years before in convincing his English and Irish friends that it was. Originally, Yeats blamed critics and scholars who failed to direct the general public toward the works of their nation's writers, but later he reached a different understanding of Whitman's lack of a national audience. He articulated it near the end of his life in an essay, written in 1937, for a volume of poems never published. Here Yeats says, "I thought when I was young—Walt Whitman had something to do with it—that the poet, painter, and musician should do nothing but express themselves." Later he had decided otherwise: "A poet is justified not by the expression of him-

self, but by the public he finds or creates, a public made by others ready to his hand if he is a mere popular poet, but a new public, a new form of life, if he is a man of genius."[106]

This is not a total rejection of Whitman — despite Yeats having once referred to his early love of Whitman as an "error" of youth — for it confers the mark of genius by its implicit acknowledgment of Whitman's having found a new, wider public when he failed to find one "ready to his hand." As Terrence Diggory has observed, "the objection lies in the 'nothing but'" of Yeats's statement, for if Whitman had done nothing but express himself and not the ideals and aims of a nation's "self," he would not have found the public he in effect created.[107] Richard Ellmann writes succinctly of the question of Yeats and audience, claiming that Yeats sang loudly his praise of the individual but wrote "for the people," and in this "he is the opposite of Whitman, who practiced the utmost concealment while he pretended to be outspoken."[108]

Just how truly Yeats wrote "for the people" is debatable, for in his essential conservatism he found something threatening in the idea of democracy. The image, in his "The Second Coming," of the rocking cradle that holds the nightmarish "rough beast" soon to be "slouching towards Bethlehem to be born" may be thought an allusion to Whitman's "Out of the Cradle Endlessly Rocking" and the "rough beast" as Yeats's depiction of the "giant," democracy, toward which Dowden believed civilization was moving and whose hand Dowden wished to shake. Yeats dismissed Dowden because of the Trinity professor's devotion to the English tradition in literature and for his lack of Irish nationalism, but of the two Dowden was more open to the pervasive trends not solely of literature but of history and was more fully aware that the ideals of a heroic past would not necessarily carry Ireland into a better future.

Yeats could, and did, reject Whitman as easily as he rejected those aspects of what was natively Irish in order to comply with his own vision of a heroic Ireland embedded in a folkloric tradition. Never truly one with the people who lived and worked and died in Galway's bogs or Dublin's streets, Yeats, unlike Whitman, remained, poetically, removed from his compatriots, aware always of the cultural and societal fragmentation both he and they had inherited and which set him apart.

Eventually Yeats turned to the creation of a national theater as the primary cultural influence, and in this endeavor he found his greatest ally in Lady Isabella Augusta Gregory. Lady Gregory joined him in the writing and production of plays for the Irish National Theater Society. She also contributed to the store of fairy- and folklore, which she gathered mainly from her Galway neighbors. In 1903 she published *Poets and Dreamers*, a collection of stories that were part of the Galway peasants' oral tradition. Her dedication of this work, "To Some Undergraduates of Trinity College," points the students to Whitman by quoting from his "A Song for Occupations" to underscore her desire for them to turn their attention away from the Anglo-Irish tradition in literature to things Irish:

> Will you seek afar off? You surely come back at last,
> In things best known to you finding the best, or as good as
>   the best;
> In folks nearest to you finding the sweetest, strongest, lovingest,
> Happiness, knowledge not in another place but this place — not
>   for another hour but this hour.

When James Joyce reviewed *Poems and Dreamers* he seized the opportunity to chide Lady Gregory for her treatment of the folk tradition, which, he claimed, was set forth "in the fulness of its senility." He concluded his review by noting the one belief shared by all of Ireland's people, "a belief in the incurable ignobility of the forces that have overcome her." His recommendation was that Lady Gregory add to the passage from Whitman that forms her dedication "Whitman's ambiguous word for the vanquished — 'Battles are lost in the spirit in which they are won.'" The editors of Joyce's critical writings point out that Joyce distorts, for his own purpose, Whitman's lines from "Song of Myself," "Have you heard that it was good to gain the day? / I also say it is good to fall, battles are lost in the same spirit in which they are won" in order to make his point — that in seeing the "folk" as its sole glory, Ireland had fallen to the level of its ignoble oppressors.[109]

With one notable exception, James Joyce, there is little evidence of Whitman's influence on twentieth-century Irish writers beyond casual references that sometimes reveal the same rejection of his poetic style as Yeats had shown. Though he believed himself to be the poet of the modern, Whitman did not fare well with the modernist poets, whose sensibilities tended in other directions. Joyce introduced a European influence into Irish literature, which enlarged his scope and which was continued in the work of Samuel Beckett, who not only chose to live in France but to write in the language of that country, eschewing entirely the language of his country's oppressors. Despite this European influence, Joyce, alone among the century's Irish writers, reveals, as discussed later, an affinity to Whitman's stylistics in persona, voice, and general ambiance.

Our bridge to twentieth-century Irish literature and its rather scant Whitman connections is Yeats's valued friend George William Russell, who chose to be known as A.E. A poet and prose writer, A.E., like Yeats, moved toward mysticism, combining it with the remote Gaelic past to form a new spiritual vision, as defined in his *Candle of Vision* (1918). A.E. had a far more varied life than most of his literary compatriots. He was not only poet and mystic, prose writer and painter, but also journalist, economist, and political figure. While his poetry reveals nothing of Whitman's influence, his political thinking at the end of the nineteenth century indicates that both his spirituality and his revolt against the institution of the Roman Catholic Church were in some way affected by his reading of *Leaves of Grass*.

In an essay titled "Ideals in Ireland: Priest or Hero" in the *Irish Theosophist* for April and May 1897, Russell demolishes an earlier ideal of the priesthood and replaces it with the heroic figures of Irish, pre-Christian, antiquity. At the outset of the essay he signals his position on the question of organized religion by quoting from "Song of Myself," where the poetic persona speaks of the condition of animals,

They do not sweat and whine about their condition,
They do not lie awake in the dark and weep for their sins,
    They do not make me sick discussing their duty to God,
. . . .
Not one kneels to another nor to his kind that lived thousands
    of years ago.

In his later years A.E. was editor of the periodical the *Irish Statesman*, where he turned his critical eye toward a multitude of topics. In one such piece, "American Culture," A.E. placed Whitman "a thousand years ahead" of that average he claimed to represent, saying Whitman's muse was "the Spread Eagle, but in its noblest and loftiest form almost out of sight of those it soared over."[110] It was not an unfamiliar assertion. A far better evaluation appeared in a piece called "Free Verse," where A.E. discusses the poetic choice of free verse as part of the general allure of freedom, which, he claims, unfortunately offers the strong possibility of disaster. The purpose of free verse, he declares, is to allow the poet greater freedom of form so that the poetry may alter with mood, "but too many have used this form to say what might as well have been said in prose." Whitman, he claimed, "the first considerable poet to attempt sustained flight in song," discarded meter and though he sometimes achieved song, "had no sustained mastery over the power that lifted the lines occasionally."[111]

In the same generation as A.E. and in the Anglo-Irish tradition was William Kirkpatrick Magee, who wrote under the pseudonym John Eglinton. Magee often invoked Whitman's name to bolster his political arguments against the social reformers of his time whose intentions he did not trust. Thus he speaks of William Blake and Walt Whitman — "of whom one was crazy and the other a poet who could not sing" — as individuals who were "as little disposed to interfere in the conduct of the world as Socrates or Jesus" and, supporting his doctrine of individualism and his praise of democracy, extols Whitman for pointing out that the average person "at last only is important"[112]

Magee defended Dowden against Yeats's criticisms, admitting that though the Trinity professor undoubtedly had "something to learn from nationalism," he was correct in insisting "that literature, like religion, is essentially international." The question of nationality did not even arise for Dowden, Magee insisted, for he was satisfied to be a citizen of the United Kingdom. "All his combative instincts were aroused on behalf of the Union," Magee claimed, "which had given him, what Swift, Goldsmith, Berkeley never really felt that they possessed, a country."[113] Magee also found a discrepancy of thought in Yeats's appreciation of Whitman offered side-by-side with his belief, in *Ideas of Good and Evil* (1903), that the awakening of reason that occurred at the time of the French Revolution had destroyed the creative imagination in all but the peasantry, who yet retained it in their folklore.[114] Indeed, there is an anomaly to be seen here, and this may well have been a factor in Yeats's distancing himself from Whitman as he moved ever more in the direction not solely of folklore but of spiritualism.

Though the issues surrounding the question of a national poetry faded somewhat over time, there were writers in the postliterary revival period who still questioned Whitman's status as "poet." One was Patrick Kavanagh, best known for his long poem *The Great Hunger* (1942). Kavanagh's career received its first boost when A.E., as editor of the *Irish Statesman*, published some of his early efforts. A.E. took Kavanagh under his wing, among other things providing him with books, including *Leaves of Grass*. Kavanagh borrowed the title of Whitman's work for a poem published posthumously in 1956. In "Leaves of Grass" Kavanagh looks back on his early misunderstanding of poetry, his belief that it was "Dreary, irrevlevant," and recalls the youth he was then, incapable of seeing what was before his eyes, "the ground / Tumultuous with living." Then,

> He hit upon the secret door that leads to the heaven
> Of human satisfaction, a purpose, and did not know it;
> An army of grass blades were at his call, million on million
> Kept saying to him, we nearly made Whitman a poet.[115]

James Joyce remains the exception among these unflattering twentieth-century Irish references. Joyce, who once wrote in a letter that he admired Whitman's "long flowing lines," paid homage to him in *Finnegans Wake* by emulating the Whitmanian line in a long continuous passage beginning "I foredreamed for thee and more than full-maked" and ending with "my tow tugs steered down canal grand, my lighters lay longside on Regalia Water."[116] The same work contains a reference to "Old Whiteman self" and an allusion to Whitman's "Out of the Cradle" that emphasizes the democracy (and perhaps the capitalism) that nurtured the American bard: "(the cradle rocking equally . . . on its law of capture and recapture)."[117]

In *Ulysses* Buck Mulligan quotes from Section 51 of "Song of Myself," "Do I contradict myself? Very well then, I contradict myself," and there is an allusion to both Whitman's "yankee yawp" and to his "Thought on Shakespere," where he is said to have referred to Shakespeare's as "the art of feudalism."[118] While on the surface these references and allusions would seem to be no more significant than those of A.E., Kavanagh, and the others, Joyce's consciousness of Whitman forms part of the deep structures of both *Finnegans Wake* and *Ulysses*. This is particularly true of *Ulysses*, and the reader who knows intimately the persona of the Whitman poems experiences a sense of recognition on encountering Leopold Bloom, who exhibits the same gigantism and the same sexual tumescence. Further, Bloom's intimate association with the city of Dublin is akin to that of the relationship to Manhattan of the *Leaves* persona, especially in Whitman's early editions. Part of this presentation of a cityscape is the inclusion, in *Ulysses*, of all classes of people, which brought into Irish literature figures from what might be termed "the lower orders" of Dublin life, just as Whitman had introduced into poetry similar characters from Manhattan's streets. There is also the matter of language and Whitman's assertion that in essence *Leaves of Grass* was "a language experiment," which *Ulysses* clearly is as well. That both *Ulysses* and *Leaves of Grass* suffered the same fate, being suppressed on charges of obscenity, cannot be overlooked, but the larger issues, of language experimentation, a democratically inclusive approach, and a bold exploration of new literary modes, are closer, more significant, ties between the two.

The autobiographies of twentieth-century Irish writers, especially those who found it necessary to leave Ireland in order to create with artistic freedom, also yield some traces of Whitman's influence. The final volume of Sean O'Casey's six-volume autobiography contains a number of references to Whitman, especially when O'Casey writes of his first visit to New York in 1934 when all of Manhattan seemed to remind him of Whitman. Quoting from "Song of the Exposition," where Whitman calls upon the muse of poetry to migrate from "Greece and Ionia" to America's shores, O'Casey uses Whitman's words to bolster his own objection to maintaining a reverential attitude toward that which was "unfamiliar to the general man."[119] This objection was the basis of his argument with those in Ireland whose idea of Irish literature, he believed, was more Anglo-Irish than that of his or of the average Irish living in the southern counties.

In the final pages of the autobiography O'Casey speaks of the Cold War and of the horrifying prospect, in the atomic age, of it becoming a full engagement. Anticipating both the flower children of the 1960s and Allen Ginsberg's poem "Bomb," O'Casey warns that the mere existence of the atom bomb has primed its maker for its use. "Zip! any minute now," he cries, adding, "Oh, Walt Whitman, saintly sinner, sing for us!" In a fifteen-line apostrophe, O'Casey seeks to conjure the spirit of Whitman so that it might bring peace to the opposing factions, "And soften the snout of the menacing cannon / With the scent and bloom of a lilac spray."[120]

Frank O'Connor's autobiography *An Only Child* (1960) includes an episode of the 1922–1923 civil war when the young O'Connor learned of the execution of Robert Erskine Childers, "a distinguished British officer with Irish family connections" who had performed a daring feat of gunrunning. Born in Ireland and educated in England, Childers, though a former clerk of the House of Commons, was a fierce supporter of Irish nationalism. He went as secretary to the delegation sent by Eamon de Valera to negotiate the terms of the Anglo-Irish Treaty in 1922 and opposed the decision to sign the treaty. In the civil war that followed he was a propagandist for the antitreaty forces and was among those tried and executed by the government of the Irish Free State for his part in the war.

O'Connor says that when he read of the execution in the newspapers, "I wrote the date over Whitman's lines on the death of Lincoln in the copy of *Leaves of Grass* that I always carried with me at the time — 'Hushed Be the Camps Today' [*sic*]." "Like everything else I did at the time," O'Connor asserts, "it reeked of literature, and yet when I recite the lines to myself today, all the emotion comes back and I know it was not all literature." [121]

Indeed, it was not all literature. Two events of decidedly nonliterary Irish association in which Whitman's poetry played a part were the 1913 labor strike and the Easter Rising of 1916. The first of these occurred under the leadership of socialists James Larkin and James Connolly. Larkin was the founder and builder of the most revolutionary labor union of his time, the Irish Transport and General Workers' Union. In 1913 a series of strikes by the union's members over their right to unionize resulted in a massive lockout of some twenty thousand workers by employers who sought to break the union. Among the workers who had earlier been fired for union membership was Sean O'Casey, who joined Larkin in the strike and in the formation of the Irish Citizens Army made up of laborers charged with the protection of striking workers. [122] Larkin, who was fond of quoting Abraham Lincoln when defending his belief in the socialist cause, claimed to have acquired his "love of comrades" by reading Whitman. His comrade in arms, James Connolly, was even more fierce in his radical socialism. Connolly saw the 1913 strike as more than just a fight for workers' right to unionize. He aimed to win recognition of labor as a force in Ireland on the grounds that labor was the country's only free institution, free of the political aspects of land policies and of capitalist exploitation. Connolly and Larkin both supported the cultural nationalism of the Gaelic League, but Connolly saw in a socialist revolution a desirable return to an early Gaelic system of communal land ownership.

The 1913 strike served to bring together labor and nationalist interests, with the result that Connolly led labor into participation in the 1916 rising. His argument for doing so was that Irish workers were serving as Irish volunteers in the British army in the World War, fighting for an empire that had oppressed the Irish for centuries. This served his socialistic agenda well, but, despite a gathering of power at this time, socialism never drew the numbers in Ireland that it did in England, where Whitman was a decided influence on many of the socialistic movements that developed there in the 1880s and 1890s.[123] Connolly's socialism was perceived as a threat to Irish nationalism, and the country's incipient socialist labor movement lost ground to the larger issue of the Anglo-Irish treaty in 1922, never to regain its force.

An eloquent speaker, in 1916 Connolly used the occasion of the anniversary of a Fenian martyrdom to move the thoughts of Dubliners forward in time to the then-current slaughter of Irishmen in the World War and to arouse them against a threatened conscription. His first biographer, Desmond Ryan, tells us that Connolly preached from "Whitman's 'defiant deed' text." This would indicate he read from "Song of the Broad-Axe," perhaps proclaiming for his audience Whitman's vision of the great city, "A great city is that which has the greatest men and women," then going on to stanza six which begins, "How beggarly appear arguments before a defiant deed!"

Connolly's evocation of the dead and dying Irish fighting for England is unmistakably Whitmanian in its cataloging cadence and its unblinking gaze at war: "All those mountains of Irish dead, all those corpses mangled beyond recognition, all those arms, legs, eyes, ears, fingers, toes, hands, all those shivering, putrefying bodies, once warm, living and tender parts of Irish men and youths — all those horrors buried in Flanders or the Gallipoli Peninsula are all items Ireland pays for being part of the British Empire. . . . And for what do we pay this price?"[124] While the outrage registered here is notably Whitmanian in its presentation, it remains within the realm of protest rhetoric rather than poetry. When a similar sentiment is expressed by the true poet Yeats, in his poem "September 1913," which remembers the labor strike of that year, nothing can be found to suggest Whitman's cadence or sweeping line, and the decision for rhyme had long since been made. Only the sense of futility in the deaths of patriots, the "delirium of the brave," as Yeats calls it, serves to remind not only of Connolly's rhetoric but of Whitman's heartbreak at the deaths of the young men in another war, waged not to sunder but to preserve a political union.

The immediate concerns of nationalism, republicanism, Home Rule, labor, and farm interests all tended to overshadow questions of Irish literary identity, especially whether or how that identity might draw on the example of the poet deemed by many — Dowden, particularly — the premiere voice of democracy. With the partitioning of Ireland into two political entities, one free and independent the other still a part of the United Kingdom, came the entrenchment of cultural division into Protestant Ulster and Catholic Ireland, foreclosing the possibility of an Irish poetic voice that would express the representational quality Whitman had striven, in America, to achieve. The fragmentation of Ireland that stemmed from its early history carried forward into the twentieth century, with the term "Irish" still offering a variety of meanings that defied the Whitmanian urge toward wholeness and toward "the knit of identity" that yet allowed for distinction, "always distinction."

9
CODA

On more than one occasion while writing this book colleagues or friends, after learning that my subject was Whitman and the Irish, have immediately asked the question: "Did he like them?" Some asked because they were aware of the *Aurora* editorials, which led them to think the answer might be a straightforward "no." Others, most often those of Irish descent, asked simply because they were curious. No one asked the question in reverse, thus according Whitman's opinion pride of place, yet I feel sure they would have done so had my topic been Whitman and the English or Whitman and the French, both studies, by the way, that have already been produced. The assumption was that Whitman was in a better position to pass judgment on, or at least to like or dislike, the Irish than they were to do the same toward him. The examination of his contacts with Irish, Anglo-Irish, and Irish Americans, however, fails to indicate he himself felt any such superiority. He accepted the immigrant, and in his New York City days the Irish were the largest immigrant group; he accepted with gratitude the adulation of the Anglo-Irish scholars; and, above all, he treasured the friendships of those individuals, both native-born Irish and Irish American, who were among the closest of his friends, O'Connor, O'Reilly, and Doyle.

One of the things this study aimed to establish is that those of the Irish literary community who were Whitman's contemporaries, as well as some who came after, responded very positively to his poetry. Clearly, he did not serve as a useful model for writers of the Irish literary revival beyond the inspiration he provided for the idea of a national poetry in modern literature and in democratic nations. There is nothing in *Leaves of Grass* that even approximates the urge felt by the Yeatsian nationalists to return to a golden age of Celtic myth and make it newly relevant. Then, too, by the time of Yeats and others who were interested in the American bard as a possible model of nationalistic poetry, Whitman was seeking to move beyond that classification to achieve the international audience he had envisioned early in his poetic career.

As early as the second edition of *Leaves*, in 1856, the poem that later became "Salut au Monde!" reveals Whitman's assumption that his democratic message would reach beyond his own country and arouse in peoples of other nations a desire to achieve democracy. The encouragement offered in "To a Foil'd European Revolutionaire" could be for no other purpose but to foster everywhere the overthrow of monarchies and the establishment of democracies; as he said to the newly radicalized Thomas W. H. Rolleston, in absentia, "I do wish you, I did wish you, Godspeed." Whitman's quick response to Rolleston's suggestions for German and Russian translations of *Leaves* bears out his desire to exert a worldwide democratizing influence, as did his belief that "America, inheritor of the past, is the custodian of the future of humanity."[1]

This sense of custodianship of a future republic to be enjoyed by all peoples underlies one of the more interesting of twentieth-century critical comments on Whitman, offered by the Ulster poet and scholar Tom Paulin. Writing in the years just after the signing of the Anglo-Irish Agreement of 1985, in which the government of Ireland was granted greater authority in the affairs of Ulster in exchange for a more determined effort at preventing republican terrorism, Paulin expresses the feelings of his fellow Ulsterites as those of a people suddenly "marginalized" by a powerful, once protective nation. His critical essays, offered in a collection titled *Minotaur*, were composed in the years after the agreement and, Paulin claims, "aim to explore the experience of marginality in relation to the nation state."[2] In one of these essays Paulin forges a not unlikely link between the republicanism of John Milton and the democratic vision of Whitman. He begins by presenting an argument for the vital and inseparable alliance between Milton's prose and poetry, though acknowledging the lack of "a [theory of] poetics for the prose" by which to correlate the two. Paulin proposes to fill the void by insisting on "topicality — the dramatic intensity of the polemical Now" as the point of connection.[3] With examples drawn from *Paradise Lost* and *Samson Agonistes*, he demonstrates Milton's creation of images and rhythms that directly convey poetic interpretations of various polemics set forth in *Of Reformation, Aeropagitica*, and others among his prose writings. Paulin quotes from *Areopagitica* and Milton's vision of the free city, "the mansion-house of liberty," where "the pursuit of Truth outstrips the pursuit of war," and where the citizens actively engage in bringing about "the approaching Reformation" by "musing, searching, revolving new notions and ideas . . . others as fast reading, trying all things, assenting to the force of reason and convincement."[4]

Paulin sees in this passage an anticipation of Whitman's "Song of Myself": "Many sweating, ploughing, thrashing, and then the chaff for payment receiving, / A few idly owning, and they the wheat continually claiming," and argues that Milton "sounds almost uncannily like Whitman democratically trying to pack every last rapid action in."[5] Then, in what proves to be his most effective drawing from Milton's prose, Paulin quotes a passage, "In short, it is the renewed cultivation of freedom and civic life that I disseminate throughout cities, kingdoms, and nations," pointing out that the voice of the poetic persona could almost be that of the persona infusing so much of Whitman's poetry. From this position of strength, Paulin concludes by asserting that it is in comparing Milton and Whitman that we can "start to see the republican poetics that structures [Milton's] prose."[6]

The argument is forceful and convincing, and the comparison offers a new pairing of visions that departs from the more familiar one, of Blake to Whitman. Since Milton and Whitman wrote in both forms, the comparison between their prose and poetry can be extended, thus offering the promise of an ever greater increase of insight. What cannot fail to impress, however, is the impulse behind the argument, which is eloquently expressed in the introduction to the collected essays, subtitled "Poetry and the Nation State." Describing the emotional and psychological effects on Ulsterites of the Anglo-Irish Agreement, Paulin speaks of a people who have no place to worship, "no place to sacrifice." It is, he says, "a version of penal times when Irish Catholics were forbidden to celebrate mass and had to do so, fearfully, at 'mass rocks' out in the hills." Driven by this sense of persecution, Paulin seeks, and finds, his place of refuge in a shared utopian vision of a free state which, conveniently, he is able first to locate in the visionary texts of the great English republican poet before finding it again in the poetic construct of an American poet describing a democractic state. More than Edward Dowden's examination of Whitman as the example of what kind of poetry a democracy will present, Paulin's essay suggests the need of so many Irish writers who felt themselves to be marginalized, adrift between two political bodies and a part of neither. Had Yeats been able to connect, via England's great polemicist and poet, to the prophet of

American democracy and his vision of its utopian future, he might not have experienced the sense of cultural fragmentation that eventually led him away even from the cultural nationalism he once embraced. In near despair, Paulin becomes an emigrant to the visionary country of Milton and Whitman, just as countless others from Ireland, north and south, had become emigrants to an alien nation. Not surprisingly for an Ulsterman, he carefully charts his route toward the envisioned state via the English literary and political tradition, which he sees as having been the custodians of the long-held vision.

Paulin's feelings of despair at the political actions of his country would not have been unknown to Whitman. The sad fact that he, too, faltered, in the 1870s, and allowed his belief in America and in himself, as the herald of democracy, to erode was the regrettable result of his declining physical and emotional health. At this point he lost his sense of mission and, rather than emphasizing the appropriateness of his message to other nations, presented himself to his European admirers as a poet neglected by his own people. Yeats, for one, saw this as the mark of failure, on Whitman's part, to achieve the national status he had expected. Yeats turned away to follow his own instincts, hearing, perhaps, in the democratic "yawp" the echo of a mob howling, which to his mind would have served only to further disunite his already politically and emotionally divided country.

The question of whether Whitman's desire for an international audience interfered, even conflicted, with the presentation of a poetic persona that claimed to speak to and for Americans brings us closer to his associations with the Irish in America.[7] There is no denying that his personal relationships with Irish and Irish Americans were warm and loving, but he seems to have found lovable in them qualities that he identified as characteristically "Irish" and which he expected to find in all who were of Irish birth or background. In short, he accepted as true the stereotype of Irish rebelliousness, fierce loyalty, and a readiness to fight, with much of which — especially the rebelliousness — he personally identified.

It also seems certain that he never overcame his objections to Catholicism and continued to view it as limiting its believers' full participation in democracy. In his defense, however, it should be said that beyond his one venture, in the pages of the 1842 *Aurora*, into a full-blown depiction of the Irish as dupes of their priests, he never again gave public utterance to such sentiments. One does wish for a fuller representation of the Irish in Whitman's poetry, especially in his poetry of Manhattan. It is a wish born of an expectation, considering the fact that the Irish constituted the largest ethnic group in New York City in the years Whitman lived and worked there. The explanation for the infrequency of their appearance that comes most readily to mind is that which also seems to explain Whitman's notice of the increasing Chinese population in Boston while never commenting on the Boston Irish: they were simply too numerous to notice and their Catholicism, which distinguished so many of them, not so immediately observable. Still, the Irish appear in the poems with sufficient frequency to register their presence among the American workers who are Whitman's principal choice of representative Americans.

It is Whitman's image of the worker, free and independent, even joyous in his or her work, that made an impress on the minds of his Anglo-Irish admirers. The sheer joy with which Whitman went about his own labor of creating a poetry of and for a nation's people struck a resounding chord among these, his earliest Irish readers. That it also took root in the hearts of some of Ireland's greatest labor leaders is obvious from their own utterances. One cannot help thinking that Whitman, whose friend and companion Peter Doyle worked on streetcars and railroads most of his adult life, would have taken special pleasure in knowing that his words had inspired the leaders of Ireland's greatest transport workers' union.

There is no denying that Whitman's democratic message was taken over by the socialists in England and in Ireland. They may have recognized what he himself did not, that his heartfelt desire for "the dear love of comrades" among workers was the ultimate "cause," to which he repeatedly referred but never defined, and that it was the genuine basis for his international appeal. In Ireland this cause was never subverted, as it sometimes was in England, by aristocratic, university-trained intellectuals whose idea of demonstrating love for the laboring class was to take a lover from among its ranks. Though they rejected him as a paradigm for their nationalistic purposes, the Irish celebrated Whitman for many of what might be termed the right reasons, his joyfulness, his humanity, even, despite themselves at times, for what he called a "heroic nudity," which encouraged them to strip away the ambiguities that flowed from cultural divisiveness and seek a unified vision of Ireland.

There is no way of knowing how popular Whitman was among the Irish Americans of his day, nor do we know if John Boyle O'Reilly was successful in promoting *Leaves of Grass* among readers of the *Pilot*.

The sexual aspect of the book may have been offputting to many of O'Reilly's readers, but the rebelliousness that led Whitman to insist on its inclusion may have proved a strong attraction for them. Whitman was not entirely wrong in accepting the Irish stereotype, for that part of it which emphasized rebelliousness was surely true — with good cause — and sparked in him a flare of recognition that must have been mutual and which seems to have carried over into other areas of mutual understanding. For evidence of this we need look no further than the cemetery worker, Ralph Moore, who, alone among those with whom Whitman discussed his final resting place, completely understood what was needed. So it had been throughout Whitman's life, that at the most elemental level of need he found understanding among the laboring class — where he could not miss finding the Irish.

NOTES

INTRODUCTION

1. Herbert Bergman, Douglas A. Noverr, and Edward J. Recchia, eds., *The Collected Writings of Walt Whitman, The Journalism, Vol. 1: 1834–1846* (New York: Peter Lang, 1998), 383 (hereafter cited as *Journalism*).

2. Charles Fanning, *The Irish Voice in America: Irish-American Fiction from the 1760s to the 1980s* (Lexington: University Press of Kentucky, 1990), 14.

3. Horace Traubel, *With Walt Whitman in Camden*, 1: 376. In his *Irish Essays* (1882), especially in "The Incompatibles," Matthew Arnold aims for a healing note and extols the Irish character to his English audience.

4. Ibid.

5. Ibid., 2: 553.

6. Gerald Griffin, *The Collegians* (New York: Frederick A. Stokes, 1940), ix. *The Collegians* was published in America in 1829, and a ten-volume edition of Griffin's works was published in 1856, 1868, and 1885 (Fanning, *The Irish Voice*, 14).

7. W. B. Yeats, "Irish National Literature, I: From Callanan to Carleton," in *Uncollected Prose by W. B. Yeats*, ed. John P. Frayne, vol. 1, *First Reviews and Articles, 1886–1896* (New York: Columbia University Press, 1970), 359–364.

8. Floyd Stovall, *The Foreground of Leaves of Grass* (Charlottesville: University Press of Virginia, 1974), 7 n14.

9. As late as 1888 Whitman also had a copy of Griffin's 1843 *Poetical Works*; see Traubel, *With Walt Whitman*, 1: 181.

10. Brown's own rationalist interests led him to write more than one utopian work, though none was published. A possible source of one of these, "The History of Carsol," is the utopian *Equality: A Political Romance* (1802) by James Reynolds, who came to America from Ireland after the 1798 rebellion and who is said to have been a brother-in-law of Wolfe Tone; see Fanning, *The Irish Voice*, 9.

11. Whitman read one of Brown's romances, *Wieland*, but did not think much of it or of the author; see Traubel, *With Walt Whitman*, 3: 138, 183.

12. Michael A. Gordon, *The Orange Riots: Irish Political Violence in New York City, 1870 and 1871* (Ithaca, N.Y.: Cornell University Press, 1993), 7.

13. Edward F. Grier, ed. *Notebooks and Unpublished Prose Manuscripts*, 6 vols. (New York: New York University Press, 1984), 2: 488 (hereafter cited as *Notebooks*).

14. Traubel, *With Walt Whitman*, 6: 405.

15. Ibid., 8: 181.

16. Ibid.

17. Ibid., 9: 282.

18. Ibid., 6: 231; 8: 66.

19. Ibid., 6: 249.

HISTORICAL BACKGROUND

1. Aidan Clarke, "The Colonisation of Ulster and the Rebellion of 1641," in *The Course of Irish History*, ed. T. W. Moody and F. X. Martin (Boulder, Colo: Roberts Rinehart, 1995), 202.

2. Hugh Kearney, in *The British Isles: A History of Four Nations* (Cambridge: Cambridge University Press, 1989), argues differently, pointing out that the Home Rule issue survived Parnell's downfall to return during the crisis years 1912–1914 (177).

NEW YORK CITY

1. Floyd Stovall, ed., *Walt Whitman, Prose Works 1892* (New York: New York University Press, 1964), 2: 369 (hereafter cited as *Prose Works*).

2. Paul A. Gilje, "The Development of an Irish American Community in New York City before the Great Migration," in *The New York Irish*, ed. Ronald H. Bayor and Timothy J. Meagher (Baltimore: Johns Hopkins University Press, 1966), 71.

3. Traubel, *With Walt Whitman*, 5: 392.

4. Quoted in Harold Syrett, *The City of Brooklyn, 1865–1898: A Political History* (New York: Columbia University Press, 1944), 18–19.

5. Quoted in Eric Homberger, *Scenes from the Life of a City: Corruption and Conscience in Old New York* (New Haven, Conn.: Yale University Press, 1994), 218.

6. Charles E. Rosenberg, *The Cholera Years: The United States in 1832, 1849, and 1866* (Chicago: University of Chicago Press, 1962), 137–138.

7. Edwin Haviland Miller, ed., *The Correspondence of Walt Whitman* (New York: New York University Press, 1961–1977), 2: 47 (hereinafter cited as *Correspondence*).

8. Thomas L. Brasher, ed., *Walt Whitman, Early Poems and the Fiction* (New York: New York University Press, 1963), 309–318 (hereafter cited as *Early Poems and Fiction*). When Whitman republished the story the cholera episode was dropped (316 n9).

9. Walt Whitman, *Leaves of Grass: A Facsimile of the First Edition*, ed. Richard Bridgman (San Francisco: Chandler, 1968), 43.

10. Hasia R. Diner, "The Most Irish City in the Union: The Era of the Great Migration, 1844–1877," in *The New York Irish*, ed. Bayor and Meagher, 92.

11. *Notebooks*, 1: 153.

12. Whitman, *Leaves of Grass Facsimile*, 75.

13. Gordon, *the Orange Riots*, 8.

14. Walt's brother Jeff suspected Jesse's condition was the result of syphilis contracted from an Irish prostitute. See Dennis Berthold and Kenneth Price, eds., *Dear Brother Walt: The Letters of Thomas Jefferson Whitman* (Kent, Ohio: Kent State University Press, 1984), 85.

15. *Correspondence*, 2: 123.

16. Ibid., 128.

17. Ibid., 126.

18. George Templeton Strong made a similar comment in his diary, noting "how little effect this orgasm of riot and bloodshed produced in side streets." *The Diary of George Templeton Strong*, vol. 4, *The Post-War Years, 1865–1875*, ed. Allan Nevins and Milton H. Thomas (New York: Macmillan, 1952), 370.

19. William D'Arcy, *The Fenian Movement in the United States: 1858–1886* (New York: Russell and Russell, 1947), 359.

20. J. T. Headley, *Great Riots of New York, 1712 to 1873* (New York: E. B. Treat, 1873; reprint, Mnemosyne, 1969), 291. Headley had been a Know-Nothing New York state senator in the 1850s; his purpose in writing on New York's riots was to push for greater protection from what he believed to be the city's "greatest danger —*mob violence*" (i).

21. Gordon, *The Orange Riots*, 221–223.

22. Christopher Gray, "An 1871 Row House Co-Designed by Calvert Vaux," *New York Times*, February 8, 1998, "Real Estate," D:7.

23. Robert Frances Hueston, *The Catholic Press and Nativism* (New York: Arno Press, 1976), 144–145.

24. Sean Wilentz, *Chants Democratic: New York City and the Rise of the American Working Class, 1788–1850* (New York: Oxford University Press, 1984), 17.

25. Ibid., 242.

26. *Journalism*, 1: 304.

27. Ibid., 313.

28. Ibid., 314–315.

29. Ibid., 340.

30. Traubel, *With Walt Whitman*, 2: 308.

31. Thomas L. Brasher, *Whitman as Editor of the Brooklyn Daily Eagle* (Detroit: Wayne State University Press, 1970), 132–133.

32. *Journalism*, 1: 340–341.

33. Robert Ernst, *Immigrant Life in New York City, 1825–1862* (Port Washington, N.Y.: Ira J. Friedman, 1949), 108.

34. *Notebooks*, 1: 239.

35. Copies of the paper available for the years 1857 and 1858 do not reveal anything identifiably Whitman's.

36. William Leonard Joyce, *Editors and Ethnicity: A History of the Irish-American Press, 1848–1883* (New York: Arno Press, 1976), 65.

37. Diner, "The Most Irish City," 92.

38. Bayor and Meagher, *The New York Irish*, 551.

39. Florence E. Gibson, *The Attitudes of the New York Irish Toward State and National Affairs, 1848–1892* (New York: Columbia University Press, 1951; reprint, New York: AMS Press, 1968), 217.

40. Diner, "The Most Irish City," 92.

41. Gibson, *Attitudes of the New York Irish*, 235.

42. Terry Golway, *Irish Rebel: John Devoy and America's Fight for Ireland's Freedom* (New York: St. Martin's Press, 1998), 9.

43. Gordon, *The Orange Riots*, 155.

44. Headley, *Great Riots*, 305.

45. Edward K. Spann, *The New Metropolis: New York City, 1840–1857* (New York: Columbia University Press, 1981), 318.

46. *Correspondence*, 2: 126–127.

47. Ibid., 128.

48. In the 1894 United States census, "Irish stock" was defined as offspring of an Irish mother whether born in Ireland or elsewhere (Bayor and Meagher, *The New York Irish*, 559).

49. Homberger, *Scenes*, 144–145.

50. *Notebooks*, 2: 783.

51. *Correspondence*, 2: 148–149.

52. Jerome Loving argues that the invective in these editorials can be laid to the owners, Anson Herrick and John F. Ropes, more than to Whitman; see *Walt Whitman: The Song of Himself* (Berkeley: University of California Press, 1999), 63.

53. Traubel, *With Walt Whitman*, 6: 379.

54. Edward L. Widmer, *Young America: The Flowering of Democracy in New York City* (New York: Oxford University Press, 1999), 32–33.

55. *Journalism*, 1: 488, 23, 22.

56. *Prose Works*, 1: 140.

57. For texts of the letters, see Arthur Golden, "Nine Early Whitman Letters, 1840–1841," *American Literature* 58 (October 1986): 342–360.

58. For "Death in the School-Room (A Fact)," see *Early Poems and Fiction*, 55–60; on its composition, see *Journalism*, 1: 145.

59. For this synopsis of the public school question I am much indebted to the full account of Vincent P. Lannie, *Public Money and Parochial Education: Bishop Hughes, Governor Seward, and the New York School Controversy* (Cleveland: Case Western Reserve University, 1968).

60. Quoted in Robert P. Whalen, "John Hughes: A Man of the People," in *The American Irish Revival: A Decade of the Recorder—1974–1983*, ed. Kevin M. Cahill (Port Washington, N.Y.: Associated Faculty Press, 1984), 492–501.

61. *Journalism*, 1: 41.

62. Ibid., 43.

63. Ibid., 57–58.

64. Ibid., 59–60.

65. Ibid., 442.

66. Ibid., 68.

67. Ibid., 88, 89.

68. Ibid., 84–86.

69. Ibid., 101.

70. Ibid., 112–113.

71. Ibid., 124–125.

72. Quoted in Lannie, *Public Money*, 180, 174.

73. In other countries where the Irish settled, such as Australia, New Zealand, and Canada, they succeeded in obtaining public funds for their parochial schools; only in the United States was this denied. Donald Harman Akenson, *The Irish Diaspora: A Primer* (Belfast: Institute of Irish Studies, Queen's University of Belfast, 1993), 273.

74. Frederick M. Binder and David M. Reimers, *All the Nations Under Heaven: An Ethnic and Racial History of New York City* (New York: Columbia University Press, 1995), 71 n49.

75. *Notebooks*, 6: 2090.

76. Dale T. Knobel, *Paddy and the Republic: Ethnicity and Nationality in Antebellum America* (Middletown, Conn.: Wesleyan University Press, 1986), 25. Though he does not cite the Whitman editorials as part of his evidence, I am much indebted to Knobel. Irish emigration to New York was already so heavy prior to 1845 that in that year New Yorkers (including Whitman) were deeply moved by a sentimental ballad, "The Irish Mother's Lament"; see *Journalism*, 1: 236.

77. *Journalism*, 1: 115.

78. Ibid., 117.

79. Ibid., 106.

80. Ibid., 285–286.

81. Ibid., 482.

82. *Notebooks*, 1: 117.

83. Ibid., 6: 2110.

84. Earl F. Niehaus, *The Irish in New Orleans, 1800–1860* (Baton Rouge: Louisiana State University Press, 1965), 49.

85. Emory Holloway, ed., *The Uncollected Poetry and Prose of Walt Whitman*, 2 vols. (Garden City, N.Y.: Doubleday, Page, 1921; reprint, Gloucester, Mass.: Peter Smith, 1932), 1: 214 (hereafter cited as *Uncollected Poetry and Prose*).

86. Emory Holloway and Ralph Adimari, eds., *New York Dissected: A Sheaf of Recently Discovered Newspaper Articles by the author of Leaves of Grass* (New York: Rufus Rockwell Wilson, 1936), 132.

87. Ibid., 237.

88. Paul O. Weinbaum, "Temperance, Politics and New York City Street Riots of 1857," *New-York Historical Society Quarterly* 59 (July 1975): 246–270.

89. Augustine E. Costello, *Our Firemen: A History of the New York Fire Department* (New York: Augustine E. Costello, 1887), 156.

90. *Journalism*, 1: 87.

91. Costello, *Our Firemen*, 158.

92. David Reynolds, *Walt Whitman's America: A Cultural Biography* (New York: Alfred A. Knopf, 1995), 253–254.

93. Clarence Gohdes and Rollo G. Silver, eds., *Faint Clews and Indirections: Manuscripts of Walt Whitman and His Family* (Durham, N.C.: Duke University Press, 1949), 233–236.

94. *Notebooks*, 2: 887. Charles Colbert, *A Measure of Perfection: Phrenology*

and the Fine Arts in America (Chapel Hill: University of North Carolina Press, 1997), uses Whitman's comments on phrenology to illuminate much of his study.

95. See L. Perry Curtis Jr., *Apes and Angels: The Irishman in Victorian Caricature* (Washington, D.C.: Smithsonian Institution Press, 1971), 5–12, for a discussion of physiognomy and racial stereotyping.

96. Whitman was conscious of the industry of these women as early as 1842 when he wrote of "Life in New York" for the *New York Aurora*, cautioning the reader, "Be careful, as you pass, lest you get a sousing from some of those Irish servant women, scrubbing the marble stoops, and dashing pails of water upon the flagging of the side walks." See *Journalism*, 1: 53–54.

97. Hasia R. Diner, *Erin's Daughters in America: Irish Immigrant Women in the Nineteenth Century* (Baltimore: John Hopkins University Press, 1983), 89, 90.

98. *Notebooks*, 1: 90–91.

99. Ernst, *Immigrant Life*, 30.

100. Of 2,000 prostitutes examined in 1858 at the penitentiary hospital on Blackwell's Island, New York City, 762 were natives of the United States; 1,238 were immigrants, of which 706 were Irish born and in the country less than five years. See ibid., 58.

101. Jerome Loving, *The Civil War Letters of George Washington Whitman* (Durham, N.C.: Duke University Press, 1975), 12n, makes the identification of Nancy Maclure.

102. Gay Wilson Allen, *The Solitary Singer* (New York: New York University Press, 1967), 308.

103. *Notebooks*, 4: 1311.

104. Traubel, *With Walt Whitman*, 1: 419. Jessie Louisa Whitman, daughter of Walt's brother Jeff, told of her uncle's fondness for the chocolate cakes baked by her parents' Irish cook, Kate: "Uncle Walt used to fairly gloat over them and he'd say, 'Kate, that cake looks too good to eat.' She used to reply, 'Go along with yez, you'll eat your share.'" It was reported that the copy of *Leaves* Whitman inscribed to his nieces Jessie and Mannahatta bore Kate's fingerprints and that she read it "with great interest and delight." Randall Waldron, "Jessie Louisa Whitman: Memories of Uncle Walt, et al., 1939–1943," *Walt Whitman Quarterly Review* 7 (summer 1989): 15–27.

105. Traubel, *With Walt Whitman*, 6: 217.

106. Spann, *The New Metropolis*, 233.

107. Ibid., 235.

108. *Journalism*, 1: 317.

109. Ibid., 213.

110. *Prose Works*, 1: 17.

111. *Uncollected Poetry and Prose*, 1: 219.

112. *Journalism*, 1: 282.

113. Blundering was not just associated with the stage Irish; Henry David Thoreau would have no Irish work with him at surveying for they were "sure to do the wrong thing for the best motives." Bradford Terry and Francis H.

Allen, eds., *The Journal of Henry David Thoreau* (Boston: Houghton Mifflin, 1906), 3: 135.

114. Sandra F. Siegel, "Transforming Conventions: The Trope of Decorum and Thomas Sheridan's Captain O'Blunder," in *Literary Imagination, Ancient and Modern: Essays in Honor of David Grene*, ed. Todd Breyfogle (Chicago: University of Chicago Press, 1999).

115. Knobel, *Paddy*, 61.

116. *Prose Works*, 1: 21.

117. Ibid.

118. William H. A. Williams, *'Twas Only an Irishman's Dream* (Urbana: University of Illinois Press, 1996), 69.

119. Ernst, *Immigrant Life*, 67.

120. *Prose Works*, 1: 595.

121. Reynolds, *Walt Whitman's America*, 103–105.

122. *Journalism*, 1: xxv n4.

123. Among the editorials from the *Brooklyn Daily Times* identified by Emory Holloway as Whitman's is one on Morrissey and a prizefight in Canada at which he would contend for title of American champion. Emory Holloway and Vernolian Schwarz, eds., *I Sit and Look Out: Editorials from the Brooklyn Daily Times by Walt Whitman* (New York: AMS Press, 1966), 105–106.

124. William L. Knapp, "I die a true American," in *The True Life of William Pool* (New York: New York Historical Society, 1855).

125. Spann, *The New Metropolis*, 255.

126. Herbert Asbury, *The Gangs of New York: An Informal History of the New York Underworld* (New York: Garden City, 1928), 105.

127. Spann, *The New Metropolis*, 47.

128. Costello, *Our Firemen*, 157.

129. Ibid., 158. "Shule, shule" was the refrain of a traditional Irish ballad, which in America became a work song.

130. Gary Schmidgall, ed., *Walt Whitman. Selected Poems 1855–1892. A New Edition* (New York: St. Martin's Press, 1999), 37, 46–47.

131. Costello, *Our Firemen*, 178.

132. Ibid., 155.

133. *Notebooks*, 2: 802.

134. Allen, *Solitary Singer*, 206.

135. Ralph Waldo Emerson, *English Traits*, ed. Howard Mumford Jones (Cambridge: Belknap Press of Harvard University Press, 1966), 34.

136. Traubel, *With Walt Whitman*, 2: 505–506.

137. Ralph L. Rusk, *The Life of Ralph Waldo Emerson* (New York: Charles Scribner's Sons, 1949), 332.

138. Ed Folsom, "Whitman and Baseball," in *Whitman's Native Representations* (Cambridge: Cambridge University Press, 1994), 27–54.

139. Holloway and Schwarz, *I Sit and Look Out*, 106–108.

140. When Whitman was editing the *Aurora* he wrote a piece about

children that began by describing just such a newsboy; see *Journalism*, 1: 122–123.

141. George C. Foster, *New York by Gas-Light and Other Urban Sketches*, ed. Stuart M. Blumin (Berkeley: University of California Press, 1990), 115–118.

142. Paul Zweig, *Walt Whitman: The Making of the Poet* (New York: Basic Books, 1984), 189.

143. Gary Schmidgall, *Walt Whitman: A Gay Life* (New York: Penguin Putnam, 1997), 92; *Notebooks*, 1: 146 n37.

144. See Betsy Erkkila, "Democracy and (Homo)Sexual Desire," in *Whitman the Political Poet* (New York: Oxford University Press, 1989).

145. *Notebooks*, 1: 146 n37.

146. Ibid., 2: 251, 256.

147. Traubel, *With Walt Whitman*, 2: 34.

148. *Notebooks*, 2: 498.

149. Ibid., 1: 467.

150. Diner, "The Most Irish City," 97.

151. *Prose Works*, 1: 19.

152. See Jerome Loving, "'Broadway, the Magnificent!': A Newly Discovered Whitman Essay," *Walt Whitman Quarterly Review* 12 (spring 1995): 209–216.

153. Whitman, *Leaves of Grass Facsimile*, 66.

154. Kenneth T. Jackson, *Crabgrass Frontier: The Suburbanization of the United States* (New York: Oxford University Press, 1985), 34; Spann, *The New Metropolis*, 285.

155. *Notebooks*, 2: 491.

156. Ibid., 1: 472–473.

157. Ibid., 2: 525.

158. Foster, *New York*, 196–197.

159. Thomas Donaldson, *Walt Whitman, the Man* (London: Gay and Bird, 1897), 203.

160. James D. McCabe, Jr., *Lights and Shadows of New York Life; or, The Sights and Sensations of the Great City* (Philadelphia, 1872; reprint, New York: Farrar, Straus and Giroux, 1970), 212.

161. Jerome Mushkat, *Fernando Wood: A Political Biography* (Kent, Ohio: Kent State University Press, 1990), 18.

162. Ibid., 68, 69.

163. *Notebooks*, 1: 272.

164. Ibid., 272–273.

165. *Prose Works*, 2: 397.

166. Knobel, *Paddy*, 89, 102.

167. *Prose Works*, 2: 371.

168. Ibid., 369.

169. James Jeffrey Roche, *Life of John Boyle O'Reilly* (Philadelphia: John J. McVey, 1891), 119–121.

1. Allen, *Solitary Singer*, 236–237.

2. William W. Thayer, unpublished autobiography, Library of Congress, Washington, D.C.

3. Thayer's opinion of, or at least his attitude toward, Whitman seems to have changed over the years. In an article in *Scribner's Monthly* in 1919 he mentioned his reluctance to visit Whitman in Camden, only doing so at the urging of a mutual friend. Despite this, he sent Whitman five dollars in November 1885. *Correspondence* 3: 408.

4. Jerome Loving, *Walt Whitman's Champion, William Douglas O'Connor* (College Station: Texas A&M University Press, 1978), 34.

5. Review of *Leaves of Grass* (1860) and William Douglas O'Connor's *Harrington, Boston Wide World*, December 8, 1860; reprinted in Kenneth Price, ed., *Walt Whitman: The Contemporary Reviews* (Cambridge: Cambridge University Press, 1996), 108.

6. Thayer, unpublished autobiography.

7. Tilden G. Edelstein, *Strange Enthusiasm: A Life of Thomas Wentworth Higginson* (New Haven, Conn.: Yale University Press, 1968), 234–236.

8. It is significant that accounts of the border incident identify the five murdered men as William Sherman, Allen Williamson, and the remaining three Irishmen, a father and two sons, simply as "three others named Doyle." The five are said to have terrorized the "free-state" community, and it had been decided they should be put to death; Brown may have anticipated the sentence. See Richard J. Hinton, *John Brown and His Men* (1894, reprint, New York: Arno Press, 1967), 87.

9. See Franklin B. Sanborn, *Recollections of Seventy Years of Concord* (Boston: Richard G. Badger, 1909), 1: 169–170 on knowledge of the use of the money. Thayer identifies two "Black Stringers," Dr. V. G. Howe and George L. Stearns, as having provided funds to Brown. Thayer, unpublished autobiography.

10. Hinton told of the meeting in a letter to the *Cincinnati Commercial*, August 26, 1871.

11. William Loren Katz, foreword to Hinton, *John Brown*.

12. William Sloane Kennedy, *The Fight of a Book for the World: A Companion Volume to Leaves of Grass* (N.Y.: privately printed, 1926), 242.

13. Loving, *Walt Whitman*, 153.

14. Whitman never had much use for Webster; in April 1846 he wrote an editorial in the *Eagle* calling him a "cynical, bad, corrupt man — distrustful of the people, and therefore distrusted by them." *Journalism*, 1: 327–328.

15. See, for instance, an editorial of March 12, 1846, in the *Eagle* where he declares, "All that it is desirable to have in government, can be obtained by the proper action of the Democratic party — thus think we." Ibid., 279.

16. Ibid., 465.

17. Thomas N. Brown, "The Origins and Character of Irish-American Nationalism," in *Irish Nationalism and the American Contribution*, ed. Lawrence J. McCaffrey (New York: Arno Press, 1976), 327–358.

18. "Slavers—and the Slave Trade," March 18, 1846; see *Journalism,* 1: 288–289.

19. *Brooklyn Daily Eagle,* December 10, 1847.

20. For Whitman on Murphy see *Uncollected Poetry and Prose,* 1: 165; 2: 1–2, 5, 225, 295.

21. See *Early Poems and Fiction,* 47.

22. "Sigma" has been identified as Lucius Manlius Sargent of Boston; see Louis Ruchames, ed., *The Letters of William Lloyd Garrison,* vol. 4, *From Disunionism to the Brink of War, 1850–1860* (Cambridge: Belknap Press of Harvard University Press, 1975), 21. Though they never met, Whitman held Garrison in high regard, saying of him, "He was of the noblest race of revolutionaries—a man who could accept without desiring martyrdom." Traubel, *With Walt Whitman,* 2: 489.

23. *Early Poems and Fiction,* 48. The year before his death Whitman agreed with Horace Traubel that "Blood-Money" was "good enough to go anywhere in 'Leaves of Grass,'" and wondered "why it is not there—in big type—along with the rest of the poems"; see Traubel, *With Walt Whitman,* 7: 393.

24. Whitman later called upon his friendship with Richard Hinton at least twice, to place his poem "The Mystic Trumpeter" in the *Kansas Magazine* of February 1872 and a prose piece, "Walt Whitman in Europe," in the same periodical for December 1872; see Justin Kaplan, *Walt Whitman: A Life* (New York: Simon and Schuster, 1980), 341. Whitman had mixed feelings about Hinton; he was appreciative of his good will but considered him an "anarchist" and had small regard for him as a writer; see Traubel, *With Walt Whitman,* 2: 396, 5: 40–41.

25. Whitman, *Leaves of Grass Facsimile,* 39.

26. Ibid.

27. Allen, *Solitary Singer,* 152.

28. *Prose Works,* 2: 690.

29. Franklin G. Sanborn, "A Visit to the Good Gray Poet," in *Whitman in His Own Time,* ed. Joel Myerson (Columbia, S.C.: Omnigraphics, 1991), 3–13.

30. John Townsend Trowbridge, *My Own Story* (Boston: Houghton Mifflin, 1903), 361.

31. *Notebooks,* 1: 422–423.

32. Loving, *Walt Whitman,* 40.

33. Traubel, *With Walt Whitman,* 1: 363. Though Whitman speaks here of Frederick Marvin as a "consistent friend," this is the only reference to him I have been able to find. He may have confused him with John B. Marvin, who published a favorable essay, "Walt Whitman," in the *Radical Review,* Boston, 1877.

34. *Notebooks,* 1: 424.

35. For population figures, see Albert J. Von Frank, *The Trials of Anthony Burns: Freedom and Slavery in Emerson's Boston* (Cambridge: Harvard University Press, 1998), 38.

36. Ibid., 92–94. Erkkila, *Whitman,* discusses the absence of Burns as an

"unintentional dimension of irony . . . which reveals as it conceals the racial phobia of Whitman and his age" (63–64). Martin Klammer, *Whitman, Slavery, and the Emergence of Leaves of Grass* (University Park: Pennsylvania State University Press, 1995), disputes this, claiming the absence is intentional and allows Whitman to focus on "his central concern: the usurpation of local rights and powers by federal authority" (108).

37. Von Frank, *The Trials*, 68.

38. Noel Ignatiev, *How the Irish Became White* (New York: Routledge, 1995), 10.

39. Ibid., 2.

40. *Journalism*, 1: 94.

41. Quoted in Ignatiev, *How the Irish Became White*, 2.

42. Ibid., 13.

43. See, for example, James Brewer Stewart, *Wendell Phillips, Liberty's Hero* (Baton Rouge: Louisiana State University Press, 1986), 111, 112.

44. Quoted in Knobel, *Paddy*, 86.

45. Ibid., 87.

46. Quoted in Edelstein, *Strange Enthusiasm*, 160.

47. Orestes A. Brownson, "Native Americanism," *Brownson's Quarterly Review*, third series, 2 (1854); 328–354.

48. Orestes A. Brownson to Charles Montalembert, December 25, 1855, Brownson Papers, University of Notre Dame Archives.

49. Traubel, *With Walt Whitman*, 1: 11.

50. Amos Bronson Alcott, *The Journals of Bronson Alcott*, ed. Odell Shepherd, in *Whitman In His Own Time*, ed. Meyerson, 339. Alcott's two letters of genuine appreciation were for Whitman's essays "Democracy" and "Personalism"; see Traubel, *With Walt Whitman*, 3: 143–145.

51. Thomas H. O'Connor, *The Boston Irish: A Political History* (Boston: Northeastern University Press, 1995). 66, 67.

52. Henry David Thoreau, *A Week; Walden; The Maine Woods; Cape Cod*, Library of America Edition (New York: Viking Press, 1985), 357.

53. Nathaniel Hawthorne, *The American Notebooks*, ed. Claude M. Simpson (Columbus: Ohio State University Press, 1972), 396–397.

54. Thoreau, *Walden*, 485.

55. Ibid., 489.

56. Torrey and Allen, *Journal*, 3: 17.

57. Ibid., 1: 414–417.

58. Thoreau, *Cape Cod*, 853.

59. Torrey and Allen, *Journal*, 4: 298.

60. Thomas Wentworth Higginson, "The Physique of Irish Americans," *Woman's Journal*, June 21, 1884.

61. Leonard N. Neufeldt and Nancy Craig Simmons, eds., *The Journals of Henry D. Thoreau* (Princeton, N.J.: Princeton University Press, 1992), 3: 155–156.

62. Margaret Ossoli Fuller, *Woman in the Nineteenth Century and Kindred Papers* (Boston: John P. Jewett, 1855), 322–323.

63. Ibid., 323.

64. Ibid., 329.

65. Traubel, *With Walt Whitman*, 8: 328.

66. O'Connor, 60.

67. Torrey and Allen, *Journal*, 3: 166.

68. Geoffrey Sill, "Whitman on 'The Black Question': A New Manuscript," *Walt Whitman Quarterly Review*, 8 (fall 1990): 69–75.

69. Knobel, *Paddy*, 90. In "Year of Meteors," Whitman's poem on the events of 1859–1860, he includes a reference to the census: "I would sing in my copious song your census returns of the States, / The tables of population and products."

70. Knobel, *Paddy*, 90.

71. Frederick Douglass, *Life and Times of Frederick Douglass, Written by Himself. His Early Life as a Slave, His Escape from Bondage, and His Complete History* (1892; reprint, New York: Macmillan, 1962), 298.

72. Colonel John W. Forney was a former Free Soiler who turned Republican over the Kansas issue; he was editor of the *Philadelphia Pennsylvanian*. On Whitman's trip, see Walter H. Eitner, *Walt Whitman's Western Jaunt* (Lawrence: Regents Press of Kansas, 1981).

73. *Prose Works*, 2: 690.

74. Traubel, *With Walt Whitman*, 2: 486.

75. See Von Frank, *The Trials*, 322.

76. Traubel, *With Walt Whitman*, 2: 489.

77. Ibid., 3: 25.

78. Ibid., 1: 193.

79. Erkkila, *Whitman*, 101.

80. Klammer, *Whitman*, 131.

81. Douglass, *Life and Times*, 298–299.

82. Ibid., 547.

WASHINGTON, D.C.

1. Loving, *Walt Whitman*, 46.

2. *Prose Works*, 1: 277.

3. Edward J. O'Brien, ed., *Collected Stories by Fitz-James O'Brien* (1925; reprint, Freeport, N.Y.: Books for Libraries Press, 1972), ix.

4. Fitz-James O'Brien, *The Diamond Lens and Other Stories* (1932; reprint, New York: AMS Press, 1969), 9–17; O'Brien, *Collected Stories*, vii-xiii; Fanning, *The Irish Voice*, 87.

5. *Notebooks*, 1: 351.

6. Harold W. Blodgett and Sculley Bradley, eds., *Leaves of Grass, Comprehensive Reader's Edition* (New York: W. W. Norton, 1965), 366.

7. *Notebooks*, 4: 1433.

8. Traubel, *With Walt Whitman*, 2: 55.

9. Blodgett and Bradley, *Leaves of Grass*, 366.

10. D'Arcy, *The Fenian Movement*, 12.

11. Ibid., 15.

12. Elizabeth McCann Kelly, "Battle, Ballad, Blarney and Ballot: The Fenians in America, 1858–1866" (Ph.D. diss., Princeton University, 1986).

13. D'Arcy, *The Fenian Movement*, 2. The Fenians frequently referred to Ireland as "Poor Old Ireland."

14. Adam Clymer, *Edward M. Kennedy: A Biography* (New York: William Morrow, 1999), 250.

15. Whitman entered Halpine's New York address in his notebook; see *Notebooks*, 2: 808.

16. Traubel, *With Walt Whitman*, 8: 342.

17. Ibid., 347.

18. William Douglas O'Connor, "What Cheer?" *Putnam's Monthly* 6 (July 1855): 8–24.

19. The theory was propounded by William Henry Smith in *Bacon and Shakespeare: An Inquiry Touching Players, Playhouses and Play-Writers in the Days of Elizabeth* (1856).

20. For Whitman's views of Donnelly's book, see Traubel, *With Walt Whitman*, 1: 135–137, 234; 2: 2; 9: 14–15, 152, 162.

21. John Townsend Trowbridge, quoted in Florence Bernstein Freedman, *William Douglas O'Connor: Walt Whitman's Chosen Knight* (Athens: Ohio University Press, 1985), 136.

22. Traubel, *With Walt Whitman*, 3: 78.

23. O'Connor, quoted in Loving, *Whitman's Champion*, 37; Whitman, preface to William Douglas O'Connor *Three Tales* (Philadelphia: David McKay, 1892), iii–iv.

24. Traubel, *With Walt Whitman*, 3: 76.

25. Ibid., 2: 491.

26. Ibid., 8: 419.

27. Ibid., 1: 277.

28. Ibid., 2: 440.

29. Clara Barrus, *Whitman and Burroughs: Comrades* (Boston: Houghton Mifflin, 1931), 14.

30. Traubel, *With Walt Whitman*, 2: 240.

31. See Loving, *Whitman's Champion*, 57–59, for a review of the case.

32. Traubel, *With Walt Whitman*, 2: 164.

33. Ibid., 7: 391.

34. Whitman did not think unmarried women or those who were not mothers could be good wartime nurses. "One of the finest nurses I met," he claimed, "was a red-faced illiterate old Irish woman; I have seen her take the poor wasted naked boys so tenderly up in her arms" (*Prose Works*, 1: 88).

35. Ibid., 49–50.

36. Edward V. Spann, "Irish in the Civil War," in *The New York Irish*, ed. Bayor and Meagher, 193.

37. Blodgett and Bradley, *Leaves of Grass*, 238–239. Whitman may have been reminded of this event when, on May 3, 1863, he saw a picture of the Prince of Wales on a Pennsylvania Avenue streetcar in Washington, D.C.; see *Notebook*, 2: 533.

38. Spann, "Irish in the Civil War," 197–198.

39. Joseph M. Hernon Jr., *Celts, Catholics and Copperheads: Ireland Views the American Civil War* (Columbus: Ohio State University Press, 1968), 18.

40. Quoted in Clymer, *Edward M. Kennedy*, 250.

41. Jerome Loving, "Caresser of Life: Walt Whitman and the Civil War," *Walt Whitman Quarterly Review* 15 (fall 1997/winter 1998): 67–86.

42. Whitman's fear that the bravery of the "Fighting Sixty-ninth" would overshadow that of other regiments was realized in 1963 when President John F. Kennedy recalled the battle of Fredricksburg on his visit to Ireland and presented the city of Dublin with one of the regiment's Civil War flags.

43. Charles Halpine, quoted in Spann, "Irish in the Civil War," 205.

44. *Notebooks*, 2: 804.

45. *Prose Works*, 2: 377.

46. Quoted in Gibson, *Attitudes of the New York Irish*, 126.

47. *Correspondence*, 1: 117.

48. Ibid.

49. Berthold and Price, *Dear Brother Walt*, 65.

50. Loving, *Civil War Letters*, 102.

51. Iver Bernstein, *The New York City Draft Riots: Their Significance for American Society and Politics in the Age of the Civil War* (New York: Oxford University Press, 1990), 18–40.

52. Traubel, *With Walt Whitman*, 1: 372.

53. Ibid., 8: 582–583.

54. Ibid., 1: 142–143.

55. Blodgett and Bradley, *Leaves of Grass*, 308–311.

56. Martin G. Murray, "'Pete the Great': A Biography of Peter Doyle," *Walt Whitman Quarterly Review* 12 (summer 1994): 1–51. I am much indebted to this article for facts on Doyle's life.

57. Ibid., 4.

58. After the war Catholic Irish in the North often claimed that Protestant Irish had sought to avoid being drafted into the Union army by using the same argument; see Gordon, *The Orange Riots*, 71.

59. Murray, "'Pete the Great,'" 7, 8.

60. Richard M. Bucke, ed., *Calamus: A Series of Letters Written during the Years 1868–1880 by Walt Whitman to a Young Friend (Peter Doyle)* (Boston: Small, Maynard, 1897), 23.

61. Traubel, *With Walt Whitman*, 2: 511; 3: 75.

62. Quoted in Murray, "'Pete the Great,'" 18.

63. Bucke, *Calamus*, 26.

64. Traubel, *With Walt Whitman*, 3: 543.

65. Ibid., 2: 512.

66. *Notebooks*, 2: 888–889.

67. Ibid., 885.

68. *Correspondence*, 2: 101.

69. Traubel, *With Walt Whitman*, 1: 349.

70. Ibid., 6: 371–372.

71. Bucke, *Calamus*, 33.

72. Ibid., 29; John Burroughs, quoted in Barrus, *Whitman and Burroughs*, 82.

BOSTON, 1881

1. *Correspondence*, 1: 15.

2. William White, ed., *Walt Whitman's Daybooks and Notebooks*, 3 vols. (New York: New York University Press, 1978), 2: 379 (hereafter cited as *Daybooks and Notebooks*).

3. Arthur Golden, "A Recovered Harry Stafford Letter to Walt Whitman," *Walt Whitman Quarterly Review* 5 (spring 1988): 40–43.

4. Manuscript Collection, Trinity College Library, Dublin, MS #4787/66. The Library of the Religious Society of Friends in Dublin, Ireland, has a manuscript autobiography of Alfred Webb, but it contains no references to Whitman, Higginson, or Phillips.

5. Oscar Wilde, "Mr. Froude's Blue Book," *Pall Mall Gazette* 49: 7511 (April 13, 1889); reprinted in Richard Ellmann, ed. *The Artist as Critic: Critical Writings of Oscar Wilde* (New York: Random House, 1969), 136–140.

6. Despite his admiration for Carlyle, Emerson had strongly objected to Carlyle's rehabilitation of Cromwell and rebuked him to his face on the subject; See Rusk, *Ralph Waldo Emerson*, 355.

7. Herbert Paul, *The Life of Froude* (London: Sir Isaac Pitman and Sons, 1905), 209.

8. *Prose Works*, 2: 543.

9. Ibid., 544. Not all the prominent New Englanders acceded to Froude's theories. Wendell Phillips responded with a public statement, "And Mr. Froude comes here to explain the situation on the ground of Irish incapacity — a bad choice of a jury, for since July 4, 1776, our political faith has been that all men are capable of self-government." Lorenzo Sears, *Wendell Phillips, Orator and Agitator* (New York: Doubleday, Page, 1909), 299.

10. See Traubel, *With Walt Whitman*, 2: 268, 196; 3: 40, 63, for Whitman's opinions of Froude's biographies. In 1846 Whitman made brief mention of Carlyle's book on Cromwell in the *Brooklyn Evening Star*, recommending it on the same basis, "*it tells the truth.*" *Journalism* 1: 249.

11. Traubel, *With Walt Whitman*, 4: 19.

12. *Correspondence*, 3: 440; 6: xxv.

13. Michael Davitt, *The Fall of Feudalism in Ireland* (New York: Harper & Brothers, 1904), 715.

14. Traubel, *With Walt Whitman*, 2: 227.

15. James Redpath, *Talks About Ireland* (New York: J. Kennedy, 1881), 81, 82.

16. Traubel, *With Walt Whitman*, 3: 459.

17. Ibid., 4: 19.

18. Ibid., 8: 23.

19. Freedman, *William Douglas O'Connor*, 141–142.

20. Loving suggests the summer, seeing as the immediate cause of the argument a petition sent in July to Senator Charles Sumner from a group of black voters seeking guidance on whom to vote for in the upcoming presidential election; see *Whitman's Champion*, 95–96. Freedman suggests the December date by pointing to some personal problems within the O'Connor family; see *William Douglas O'Connor*, 254–257.

21. Barrus, *Whitman and Burroughs*, 96.

22. Traubel, *With Walt Whitman*, 3: 75–76.

23. Ibid., 8: 418.

24. *Daybooks and Notebooks*, 1: 191; Traubel, *With Walt Whitman*, 5: 461.

25. Traubel, *With Walt Whitman*, 5: 198–299.

26. Ibid., 461.

27. Ibid.

28. *Correspondence*, 4: 369; Traubel, *With Walt Whitman*, 5: 469.

29. *Prose Works*, 1: 264.

30. Traubel, *With Walt Whitman*, 2: 459.

31. In 1876 O'Reilly and Boston's archbishop John Williams purchased the paper from Patrick Donohue.

32. Aldrich continued his rise; in 1881 he became editor of Boston's prestigious *Atlantic Monthly*.

33. Traubel, *With Walt Whitman*, 2: 38.

34. Ibid., 37.

35. Ibid., 361, 371.

36. Davitt, *The Fall of Feudalism*, 129.

37. Roche, *John Boyle O'Reilly*, 117–121.

38. Yeats's poem "How Ferenez Renyi Kept Silence" appeared in the *Pilot* in 1887. Yeats later contributed a regular "Irish Letter" to the paper; these and similar letters published in the *Providence (Rhode Island) Sunday Journal* were collected in Horace Reynolds ed., *Letters to the New Island* (Cambridge: Harvard University Press, 1934).

39. John R. Betts, "The Negro and the New England Conscience in the Days of John Boyle O'Reilly," *Journal of Negro History* 51 (October 1966): 246–261.

40. John Boyle O'Reilly to Edwin P. Whipple, March 20, 1878; quoted in Francis R. Walsh, "John Boyle O'Reilly, the Boston *Pilot*, and Irish-American Assimilation, 1870–1890," in *Massachusetts in the Gilded Age: Selected Essays*, ed. Jack Tager and John W. Itkovic (Amherst: University of Massachusetts Press, 1985), 148–163.

41. Francis G. McManamin, *The American Years of John Boyle O'Reilly, 1870–1890* (New York: Arno Press, 1976), 138.

42. Horace Traubel, "Walt Whitman and His Boston Publishers," *Conservator*, December 1895.

43. Ibid.

44. Whitman's memorandum of the Boston visit in the Library of Congress includes three such maps published by J. H. Daniels, 1879.

45. Sylvester Baxter, "Walt Whitman in Boston," in *Whitman in His Own Time*, ed. Myerson, 76–89.

46. *Daybooks and Notebooks*, 1: 256.

47. Ibid., 238–239.

48. Baxter, "Walt Whitman," 82, 83.

49. Traubel, *With Walt Whitman*, 2: 70.

50. Ibid., 1: 8.

51. Ibid., 3: 17.

52. See *Notebooks*, 3: 1115; and *Prose Works*, 1: 275–276, for the article; see also Ed Folsom, *Walt Whitman's Native Representations* (Cambridge: Cambridge University Press, 1994), 62–65.

53. Doris Ostrander Dawdy, *Artists of the American West: A Biographical Dictionary* (Chicago: Swallow Press, 1974), 165–166; Peter Hastings Falk, ed., *Who Was Who in American Art* (Madison, Conn.: Sound View Press, 1985), 437.

54. *Prose Works*, 1: 282.

55. Anonymous review, *Critic*, November 5, 1881; reprinted in Milton Hindus, *Walt Whitman: The Critical Heritage* (New York: Barnes and Noble, 1971), 182–185.

56. Whitman once told Traubel that O'Reilly had sent him a copy of an article O'Reilly had written in the *Pilot* pointing out the strong influence of Whitman's "Old Ireland" on a poem written by a local Irish poet (Traubel, *With Walt Whitman*, 2: 372). I have not been able to locate the poem in question.

57. Ibid., 421.

58. The facetious subtitle, "Raising a New 'Barbaric Yawp' Over the Roofs of the World/Red-Hot and Dead Earnest," is almost certainly the work of an editor.

59. On O'Connor's references to Emerson, see Loving, *Whitman's Champion*, 129–131.

60. About this time O'Connor also defended Whitman to Lafcadio Hearn, born in Greece to a Greek mother and Irish father. Hearn claimed he secretly admired Whitman — and openly admired O'Connor for championing him — but could not write about him because the newspapers, for which he then wrote, "always tell you to remember that their paper 'goes into respectable families.'" Freedman, *William Douglas O'Connor*, 322.

61. *Notebooks*, 3: 1136; *Correspondence*, 3: 218.

62. William Sloane Kennedy, "A Study of Whitman," *Californian* 111 (February 1881): 149–158.

63. Traubel, *With Walt Whitman*, 2: 156.

64. In 1896 Kennedy published *Reminiscenses of Walt Whitman* and in 1926 *The Fight of a Book for the World: A Companion Volume to Leaves of Grass*. In 1904 he edited *Walt Whitman's Diary in Canada*, now included in *Daybooks and Notebooks*.

65. Golway, *Irish Rebel*, 72.

66. Davitt, *The Fall of Feudalism*, 547.

67. Thomas N. Brown, *Irish-American Nationalism, 1870–1890* (Philadelphia: Lippincott, 1966), 77.

68. The article, "Ireland's Opportunity—Will It Be Lost?" is reprinted in Roche, *John Boyle O'Reilly*, 208–212.

69. Davitt, *The Fall of Feudalism*, 359.

70. On Whitman's meeting with Bagenal, see Traubel, *With Walt Whitman*, 1: 399; 2: 38; and Horst Frenz, ed., *Whitman and Rolleston: A Correspondence* (Bloomington: Indiana University Press, 1951), 63n.

71. Traubel, *With Walt Whitman*, 7: 293.

72. Ibid., 349–350.

73. Ibid., 373.

74. Ibid., 9: 14.

75. Ibid., 3: 19.

76. See *Early Poems and Fiction*, "Death," 55–60; "'Bervance," 80–87.

77. *Prose Works*, 1: 101.

78. Traubel, *With Walt Whitman*, 3: 113, 19.

79. Ibid., 3: 6; 2: 540–541.

80. Ibid., 3: 113.

81. Whitman and O'Connor had reconciled by this time, and Whitman sent the *Transcript* containing the poem to O'Connor. As he told Traubel, "I know O'Connor always keeps up with such things" (ibid.).

82. Ibid., 113–114.

83. McManahim, *American Years*, 123.

84. Ibid., 197.

85. Roche, *John Boyle O'Reilly*, 468.

86. Ibid., 416.

87. McManahim, *American Years*, 239.

88. Roche, *John Boyle O'Reilly*, 520.

89. Quoted in the *Pilot*, April 23, 1881.

90. Trowbridge, *My Own Story*, 188.

91. Wilde, "Mr. Froude's Blue Book," 136.

92. Traubel, *With Walt Whitman*, 7: 48.

93. Traubel invited O'Reilly to Whitman's birthday celebration, but O'Reilly sent regrets that his schedule would not permit it; see Horace Traubel, "John Henry Newman: John Boyle O'Reilly," *Conservator*, August 1890.

94. Traubel, *With Walt Whitman*, 6: 468.

95. O'Reilly ordered two copies of *Leaves of Grass* from Whitman in March of 1885; one was probably a gift to Kelley; see *Daybooks and Notebooks*, 2: 353.

96. Traubel, *With Walt Whitman*, 1: 8.

97. Traubel, "John Henry Newman."

98. Traubel, *With Walt Whitman*, 7: 68.

99. Ibid., 58.

100. Ibid., 72–73. Tucker was then editing his own periodical, *Liberty*, where this appeared. He was a Free Love advocate who, at the time of the

suppression of the 1881 *Leaves*, offered to republish the book; see ibid., 2: 253–254.

101. Ibid., 7: 73.

CAMDEN & EMINENT VISITORS

1. *Correspondence*, 3: 263.

2. Quoted in Terence De Vere White, *The Parents of Oscar Wilde* (London: Hodder and Stoughton, 1967), 86.

3. Davis Coakley, *Oscar Wilde: The Importance of Being Irish* (Dublin: Town House, 1994), 10–11.

4. Rupert Hart-Davis, ed., *More Letters of Oscar Wilde* (New York: Vanguard Press, 1985), 47–48. A "dado" is the lower part of a wall if it is decorated differently from the upper part. It was one of the decorative techniques popular among the aesthetes.

5. Rupert Hart-Davis, ed., *The Letters of Oscar Wilde* (New York: Harcourt Brace, 1962), 26–27.

6. "Oscar Wilde and Whitman," *Philadelphia Press*, January 19, 1882; reprinted in E. H. Mikhail, ed., *Oscar Wilde: Interviews and Recollections* (New York: Harper and Row, 1979), 1: 46–48.

7. Ibid.

8. Ibid.

9. Richard Ellmann, *Oscar Wilde* (New York: Alfred A. Knopf, 1987), 171.

10. *Philadelphia Press*, January 17, 1882; quoted in ibid., 167.

11. For Whitman's account of this see *Prose Works*, 1: 230–233.

12. Ellmann, *Oscar Wilde*, 167.

13. Traubel, *With Walt Whitman*, 1: 75, 73.

14. Ellmann, *Oscar Wilde*, 32.

15. Edward Carpenter was made a life member of the Society for the Study of Sex Psychology and in 1905 delivered a paper later privately published to the society, *Some Friends of Walt Whitman: A Study in Sex Psychology*.

16. Jeffrey Weeks, *Coming Out: Homosexual Politics in Britain from the Nineteenth Century to the Present* (New York: Quartet, 1977), 122, 123.

17. Ellmann, *Oscar Wilde*, 171.

18. Ibid.

19. Jerome Loving, *Walt Whitman: The Song of Himself* (Berkeley: University of California Press, 1999), 413.

20. Whitman, "What Think You I Take My Pen in Hand?" in Blodgett and Bradley, *Leaves of Grass*, 133.

21. Mikhail, *Oscar Wilde*, 48.

22. Traubel, *With Walt Whitman*, 2: 192; Edwin Haviland Miller, "Amy H. Dowe and Walt Whitman," *Walt Whitman Review* 13 (September 1967): 73–79.

23. *Correspondence*, 3: 266.

24. See Miller, "Amy H. Dowe."

25. Horace Traubel to J. W. Wallace, April 8, 1895, Bolton Metropolitan

Library, Bolton, England; see Joann P. Krieg, "Without Walt Whitman in Camden," *Walt Whitman Quarterly Review*, 14 (fall 1996/winter 1997): 85–112.

26. Barrus, *Whitman and Burroughs*, 235.

27. Traubel, *With Walt Whitman*, 2: 289.

28. Ibid., 279.

29. Helen Gray Cone, "Narcissus in Camden," *Century Magazine* 25 (November 1882): 157–159.

30. Lloyd Louis and Helen Justin Smith, *Oscar Wilde Discovers America* (New York: Harcourt Brace, 1936), 115–116.

31. See Joy S. Kasson, *Marble Queens and Captives: Women in Nineteenth-Century American Sculpture* (New Haven, Conn.: Yale University Press, 1990).

32. Thomas Wentworth Higginson, "Unmanly Manhood," *Woman's Journal*, February 4, 1882; reprinted in Karl Beckson, ed., *Oscar Wilde: The Critical Heritage* (New York: Barnes and Noble, 1970), 50–52.

33. The "Pale" refers to the varying portion of Irish territory which the Anglo-Normans conquered and governed for several centuries after their twelfth-century invasion of Ireland.

34. Beckson, *Oscar Wilde*, 50.

35. Louis and Smith, *Oscar Wilde*, 122.

36. Traubel, *With Walt Whitman*, 2: 14.

37. Ibid., 6: 62.

38. Ibid., 7: 253.

39. Ibid., 2: 372.

40. In *Between Men: English Literature and Male Homosocial Desire* (New York: Columbia University Press, 1985), 201–217, Eve Kosofsky Sedgwick discusses the nineteenth-century circle of homosexual English readers of Whitman, among whom she includes Wilde. Her perspective is largely one of class distinctions.

41. Edmund Gosse and Thomas James Wise, eds., *Complete Works of Algernon Charles Swinburne*, vol. 6, *Prose Works* (New York: Russell and Russell, 1925), 342.

42. Ibid., vol. 2, *Poetical Works*, 184–188.

43. In this essay Swinburne also makes a point that bears on Dowden's attention to Whitman as the poetic expression of democracy: Swinburne argues that the poet in Whitman is often overwhelmed by the democrat, with the result that "high poetry [becomes] puddled and adulterated with mere doctrine in its crudest form." Ibid., vol. 6, *Prose Works*, 377–444.

44. Traubel, *With Walt Whitman*, 2: 288.

45. William Rossetti to Edward Dowden, January 17, 1884, in Roger W. Peattie, ed., *Selected Letters of William Michael Rossetti* (University Park: Pennsylvania State University Press, 1990), 460.

46. Gosse and Wise, vol. 5, *Poetical Works*. Terry L. Meyers, "Swinburne and Whitman: Further Evidence," *Walt Whitman Quarterly Review* 14 (summer 1996): 1–11, has pointed out the equivocation in all of Swinburne's utterances, public and private, on Whitman.

47. Though often quoted, Swinburne's allusion is seldom explained. Early in the nineteenth century a South African woman, Sartje Baartman, known as "the Hottentot Venus," was exhibited throughout Europe as a racial "curiosity" because of a disfiguring condition, steatopygia, which caused large fatty deposits in her buttocks. At her death in 1815 an autopsy was done and her genitals removed; they remain in a jar to this day at the Museé de l'Homme in Paris; see Rosemarie Garland Thomson, *Extraordinary Bodies: Figuring Physical Disability in American Literature and Culture* (New York: Columbia University Press, 1997), 71, 76. Interest in such deformities was part of the century's concern for racial characteristics, discussed in chapter 1.

48. Gosse and Wise, vol. 15, *Prose Works*, 316.

49. Ibid., vol. 5, *Poetical Works*, 307.

50. In a few years Swinburne would himself, along with Wilde and Rossetti, become the objects of Dr. Max Nordau's medical diagnosis in *Degeneration* (1893). Nordau suspected all extraordinarily talented individuals of being either physically or mentally impaired.

51. Peter Bayne, "Walt Whitman's Poems," *Contemporary Review* 27 (1875); reprinted in Hindus, *Walt Whitman*, 156–178.

52. Meyers, "Swinburne and Whitman," 7.

53. Gosse and Wise, vol. 5, *Poetical Works*, 307–318.

54. William Sloane Kennedy, *Reminiscences of Walt Whitman* (London: Alexander Gardner, 1896), viii.

55. Oscar Wilde, *Pall Mall Gazette*, January 25, 1889; reprinted in *The Complete Works of Oscar Wilde*, vol. 12, *Criticisms and Reviews* (New York: William H. Wise, 1927), 429–438.

56. Horace Traubel also declared "Homosexuality is disease" in an 1893 letter to J. W. Wallace, a Whitman devotee in Bolton, England. At the time, Traubel, though married, was involved in a highly seductive relationship with another Whitmanian, Philip Dalmas. See Krieg, "Without Walt Whitman."

57. Harold Blodgett, *Walt Whitman in England* (New York: Russell and Russell, 1973), 120.

58. Traubel, *With Walt Whitman*, 3: 394.

59. David F. Greenberg, *The Construction of Homosexuality* (Chicago: University of Chicago Press, 1988), has a chapter entitled "The Medicalization of Homosexuality," which covers these years in England.

60. Wilde asked the actor playing the role of a dandy, Lord Darlington, in his *Lady Windermere's Fan* to wear a green carnation in his lapel on opening night in February 1892. He arranged to have a number of male homosexuals in the audience wearing the same flower, which had become a symbolic emblem among Parisian gays. Ellmann, *Oscar Wilde*, 365.

61. Ibid., 104.

62. Traubel, *With Walt Whitman*, 4: 180–185.

63. Schmidgall, *Walt Whitman*, 115–116, sees this as an admission of Stoker's homosexuality.

64. Traubel, *With Walt Whitman*, 4: 185.

65. Ibid., 185–186.

66. Bram Stoker, *Personal Reminiscences of Henry Irving* (New York: Macmillan, 1906), 2: 97.

67. *Correspondence*, 5: 3.

68. Hugh Anderson, *Bernard O'Dowd* (New York: Twayne, 1968), preface.

69. Traubel, *With Walt Whitman*, 4: 212–217.

70. Ibid., 212.

71. Donaldson, *Walt Whitman*, 210.

72. Mary Costelloe to Walt Whitman, September 1, 1888, Library of Congress, Washington, D.C.

73. Traubel, *With Walt Whitman*, 2: 384.

74. Ibid., 390.

75. Costelloe to Whitman, October 21, 1888, Library of Congress.

76. *Pall Mall Gazette*, October 18, 1888, 2.

77. Ibid.

78. Traubel, *With Walt Whitman*, 3: 14.

79. The visits to New York were probably necessitated by O'Donovan's having been awarded a commission for two life-size equestrian bronzes of Abraham Lincoln and Ulysses S. Grant for the Soldiers' and Sailors' Memorial Arch in Brooklyn.

80. Traubel, *With Walt Whitman*, 8: 176.

81. Ibid., 301.

82. I have found no record of a completed Whitman bust. The work in progress can be seen in a photograph taken of O'Donovan and Eakins in the Philadelphia studio. The two men, along with Samuel Murray, took a plaster cast of Whitman's face in death, from which a death mask was made.

83. Traubel, *With Walt Whitman*, 8: 516.

84. *Prose Works*, 2: 541, 545.

DUBLIN

1. Barrus, *Whitman and Burroughs*, 74–75.

2. Ibid., 76.

3. Ibid., 78.

4. Traubel, *With Walt Whitman*, 1: 224.

5. William Kirkpatrick Magee, *Anglo-Irish Essays* (1918; reprint, Freeport, New York: Books for Libraries Press, 1968), 85.

6. Edward Dowden to William Michael Rossetti, in *Rossetti Papers, 1862 to 1870: A Compilation by William Michael Rossetti* (London: Sands, 1903), 517.

7. Stoker, *Reminiscenses*, 2: 95.

8. *The Letters of Edward Dowden and His Correspondents* (New York: E. P. Dutton, 1919), 40.

9. *Rossetti Papers*, 517.

10. *Westminster Review* 74 (October 1, 1860), 590; reprinted in Price, *Contemporary Reviews*, 107.

11. All quotations are from Edward Dowden, *Westminster Review* 96 (July 1871); reprinted in Price, *Contemporary Reviews*, 181–208.

12. Edward Dowden, from notes on "Poets and Politicians," Trinity College Library.

13. Alexis de Tocqueville, *Democracy in America*, ed. Richard D. Heffner (New York: New American Library, 1960). All quotations from Tocqueville are from the section "Of Some Sources of Poetry Amongst Democratic Nations," 178–183.

14. All quotations are from Dowden, *Westminster Review* 96 (July 1871); reprinted in Price, *Contemporary Reviews*, 181–208.

15. Ibid., 189.

16. Dowden to Rossetti, February 10, 1870, *Rossetti Papers*, 520.

17. *Correspondence*, 2: 128.

18. Traubel, *With Walt Whitman*, 2: 132.

19. Edward Dowden to John Todhunter, December 1, 1875; reprinted in *Letters of Edward Dowden*, 86–87.

20. Traubel, *With Walt Whitman*, 2: 496.

21. Ibid., 497.

22. Stoker, *Reminiscenses*, 2: 94.

23. Dowden Collection, Trinity College Library, Dublin.

24. Stoker, *Reminiscenses*, 2: 94.

25. Frenz, *Whitman and Rolleston*, 97, 121.

26. Ramsay Colles, *In Castle and Court House, Being Reminiscences of 30 Years in Ireland* (London: T. Werner Laurie, 1911), 94. The book includes an autographed reproduction sent to Colles by Whitman of the photograph taken in September 1872, which was the frontispiece for *Two Rivulets*.

27. Ibid., 95. Colles quotes the letter as he received it; it differs slightly from the version that appears in *Correspondence*, 4: 54.

28. *Spectator*, June 15, 1877.

29. *John Bull*, April 27, 1878.

30. There is some confusion between Dowden's and Stoker's accounts as to the exact dates of, and papers read at, these Fortnightly Club meetings, but the major points coincide.

31. Traubel, *With Walt Whitman*, 3: 218.

32. Ibid., 3: 42; 1: 135.

33. Ibid., 1: 196.

34. *Correspondence*, 5: 72–73.

35. Edward Dowden, *Fragments from Old Letters, E. D. to E. D. W., 1869–1892* (London: J. M. Dent, 1914), 15.

36. *Correspondence*, 2: 134.

37. Traubel, *With Walt Whitman*, 1: 302.

38. Ibid.

39. Ibid., 303.

40. Robert Y. Tyrrell, *Echoes from Kottabos* (London: E. G. Richards, 1906), 49, 52.

41. "The Banshee" is quoted in Yeats's review, which is reprinted in John P. Frayne, ed., *Uncollected Prose of William Butler Yeats* (New York: Columbia University Press, 1970–1976), 1: 215–218.

42. Tyrrell, *Echoes*, 96.

43. Barrus, *Whitman and Burroughs*, 62.

44. Ibid., 67.

45. *Correspondence*, 2: 152 n20.

46. Traubel, *With Walt Whitman*, 3: 42.

47. Ernest A. Boyd, ed., *Standish O'Grady: Selected Essays and Passages* (New York: Frederick A. Stokes, 1918), 272, 273.

48. *Correspondence*, 3: 27.

49. Traubel, *With Walt Whitman*, 7: 123.

50. Ibid.

51. Ibid., 1: 400.

52. Ibid.

53. In October 1881, the same month in which O'Grady wrote to Whitman, the first magazine devoted to the modern Irish language was published in Brooklyn by Michael Logan, an immigrant from Galway. Called *An Gaodhal* (The Gael), its masthead read, "The Gael, a Monthly Journal devoted to the Preservation and Cultivation of the Irish Language and the Autonomy of the Irish Nation." Philip O'Leary, *The Prose Literature of the Gaelic Revival, 1881–1921* (University Park: Pennsylvania State University Press, 1994), 7.

54. Traubel, *With Walt Whitman*, 3: 219.

55. Ibid., 1: 398.

56. Ibid.

57. Ibid., 400.

58. Ibid.

59. Edward Dowden to Bertram Dobell, August 6, 1885, *Letters of Edward Dowden*, 214.

60. Dobell, introduction to *Walt Whitman: The Man and The Poet*, by James Thomson (London, 1910), xviii.

61. Ibid., xxi.

62. Herbert Howarth, "Whitman and the Irish Writers," in *Comparative Literature, Proceedings of the Second Congress of the International Comparative Literature Association*, ed. Werner P. Friederich (Chapel Hill: University of North Carolina Press, 1959), 2: 480–488.

63. *Correspondence*, 2: 154.

64. Traubel, *With Walt Whitman*, 2: 154–155.

65. In January 1871 Whitman had applied for the position of pardon clerk in the Department of Justice and was turned down (*Correspondence*, 1: 117); on January 1, 1872, the same month as his letter to Dowden, he received a notice of transfer to the Solicitor's Office and immediately planned to request leave as of February 1 (ibid., 2: 148, 157). It is possible that some feelings of anger led him to rehearse to Dowden his earlier dismissal.

66. Ibid., 3: 67.

67. Traubel, *With Walt Whitman*, 1: 343.

68. Ibid., 343–344.

69. Ibid., 429.

70. Ibid., 224, 225.

71. Dowden, *Academy* 22 (November 18, 1882): 357–359; reprinted in Price, *Contemporary Reviews*, 282–285.

72. Quoted in Richard M. Bucke, *Walt Whitman* (Philadelphia: David McKay, 1883), 253.

73. Frenz, *Whitman and Rolleston*, 34.

74. *Correspondence*, 3: 259; *Prose Works*, 2: 511–512.

75. Frenz, *Whitman and Rolleston*, 56.

76. Dowden concurred in this poor opinion of Wilde's poetry. On December 3, 1881, he wrote to Todhunter that Wilde "has literary talent but a want of sincerity and of original powers of thought" (Trinity College Library).

77. Frenz, *Whitman and Rolleston*, 56.

78. Part of the lecture was translated into English by Horace Traubel's father and appeared in the *Camden Daily Post* the following year (*Correspondence*, 3: 349 n90). Other portions of it were translated by Alfred Forman and Richard M. Bucke and published in Horace Traubel, Richard M. Bucke, and Thomas Harned, eds., *In Re Walt Whitman* (Philadelphia: David McKay, 1893).

79. Frenz, *Whitman and Rolleston*, 22.

80. Ibid., 26.

81. Ibid., 27.

82. In *Hail and Farewell* George Moore recounts a conversation in which he was told that "after a few lessons in Irish history Rolleston donned a long black cloak and a slouch hat, and attended meetings, speaking in favor of secret societies, persuading John O'Leary to look upon him as one that might rouse the country." (New York: D. Appleton, 1912), 1: 147.

83. Traubel, *With Walt Whitman*, 4: 114.

84. Ibid., 114–115.

85. Frenz, *Whitman and Rolleston*, 121.

86. Ibid., 62–63.

87. Ibid., 100; Traubel, *With Walt Whitman*, 3: 86.

88. In 1892 Yeats reformed the Young Ireland Society into the Irish Literary Society, London, of which Rolleston was a vice president. It was this organization that led the literary revival.

89. Todhunter's only significant contribution to the creation of an Irish literature was his *Life of Patrick Sarsfield* (1895), a project originally planned by Lady Wilde, Oscar Wilde's mother.

90. C. H. Rolleston, *Portrait of an Irishman: A Biographical Sketch of T. W. Rolleston* (London: Methuen, 1939), 15.

91. Frenz, *Whitman and Rolleston*, 102.

92. Ibid. Though the Young Ireland movement was not a part of it, the socialistic Fellowship of the New Life, based in Surrey, England, was founded in 1884 and was the forerunner of the Fabian Society. According to Yeats, it

sought "to carry out some of the ideas of Thoreau and Whitman"; see Yeats to Katharine Tynan, May 31, 1887, in John Kelly, ed., *The Collected Letters of William Butler Yeats*, vol. 1: 1865–1895 (Oxford: Clarendon Press, 1986), 18. Yeats's first important poem, *The Wanderings of Oisin* (1889), owes some of its splendor to William Morris.

93. Traubel, *With Walt Whitman*, 1: 84.

94. Yeats, introductory sketch of Allingham in Alfred Miles, ed., *The Poets and the Poetry of the Century* (London, 1892), reprinted in Frayne, *Uncollected Prose*, 259–261. Allingham was not capable of doing with Ballyshannon what Thomas Hardy would later achieve with the imaginary county of Wessex in England or what William Faulkner did in creating the world of Yoknapatawpha County; the contemporary Irish dramatist Brian Friel has effectively used a mythical Donegal village, Ballybeg, as his "touchplace" for the human experience.

95. Yeats, "The Poetry of Sir Samuel Ferguson," in Frayne, *Uncollected Prose*, 87–104.

96. Dowden's first impressions of Yeats were not positive. In August 1886 he wrote to John Todhunter, "I sometimes see Willie Yeats: he hangs in the balance between genius and (to speak rudely) fool; I shall rejoice if he be the first, but it remains doubtful" (Trinity College Library).

97. Traubel, *With Walt Whitman*, 4: 86.

98. Ibid., 348–349.

99. Ibid., 349.

100. See Blodgett, *Whitman in England*, 169–171.

101. Roger McHugh, ed., *W. B. Yeats, Letters to Katharine Tynan* (New York: McMullen, 1953), 44, 46.

102. Kelly, *Collected Letters*, 408–409.

103. W. B. Yeats, "The Irish Intellectual Capital: Where Is It?" in Frayne, *Uncollected Prose*, 222–225.

104. Declan Kiberd, *Inventing Ireland* (Cambridge: Harvard University Press, 1996), 56.

105. Kelly, *Collected Letters*, 9.

106. William H. O'Donnell, ed., *William Butler Yeats: Later Essays* (New York: Charles Scribner's Sons, 1994) 219.

107. Terrence Diggory, *Yeats and American Poetry: The Tradition of the Self* (Princeton, N.J.: Princeton University Press, 1983), 29.

108. Richard Ellmann, *Yeats: The Man and the Masks* (New York: E. P. Dutton, 1948), 293.

109. Ellsworth Mason and Richard Ellmann, eds., *The Critical Writings of James Joyce* (New York: Viking Press, 1959), 105.

110. Reprinted in Monk Gibbon, ed., *The Living Torch* (1937; reprint, Freeport, New York: Books for Libraries Press, 1970), 319–323.

111. Ibid., 233–236.

112. William Kirkpatrick Magee, *Pebbles from a Brook* (Dublin: O'Grady, 1901), 13; Magee, *Anglo-Irish Essays*, 123. Perhaps following the Rossetti

lead, many Irish commentators linked Whitman with Blake, even as late as Sean O'Casey, who pairs Blake's "deep-desiring vision" with Whitman's "expansive one of brotherhood." See Sean O'Casey, *Autobiographies, Sunset and Evening Star* (London: Macmillan, 1981), 313.

113. John Eglinton (Magee), *Irish Literary Portraits* (1935; reprint Freeport, New York: Books for Libraries Press 1967), 66.

114. Magee, *Anglo-Irish Essays*, 42.

115. Quoted in Antoinette Quinn, *Patrick Kavanagh: A Critical Study* (Syracuse, New York: Syracuse University Press, 1991), 395–396.

116. Richard Ellmann, ed., *James Joyce Letters* (New York: Viking Press, 1966), 2: 203; James Joyce, *Finnegans Wake* (New York: Viking Press, 1955), 551.

117. Joyce, *Finnegans Wake*, 263, 81–82. These identifications were made by James Atherton, *The Books at the Wake: A Study of Literary Allusions in James Joyce's Finnegans Wake* (New York: Viking Press, 1960).

118. James Joyce, *Ulysses: A Critical and Synoptic Edition* (New York: Garland, 1984), l.517, 9.139, 9.626. The identifications are made in Don Gifford, ed., with Robert J. Seidman, *Ulysses Annotated* (Berkeley: University of California Press, 1988). Don Summerhayes, "Joyce's *Ulysses* and Whitman's "Self": A Query," *Wisconsin Studies in Contemporary Literature* 4 (1963): 216–224, makes further suggestions.

119. O'Casey, *Autobiographies, Sunset and Evening Star*, 633.

120. Ibid., 657–658.

121. Frank O'Connor, *An Only Child* (London: Macmillan, 1961), 237.

122. Maureen Murphy, "O'Casey and the Labor Movement," in *The American Irish Revival, a Decade of The Recorder—1974–1983*, ed. Keven M. Cahill (Port Washington, New York: Associated Faculty Press, 1984), 188–196.

123. On Whitman and British socialism see Paul Salveson, "Loving Comrades: Lancashire's Links to Walt Whitman," *Walt Whitman Quarterly Review* 14 (fall 1996/winter 1997): 57–84.

124. Desmond Ryan, *James Connolly* (Dublin: Talbot Press, 1924), 122–123.

CODA

1. *Prose Works*, 2: 513.

2. Tom Paulin, *Minotaur, Poetry and the Nation State* (Cambridge: Harvard University Press, 1992), 16.

3. Ibid., 23.

4. Ibid., 29.

5. Ibid., 30.

6. Ibid., 31.

7. Clarence Ghodes, "Nationalism and Cosmopolitanism in Whitman's *Leaves of Grass*," in *Comparative Literature*, ed. Friederich, 472–479. Ghodes finds an obvious and "violent" conflict between the two, which he sees as "one of the chief sources of Whitman's notorious contradictions" (478).

INDEX

Abolitionism, Irish and, 98–99, 100–101

Address from the People of Ireland, 89, 91, 130, 133

Advertiser (New York), 19

Alcott, Amos Bronson, 84, 93

Aldrich, Thomas Bailey, 138

Allen, Richard, 89

Allingham, William, 218

American Land League, 152, 215, 216

Anglo-Irish, 191–192

Astor, John Jacob, 57–58

Aurora (New York), 34, 36, 41, 42, 43, 44, 46, 49, 50, 89, 90, 235

Bagenal, Philip, 153

baseball, Irish and, 64

Batchelder, James, 88, 92, 96, 143

Battle of the Boyne, 22, 23, 29, 122

Bayne, Peter, 179, 212

Beaumont, Gustave de, 197

Beckett, Samuel, 224–225

Beecher, Henry Ward, 131

Benjamin, Park, 49

Bennett, James Gordon, 42

Blake, William, 221, 234

"blunderer" (Irish stereotype), 58

Boston Pilot, 27, 91, 140, 141, 144, 146, 149, 150, 152, 157, 160, 161, 165, 174, 236

Boucicault, Dion, 59, 173

"Bowery b'hoys," 59–60

"boycotting," 135

Brinton, Daniel, 171

Brooklyn Daily Eagle, 24, 25, 41, 45, 48, 57, 58, 79, 80, 81, 85

Brooklyn Daily Times, 64

Brooklyn Navy Yard, 17

Brooklyn Standard, 110

Brougham, John, 59

Brown, John, 77–78, 82, 83, 92, 100, 134

Brownson, Orestes, 43, 92–93, 141

Bryant, William Cullen, 131

Buchanan, Robert, 177, 178, 191

Bucke, Richard Maurice, 114, 136, 147, 148, 212

Burns, Anthony, 83, 85, 88, 92, 143

Burroughs, John, 114, 126, 135, 136, 149, 171, 190, 206

Carlyle, Thomas, 131, 133, 210

"The Carpenter," 135

Carroll Hall, 24, 39, 42

Catholic school controversy, 37–44

Chainey, George, 148

Chanfrau, Francis S., 59, 63

"Charmides," 174

Childers, Robert Erskine, 228–229

cholera, 18–19

Churchill, Lord Randolph, 209

Civil War, Irish in, 117–120, 128

Clapp, Henry, 104

Clare, Ada, 105

Cleveland, Grover, 156

Clinton, De Witt, 17

Colles, Richard William, 201–202

Collins, James, 94

Cone, Helen Gray, 172

Connolly, James, 229–230

Connolly, Richard B., 23, 32

Corcoran, Michael, 117

Costelloe, Frank, 185, 186

Costelloe, Mary Whitall Smith, 185, 186
Cromwell, Oliver, 131
Cushman, Charlotte, 59

Davis, Mary, 55
Davis, Thomas, 106, 193
Davitt, Michael, 134, 139, 150, 151, 153, 215, 217
Dead Rabbits, 59, 61, 70
Democratic Review, 18, 34, 35–36
Devoy, John, 29, 139, 150, 151
Diamond, John ("Master"), 64
Diggory, Terrence, 223
Dobell, Bertram, 209–210
Donaldson, Thomas, 181, 185
Donnelly, Ignatius, 112
Douglas, Stephen A., 120
Douglass, Frederick, 99, 101–102, 134
Dowden, Edward, 21, 131, 134, 163, 177, 190, 191–192, 215, 217, 219, 221, 223, 226, 230, 234
Dowden, Elizabeth West, 206
Dowden, John, 194, 206
Doyle, Francis, 32–33, 126
Doyle, Peter, 22, 31, 32, 33, 66, 71, 124, 125–128, 130, 136, 162, 167, 185, 194, 211, 232, 236
D'Oyly Carte, Richard, 166–167
Dracula, 181
Dublin University Review, 217, 219
Duffy, Charles Gavan, 165

Eakins, Thomas, 187–188
Eglinton, John, see Magee, William Kirkpatrick
Eighty-fourth Regiment (New York), 30
Eldridge, Charles, 75–79, 103, 104, 110, 113
Eliot, George, 221
Ellis, Edwin, 206

Ellmann, Richard, 168, 223
Emerson, Ralph Waldo, 63–64, 84, 93, 100, 131, 141, 142, 143, 168, 218
Erie Canal, 17
Erkkila, Betsy, 101

Fellows, Colonel John, 36
Fenian Brotherhood, 23, 108, 109, 139
Ferguson, Sir Samuel, 192, 195, 198, 218, 219, 220, 221
Fifty-first Regiment (New York), 103, 118–119, 124
Fitzhugh, George, 90
Five Points, 18, 40
Flynn, Richard, 136–137
Forrest, Edwin, 59
Folsom, Ed, 64
Fowler, Lorenzo, 51
Fowler, Orson, 51, 52
Free Soil Party, 81, 86, 93
Froude, James Anthony, 130–132, 189
Fuller, Margaret Ossoli, 96–98

Galaxy, 21
Galbraith, Joseph S., 201
Garrison, William Lloyd, 78, 82, 89, 112
Gilchrist, Anne, 21, 136, 190
Gilchrist, Herbert, 56
Ginsberg, Allen, 228
Gladstone, William, 153, 186, 187
The Good Gray Poet, 115, 135, 147, 218
Grace, William, 20
Greeley, Horace, 61, 97
Gregory, Lady Isabella Augusta, 193, 223–224
Griffin, Gerald, 59

Hall, A. Oakey, 28
Haley, Thomas, 116–117, 119

Halpine, Charles G., 105, 110, 119, 120, 159
Harlan, James, 115
Harrington, 76, 77, 85
Hawthorne, Nathaniel, 94, 143
Higginson, Thomas Wentworth, 77, 88, 96, 131, 156, 173–176
Hinton, Richard J., 78, 82, 99, 114
Hoffman, John T., 28, 29
Holmes, Oliver Wendell, 140, 141, 173
Home Rule, 133, 152, 185, 187, 214, 230
Howe, Julia Ward, 173, 174, 175
Howells, William Dean, 138
Hughes, Rev. John, 33, 37, 38–39, 40, 42, 43, 45, 53, 89, 91, 123, 188
Hyde, Douglas, 216

Ignatiev, Noel, 89
immigration, Irish, 27–29
Ingersoll, Robert, 208
Irish-American (New York), 27, 120
Irish Coercion Bill, 46
Irish Emigrant Society, 53
Irish National Land League, 151, 209, 214
Irish servant girls, 53–54, 55–56
Irish Times, 132
"Irish Town" (Brooklyn), 19
Irving, Henry, 181, 189
Ives, George Cecil, 169, 170, 179

Jackson, Andrew, 27
Joyce, James, 224–225, 227–228

Kavanagh, Patrick, 226–227
Kelly, John, 20
Kennedy, William Sloane, 148–149, 180
Klammer, Martin, 101
Knobel, Dale T., 71, 98

Knortz, Karl, 214
Kottabos, 204–206, 213, 214
Krafft-Ebing, Richard von, 179, 180

labor, Irish and, 24–26
Laborers' Union Benevolent Society, 20
Lane, William Henry ("Juba"), 64
Larkin, James, 229
Larminie, William, 222
Law, George, 48
Lee, John Fitzgerald, 213
Lincoln, Abraham, 120, 137, 191, 229
Literary World (Boston), 133
London Times, 132
Longfellow, Henry Wadsworth, 131, 140, 168, 173, 195
Long Island Patriot, 80, 81
Longshoremen's United Benevolent Society, 26
Loving, Jerome, 85
Lowell, James Russell, 173
Lynch, Patrick, 27

Macpherson, James, 105, 145, 192
Macready, William, 38–39
Magee, William Kirkpatrick (John Eglinton), 193, 222, 226
Mangan, James Clarence, 195
Mathew, Theobald, 94
McKay, David, 147
Meagher, Thomas, 117–118, 158
Melville, Herman, 46
Metropolitan Police, 23, 70
Meyers, Terry L., 179
Milton, John, 233–235
Molloy, Fitzgerald, 213
Moore, Ralph, 237
Moore, Thomas, 106, 140
Morris, William, 217
Morrisey, John, 61
Mulvaney, John, 144, 145

Murphy, Henry C., 80, 81
Murray, Samuel, 188

"Narcissus in Camden," 172–173
national character, Irish and,
  95–98
National Land League, 134, 151
nationalistic literature, Irish and,
  217–223
Native American Party, 41, 42, 61
New Era (New York), 41, 42
Newman, John Henry, 161, 206
New Orleans Crescent, 48, 57
New York City: Astor Place riots,
  58–59; draft riots, 121–123;
  firemen, 62–63; gangs, 61, 70;
  "loafers," 60; newsboys, 64–65;
  Orange riots, 22–23, 29–31, 33,
  140 199; police, Irish and, 16,
  31, 71–74; "roughs," 60; stage
  drivers, 68–69
New York Herald, 42, 134, 138,
  159
New York Hospital, 68
New York Leader, 105, 109, 110,
  119
New York Times, 17, 30, 118, 119,
  132
New York Tribune, 34, 132, 144,
  145, 148, 201
New York World, 22
Nettleship, John, 206
Noel, Roden, 194

O'Brien, Fitz-James, 104, 105
O'Casey, Sean, 228, 229
O'Connell, Daniel, 59, 88, 91, 92,
  108, 164, 192
O'Connor, Ellen Tarr, 110, 112,
  136
O'Connor, Frank, 228–229
O'Connor, William Douglas, 22,
  31, 33, 71, 76, 85, 87, 93, 99,
  100, 103, 104, 110, 111–116,
  126, 127, 129, 135–136,
  138–139, 142, 147, 148, 155,

162, 175, 185, 194, 199, 203,
  208, 211, 218, 220, 232
O'Donovan, William R., 187–188
O'Dowd, Bernard, 184
O'Grady, Standish James, 191,
  193, 195, 198, 206–209, 210,
  212, 213, 214, 217, 218
O'Halloran, Sylvester, 193
O'Leary, John, 140, 215, 217, 218
Opdyke, George, 123
Osgood, James R., 133, 141, 142,
  146, 147, 149, 175
Ossian, 105, 145, 192
O'Sullivan, John L., 18, 34–36

"Paddy" (Irish stereotype), 44, 45,
  47, 48, 52, 58, 71, 74, 87
Paine, Thomas, 36
Pall Mall Gazette, 186, 187
Parker, Theodore, 78, 92, 95, 188
Parnell, Charles Stewart, 151, 152,
  153, 154, 216
Paulin, Tom, 233–235
*Personal Reminiscenses of Henry
  Irving*, 181, 184
Pfaff's, 104, 105
Phillips, Wendell, 78, 87, 89, 92,
  140
phrenology, 51
physiognomy, 52
Poe, Edgar Allan, 17–18, 168
Poems of Walt Whitman, 134, 184,
  201
"The Poetry of Democracy:
  Walt Whitman," 21, 131, 193,
  194–199
Poole, William ("Butcher Bill"),
  60–61
Powers, Hiram, 174
Pre-Raphaelites, 166
Public School Society, 37, 39, 40
Putnam's Monthly, 111, 135

Redpath, James, 77–78, 84,
  124–135, 153
Riis, Jacob, 18

Rolleston, Thomas W. H., 212, 213–217, 219, 233
Rossa, Jeremiah O'Donovan, 29, 216
Rossetti, William Michael, 134, 165, 176, 177, 178, 184, 190, 193, 199, 200, 201, 207, 211
Ruskin, William, 210
Russell, George (A.E.), 216, 222, 225–226, 227
Ryan, Desmond, 230, 265

Sackville-West, Sir Lionel, 156
Sanborn, Franklin B., 84, 99, 143
Sarony, Napoleon, 171
"The Second Coming," 223
Seward, William, 37
Sixty-ninth Regiment (New York), 110, 117, 118, 119, 123, 124, 158
Smith, Hannal Whitall, 185
Smith, Robert Pearsall, 185
Spartan Band, 45, 56
"Speranza," see Wilde, Lady Jane Francesca
Stafford, Harry, 171
Stedman, Edmund Clarence, 207
Stevens, Oliver, 146, 147, 148, 149
Stoddard, Joseph M., 163, 164, 169, 170
Stoker, Abraham (Bram), 181–185, 190, 201, 202–203, 204
Stowe, Harriet Beecher, 96
Studies in Literature, 202
Sullivan, "Yankee," 47, 50
Sumers, William, 185–187
Sweeny, Peter Barr, 23
Swinburne, Algernon Charles, 21, 166, 176–181, 183, 189, 191, 194, 202, 212
Symonds, John Addington, 169, 178, 179, 183, 190, 203–204

Tammany, 23, 24, 28, 29, 32, 36, 38, 41, 42, 49, 56, 61, 86
Tasistro, Louis Fitzgerald, 129–130

Tennyson, Alfred Lord, 21, 168, 190, 218
Thayer, William, 75–76, 77–79, 104, 113
Thomson, James, 209–210
Thoreau, Henry David, 84, 94–96, 98, 143
Ticknor, Benjamin, 141, 176
Tocqueville, Alexis de, 197–198
Todhunter, John, 200, 204, 205, 212, 216, 217
Traubel, Horace, 55, 56, 99, 114, 116, 123, 124, 133, 135, 137, 141, 142, 144, 153, 154, 156, 160, 161, 170, 171, 175, 180, 185, 186, 188, 191, 203, 207, 208, 211, 212, 215, 219, 221
Trinity College, Dublin, 21, 131, 163, 182, 190, 191, 194, 195, 201, 204, 219
Trowbridge, John Townsend, 84, 85, 114
Tucker, Benjamin R., 161
Tweed, William A., 23, 28, 29, 32
Tynan, Kathleen, 216
Tyrrell, Robert Yelverton, 201, 204, 212

Upward, Allen, 184–185

Valera, Eamon de, 228
Van Buren, Martin, 36, 81
Vaux, Calvert, 24
Von Frank, Albert J., 88

Walsh, Mike, 45, 54, 56–57, 58, 59, 86, 93
Washington Temperance Society, 49
Webb, Alfred, 89, 130, 132, 133–134, 153, 190
Webb, Richard Davis, 89, 130, 133, 134
Westminster Review, 191, 194, 199, 204, 210, 212
Whitman, Andrew, 20, 54

Whitman, Edward, 20

Whitman, George, 100, 103, 118, 120, 122, 124, 125, 127, 136, 171

Whitman, Jesse, 19, 20

Whitman, Louisa (mother), 20, 121

Whitman, Louisa (sister-in-law), 163, 170

Whitman, Mattie, 20

Whitman, Nancy McClure, 54

Whitman, Thomas Jefferson (Jeff), 20, 120, 122

Whitman, Walt: and abolitionism, 79, 80–81, 99–102; and Home Rule, 133; and New York City police, 71–74; and slavery, 79–83

Whitman, Walt: works by, "A Backward Glance O'er Travel'd Roads," 180; "A Boston Ballad," 83, 88; "Beat! Beat! Drums," 105, 118; "Black and White Slaves," 90; "Blood-Money," 79, 81–82, 101; "Calamus," 168, 196, 203–204, 207; "City Photographs," 105; "Custer's Last Rally," 144; "The Dalliance of the Eagles," 147; "Death in the School-Room," 37, 155; *Democratic Vistas*, 21, 70, 71, 72, 73, 120, 194, 198, 204, 207; *Drum-Taps*, 110, 120, 129; "The Eighteenth Presidency!," 82; "Faces," 52; "Fifty-First New York City Veterans," 118–119; *Franklin Evans*, 49, 50; *Good-bye My Fancy*, 99; "The House of Friends," 82; "I Saw in Louisiana a Live-Oak Growing," 62–63; "I Sing the Body Electric," 147; *Leaves of Grass*, 19, 21, 60, 69, 75, 76, 79, 82, 84, 101, 104, 108, 113, 115, 124, 133, 135, 136, 141, 142, 144, 145, 148, 149, 158, 160, 171, 174, 175, 176, 177, 182, 184, 188, 193, 196, 199, 201, 202, 204, 209, 210, 211, 213, 214, 218, 221, 229, 233, 336; *November Boughs*, 132, 133, 180, 188; "Of the black question," 98; "Old Ireland," 105–110, 120, 146, 187, 205; "One's-Self I Sing," 52, 53; "Our Eminent Visitors," 132, 188; "Out of the Cradle Endlessly Rocking," 104, 149, 222, 223; *Passage to India*, 21; "Patrick McDray," 48; "Pioneers! O Pioneers!," 99; "The Return of the Heroes," 107; "Revenge and Requital," 18; "Salut au Monde!," 233; "Shakspeare-Bacon's Cipher," 112; "The Sleepers," 19–20; "Song for Certain Congressmen," 81, 101; "Song of Myself," 19, 29, 62, 67, 82, 101, 224, 225; "A Song of Occupations," 55; "Song of the Broad-Axe," 70–71, 230; *Specimen Days*, 57, 66, 116, 137, 201, 212; "Spontaneous Me," 147; "Starting from Paumanok," 50; "Tear Down and Build Over Again," 57; "Thou Mother with Thy Equal Brood," 107; "To a Common Prostitute," 147, 148; "To a Foil'd European Revolutionaire," 233; "To Think of Time," 67–68; *Two Rivulets*, 201; "Wants," 53–54; "Wild Frank's Return," 155; "A Woman Waits for Me," 147; "Year of Meteors," 117

"Whitmania," 177–180, 194, 202

Whittier, John Greenleaf, 131, 140, 141, 173

Wilde, Lady Jane Francesca, 164, 165, 175, 193

Wilde, Oscar, 131, 140, 159, 163–175, 177–180, 181, 183, 189, 190, 214

Wilentz, Sean, 24
Wilkins, William, 214
Williams, Rev. John J., 138, 149, 150
Wood, Fernando, 32, 61, 69, 86

Yeats, Jack, 206
Yeats, John Butler, 206, 216

Yeats, William Butler, 107, 191, 193, 195, 198, 205, 208, 210, 215, 216, 217, 218, 219–223, 226, 230, 232, 234, 235
Young Ireland, 105, 108–109, 165, 193, 217

Zweig, Paul, 65